Actor training

Actor Training

Second Edition

Actor Training expands on Alison Hodge's highly-acclaimed and bestselling *Twentieth Century Actor Training*. This exciting second edition radically updates the original book making it even more valuable for any student of the history and practice of actor training. The bibliography is brought right up to date and many chapters are revised. In addition, eight more practitioners are included – and forty more photographs – to create a stunningly comprehensive study.

The practitioners included are:

Stella Adler
Eugenio Barba
Augusto Boal
Anne Bogart
Bertolt Brecht
Peter Brook
Michael Chekhov

Joseph Chaikin
Jacques Copeau
Philippe Gaulier
Jerzy Grotowski
Maria Knebel
Jacques Lecoq
Joan Littlewood
Sanford Meisner

Vsevolod Meyerhold
Ariane Mnouchkine
Monika Pagneux
Michel Saint-Denis
Włodzimierz Staniewski
Konstantin Stanislavsky
Lee Strasberg

The historical, cultural and political context of each practitioner's work is clearly set out by leading experts and accompanied by an incisive and enlightening analysis of the main principles of the practitioners' training, practical exercises and key productions.

This book is an invaluable introduction to the principles and practice of actor training and its role in shaping modern theatre.

Alison Hodge has been a professional director since 1982. She was assistant director for Gardzienice Theatre and co-authored, with Włodzimierz Staniewski, *Hidden Territories: the Theatre of Gardzienice* (Routledge, 2004). She is director of The Quick and the Dead, an international theatre research company, and a Reader in Theatre Practice at Royal Holloway College, University of London. Her website can be found at www.alisonhodge.net

Actor Training

Second Edition

Edited by

Alison Hodge

 Routledge
Taylor & Francis Group

LONDON AND NEW YORK

First published 2010
by Routledge
2 Park Square, Milton Park, Abingdon, Oxon OX14 4RN

Simultaneously published in the USA and Canada
by Routledge
270 Madison Avenue, New York, NY 10016

Routledge is an imprint of the Taylor & Francis Group, an informa business

Selection and Editorial Material © 2010 Alison Hodge
Individual Chapters © the contributors

Typeset in Joanna MT and Bell Gothic by
RefineCatch Limited, Bungay, Suffolk
Printed and bound in Great Britain by
TJ International Ltd, Padstow, Cornwall

British Library Cataloguing in Publication Data
A catalogue record for this book is available from the British Library

Library of Congress Cataloging-in-Publication Data
Actor training / edited by Alison Hodge. – 2nd ed.
      p. cm.
   Previously published under title: Twentieth century acting training,
   2000.
   Includes bibliographical references and index.
   1. Acting – Study and teaching.   I. Hodge, Alison, 1959–
   II. Twentieth century acting training.
   PN2075.T94 2010
   792.02'807 – dc22   2009028309

ISBN10: 0-415-47167-2 (hbk)
ISBN10: 0-415-47168-0 (pbk)
ISBN10: 0-203-86137-X (ebk)

ISBN13: 978-0-415-47167-1 (hbk)
ISBN13: 978-0-415-47168-8 (pbk)
ISBN13: 978-0-203-86137-0 (ebk)

For Sophie and Hannah

And, in gratitude, to Janice Barton, Tatiana Bre, Daniela Garcia Casilda, Chiara D'Anna, Luis Gallo Mudarra, Alexia Kokkali and Göze Saner

Contents

Illustrations

Contributors

Frances Babbage is Senior Lecturer in Drama at the University of Sheffield where she is also Director of the MA in Theatre and Performance Studies. She is the author of *Augusto Boal* (Routledge Performance Practitioners, 2004) and editor of *Working Without Boal: Digressions and Developments in the Theatre of the Oppressed* (Contemporary Theatre Review 3:1, 1995). She has regularly worked as a facilitator using methods derived from Boal's practice and more generally as a performer and deviser. Her research has been published in journals including *New Theatre Quarterly*, *Modern Drama* and *Comparative Drama*.

Jane Baldwin taught modern drama, acting, introduction to theatre and humanities at the Boston Conservatory, USA. Her books include *Michel Saint-Denis and the Shaping of the Modern Actor, Theatre: The Rediscovery of Style and Other Writings*, which she edited (Routledge), and *Vie et morts de la création collective/Lives and Deaths of Collective Creation*, co-edited with Jean-Marc Larrue and Christiane Page (Vox Theatri). Her articles have appeared in *Theatre Topics*, *L'Annuaire théâtral*, *Theatre Notebook*, and *Theatre History Studies*, among others. She is presently writing *A National Drama: Jean Gascon and the Canadian Theatre*. She has been an actress and director throughout her career.

Clive Barker began his career in the early 1950s as an actor with Joan Littlewood's Theatre Workshop company at the Theatre Royal Stratford East, appearing in, amongst others, Brendan Behan's *The Hostage* and the company's devised show, *Oh What A Lovely War!* He directed productions, wrote plays and recorded documentaries for radio and television. From the mid-1960s he combined professional work with lecturing at the universities of Birmingham and Warwick. His actor training methods and ideas are set out in *Theatre Games* (Methuen, 1977) and he was joint editor of *New Theatre Quarterly* (Cambridge University Press). Clive Barker died in 2005.

Sharon Marie Carnicke is Professor of Theatre and Slavic Studies as well as Associate Dean for the School of Theatre at the University of Southern California. Her book, *Stanislavsky in Focus*, is now in its second edition. She has professional experience on stage and a Ph.D. in Russian from Columbia University, and her research and teaching melds theatrical practice with historical scholarship. A widely published author, her works include *Reframing Screen Performance* (with Cynthia Baron), *The Theatrical Instinct* (a study on the avant-garde director Nikolai Evreinov), *Chekhov: 4 Plays and 3 Jokes* which includes her Kennedy Center award-winning translation of Anton Chekhov's *The Seagull*, and articles on topics from the Ballets Russes to performance in the town festivals of Puerto Rico.

Franc Chamberlain lectures in Drama and Theatre Studies at University College Cork, Ireland and is Visiting Professor in Performance Studies and Creative Practice at the University of Northampton, UK. He is series editor for Routledge Performance Practitioners and the author of *Michael Chekhov* (Routledge, 2003) and co-editor (with Ralph Yarrow) of *Jacques Lecoq in the British Theatre* (Routledge, 2002) and (with Thomas Leabhart) of *A Decroux Companion* (Routledge, 2008). He has also prepared a new edition of Craig's *On the Art of the Theatre* (Routledge, 2008).

Royd Climenhaga teaches in the Theater and Arts in Context programmes at Eugene Lang College/The New School University in New York City. He writes on intersections between dance and theatre, with a book on Pina Bausch published through the Routledge Performance Practitioner Series. He has created and directed several new theatre pieces and develops and produces new physical performance works as Co-Artistic Director of Human Company.

Alison Hodge has worked as professional director since 1982 when she co-founded the storytelling company Theatre Alibi. She was assistant director at Gardzienice Theatre and co-authored, with Włodzimierz Staniewski, *Hidden Territories: the Theatre of Gardzienice* (Routledge, 2004). She is director of The Quick and the Dead, an international theatre research company and a Reader in Theatre Practice in the Department of Drama and Theatre, Royal Holloway College, University of London. Her website can be found at www.alisonhodge.net

Dorinda Hulton is a Senior Lecturer in Drama and a freelance director and dramaturg. Her research, professional practice, and teaching focus on processes that facilitate innovative theatre making. Her publications include 'the creative actor' in *Theatre Praxis* (Macmillan) and articles in *Performance and Art Journal* and *Studies in Theatre and Performance*, DVD-ROM for The Open University and The Archive of Performances of Greek and Roman Drama, Oxford University. With Echo Arts, Cyprus, she acted as dramaturg for an interdisciplinary performance of new work, which represented Cyprus at the New Plays from Europe Festival (2006). She is Artistic Consultant to Theatre Alibi, UK.

David Krasner (PhD) is Head of the Acting Program at Emerson College. He is an actor and director and has been a teacher of acting for thirty years. He is the author/editor of eight books and co-editor of the University of Michigan Series *Theater: Theory/Text/Performance*. He is currenty at work on a book on acting, practice and theory, and another on the history of modern drama for Blackwell Press.

Robert Leach taught drama and theatre arts at Birmingham University and English Literature at Edinburgh University. He directed the Russian premiere of the formerly banned *I Want a Baby* by Sergei Tretyakov for the Teatr u Nikitskikh Vorot, Moscow, where it remained in the repertoire for over five years. His theatre books include *Revolutionary Theatre* (Routledge), *Stanislavsky and Meyerhold* (Peter Lang) and *Theatre Workshop: Joan Littlewood and the Making of Modern British Theatre* (Exeter University Press), which was short-listed for Theatre Book of the Year, 2006.

Lorna Marshall trained in Japanese Theatre (Noh, Kabuki and Butoh) and Physical Performance (Jacques Lecoq and Etienne Decroux). She has worked in a range of styles including classical drama, circus, opera and physical theatre with companies such as the Royal Shakespeare Company, the National Theatre and Shared Experience. She is Honorary Research Fellow at RADA, Advisor on Training at the New National Theatre (Tokyo) and Visiting Lecturer at the Shanghai Theatre Academy. She has a long-standing collaboration with Yoshi Oida, co-writing three books with him, including *The Invisible Actor*, and assisting several productions. Her writing includes *The Body Speaks* (second edition, Methuen, 2008).

Simon Murray is Senior Lecturer in Theatre Studies at the University of Glasgow. He was recently Director of Theatre at Dartington College of Art, and has been a professional performer and director, working particularly in the field of devised theatre. He trained in Paris for a year during the late 1980s with Philippe Gaulier and Monika Pagneux. He is the author of *Jacques Lecoq* (Routledge, 2003) and joint author/editor (with John Keefe) of *Physical Theatres: A Critical Introduction* and *Physical Theatres: A Critical Reader* (Routledge, 2007). He is joint editor with Jonathan Pitches of *Theatre, Dance and Performance Training*, Routledge.

Helen E. Richardson is Associate Professor of Theatre at Brooklyn College and has her PhD in Directing from the University of California at Berkeley, where her studies focused on the work of the Théâtre du Soleil. From 1991 to 1994 she served as Artistic Director of the award-winning Stalhouderij Theatre Company, Amsterdam's resident English-language theatre, which featured an international ensemble of actors creating new works. She is currently Artistic Director of Tiyatroglobal, an international theatre, based in NY. Recently Tiyatroglobal was invited by the United Nations to create a piece for the Elimination of Violence Against Women Day.

John Rudlin was formerly Senior Lecturer in Drama, University of Exeter. His publications include: *Jacques Copeau* (Cambridge University Press, 1986) and

Commedia dell'Arte: an actor's handbook (Routledge, 1994). He edited and translated *Copeau, Texts on Theatre* (Routledge, 1990) with Norman Paul.

Peter Thomson is Emeritus Professor of Drama at the University of Exeter. His work on Brecht includes (with Jan Needle) *Brecht* (Blackwell, 1981) and *Mother Courage and Her Children* (Cambridge University Press, 1997). With Glendyr Sacks he edited *The Cambridge Companion to Brecht* (revised edition Cambridge University Press, 2006). Other publications include *Shakespeare's Professional Career* (Cambridge University Press, 1992) and *On Actors and Acting* (University of Exeter Press, 2000). He is editor of the journal *Studies in Theatre and Performance*.

Ian Watson teaches at Rutgers University-Newark where he is the Chair of the Department of Visual and Performing Arts as well as the Coordinator of the Theatre Program. He is the author of *Towards a Third Theatre: Eugenio Barba and the Odin Teatret* (Routledge, 1993, 1995) and *Negotiating Cultures: Eugenio Barba and the Intercultural Debate* (Manchester University Press, 2002). He edited *Performer Training Across Cultures* (Harwood/ Routledge, 2001) and has also published numerous articles in journals such as *The Drama Review, New Theatre Quarterly, The Latin American Theatre Review, Asian Theatre Journal, Latin American Theatre Review*, and *Gestos*. He is an Advisory Editor for *New Theatre Quarterly*.

David Williams is currently Reader in Drama and Theatre at Royal Holloway College, University of London after many years at Dartington College of Arts. He has taught and made performance in Australia, Germany and England, in theatre, dance and spaces in between. Publications include books on Peter Brook's Centre, the Théâtre du Soleil and contemporary directors; and he has been a contributing editor to *Performance Research* (Routledge) and *Writings on Dance* (Melbourne, Australia). He is the dramaturg for Lone Twin Theatre.

Lisa Wolford (now Lisa Wolford Wylam) is Graduate Programme Director and Associate Professor of Theatre at York University in Toronto, Canada. She is author of *Grotowski's Objective Drama Research* (1996) and co-editor (with Richard Schechner) of *The Grotowski Source Book* (Routledge, 1998). Her writings have appeared in *TDR, Slavic and Eastern European Performance, New Theatre Quarterly* and *Text and Performance Quarterly*. She recently co-edited a special issue of *TDR, Re-Reading Grotowski*, in collaboration with Kris Salata and is currently completing a collected volume on Grotowski and the Workcenter in collaboration with Professor Antonio Attisani and Workcenter Associate Director Mario Biagini.

Acknowledgements

I SHOULD LIKE TO THANK the following individuals and institutions for permission to reproduce the various photos enclosed: Anatoly Smeliansky and the Moscow Art Theatre Archives; Andrew N. Makarovsky, Tina Henle and the Fritz Henle Estate; Martin Barber and the Sanford Meisner Institute; Dartington Hall Trust Archive and Collection, Julien and Rosine Gautier, Mel Gordon, the Bertolt Brecht Archive; Murray Melvin, the Theatre Workshop Archive; Open Theater Archive, Kent State University Libraries, Department of Special Collections and Archives; Nina Soufy, CICT; Hugh Hill, Adela Karsznia-Karpowicz, the Grotowski Institute; Getty Images, The Hulton Archive, Madame Fay Lecoq, L'Ecole Internationale de Theatre Jacques Lecoq, Philippe Gaulier, Monika Pagneux, Complicite, Włodzimierz Staniewski and the Centre for Theatre Practices Gardzienice; Rita Skeel, Odin Teatret, SITI company, Maciej Stawinski and Cardboard Citizens. For permission to publish extracts, we gratefully acknowledge The Samuel Beckett Estate; the Calder Educational Trust and Grove/Atlantic, Inc; and Arts Archives. Every effort has been made to contact copyright holders. Where this has not been possible, we would be pleased to hear from the parties concerned.

I want to thank Talia Rodgers, my commissioning editor at Routledge and Ben Piggott and Hilary Faulkner for their patience and efficiency. I would also like to thank the following individuals: Ania Dabrowska, Mariusz Gołaj, Joanna Holcgreber, Dorinda Hulton, Peter Hulton, Chris Mazeika, Dick McCaw, Yana Sistovari-Zarifi and, Chris Hurford, for his invaluable advice.

Preface

THE SECOND EDITION of this book is a considerably expanded version of the original, including six new essays on the work of eight practitioners: Michel Saint-Denis, Maria Knebel, Jacques Lecoq, Philippe Gaulier, Monika Pagneux, Ariane Mnouchkine, Anne Bogart and Augusto Boal. In addition, a number of the original chapters have been revised. You will also find updated bibliographies and many new photographs.

From a twenty-first-century perspective, the original title, *Twentieth Century Actor Training* no longer seems appropriate since a significant number of the directors and trainers included continue to be regarded as leading practitioners worldwide. Moreover, many of the systems, methods and protocols that were developed throughout the twentieth century remain the basis of professional training in the twenty-first. I have, therefore, simply retitled the book, *Actor Training*.

Introduction

ACTOR TRAINING is a collection of introductory essays to what is arguably the most important development in modern Western theatre making. European and North American cultures have sustained a long history of actor apprenticeship, but not the systematic training traditions of Eastern performance cultures, such as those of Japanese Noh theatre, Balinese dance drama and Indian Kathakali. The first system of actor training in Europe and North America emerged at the beginning of the twentieth century after the Russian actor and director Konstantin Stanislavsky perceived the need to harness the actor's creativity, inspiration and talent through the introduction of disciplined techniques. In 1906, feeling that his acting had become stale, 'he hid away in a darkened room, smoked endlessly and surrounded himself with twenty years of notebooks . . . He began a complicated and soul-searching attempt to organize formally a practical acting "system" ' (Merlin 2003: 19). He subsequently developed a system of training through his work at the Moscow Art Theatre and related studios, and published his ideas in seminal texts translated into English as *An Actor Prepares* (1936), *Building a Character* (1949) and *Creating a Role* (1961).[1]

In the light of the work of Stanislavsky and of those that followed, actor training came to be central to theatrical innovation in the twentieth century, with many of its key practitioners also being responsible for landmark productions in North American and European theatre.

The essays in this collection begin with an exploration of the work of five early pioneers of European actor training: Stanislavsky, Vsevolod Meyerhold, Michael Chekhov, Jacques Copeau and his nephew, Michel Saint-Denis. Their influence is then traced to Maria Knebel, who furthered both Stanislavsky's and Chekhov's legacies in Russia, and to Bertolt Brecht, who had already laid down the central tenets of acting for his Epic theatre in 1930s Germany. This influenced the innovative ensemble work of Joan Littlewood in the UK, whilst the North American exponents of the Method – Lee Strasberg, Stella Adler and Sanford Meisner – shaped several generations of actors for film and theatre in the US.

The chapters go on to explore training practices in the second half of the twentieth century, such as the experimental work of Joseph Chaikin in the US, and the deep research processes of Jerzy Grotowski, Eugenio Barba and Włodzimierz Staniewski in Europe. Three teachers, Jacques Lecoq, Phillippe Gaulier and Monika Pagneux, developed physically orientated pedagogies which are both distinct and interconnected, and are considered in a single chapter. Two prolific directors whose work has straddled both centuries, Peter Brook and Ariane Mnouchkine, are dis-cussed as examples of directors whose ensemble training with actors underpins their innovative performances. Returning to the US, Anne Bogart's transcultural approach to training is analysed through her alignment of Japanese and North American methods. Finally the work of the Brazilian director, Augusto Boal, is assessed through his radical approach to acting, in which actors and non-actors use theatre as a force for social and political change.

Whilst much has been written about these figures individually, this book con-siders the breadth and lineage of the development of actor training from Stanis-lavsky's early investigations to the plethora of approaches by recent practitioners. In each chapter the historical, cultural and political context provides an introductory background to key elements in the practitioner's work. This is followed by the main principles of training, tracing their exploration through specific exercises and, where relevant, to their manifestation in theatre production.

EARLY THEORETICAL INFLUENCES

The conceptual roots of early European actor training can partly be traced to early nineteenth-century France. Denis Diderot's *Le Paradoxe sur le comédien*, first published in 1830, initiated a sustained debate in Western Europe over issues such as inspiration versus technique in the actor's process. It was Diderot's materialist analysis of the acting of his time which laid bare an essential paradox: that while the actor appeared to be experiencing 'real' feelings, the opposite was more probably true. His solution, propounded in *Le Paradoxe*, was that an actor should be capable of mechanically reproducing emotion in performance, achieving technical control and the avoidance of emotional engagement.

However, as Joseph Roach reveals in *The Player's Passion*, a more subtle read-ing than this of Diderot's ideas on acting is necessary. Diderot became increasingly aware of the hugely complex and interrelated personal processes and instincts that were at play during an actor's performance. Indeed, his further investigations into the psychophysical aspects of the human body anticipated 'emotion memory, imagination, creative unconsciousness, public solitude, character body, the score of the role and spontaneity' (Roach 1993: 117).[2]

Stanislavsky's theoretical research was likely to have included Diderot's writings. He was also greatly interested in scientific investigations into the inseparability of the mind and body, in particular, the proposition of the French psychologist Théodule Ribot, who claimed that emotion cannot exist without a physical consequence. As Carnicke points out in her chapter, Stanislavsky echoed Ribot with his assertion that: 'In every action there is something psychological, and in the psychological, something physical' (Stanislavskii 1989: 258). The emphasis on both is important because theories concerning the body/mind dynamic remain a continuous source of investigation for all subsequent actor training practitioners.

Stanislavsky's psychophysical approach emphasised the actor's deep immersion in the role in order to achieve a fully rounded 'characterisation'. The 'self' and the character represented are held in creative tension as the actor's 'inner life' is channelled into the formation of the character. Sharon Carnicke identifies two key strands of Stanislavsky's training here: the actor's work on the self and the actor's work on the role. This dual approach to training is characteristic of many of the methods that followed, though these diversified greatly in their assumptions about the self, consciousness, notions of character and the nature of representation.

Despite having trained with Stanislavsky at the Moscow Art Theatre, Vsevolod Meyerhold was one of the first practitioners to propose an alternative system of training. It is generally held that Stanislavsky's point of orientation was psychology: to reach the unconscious through the conscious. By contrast, Meyerhold's was more sociological – with its primary focus on the actor's relationship to the audience within the theatrical event. In turning to popular theatre traditions, which actively acknowledged the spectator, Meyerhold aimed to transform theatre into a revolutionary cultural force, by encouraging the audience to engage with the ideas of the performance over the emotional narrative of individual actors.

Meyerhold defined the basic elements of an anti-illusionist theatre as gesture, mask and movement. In describing Meyerhold's biomechanical training, Robert Leach notes that the actor is not 'to identify with the part' but to 'decide on the physical formulation': to embody a social paradigm or 'type' rather than inhabit a fully realised psychological characterisation. The audience would be enabled to retain their awareness of both the actor and the character-type presented through the actor's self-reflexive, 'embodied' experience. As Erika Fischer-Lichte observed:

> The human body which had been limited to serving as the natural sign of an individual's soul, now became a theatrical sign system which would be eminently suitable for expressing and presenting widely different phenomena, conditions and processes.
>
> (Fischer-Lichte 2002: 298)

Stanislavsky and Meyerhold's theoretical positions can be somewhat simplistically but usefully characterised as diametrically oppositional – the 'psychological' approach versus the 'social' – to define the parameters of one of the central debates within actor training. However, as the essays on the two practitioners make clear, in practice, both Stanislavsky and Meyerhold evolved more complex and wide-ranging approaches to training actors.

ASIAN INFLUENCES

A significant number of early Western practitioners incorporated aspects of Asian techniques into their own methods of training. In her revised essay, Sharon Carnicke emphasises Stanislavsky's holistic vision of the actor, which was influenced by a knowledge of Yoga as early as 1911, while Robert Leach notes that Meyerhold's experiments with character and form owed much to both Japanese and Chinese performance traditions. In 1935, on a visit to Moscow, Brecht was impressed by the alienation effect employed by actors in Beijing opera, which would help him formulate the basic tenets of Epic Theatre. Later practitioners such as Littlewood, Brook and Mnouchkine also explored Asian performance techniques, not only in training but through their incorporation in non-naturalistic productions.[3]

Inevitably, Asian actor training traditions run the risk of being exoticised or simplistically appropriated by practitioners in the West. In her chapter, Lisa Wolford describes how Grotowski concluded that actors should look to Asian theatre practices 'as a model for a rigorous work ethic' rather than 'attempting to appropriate codified exercises'. However, later practitioners have undertaken intercultural activities with specific intentions. For Staniewski, traditional techniques are never to be copied. Instead he seeks a correspondence with Gardzienice's own vocal and physical techniques through encounters with indigenous practices. For Anne Bogart, both rigorous training and codified form have been embraced through the co-founding of SITI theatre with Japanese director, Tadashi Suzuki. The SITI actors have adopted the Suzuki method, which is practised together with North American 'Viewpoints' in a transcultural approach to training. Rather than deeply engaging with a single form in this way, Eugenio Barba has approached Eastern techniques on an anthropological level, analysing the underlying principles of a huge range of codified performance forms in his study of the source of the actor's 'pre-expressive' performance techniques.

ANTONIN ARTAUD

The writings of the French actor, director and poet Antonin Artaud (1896–1948) have provided a significant reference point for many actor training practitioners in the second half of the twentieth century. His seminal collection of essays, *The Theatre and its Double*, was first published in English in 1958. Artaud rejected what he regarded as the rationalist and reductive tendencies of Western theatre. He called for a theatre which celebrated the non-verbal elements of consciousness that could ultimately arouse therapeutic emotions within his spectators. It was Artaud's passionate belief that 'theatre will never recover its own specific powers of action until it has also recovered its own language' (Artaud 1970: 68).

As a result, Artaud felt it was necessary to 'create word, gesture and expressive metaphysics, in order to rescue theatre from its human, psychological prostration' (Artaud 1970: 69). As Grotowski points out: 'Artaud left no concrete technique behind him, indicated no method. He left visions and metaphors' (Grotowski 1969: 86). However, these visions and metaphors have offered inspiration to many in practice, perhaps, most explicitly, Peter Brook and actors from the Royal Shakespeare Company in the Theatre of Cruelty season of 1964.

THE DIRECTOR AND THE ACTOR

The relatively recent rise of the specialist role of theatre 'director' brought about a seismic shift in the process of theatre making. As the dual functions of the nineteenth-century actor/manager gave way to the more specialist position of the modern director, work with actors became further refined. Firstly, and most obviously, the director has furthered the opportunity for a more objective examination of the nature of the actor's work – in particular the development of systems and disciplines of training. Secondly, and more fundamentally, the director has helped to mediate and negotiate the central issue of acting: the tension between the actor's self and the actor's role.

Consequently, directors have utilised training as a means to incorporate the actor in a revitalised role as a theatre maker. Performers often formed intensive collaborative relationships with directors, and have been central to the realisation of a new aesthetic – Ryszard Cieslak in Grotowski's Poor Theatre, for example. During intimate, preparatory work with Cieslak while developing his role in *The Constant Prince*, Grotowski acknowledges that 'for months and months Cieslak worked alone with me' (Richards 1995: 122).

The actor's shift in role from interpreter of text to co-deviser became more prevalent in the 1960s as avant-garde artists explored the dynamic opposition between presence and representation, actor and dramatic character; and where the performance text was more often drawn from the actor's personal material or research. Joseph Chaikin's Open Theater is a paradigm of this collaborative and personal process: 'it has sometimes been possible to join with others in a common effort so intense that at the end of a project I have been unable to say which part was my work and which part belonged to someone else' (Chaikin 1972: xi).

Within another collaborative model, play and improvisation became key aspects of training for the physical theatres of Jacques Lecoq, Philippe Gaulier and Monika Pagneux. In particular, Lecoq's 'autocours' encouraged a view of the actor as co-creator, stressing the significance of the ensemble and the actor's physicality in an independent devising process. Towards the end of the twentieth century, physical scoring and composition work became protocols in the training of Eugenio Barba and Anne Bogart respectively, and testify to the increasing formalisation of the actor's theatre-making skills with or without the director as a guide.

THE ACTOR'S PRESENCE

An actor's real-time encounter with the audience relates to a highly valued concept in live performance, namely, that of the actor's presence. Jane Goodall cites two distinctive definitions: firstly, presence as an intrinsic, mysterious, essential 'inner power being radiated outwards' by the actor and, secondly, presence as constructed through skills and techniques that actors can acquire through training (Goodall 2008: 8). Erika Fischer-Lichte also distinguishes between the innate 'sheer presence' of the actor's phenomenal body and the actor's active ability 'to command both space and the audience's attention' through a 'mastery of certain techniques and practices to which the spectators respond' (Fischer-Lichte 2008: 96).

The idea that presence can be galvanised through an active relationship with the audience is explored in the training methods of many practitioners. One key aspect of this complex process has been to focus the actor's attention within the present moment as a source of energy and power. Stanislavsky recognised this early, referring to acting as 'experiencing'. Lecoq encouraged the actor's energetic response through playful spontaneity, Meisner stressed 'the reality of doing', Grotowski focused on 'the cycle of living impulses' and Brook seeks a state of 'openness and immediacy' in the actor which he calls 'transparency'.

While various definitions of presence obtain, it is understood within most forms of actor training as potentially a constructed phenomenon that can be realised by coordinating the actor's body/consciousness and the circulation of energy. For example, Ian Watson describes Barba's study of the actor's presence through his anthropological analysis of Oriental techniques. Barba identifies two main sources: 'the use of learned body techniques designed to break the performer's daily responses' and the 'codification of principles which dictate the use of energy during performance'.

In her chapter in this volume Dorinda Hulton's definition of presence relates to Chaikin's sound and movement exercise. Within this context she suggests the actor is not uniquely concerned with the presence of 'self' but is more concerned with being 'in operation with imagery'. The actor's attention is completely absorbed in this interactive task. When the full engagement of the actor with an immediate process

> allows a particular kind of shifting balance, or dialogue, between body and mind, in listening to and watching for the emerging form, the emerging image, and is able, moment to moment, to come into alignment with it . . . [Then] there is a perceptible quality of 'presence'.
>
> (p. 161)

CROSS FERTILISATION

The cross fertilisation of ideas and practices between later practitioners is complex. In a number of cases practitioners have been trained within each other's systems. In addition to Meyerhold, both Chekhov and Knebel were former actors with Stanislavsky at the Moscow Art Theatre. Both went on to develop their own very distinct working methods. Chekhov retained a certain amount of his former director's ideas, although he reinterpreted or transformed many of them, particularly in the light of his study of Steiner's anthroposophy, which led to his belief in the importance of establishing a distance between the actor and their emotions. Knebel studied acting with Chekhov and active analysis with Stanislavsky, and went on to develop and apply ideas from both systems as Artistic Director of the State Children's Theatre and in her capacity as a teacher at the State Institute of Theatrical Arts (GITIS) from 1948 until her death in 1985.

John Rudlin maps out Copeau's immense legacy through those who trained with him, such as Michel Saint-Denis, Jean Dasté and Etienne Decroux, and those who were influenced by him in other ways, such as Jean-Louis Barrault, Jacques Lecoq and Ariane Mnouchkine. Copeau's ideas were further developed by his nephew, Michel Saint-Denis, and Jane Baldwin traces his extraordinary contribution to the foundation of theatre schools in the UK, France, Canada and the US.

Brecht's anti-illusionist acting techniques offer interesting parallels to Meyerhold's. His influence on Western theatre in the second half of the twentieth century has been hugely significant and his techniques have informed a wide range of practitioners, from Littlewood, Brook, Chaikin and Mnouchkine to Boal.

Other practitioners have reinterpreted elements of former approaches. The clearest example of this is the Method, both in terms of its connections to the Stanislavskian system through its concern with psychological revelation, and also through the contrasting interpretations of it by three of its foremost exponents: Strasberg, Adler and Meisner. Joan Littlewood also drew on Stanislavskian approaches, but combined them with the movement training of Rudolf Laban (and, to some extent, Meyerhold's biomechanics). Thus, rather than reinterpreting Stanislavsky, she found an interface with completely different systems of movement training. Other practitioners even rejected their own training: Chaikin worked as a Method actor before wholeheartedly abandoning its tenets to formulate his own – partially out of exasperation with what he saw as its dogmatic assumptions.

Given this extraordinary fluidity of influences, collaboration is, unsurprisingly, a prevalent characteristic among later avant-garde practitioners. For example, Brook, Barba, Staniewski and Chaikin all worked with Grotowski in various ways. Barba and Staniewski both actively participated in Grotowski's Laboratory Theatre. Chaikin and Brook invited Grotowski to introduce his training techniques to their actors but, as Chaikin points out, whilst his 'inspiration and urgent sincerity have affected me and many others . . . still, we are on different journeys' (Chaikin 1972: xi).

Of the physical theatre trainers, both Gaulier and Pagneux taught at Lecoq's school before leading their own courses, each with a different emphasis on the actor's physical expressivity. Pagneux also worked as a movement director for Peter Brook, whilst her teaching draws on the work of the influential Israeli movement teacher, Moshe Feldenkrais and the early contemporary dancer Mary Wigman. Mnouchkine also trained with Lecoq and acknowledged his significant influence on her mask, improvisation and body work.

SYSTEMS OR PRINCIPLES

The search for methodologies of Western actor training in the twentieth century precipitated debate around two key questions. Firstly, could a single, universal system be achieved which would contain a complete method of actor training? This was Stanislavsky's initial project but, as Carnicke emphasises in her chapter, the system ultimately suggests various pathways for the actor: 'In choosing a path, each actor reinvents and personalises the System.' Stanislavsky's hope was for 'a guide . . . a handbook, not a philosophy' (pp. 33–4).

Secondly, could the fundamental techniques of one acting system be applicable in the creation of any form of theatre? This again was Stanislavsky's belief. But some practitioners have found limitations within his system, particularly when attempting to move away from psychological realism and the interpretation of existing texts.

Meyerhold reacted against the psychological assumptions of naturalistic theatre. Through a sustained and intensive training of the body he too sought a methodology that would cope with a range of styles, but through a greater articulation of the performer's physical, spatial and rhythmical vocabulary. Later practitioners resisted the notion of anything as absolute as a universally applied method. It was, for example, Chaikin's belief that systems were recorded as ground plans, not to be followed any more than rules of courtship. We can get clues from others, but our own culture and sensibility and aesthetic will lead us to a totally new kind of expression, unless we imitate both the process and findings of another. The aesthetic remakes the system.

(Chaikin 1972: 21)

Ultimately, practitioners have eschewed the notion of a comprehensive system in favour of identifying first *principles* within their own particular context. These principles are made manifest through specific actor training techniques and amplify distinctive ethical positions, but do not in themselves constitute a 'system'. Copeau speaks of understanding the 'dramatic principle in oneself' in his quest for sincerity on stage. Brecht's actor cannot simply observe without at the same time interrogating the social forces at play. Strasberg describes an actor as the individual who can 'create out of himself', but in order to achieve this, the actor must be prepared to 'appeal to the unconscious and the subconscious' (Strasberg 1965: 82). Mnouchkine propounds 'a commitment to collective and community, which may include collective creation' (Miller 2007: 105).

But while the contexts in which these training principles evolved remain an essential part of their identification, many have endured, and influenced the work of those who followed. This suggests that some principles are fundamental, capable of transcending their origins and therefore justifiably can be recognised as part of a matrix of key concepts in contemporary actor training. Collectively, the essays included here begin to uncover these key ideas.

Alison Hodge, July 2009

Notes

1   See Sharon Carnicke's chapter for the complex history of Stanislavsky's first publications. *An Actor Prepares* and *Building a Character* were edited and re-translated by Jean Benedetti as *An Actor's Work: a student's diary* and published by Routledge in 2008.

2   Roach points out that the *Paradoxe sur le Comédien* was conceived by Diderot very closely with other works of that period, *Eléments de physiologie* and the *Rêve de d'Alembert*, and that the three works, which each take the human body as a central theme, 'may usefully be interpreted as a triptych . . .' (Roach 1993: 129).

3   For example, Peter Brook has famously founded an international centre for theatre research in Paris, employing Asian training techniques in a wide range of projects. Ariane Mnouchkine drew on several (Kabuki, Noh and Balinese dance) in her warrior-like interpretation of Shakespeare's *Richard II* (1981).

Selected bibliography

Artaud, A. (1970) *The Theatre and its Double*, trans. V. Corti, London: Calder and Boyars.

Barba, E. (1979) *The Floating Islands: Reflections with Odin Teatret*, trans. J. Barba, F. Perdheilhan, J.C. Rodesch, S. Shapiro, J. Varley, Denmark: Thomsens Boytrykheri.

Chaikin, J. (1972) *The Presence of the Actor*, New York: Atheneum.

Cole, T. and Chinoy, H. Krich (1970) *Actors on Acting, The Theories, Techniques, and Practices of the World's Great Actors, Told in Their Own Words*, New York: Three Rivers Press.

Diderot, D. (1883) *The Paradox of Acting*, trans. Walter Herries Pollock, London: Chatto Windus.

Fischer-Lichte, E. (2002) *History of European Drama and Theatre*, London and New York: Routledge.

—— (2008) *The Transformative Power of Performance*, London and New York: Routledge.

Goodall, J. (2008) *Stage Presence*, London and New York: Routledge.

Grotowski, J. (1969) *Towards a Poor Theatre*, trans. M. Buszewicz and J. Barba, ed. E. Barba, London: Methuen.

Merlin, B. (2003) *Konstantin Stanislavsky*, London and New York: Routledge.

Miller, J.G. (2007) *Ariane Mnouchkine*, London and New York: Routledge.

Nemirovitch-Dantchenko [*sic*], V. (1937) *My Life in the Russian Theatre*, trans. John Cournos, London: Geoffrey Bles.

Ribot, T. (1897) *The Psychology of Emotions*, London: Walter Scott Ltd.

Richards, T. (1995) *At Work with Grotowski on Physical Action*, London: Routledge.

Roach, J. (1993) *The Player's Passion, Studies in the Science of Acting*, The University of Michigan Press.

Schmidt, P. (1996) *Meyerhold at Work*, trans. P. Schmidt, I. Levin, V. McGee, New York and London: Applause.

Stanislavski, C. (1980) *An Actor Prepares*, trans. E. Hapgood, London: Methuen.

—— (1983) *Building a Character*, trans. E. Hapgood, London: Methuen.

—— (1983) *Creating a Role*, trans. E. Hapgood, London: Methuen.

Stanislavki, K. (2008) *An Actor's Work: A Student's Diary*, trans. and ed. J Benedetti, London and New York: Routledge.

Stanislavskii, K.S. (1989) *Sobranie sochinenii*, vol. 2 [*An Actor's Work on Himself, Part 1*], Moscow: Iskusstvo.

Strasberg, L. (1965) *Strasberg at the Actor's Studio: Tape-Recorded Sessions*, ed. R. Hethmon, New York: Theatre Communications Group.

Zarrilli, P. (1995) *Acting (Re)Considered, Theories and Practices*, London and New York: Routledge.

Zeami, M. (1984) *On the Art of No Drama: The Major Treatises of Zeami*, trans. J. Thomas Rimer, Y. Masakazu, Princeton, N.J.: Princeton University Press.

Chapter 1

Sharon Marie Carnicke

STANISLAVSKY'S SYSTEM: PATHWAYS FOR THE ACTOR

O**UR COMMON KNOWLEDGE GENERALLY** associates the Stanislavsky System with the twentieth century's infatuation with psychological realism on stage. However, a closer look at the full trajectory of his life and work offers much of value to twenty-first-century actors. For example, his long-overlooked interest in Yoga dovetails with current curricula in many acting schools, and his holistic view of psychology anticipates ground-breaking discoveries in cognitive science which impact on acting (Blair 2008). This chapter suggests how Stanislavsky's insights on actor training are more holistic, more complex and more elastic than twentieth-century views allow.

LIFE AND CAREER

Born in 1863, Stanislavsky saw profound scientific and social changes take place as the nineteenth century became the twentieth. Living in Russia, he experienced artistic traditions from both Europe and Asia. Before his death in 1938, he witnessed three great revolutions: realism's overturn of nineteenth-century histrionics, modernism's rejection of realism, and Russia's political move from monarchy to communism. The first two shaped his career and made him world famous; the last turned him from a wealthy man into a poor one, from an artist who shaped modern theatre into one who was shaped by political forces. 'In truth, many changes occurred during my life', he wrote, 'and more than once were they fundamental' (Stanislavskii 1988b: 3).

Born Konstantin Sergeevich Alekseev into one of Russia's wealthiest manufacturing families, he lived a privileged youth. He regularly visited plays, circuses, ballets and the opera. He expressed adolescent theatrical impulses in a fully equipped theatre, built by his father in 1877 at the family estate, and as he grew, he often used his wealth to further his talents as actor and director. Until the communist revolution, he personally financed many of his most productive artistic experiments: in 1888 he founded the critically acclaimed theatrical enterprise the Society of Art and Literature; in 1912 he started the First Studio to develop his System for actor training.

Until the age of thirty-three, Stanislavsky performed and directed only as an amateur. In early nineteenth-century Russia, many actors had been serfs, appearing at the behest of their owners; even after the abolition of serfdom, actors continued to be regarded as lower-class citizens. Hence, whilst the Alekseev family loved theatre, they discouraged their children from professional aspirations which threatened social embarrassment. The critics, too, respected decorum when they tactfully praised an anonymous 'K. A–v' for outstanding performances in productions by the Society of Art and Literature. In 1884, Konstantin Alekseev began to act without his family's knowledge, under the stage name Stanislavsky.[1]

With the founding of the Moscow Art Theatre in 1897, Stanislavsky turned professional. The playwright and theatre educator Vladimir Nemirovich-Danchenko had chosen the impressive amateur as his co-director in an idealistic effort 'to reconstruct [theatre's] plays' (Nemirovitch-Dantchenko [sic] 1937: 68). Their first meeting at a Moscow restaurant lasted a legendary eighteen hours. Their conversation set in motion the company that would bring the latest European ideas in stage realism to Russia, and new standards in acting to the world.

In order to understand the revolutionary impact of their endeavour one need only compare the 1896 production of Chekhov's *The Seagull* at the Imperial Aleksandrinsky Theatre with the Moscow Art Theatre's staging two years later. The first relied on nineteenth-century conventions. It served as a benefit for a popular comic actress and featured a star. The cast met for a few rehearsals, learning their parts on their own and supplying their own costumes. The theatre used sets from the existing stock. Despite its mythic failure on opening night, *The Seagull* attained, in Danchenko's

Figure 1.1 Konstantin Stanislavsky (1922).

Figure 1.2 Stanislavsky as Astrov in Chekhov's *Uncle Vanya* (1899).

words, 'routine' success (Nemirovitch-Dantchenko [sic] 1937: 63). By this, he meant that the Aleksandrinsky production entertained its audiences in typically nineteenth-century fashion, without any concessions in staging or acting to Chekhov's twentieth-century innovations in drama. In contrast, the Moscow Art Theatre put eighty hours of work into thirty-three rehearsals in order to cultivate an ensemble of actors without stars. Sets, costumes, properties and sound (including humming crickets and barking dogs) were all carefully designed to support a unified vision of the play. The directors held three dress rehearsals. Even so, Stanislavsky considered the 1898 *Seagull* under-rehearsed (Benedetti 1990: 82).

With this production, Stanislavsky became known as Chekhov's definitive director, and the Moscow Art Theatre took its place in the history of twentieth-century theatre.[2] Moreover, from this point forward, Stanislavsky's name and that of the Art Theatre became inextricably linked. His work on Chekhov's major plays (1898–1904), Gorky's *The Lower Depths* (1902), Ibsen's *An Enemy of the People* (1900), and his playing of such roles as the fussy old Famusov in Griboedov's *Woe From Wit* (1906) created his reputation as a leading realistic director and a gifted character actor.

No sooner had the Moscow Art Theatre established itself as the leader in realism, than symbolist playwrights and theatricalist directors revolted against representational theatre. Symbolists wanted to get beyond the illusions of reality by creating poetic expressions of the transcendental and spiritual. Theatricalists enjoyed making spectators aware of the conventions of performance, sets and costumes, much as abstract artists bring viewers' attention to canvas and paint. Both groups fostered non-realistic theatrical forms. Whilst Stanislavsky tackled the new styles with productions of symbolist plays in 1907 and 1908,[3] these efforts left little imprint on the character of the Art Theatre, which remained a bastion of realism.

Stanislavsky, however, wished to explore more widely. At various times during his career he experimented with symbolism, verse, opera, Western psychology, Yoga and Eastern ideas on the mind/body continuum, modern dance, and trends in criticism of art and literature. In short, he willingly embraced anything that could illuminate acting and drama. Paradoxically, whilst the Moscow Art Theatre fostered his fame as a master of psychological realism, it also clipped his wings in other directions. Whilst the actors saw his experimentation as eccentric, Nemirovich-Danchenko considered 'Stanislavskyitis' as dangerous to the stability of their theatre (2005: 294). As a sharp businessman, Danchenko insisted that they continue to build upon their initial success with realistic styles. As a consequence, Stanislavsky moved his experiments to a series of studios, adjunct to the main stage and independently financed.

Take the System as a case in point. Stanislavsky became the first practitioner in the twentieth century to articulate systematic actor training, but he did so largely outside the confines of the Moscow Art Theatre. He began to develop what he called a 'grammar' of acting in 1906, when his performances as Dr Stockmann (*An Enemy of the People*) had begun to falter. He brought his new ideas and techniques to his home company in 1909 whilst rehearsing Turgenev's *A Month in the Country*. Although he had banned Danchenko from attending these rehearsals so as to alleviate tension, he still met with resistance from the actors, who had succeeded in Chekhov's plays without any 'eccentric' exercises. In 1911, a frustrated Stanislavsky threatened to resign if the company did not adopt his System as its official working method. Danchenko relented, but reluctantly. After one year, the seasoned actors still remained sceptical and Stanislavsky finally stepped outside of the Art Theatre and created the First Studio in order to work with more willing actors.

The Bolshevik Revolution of 1917 left Russia in chaos. Civil war raged until 1921, food and necessities became scarce and inflation made the rouble all but worthless. In the upheaval, Stanislavsky lost the wealth and privileges of his youth. The Soviets confiscated his family home and factory. He began to sell his remaining possessions to survive. 'My life has completely changed', he wrote. 'I have become proletarian' (Stanislavskii 1999: 18). When his son fell ill with tuberculosis, he could not afford treatment (Stanislavskii 1999: 110). Facing eviction in 1920, Stanislavsky turned for help to Lenin's newly appointed Commissar of Enlightenment, Anatoly Lunacharsky, who was himself a playwright. Lunacharsky pleaded with Lenin on Stanislavsky's behalf, stressing that he was 'about to see his last pair of trousers' (Hecht 1989: 2). The state relented by allocating Stanislavsky a modest house with two rooms for rehearsals.[4]

The Moscow Art Theatre also struggled in post-revolutionary Russia. At the time of the Revolution, the theatre required 1.5 billion roubles to operate, whilst its box office receipts totalled only 600 million (Benedetti 1990: 250). Without more profit or governmental subsidy the theatre could not survive. Both sources of income proved impossible in the wake of the Revolution. The theatre mounted only one new production between 1917 and 1922 – Byron's *Cain*. Its set could not be built as designed, due to the lack of funds. Therefore, Stanislavsky decided to use a simple black backdrop for the production. Even so, enough velvet to enclose the full stage could not be found (Benedetti 1990: 244).

Stanislavsky and the Moscow Art Theatre looked to the West, and more specifically to America, for financial survival. As Stanislavsky soberly wrote to Danchenko in 1924: 'America is the sole audience, the sole source of money for subsidy, on which we can count' (Stanislavskii 1999: 138). Thus, the company split into two. Stanislavsky led the most famous actors on tour throughout Europe and the United States; Danchenko kept the theatre open in Moscow. The tours lasted two years (1922–24) and were unabashedly intended to make money for the floundering theatre. Only fame, however, resulted.

Many of the Moscow Art Theatre's talented actors traded their fame for employment in the West as actors, directors and teachers, rather than return to difficult lives in the new Soviet Union. These émigrés (Richard Boleslavsky, Maria Ouspenskaya and Michael Chekhov amongst them) promoted Stanislavsky's ideas on actor training. They helped move the System beyond the bounds of Russia.

Whilst on tour, Stanislavsky turned to writing for personal income. He published *My Life in Art* and *An Actor Prepares* in the United States in English (a language which he could neither speak nor read) so that he could gain control over international royalties. The Soviet Union had not yet signed the International Copyright Agreement, and therefore Russian publication would not protect his rights (Carnicke 2008: 80). His decision to publish abroad undeniably helped to promote the System throughout the world.

Upon returning to Moscow, Stanislavsky and his theatre faced growing Soviet control over the arts. The state deemed realism superior to any type of formal or abstract art, and the physical, material world superior to anything spiritual or transcendental. Danchenko had read the writing on the wall. In recognizing the importance of realism to the Soviet regime, he had sent the company's oldest, most realistic productions to the West (Carnicke 2008: 27–39). In contrast, Stanislavsky found it harder to learn the new, post-revolutionary rules. In 1928 he betrayed his utter lack of political savvy when, at the thirtieth anniversary of the Moscow Art Theatre, before an exclusively communist audience, he praised a wealthy capitalist for initially funding the enterprise (Stanislavskii 1994: 297). Vicious attacks followed in the press, triggering the severe heart attack that ended Stanislavsky's acting career (Autant-Mathieu 2003: 73). Until his death, he struggled to comprehend the new, inscrutable society that surrounded him, composed of 'actually new people' with radically different attitudes from his own (Stanislavskii 1999: 656).

By 1934, when Socialist Realism became the only lawful artistic style, governmental control turned into a stranglehold. The Soviets co-opted Stanislavsky, too, for the political cause. By focusing on his early career and willfully ignoring his experimental interests, the press of the 1930s turned Stanislavsky into a model for theatrical Socialist Realism. In 1932, when the regime decided to create a standard, politically correct curriculum for the nation's theatre institutes, the acting manuals which Stanislavsky was then writing became the state's business. A Soviet commission was thus appointed to bring them into agreement with Marxist materialism (Carnicke 2008: 94–109). In short, censors modified everything that Stanislavsky published in Soviet Russia. Only with the fall of the USSR in 1991 and the consequent emptying of hidden archives has the full extent of this censorship been revealed.[5]

The private man did not match the public image, and Stanislavsky's System contained more than the official curriculum allowed. Despite his early, much publicised work on psychological realism, Stanislavsky had continued with his politically incorrect interests in Yoga, symbolism and the formal structures of drama and action. No one style in art could ever suffice. As Stanislavsky explains, 'Human life is so subtle, so complex and multifaceted, that it needs an incomparably large number of new, still undiscovered "isms" to express it fully' (Stanislavskii 1989: 458). Hence, he supported his former student, the theatricalist director Meyerhold, at the very time when Stalin sentenced such artists to hard labour and execution. Stanislavsky even dared to criticise the now mediocre, propagandistic repertory at the Art Theatre.

To keep Stanislavsky's public image as a Socialist Realist intact, the regime hid the truth. Stanislavsky lived the last four years of his life in internal exile, according to Stalin's policy of 'isolation and preservation' reserved for internationally known Soviet citizens. The ageing Stanislavsky, now frail, with a heart condition, made such confinement relatively easy to explain in the press. From 1934 to 1938 he left his home only for brief visits to doctors, whilst his nurses and close associates – his 'wardens' – monitored what information reached him from the outside world (Smeliansky 1991: 9). But for his international fame, Stanislavsky might have suffered more than the internal exile which Stalin imposed upon him in 1934.

Ironically, Stanislavsky conducted his most non-realistic work during these last years. In the privacy of his home, he experimented with opera, Shakespeare's plays, new plays devised through his actors' improvisations and Molière's *Tartuffe*. However partial Stanislavsky's public image, his System embodies a holistic and multivariant approach to acting that escapes the bounds of politics.

THE SYSTEM

Stanislavsky's name has become omnipresent in Western theatrical discourse because of his lifelong, obsessive passion to turn the practice of acting into a system. 'I believe that all masters of the arts need to write', he said, 'to try and systematise their art' (Filippov 1977: 58). He had begun to do so at the age of fourteen, keeping detailed notebooks on every performance he gave or saw. His project culminated in an auto-biography, piles of drafts for three acting manuals, a myriad of unpublished notes, lesson plans and jottings. However, he never deemed his System or his books complete; they remain dynamic, experimental explorations of the unique communicative power of theatre. At his death, he had finished only two volumes: *My Life in Art* and the first volume of *An Actor's Work on Himself*, or what we in the West generally know as *An Actor Prepares*.[6]

Stanislavsky's effort to 'systematise' his art in writing was far from easy. Acting, like riding a bicycle, is easier to do than to explain. No wonder acting is more effectively taught in classrooms than through textbooks. In order to surmount this difficulty, Stanislavsky chose to write his manuals as if they were 'the System in a novel' (Stanislavskii 1999: 99). He thus creates a fictional classroom to portray, rather than explain, the process of acting. He introduces characters who struggle to act well, and their teacher who struggles to help them. Stanislavsky puts his characters into changing contexts which continually challenge their ideas about what it means to act. In endless Socratic dialogue, they explore the mysteries of acting, they argue their various points of view and they sometimes break through to clear understandings of their intractable art.

Taken together, Stanislavsky's books and manuscripts encode a coherent and remarkably consistent set of assumptions about acting. All his exercises, techniques and interests partake of these essential ideas.

Figure 1.3 Stanislavsky as Satin in Gorky's *The Lower Depths* (1902).

The first, most pervasive of these is Stanislavsky's holistic belief that mind, body and spirit represent a psychophysical continuum. He rejects the Western conception that divides mind from body, taking his cue from French psychologist Théodule Ribot, who believed that emotion never exists without physical consequence. Echoing Ribot's assertion that 'a disembodied emotion is a non-existent one' (Ribot 1897: 95), Stanislavsky insists that: 'In every physical action there is something psychological, and in the psychological, something physical' (Stanislavskii 1989: 258).

In his holistic System, Stanislavsky also links spirit to the human psyche by embracing Yoga, which views the physical as a threshold into the spiritual. The 'organic connection of body and soul' is so strong, he insists, that artificial respiration revives not only flesh, but also 'the life of the spirit' (Stanislavskii 1989: 349). He first encountered Yoga in 1911, whilst discussing his latest ideas on acting with his family. His son's tutor (a young medical student) recognised the yogic impulse behind his employer's words and suggested that he read *Hatha Yoga* by Ramacharaka (Vinogradskaia 2003: 294).[7] From that time on, Stanislavsky borrowed ideas, terms, images and exercises from Ramacharaka as explicitly as he did from Western psychology.

Many critics and teachers privilege one element in this continuum over the other. In the United States, Stanislavsky's work with emotion answered the American fascination with Freudian psychology. In the Soviet Union, Stanislavsky's work with physical aspects of acting made his System better conform to the tenets of Marxist materialism. This bifurcation of the System is mistaken (Carnicke 2008: 162–64, 185–89). For Stanislavsky, the mental and spiritual is always imbued with the physical and vice versa. Only three months before his death, he cautioned his directing students that: 'One must give actors various paths. One of these is the path of [physical] action. But there is also another path: you can move from feeling to action, arousing feeling first' (Stanislavskii 2000: 498).

Following from this first assumption, Stanislavsky posits that physical tension is creativity's greatest enemy, not only paralysing and distorting the beauty of the body, but also interfering with the ability to concentrate and fantasise. Performance demands a state of physical relaxation, in which the actor uses only enough muscular tension to accomplish what is necessary. Stanislavsky suggests that actors practise yogic breathing to build habits of relaxation. He also teaches progressive relaxation, contracting and releasing each muscle of the body in turn, in order to learn the experiential difference between the two.

A second major assumption behind the System involves Stanislavsky's belief that successful acting places the creative act itself in the laps of the audience. By insisting on the immediacy of performance and the presence of the actor, Stanislavsky argues against nineteenth-century traditions, which taught actors to represent characters from the stage through carefully crafted intonations and gestures. However well rehearsed, Stanislavskian actors remain essentially dynamic and improvisatory during performance. Stanislavsky calls such acting (which 'is cultivated in our theatre and mastered here in our school') 'experiencing' (Stanislavskii 1989: 59). He adopts this idiosyncratic term from novelist Leo Tolstoy, who had argued that art communicates felt experience, not knowledge (Tolstoi 1964: 85–86; Carnicke 2008: 113–47).

Stanislavsky relates 'experiencing' to states of mind that seem more familiar: 'inspiration', 'creative moods', the activation of the 'subconscious'. He compares it to the sensation of existing fully within the immediate moment – what he calls 'I am' (taken from Yoga) and what Western actors generally call 'moment-to-moment' work. He describes this state as 'happy', but 'rare', when the actor is 'seized' by the role (Stanislavskii 1993: 363). The Russian word carries many different nuances, amongst them 'to experience', 'to feel', 'to become aware', 'to go through', 'to live', 'to live through', etc. (Carnicke 2008: 132–33).

Following from this second assumption, Stanislavsky designs the whole System to foster 'experiencing'. From a theoretical point of view, the System merely collects and codifies the principles of human creativity necessary to the actor. Stanislavsky assumes that the ideal creative state occurs of itself when the actor works through the various elements that comprise the 'natural laws' of the actor's 'organic creativeness' (Stanislavskii 1988b: 495). From a practical point of view, the System suggests specific techniques that help actors develop a state of mind and body that encourages 'experiencing'. Stanislavsky believes that this 'sense of self' (as he calls it) provides the 'soil' (Stanislavskii 1989: 95, 265) from which the role can grow. It combines two alternating, nearly simultaneous perspectives: being on stage and being within the role (Carnicke 2008: 142–44). It is 'proper to the stage', 'inner' in its concentration, 'outer' in the actor's physical presence and 'creative'.

The following exercises from the System[8] reveal the wide spectrum of Stanislavsky's interests. They fall into two broad groups: techniques that foster a proper 'sense of self' and hence induce in the actor a creative state of 'experiencing', and methods that offer pathways into dramatic texts for the successful creation of characters.

GROUP I

The actor develops a theatrical *sense of self* by learning to control the skills of *concentration*, *imagination* and *communication*. Many exercises in this group derive from Stanislavsky's fascination with Yoga.

Concentration

Stanislavsky expects total mental and physical concentration on stage. He calls this psychophysical state *public solitude*. In it, actors tune out anything external to the world of the play. They behave in public as if in private. Stanislavsky teaches the importance of such a state of absorption by relating the Hindu story of a maharaja who offers the position of governmental minister to the person able to carry a pitcher of milk around the walls of the bustling city without spilling a drop (Stanislavskii 1989: 164).

1   Psychophysical concentration begins with sharpening the senses through observation (Stanislavskii 1990: 400).

Sight

● Look at an object or person for thirty seconds, look away, and give an accurate description.
● The classic mirror exercise: two partners face each other; one reflects the other as an image in a mirror. The leader moves, and the image follows so exactly that an observer should not be able to tell who leads and who follows.

Hearing

● Close your eyes, relax, and listen only for sounds in the surrounding room; broaden your focus to sounds within the building; broaden your focus once more to sounds from the street. Open your eyes, and describe what you have heard as precisely as possible.

Touch

● Close your eyes; someone will hand you an object. Examine it thoroughly through touch alone. Return the object, open your eyes, and describe it as exactly as possible.

Smell

- Close your eyes, relax, and focus on what you can smell within the surrounding room. Open your eyes, and recall precisely what you sensed.
- Imaginatively recreate familiar smells: the sea, hot chocolate, roses.

Taste

- Describe the present taste in your mouth to another person.
- Imaginatively recreate familiar tastes: lemon, vinegar, sugar.

Affect

In addition to the five physical senses, Stanislavsky adds a sixth, emotion. Indeed, in Russian the word for 'feelings' applies equally to emotional and physical sensations. To illustrate the link between emotion and other senses, Stanislavsky relates two anecdotes. The first involves two travellers, who stop at a precipice overlooking the sea. As they look down at the raging water, one recalls all the details of a near-drowning, 'how, where, why'. The other recalls the same incident but with details that have lost clarity over time. Only the first exhibits the heightened affective sensibility (*emotional memory*) helpful to actors. The second story tells of two men who hear a familiar polka. As they try to remember where they have heard it before, one recalls sitting near a column with the other at his side. 'We were eating fish', he reminds his friend, as the smell of perfume wafted by. Suddenly the memories of the polka, fish and perfume bring back to them their bitter, drunken quarrel that night (Stanislavskii 1989: 284–85).[9] Stanislavsky advocates that actors sharpen their emotional memories, just as they do other senses, through exercise.

- Read voraciously (newspapers, novels, anything in print), visit museums, concerts and art exhibits. In short, develop your experience of the world and your ability to empathise with others through a broad, liberal education (Stanislavskii 1989: 316).
- Recall your mood when you last sat on the beach at daybreak (Stanislavskii 1990: 502).
- Recall a moment of joy, sadness, ecstasy, or any other emotion or mood (Stanislavskii 1990: 502).

2   Stanislavsky further trains concentration through *circles of attention* that can be *small, medium,* or *large.* He calls points of focus on stage (whether animate or inanimate, visible or imagined) *objects of attention*. Actors learn to limit their focus to only those objects within defined circles. In his fictional classroom, Stanislavsky uses pools of light to help his students understand such focus. He first trains a spotlight on a table, illuminating only the small number of objects lying upon it – a small circle of attention; light then pools over the table, its chairs and a sofa nearby – a medium circle; then finally light floods the entire stage – a large circle (Stanislavskii 1989: 158–63).[10]

  - Walk in a small circle and notice what objects fall within it; broaden your walk to a circle of medium size, adding more objects of attention;

finally, walk in as big a circle as the room allows, taking in all objects as you walk.
- Sitting still, mentally establish a small circle around you and notice what falls within it; broaden your attention to a medium circle; take in the whole room as the largest circle of attention available to you.
- When performing, define your circles of attention carefully to include all objects necessary to the scene. However, if your attention starts to wander, create a small circle in order to re-focus your concentration.

Imagination

The System values an actor's capacity to treat fictional circumstances as if real, to visualise the details of a character's world specifically, and to daydream or fantasise about the events of the play. Stanislavsky taught that an actor should not speak without an image in the mind's eye and suggests developing a 'filmstrip' of images to accompany the performance of every role (Stanislavskii 1989: 130). Such *visualisation* energises the imagination.

1   Training the imagination begins by strengthening inner vision.

Visualisation

- Close your eyes and imagine that you are a tree. Define your species (see the shape and colour of the leaves), how old you are (see how thick your trunk, how high your branches), and conjure a vision of where you grow. Then, pick a particular moment from your life and create it imaginatively. What was the weather? The time of day? What could you feel? See? Hear? What event (perhaps historical like a battle, or romantic like a lovers' tryst) occurred beneath your boughs that day? Specify all details as precisely as possible (Stanislavskii 1989: 133–36).
- Choose several words at random; using them all, imagine a single, harmonious picture (Stanislavskii 1990: 400).
- Take a familiar event (your acting class, a ball game, a concert). Progressively change the circumstances under which it occurs: time of day, weather, number of participants. Find an explanation to justify each change, and fantasise how the event would unfold differently (Stanislavskii 1990: 400).

2   Stanislavsky further trains imagination by invoking the *magic if*. He borrowed this technique from his six-year-old niece, with whom he loved to play 'what if' games (Stanislavskii 1989: 119).

The magic if

- Pass around different objects using 'what if' to change your relationship to them. What if this glass of water were poison? What if this glass ashtray were a frog? What if this book were a bomb? (Stanislavskii 1989: 99–100).

- Take an object and change your relationship to it in successive moments: my book, the library's book, my mother's book (Stanislavskii 1990: 401).

Communication

For Stanislavsky, there can be no drama without interaction among scene partners and between actors and audience. Words are one vehicle for such interaction, but dialogue represents only a part of the play's total communicative power. Hidden beneath the words is *subtext*, a term that describes anything a character thinks or feels but does not, or cannot, put into words. Actors infer the content of subtext by noticing inconsistencies between what is said and done, or by apparently nonsensical shifts in conversation. Actors communicate subtext through non-verbal means (body language, the cast of the eyes, intonations and pauses). Influenced by Yoga, Stanislavsky imagines communication as the transmitting and receiving of *rays of energy*, much like psychic radio waves. Our breathing puts us in touch with these rays. With every exhalation, we send rays out into the environment, and with every inhalation we receive energy back into our bodies (Stanislavskii 1986: 220–21).

1   To control non-verbal expression, Stanislavsky teaches actors to recognise and manipulate the rays of energy that carry communication.[11]

Rays of energy

- Close your eyes, relax, and feel your breath moving through your body. Visualise the breath as warm, yellow sunlight, energising you. As you inhale, see the light travelling from the top of your head down to your toes; as you exhale, reverse the direction of the breath.
- Close your eyes, relax, and feel your breath moving through your body. As you inhale, breathe the energy in from the surrounding room; as you exhale, send the energy back out into the furthest corner.
- Stand apart from the group, hands held with palms outward. Radiate energy from your hands to someone else in the room. Does anyone in the room feel a transmission?
- One actor stands behind another in single file. The person behind concentrates on a simple command (open the door, sit down, shake my hand), then radiates it to the person in front, who carries out the command.

2   Stanislavsky teaches actors to refine non-verbal communication by improvising situations that involve naturally silent moments.

Improvisations on silent moments

- In a library, A wishes to greet B, who resembles a famous actor; B does not wish to be disturbed.
- After a serious argument, A and B have fallen silent; A wants to make up, but doesn't wish to say so.
- A blind person is at home, when a thief breaks in.

- A sits on a park bench, wanting to meet B, but C has just sat down on the same bench to read a paper. A wants C to leave.
- Recreate a dentist's waiting room.
- Recreate the platform at a rail-road station (Stanislavskii 1990: 404).

3   The actors incorporate words as elements of communication only after a firm grounding in non-verbal means. Stanislavsky asks actors to improvise familiar situations using their own words.

Improvisations using words

- An art exhibit. Several visitors and one art dealer.
- A thrift store. Several customers and one salesperson.
- A is waiting for B, but C arrives instead.
- A visits B to ask for money; B refuses.
- A day at work: the boss, the secretary, the janitor (Stanislavskii 1990: 405–7).

GROUP II

The System offers actors a variety of ways to *work on roles*. Some begin with imagination and intellect: *affective cognition and the scoring of actions*. Others rely on physicalisation: *the method of physical actions* and *active analysis*. All assume that careful reading of the play precedes rehearsal. When his fictional students admit that they have 'read' *Othello* on trolleys and buses, from books with pages missing, by studying only their own parts, or by recalling productions they once saw, Stanislavsky reprimands them. 'The first acquaintance with a role is the first stage of creative work' (Stanislavskii 1991: 279). In an extended metaphor, he compares this acquaintance to the first meeting of lovers, in which the author seduces the actor. Rehearsals bring them ever closer, resulting in their marriage. The relationship eventually leads to the birth of a new human being, the character (Stanislavskii 1989: 456–66).

Affective cognition (also called cognitive analysis)

This technique for analysing a play consists of two parts. First, the cast come together to discuss each element in the play and all the historical details of its world in extended *sessions at the table*. (This work relies on intellect, hence 'cognition'.) Second, actors work individually by visualising distinct moments from their characters' lives, thus imaginatively empathising with them. (Visualisations trigger emotional, hence 'affective', responses.) Such fantasy incorporates the elements and details discovered by the cast as a whole. Stanislavsky's work on the role of Famusov (Griboedov's *Woe from Wit*) utilises this technique. He mentally sees himself in Famusov's house, walking through its many rooms, visualising himself sitting in the study, sleeping in the feather bed, ascending the staircases. Thus, Stanislavsky creates a personal vision, a 'filmstrip', of himself in the role (Stanislavskii 1991: 69–74).

The process of affective cognition

- Analyse all details in a play to illuminate the lives of the characters.
- Research the history and social world of the play.
- Visualise your character going through a typical day, walking through the house, eating, working, sleeping, socialising. Incorporate all the details discovered in your analysis of the play and your research.

The scoring of actions

Stanislavsky believes that *action* distinguishes drama from all other arts, citing as proof Aristotle's definition of tragedy as the 'imitation of action'. Stanislavsky also invokes the etymology of *drama* from the Greek root *dran*, 'to do' (Stanislavskii 1989: 88). 'People on stage act', he writes, 'and these actions – better than anything else – uncover their inner sorrows, joys, relationships, and everything about the life of the human spirit on stage' (Stanislavskii 1923: 165).

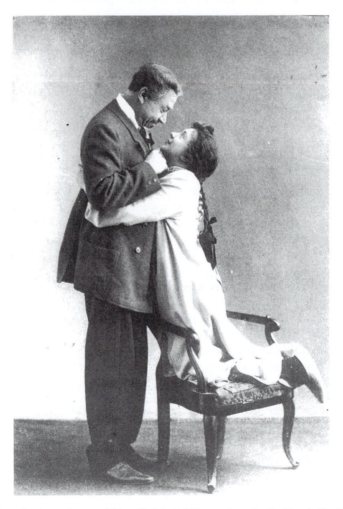

Figure 1.4 Stanislavsky as Gaev and his wife Maria Lilina as Anya in Chekhov's *The Cherry Orchard* (1904).

In the System, *action* denotes what the actor does to solve the *problem*, set before the character by the *given circumstances* of the play and production. Thus, action seeks to accomplish something: to persuade an opponent, to climb the ladder of success, to revenge one's father's death. Expressed as an active verb, action is both 'mental'/'inner' and 'physical'/'outer'; it must be 'apt' in relationship to the circumstances. Moreover, Stanislavsky distinguishes between *actions*, through which the events of the play unfold, and *activities* (such as eating, cleaning the house, dressing), that create contexts for scenes. For example, in Shakespeare's *Macbeth*,[12] Act III scene 4, Lady Macbeth 'hosts' her husband's banquet (her activity), and simultaneously 'covers up' (her action) for her husband's crazed reaction at seeing Banquo's ghost (Shakespeare 1974: 1326–27).

Taken together, the actions of all the scenes tell the story of the play, much as a score of music organises sound. As actors rehearse, they write down the sequence of their actions, creating personal *scores of actions* which guide them during performances. Each action follows 'logically' and 'consecutively' from what precedes it. Moreover, each actor searches for a uniting thread that links together all the characters' actions to produce an overall sense of what the play conveys to the audience. Stanislavsky calls this unifying force *through-action*. Lady Macbeth might strive to control the uncontrollable, a through-action that might explain her trust in the witches, her ambition to be queen, her ability to overlook the immorality of Duncan's murder. Simultaneously, because one can never succeed in controlling the uncontrollable, this overarching action also logically leads to her breakdown and suicide. Stanislavsky warns his students not to be too hasty in defining what unites a role. Often, an actor finds a through-action in the last stages of rehearsal or even during performance.

1   Begin with distinguishing between actions and activities and learning to execute them.

Exercises on actions

● Strike a pose; observers select an active verb expressed by your pose. Now, improvise a scene using the verb.
● Choose active verbs and execute them, changing the circumstances under which they are performed. *Sit down* in order to relax, in order to hide, in order to better hear what's happening in the next room, in order to read a book; *enter the room* in order to visit close friends, in order to meet your lover, in order to interview for a job; *shake your partner's hand* in order to apologise, in order to be hospitable, in order to meet a famous casting agent.
● Change the object of attention for various actions. *Wait* for your spouse, your friend, your child; *write a letter by hand* defining who you are (spouse, lover, spy, lawyer) and to whom you are writing (lover, client, opponent, boss, parents) (Stanislavskii 1990: 402, 408–9, 411).

2   The process of identifying actions begins with breaking the play into segments, what Stanislavsky calls *bits* and what have come to be called colloquially 'beats'.[13] Each bit embodies a single action and begins whenever the action of the scene shifts, not with the playwright's divisions of the play. For each bit, the actor first examines the given circumstances and describes the character's situation in an adjective. For example, in *Macbeth*'s banquet scene, Lady Macbeth

is 'embarrassed' by her husband's crazed behaviour in public (Shakespeare 1974: 1326–27). Note that Stanislavsky includes in the given circumstances not only all details in the play, but also historical and social research as well as whatever the director and designers of the production have decided. The chararacter's situation, thus described, poses a *problem*, which must be solved by means of action.[14] The actor next decides what the character needs to do in order to solve the defined problem, thus leading naturally to the specific *action* for that segment of the play. In an effort to deal with her embarrassment, Lady Macbeth 'covers up' for her husband's behaviour. Stanislavsky also advocates using the *magic if* to help identify action. 'What would I do if I found myself in the circumstances of the scene?' The answer, expressed as a verb, suggests the action (Stanislavskii 1989: 96–97).[15]

During performance, the actor places full attention on carrying out the required action, with the character's emotions arising as a natural result. By focusing solely on action, the actor experiences something akin to the role's emotional life as a subsidiary effect. As Stanislavsky explains, 'If our preparatory work is right, the results will take care of themselves.' He concludes by warning that actors make a common mistake when they worry about the result, rather than the action (Stanislavskii 1989: 212–14).

The process of identifying an action

- Isolate a single bit within any scene on which you are working. Be sure that you identify a single segment.
- Define your character's circumstances as an adjective.
- Then ask yourself, 'What would I do if I were in this situation?' Be sure to answer with an active verb that can be employed during the performance of the scene.

The method of physical actions

This rehearsal technique assumes that emotional life may sometimes be more easily aroused and fixed for performance through work on the physical life of the role, rather than through inner work. In this method, the actor discovers and then performs the logical sequence of physical actions necessary to carry out the inner, purposeful actions of a scene (as identified above). Stanislavsky gives an example of such a sequence. An actor who plays the character of Salieri in Pushkin's *Mozart and Salieri* murders Mozart (the action) by means of a series of physical actions: first by choosing a wine glass, next by pouring the wine, next by dropping in the poison, and only then by handing the glass to his rival (Stanislavskii 1989: 217). Such physical actions are best suggested to actors by the text. In the banquet scene, Lady Macbeth carries out her overall action, 'to cover up' for her husband's mad address to a ghost, through a number of strategic physical moves. First she seats her startled guests, thereby reassuring them that her husband is well ('Sit, worthy friends. My lord is often thus'). She then takes her husband aside in order to shame him into better behaviour by upbraiding him like a child ('O, proper stuff!/This is the very painting of your fear'). Next she returns him to the table ('My worthy lord, your noble friends do lack you'). Finally she turns her attention back to the guests, reiterating her first reassurance ('Think of this, good peers/But as a thing of custom'). This series of physical and strategic actions helps her accomplish her 'cover up' (Shakespeare 1974: 1326–27).

Stanislavsky refers to the sequence of physical actions as a score. Notice that he uses the same word here as he does for the sequence of psychophysical actions throughout the play (see above). Do not confuse the two. *The score of physical actions* includes the many external moves and strategies that the actor needs to carry out the overarching purposeful psychophysical action, which has been identified as necessary to the scene. The larger *score of actions* gives all the inner and purposeful actions that the character carries out from the beginning to the end of the play.

The actor tests the physical score by executing it silently, what Stanislavsky calls *the silent étude*. In such improvisation, actors perform the segment of the scene completely: they establish circumstances and activities, carry out the sequence of physical actions, and accomplish the overarching psychophysical action. Unlike a standard rehearsal, however, they do so without using words. Such non-verbal acting helps physicalise the scene. Actors avoid pantomime, however, using credible gestures and blocking that could conceivably be transferred to a spoken performance. If the actors successfully communicate the key elements of the scene in a *silent étude*, they have created useful scores for performance (Kovshov 1983: 108–28; Knebel' 1971: 72–75).[16]

Steps in the method of physical actions

- Identify the inner, purposeful action of the bit on which you are working.
- Compile your score by listing all the physical actions necessary to carry out this action.
- Test your score by means of a *silent étude*, playing that bit of the scene without words.

Communists, who were expected to adapt Stanislavsky to Marxist materialism, found Stanislavsky's experiments with physical actions helpful. It allowed them to tell a politically acceptable story, which goes something like this: Stanislavsky erroneously emphasised emotion and spirituality in his early work, but, as he matured, he rejected these embarrassing ideas. By the end of his life, he had finally discovered the scientific, material basis for acting and thus created The Method of Physical Actions (see the chapter on Knebel below; Carnicke 2008: 185–89). Alas, nothing could be further from the truth. Stanislavsky maintained his holistic views until his death, as his work with active analysis proves.

Active analysis

Stanislavsky hammered out his last, most unique rehearsal technique in workshops conducted in his home from 1934 to 1938. He bases active analysis upon a literary assumption which he took from Russian Formalist critics and adapted to drama: that plays encode 'structures of action'. Thus, he speaks metaphorically of the 'anatomy of the role and the play', of a role's 'skeleton', its 'arteries, nerves, pulse' (Stanislavskii 1991: 58, 131, 64, 135). One of his last students expressed this assumption well.

'The idea of any artistic work is contained not only in its words, but in its structure, and in the very medium of art' (Kovshov 1983: 45).[17]

In active analysis, actors grasp a play's anatomy before memorising lines. To do so, they read a play as if it were a system of clues that imply potential performance, just as musicians read musical scores. Stanislavsky calls these clues the *facts*, to which actors accommodate performance. Such facts can be obvious. After Duncan's murder, when Lady Macbeth (Act II, scene 2) says 'My hands are of your colour', we know that she must appear bloodied. However, facts may also entail sophisticated literary observations. In the same speech, Lady Macbeth speaks only in short phrases, broken by ends of lines and punctuation: 'Hark! More knocking./Get on your night-gown, lest occasion calls us/And show us to be watchers. Be not lost/So poorly in your thoughts' (Shakespeare 1974: 1320). This rhythm suggests that she has been running from the murder chamber and is out of breath. In this technique, the actor learns to read each line not only for semantic meaning, but also for style, literary images and rhythms, which betray the action of the scene and the personality of the character.

The 'facts' of each scene encode an *event* that occurs between the characters before the scene concludes. For each individual event, actors discover the *action* (that *impels* or moves the scene forward) and the *counteraction* (that *resists* the scene's forward momentum). When action meets counteraction *conflict* results. Consequently, actors must identify situations and problems that are *contradictory*. Take, for example, Act I, scene 7 from *Macbeth*. The scene between husband and wife occurs when Macbeth has begun to falter in his resolve to kill the King to gain the throne. The key event takes place when Lady Macbeth persuades her husband to proceed. Macbeth's action (to say 'no') meets Lady Macbeth's counteraction (to persuade him to say 'yes'). Whilst he impels the scene, her resistance ultimately carries it, producing the event. She uses a number of different active strategies – calling him inconstant in his love, naming him a coward and finally attacking his manhood. Her verbal images embody sarcasm, taunting and challenge. Her last approach clearly weakens his position, and instead of further resistance, he questions her, 'If we should fail?' (Shakespeare 1974: 1318). This moment marks a *reversal point*, when Macbeth's action begins to be modified by his wife's, paving the way for the event to occur.

A play reveals its anatomy through the *chain of events*, which tells the story. Each event carries different weight according to its sequence and function within the play. The event that begins the play is the *inciting* event; the one which resolves the through-action is *climactic*. Others may be *main* or *incidental*, depending on their relative importance to the story or to subplots within it (Kovshov 1983: 84–95; Knebel' 1971: 57–62).

Stanislavsky means active analysis to be far from a mere intellectual exercise. He asks actors to discover the play's anatomy not through discussion, but *on their feet*. Analysis is 'active' because actors test their understanding of how characters relate to and confront each other through improvisations of scenes in the play. These *études* serve as successive 'drafts' for future performance, each draft embodying and actualising the text better than the last (Knebel' 1971: 52). 'The best way to analyse the play', Stanislavsky said, 'is to take action in the given circumstances' (Stanislavskii 1991: 332–33).

The process of active analysis

- Carefully read and assess the facts of the scene on which you are working. Determine the event, the impelling and resisting actions that create its dynamics, and notice the style, language, images and rhythms of each character's language.
- Immediately play the scene using your own words; incorporate any 'facts' that you remember. (You may also use *silent études* to test your understanding of action, counteraction and event.)
- Re-read the scene and compare it with what happened in your improvisation. Did you retain the scene's basic dynamics and sequence? What images, styles, rhythms were you able to retain, and which did you forget? Did the event occur?
- Repeat the improvisation again, and again check your work against the text. Continue this repetition until you come as close as you can to the scene without actually memorising it. Each time, add something specific from the scene, using images, phrases, lines as written.
- Now memorise the scene for performance.

Whilst Stanislavsky had always expected actors to use all their faculties equally (mental, intellectual, emotional, spiritual, and physical), the alternation of reading and improvising in active analysis set the actor up for precisely this kind of holistic work.

PRODUCTIONS

Stanislavsky staged Chekhov's plays without a System. He strictly controlled the external elements of production to create realistic illusion. Three-dimensional rooms with real knobs on real doors and historically accurate props and costumes reproduced reality as closely as was then technologically possible. Blocking too helped to sculpt credible space. For example, in Act I of *The Seagull* (1898) Stanislavsky places Sorin on a bench with his back to the audience, thus making the invisible 'fourth wall' palpable and reminding spectators of their role as eavesdroppers (Stanislavskii 1981: 61). These early Moscow Art Theatre productions borrowed the latest techniques in realism from European directors like Germany's Duke Georg of Saxe-Meiningen (who used an ensemble of actors and visual perspective to produce believable crowd scenes) and France's André Antoine (who created three-dimensional interior rooms on stage and coined the term 'fourth wall'). In short, Stanislavsky used means familiar throughout Europe to join the aesthetic revolution of his time. His promptbooks for Chekhov's plays betray his technical approach. They describe movements, gestures, *mise en scène*, not inner action and subtext.

Moreover, in these early productions the Moscow Art Theatre overturned the star system, then current on Russian stages, in order to forge an ensemble of actors who worked together seamlessly. Grounded in Stanislavsky's oft-quoted motto 'There are no small parts, only small actors' (Stanislavskii 1988b: 250), the Art Theatre's ensemble distinguished its productions from others at the time. However, the Chekhov promptbooks tell us little of how that ensemble was forged. Sound effects best suggest Stanislavsky's attitude towards actors during rehearsal. He ended Act I of *The Cherry Orchard* with a plethora of sound: 'A shepherd plays on his pipe, the neighing of horses, the mooing of cows, the bleating of sheep and the lowing of cattle are heard' (Stanislavskii 1983: 337). Whilst his critics, including Chekhov, complained that such details cluttered the play,[18] Stanislavsky inserted them primarily for the actors' inspiration. He assumed that the more actors could believe in the reality of the play's environment, the better they would act. Therefore, all production details, and most especially sound, served to stimulate the actors' imaginations by creating distinct 'atmospheres'. In the same spirit, Stanislavsky allowed his actors to use make-up and costumes as early as two months before a play opened (Nemirovitch-Dantchenko [sic] 1937: 100).

In 1907 and 1908, coincident with his staging of symbolist plays, Stanislavsky turned his directorial attention away from external details and towards the inner worlds of characters and plays (Soloveva 1988: 51). His plan for Turgenev's *A Month in the Country* (1909), a production for which he used the nascent System, best embodied this change.

This Russian classic dramatises the story of Natalia Petrovna, a wife and mother who falls hopelessly in love with her son's tutor. In choosing this play, Stanislavsky was moved by a married woman who, at twenty-nine, experiences first love (Soloveva 1988: 62). He used everything in the production to express the play's central conflict: Natalia's illicit passion, frustrated by the conventional rigours of her loveless marriage. Simple and symmetrical sets portrayed the calm restraint of her environment; paintings on the wall (a storm at sea and the eruption of Mount Vesuvius) suggested her inner turmoil. In his promptbook, Stanislavsky describes Natalia's situation: 'All her life she has been corseted' (Chevrel 1979: 282). His comment is both literal and metaphorical. Stanislavsky saw the tutor, with his youthful, unfettered energy, as fresh air in Natalia's stuffy salon. The production embodied great continuity between visual and interpretative elements. Its economy of expression unmistakably showed that Stanislavsky had learned from the symbolists. He directed Turgenev as Chekhov would have wanted his own plays directed.

Figure 1.5 Stanislavsky as Mikhailo Raikitin and Olga Knipper as Natalya Petrovna in Turgenev's *A Month in the Country* (1909).

In sharp contrast to the elaborate blocking in his Chekhov productions, Stanislavsky now reduced gesture and movement to a minimum. In the Turgenev promptbook, Stanislavsky describes not bodily movement but states of mind for nearly every line. Moreover, by cutting extensively from long monologues, he enriches the unspoken subtext. Quoting one of Natalia's lines, Stanislavsky writes that with this production he intended to expose 'the subtlest lacework of invisible, spiritual sensations' amongst the characters (Soloveva 1988: 50). His work with the actors certainly aimed to do so. Rehearsals for *A Month in the Country* began with two months 'at the table', discussing the nuances behind every line. Once 'on their feet', Stanislavsky conducted a series of exercises on feelings, concentration and communication. At one rehearsal the actors explored remembered emotions, transitions from one feeling to another and simplicity of expression. The next day, they tested circles of attention. These exercises, as well as others on communicating with the eyes alone, speaking without gestures and playing scenes without words (*silent études*), clearly anticipate the System's inner techniques.

The Turgenev promptbook also anticipates the System's overarching emphasis on action. Stanislavsky gives active verbs for most lines. In Act I, when the tutor enters, Natalia 'observes' him closely, 'flirts' and 'pets' her son (Stanislavskii 1988a: 385). For many scenes, Stanislavsky also distinguishes between activities and actions. He notes that when the curtain opens, Natalia and her would-be lover Rakitin carry on a desultory conversation (their *activity*). However, Natalia's absorption with the tutor and Rakitin's unsuccessful flirtation form the hidden, subtextual *action*. 'She concentrates [inwardly]', Stanislavsky explains, 'and that is why she seems externally distracted' (Stanislavskii 1988a: 377). Her external distractions (listening to Rakitin reading aloud, his chatter and his story about a neighbour) contrast with the objects of her real attention (her contemplation of the tutor and her dissatisfaction with her own life). She inadvertently reveals herself when she interrupts Rakitin by asking, 'Have you seen how they make lace?' She imagines lace makers 'in airless rooms, no one moving from their places. . . . Lace – a beautiful thing, but a gulp of fresh water on a hot day is a much better thing.' Her remark shakes Rakitin out of his chatter and forces a moment of true communication between them. In performance Rakitin, together with the audience, understood that Natalia spoke about herself (Stanislavskii 1988a: 382–83).

Stanislavsky's last production, Molière's *Tartuffe*, opened posthumously in December 1939 under the direction of Mikhail Kedrov, who played the title role and would later promote the Sovietised version of The Method of Physical Actions (see the chapter on Knebel below). Stanislavsky conducted rehearsals at his home between March 1936 and April 1938. His choice of material was significant. Molière's story of Tartuffe, the cunning religious hypocrite who hoodwinks the trusting Orgon, is told in rhyme; the play could not be further from Chekhov. Whilst psychological realism had been the style for which Stanislavsky had become best known, he always resisted association with any particular style. That his System should be perceived as universally applicable became an obsession in his last four years. In choosing a classic seventeenth-century comedy in verse, he insisted on the wide applicability of his techniques.

Stanislavsky had used this production to explore new rehearsal techniques. He had seen how affective cognition (and its long discussions 'at the table') left actors 'with a stuffed head and an empty heart' (Stanislavskii 1991: 325–26). He therefore replaces 'analysis of feelings' with 'active analysis', obviating the need to translate imagination into actuality. From the first, the actors were on their feet. Stanislavsky began by asking the cast to turn their rehearsal space into Orgon's house. They located each room, arguing over which area would be better suited for dining or for sleeping (Stanislavskii 1991: 69–74). Thus, collective fantasy replaces individual imagination. Such initial work makes the play more palpably present. 'Here, today, now', resounds throughout Stanislavsky's writing from this period (Stanislavskii 1991: 331).

Rehearsal records show that Stanislavsky dissected the play, ascertaining its 'anatomy'. He divided the cast into two camps, one led by Tartuffe (with Orgon in tow), the other composed of those who see through Tartuffe's chicanery (Orgon's wife, his daughter, brother-in-law and clever servant). Each camp's set of problems was chosen to conflict with those of the other camp, thus prompting actions and counteractions. Stanislavsky then broke the play into twelve bits, each one defined in terms of a key event that embodies struggle. He includes 'a protest against the oppression of Tartuffe', '[the servant's] counteroffensive', 'Orgon's counterattack by his promise to marry [his daughter] to Tartuffe' (Stroeva 1977: 374). The war-like metaphors reveal that conflict is the essence of dramatic structure for him.

Improvisations served to recreate both the world of the play and its dynamic structure. In early rehearsals, Stanislavsky encouraged improvisations on any aspect of the play's story: how Orgon's family dine, how they play cards, Orgon's first meeting with Tartuffe. Whilst these events do not occur in the play proper, they establish context and environment. As rehearsals continued, Stanislavsky turned to the exact structure of Molière's play for true active analysis. The actors paraphrased each scene over and over again to discover each action, counteraction and event. With each paraphrase, they incorporated more of the text (images, style, rhythms, even lines) until, as one of Stanislavsky's actors reports, 'we could move on to the next stage in our rehearsals, the stage when we needed the words'. The successive drafting of performance through paraphrase now 'found greater expressiveness and completion in [the author's] thoughts and words'. Moreover, this process 'happened by itself, gradually as a result of our growing inner need' (Toporkov 2002: 197–98).

Just as Stanislavsky's System for actor training remained experimental and dynamic to the end, his rehearsal methods reflect his ever-changing views on how best to establish connection between actors and their roles. From his early work on Chekhov, which features directorial control over the external aspects of production, he turned his attention to the inner realm of non-verbal communication. His last experiments connected actor with text through a unique process of dramatic analysis.

CONCLUSION

Throughout his career, Stanislavsky believed that there are three basic drivers behind creativity: 'mind' (for analysis and understanding), 'will' (for control) and 'feeling' (which fosters passionate and zestful relationships with the characters we create). At various times, both in classrooms and in rehearsal halls, he focused on one or another of these drivers. Ultimately, however, he saw them as inextricably linked to each other in a tightly wound 'knot' or 'bundle' (Stanislavskii 1989: 395, 417). The successful actor, by whatever path, arrives always at the same place, where mind, will and feeling together produce a satisfying performance. 'How astounding a creation is our nature!' he writes. 'How everything in it is bound together, blended, and interdependent!' Like a 'harmonious' musical chord, in which one false note creates disharmony, all elements of the system work together (Stanislavskii 1991: 314).

The System's techniques suggest various pathways for actors to follow as they strive towards successful performances. In choosing a path, each actor reinvents and personalises the System. This reinterpretation and adaptation is exactly what Stanislavsky hoped to inspire in actors. He hated the dogmatic teacher who insists upon a single correct way. Thus, in his last years he advised his students that:

> The System is a guide. Open and read. The System is a handbook, not a
>   philosophy.
> The moment when the System begins to become a philosophy is its end.
> Examine the System at home, but forget about it when on stage.
> You can't play the System.
> There is no System. There is only nature.
> My lifelong concern has been how to get ever closer to the so-called
>   'System', that is to get ever closer to the nature of creativity.
>
> (Stanislavskii 1990: 371)

The history of actor training from the twentieth-century onward can be seen as a series of explorations, inspired by Stanislavsky's guide, and each probing a different pathway into the actor's unique creativity as a performer.

Notes

1   Stanislavsky adopted the name of his favourite Polish ballerina. In one surreptitious production, he met his future wife; she too was acting on the sly as Maria Lilina.
2   No wonder the Moscow Art Theatre adopted a seagull as its visual logo.
3   These productions were Hamsun's *The Drama of Life*, Andreev's *The Life of Man* and Maeterlinck's *The Blue Bird*.
4   This house has since become one of Moscow's museums.
5   Unfortunately, Stanislavsky's books (*My Life in Art*, *An Actor's Work on Himself*, *Parts I and II* and *An Actor's Work on the Role*) in whatever language will forever bear the censor's marks. One can get beyond the censorship, however, by looking for Stanislavsky's subtexts in the same ways that Russian readers did. By examining the rules of Soviet censorship, I offer a guide to reading this way in Chapter 6 of *Stanislavsky in Focus* (2008).
6   Until 2008, the only English-language translations of Stanislavsky's manuals were abridged versions by Elizabeth Reynolds Hapgood: *An Actor Prepares* (1936), *Building a Character* (1949) and *Creating A Role* (1961). Moreover, these versions were translated into most of the world's languages. Consequently, her translations and abridgements have had a significant impact on how theatre practitioners and scholars outside Russia have understood the System (Carnicke 2008: chapter 5). Jean Benedetti's competing translation of *Parts I and II* of *An Actor's Work on Himself* (published as *An Actor's Work* by Routledge in 2008) breaks the Hapgood hegemony and offers readers the opportunity to encounter Stanislavsky in more than one English version. I base my analysis of the System and its exercises on the Russian-language manuals and on drafts and notebooks in K. S. Stanislavskii, *Sobranie sochinenii* [*The Collected Works*], Moscow, 1988–99. I also draw upon my work as assistant director and interpreter for Sam Tsikhotsky of the Moscow Art Theatre whilst he was in residence at the Actors Studio (New York) in 1978, and classes at the Moscow Art Theatre School and the Russian Academy of Theatrical Arts.
7   Ramacharaka was the pen-name of William Walker Atkinson (1862–1932), an American lawyer who introduced the West to Eastern metaphysics in a series of twelve books (see Carnicke 2008: chapter 9 and White 2006). Ramacharaka's works were translated into Russian in the 1910s and Stanislavsky owned several of them.

8   This grouping of exercises is mine. All cited exercises are adapted from either Stanislavsky's published acting manuals or his notes on training (Stanislavskii 1990).

9   Stanislavsky borrows these anecdotes from Ribot (1897: 152–53). Whilst The Method would later turn them into models for its famous affective memory exercise, Stanislavsky uses them as mere examples of the range of emotional recall discovered by Ribot.

10   Notice that the exercise on hearing assumes the actor's ability to use 'circles of concentration'.

11   I observed the following exercises at Moscow's Russian Academy of Theatrical Arts (formerly GITIS), 1989.

12   All examples from *Macbeth* are my own.

13   'Beats' may derive from the 'bits' of the play strung together like 'beads' on a necklace, when pronounced in English with a Russian accent by émigré teachers.

14   The Russian word, *zadacha*, has been translated as 'objective' by Elizabeth Reynolds Hapgood and as 'task' by Jean Benedetti. It can also be rendered as 'problem.' When Stanislavsky explains his usage of the word, he compares the actor's *zadacha* to an arithmetic problem that a child is given to solve (Stanislavskii 1989: 212). Therefore, I favour 'problem' as the clearest translation.

15   Lee Strasberg rejected this formulation, adopting what he thought to be Evgeny Vakhtangov's modification: 'What would motivate me, the actor, to behave in the way that the character does?' This question allows the actor to replace the play's circumstance with a personal one, called a 'substitution' (Strasberg 1987: 85–86).

16   I observed master teacher Natalia Zvereva and director Leonid Kheifetz teach *silent études* and other aspects of active analysis in Paris at the international symposium 'Le Siècle Stanislavski' (Centre Georges Pompidou, 2–6 November 1988) and at their home institution in Moscow, the Russian Academy of Theatrical Arts (formerly GITIS) during 1989 and 1990.

17   The Group Theatre's use of the word 'spine' also reflects Stanislavsky's metaphor.

18   Chekhov threatened to write an opening line for his next play that reads, 'How wonderful, how quiet! Not a bird, a dog, a cuckoo, an owl, a nightingale, or clocks, or jingling bells, not even one cricket to be heard' (Benedetti 1990: 135).

Bibliography

All translations from Russian sources are the author's unless otherwise indicated.

Autant-Mathieu, Marie Christine (2003) 'Stalin and the Moscow Art Theatre', *Slavic and East European Performance* 28 (3): 70–85.

Benedetti, Jean (1990) *Stanislavski: A Biography*, New York: Routledge.

Blair, Rhonda (2008) *The Actor, Image, and Action: Acting and Cognitive Neuroscience*, London: Routledge.

Carnicke, Sharon Marie (2008) *Stanislavsky in Focus: An Acting Master for the Twenty First Century*, 2nd Edition, London: Routledge.

Chevrel, Claudine Amiard (1979) *Le Théâtre Artistique de Moscou (1898–1917)* [The Moscow Art Theatre], Paris: Editions du CNRS.

Filippov, Boris (1977) *Actors Without Make-Up*, trans. Kathelene Cook, Moscow: Progress Publishers.

Hecht, Leo (1989) 'Stanislavsky's Trips to the United States', paper for the American Association of Teachers of Slavic and East European Languages, Washington, DC.

Knebel', M.O. (1971) *O tom, chto mne kazhetsia osobenno vazhnym* [*What Seems Most Important to Me*], Moscow: Iskusstvo.

Kovshov, N. (1983) *Uroki M.N. Kedrova* [*The Classes of M.N. Kedrov*], Moscow: Iskusstvo.

Nemirovitch-Dantchenko [sic], Vladimir (1937) *My Life in the Russian Theatre*, trans. John Cournos, London: Geoffrey Bles.

Nemirovich-Danchenko, V.I. (2005) *Pis'ma O.S. Bokshanskoi*, vol. 2 [letters to his secretary], Moscow: Moskovskii khudozhestvennyi teatr.

Ribot, Théodule (1897) *The Psychology of Emotions*, London: Walter Scott, Ltd.

Shakespeare, William (1974) *The Riverside Shakespeare*, Boston, MA: Houghton Mifflin Co.

Smeliansky, Anatoly (1991) 'The Last Decade: Stanislavsky and Stalinism', *Theater*, 12, 2: 7–13.

Soloveva, I.N. (1988) 'Puti iskanii' ['Experimental Paths'], in K.S. Stanislavskii, *Rezhisserskie ekzempliary K.S. Stanislavskogo*, vol. 5 [directing plans], Moscow: Iskusstvo.

Stanislavskii, K.S. (1923) Untitled draft typescript, Bancroft Library, University of California, Berkeley.

—— (1981) *Rezhisserskie ekzempliary K.S. Stanislavskogo*, vol. 2 [directing plans], Moscow: Iskusstvo.

—— (1983) *Rezhisserskie ekzempliary K.S. Stanislavskogo*, vol. 3 [directing plans], Moscow: Iskusstvo.

—— (1986) *Iz zapisnykh knizhek* [From the *Artistic Notebooks*], vol. 2, Moscow: VTO.

—— (1988a) *Rezhisserskie ekzempliary K.S. Stanislavskogo*, vol. 5 [directing plans], Moscow: Iskusstvo.

—— (1988b) *Sobranie sochinenii*, vol. 1 [*My Life in Art*], Moscow: Iskusstvo.

—— (1989) *Sobranie sochinenii*, vol. 2 [*An Actor's Work on Himself, Part I*], Moscow: Iskusstvo.

—— (1990) *Sobranie sochinenii*, vol. 3 [*An Actor's Work on Himself, Part II* and notes on exercises], Moscow: Iskusstvo.

—— (1991) *Sobranie sochinenii*, vol. 4 [*An Actor's Work on the Role* and *From the Artistic Notebooks*], Moscow: Iskusstvo.

—— (1993) *Sobranie sochinenii*, vol. 5, part 2 [*From the Artistic Notebooks*], Moscow: Iskusstvo.

—— (1994) *Sobranie sochinenii*, vol. 6 [*Essays, Speeches, Memoirs, Artistic Notebooks*], Moscow: Iskusstvo.

—— (1999) *Sobranie sochinenii*, vol. 9 [letters], Moscow: Iskusstvo.

—— (2000) *Stanislavskii repetiruet: Zapisi i stenogrammy repeticii* [*Stanislavsky Rehearses: Notes and Transcripts*], ed. I. Vinogradskaia, Moscow: Moskovskii khudozhestvennyi teatr.

Strasberg, Lee (1987) *A Dream of Passion: The Development of the Method*, Boston, MA: Little, Brown and Company.

Stroeva, M.N. (1977) *Rezhisserskie iskaniia Stanislavskogo: 1917–1938* [*The Directorial Experiments of Stanislavsky*], Moscow: Nauka.

Tolstoi, L.N. (1964) 'Chto takoe iskusstvo?' ['What is Art?', written in 1897] in *Sobranie sochinenii*, vol. 15, Moscow: Khudozhestvennaia literatura.

Toporkov, V.O. (2002) *K.S. Stanislavskii na repetitsii* [*Stanislavski in Rehearsal*], Moscow: AST Press, Skd.

Vinogradskaia, I. (ed.) (2003) *Zhizn' i tvorchestvo K. S. Stanislavskogo: Letopis'* [*The Life and Work of K.S. Stanislavsky: A Chronology*], vol. 2, Moscow: Moskovskii khudozhestvennyi teatr.

White, R. Andrew (2006) 'Stanislavsky and Ramacharaka: The Influence of Yoga and Turn-of-the-Century Occultism on the System,' *Theatre Survey*, 47 (1):73–92.

Chapter 2

Robert Leach

MEYERHOLD AND BIOMECHANICS

Training! Training! Training! But if it's the kind of training which exercises only the body and not the mind, then No, thank you! I have no use for actors who know how to move but cannot think.[1]

THROUGHOUT HIS CAREER, VSEVOLOD Meyerhold sought to train the brains and bodies of actors so that they would be able to participate in his lifelong quest for a theatre which would not attempt to reproduce the surface reality of living, but would be, rather, 'theatrical'. Yet largely because of accidents of history, which cruelly silenced him and fortuitously aided the ideas of his mentor, colleague and ideological rival, Konstantin Stanislavsky, the significance of his quest is, even in the twenty-first century, rarely recognised or acknowledged. His contemporaries believed that he was Stanislavsky's equal, and that this was as true for his ideas about actor training as about stage production. It is probably fair to say that virtually all those scholars, especially Western scholars, who have discussed his work since his 'rehabilitation' in 1955, have underestimated the importance of his pedagogy.[2] But many of his ideas were preserved through dark times by his pupils, and his pupils' pupils, who are now promulgating them energetically, and the time has perhaps come for a new assessment of Meyerhold's work on training actors.

Meyerhold's own troupe, the Comrades of the New Drama, was founded in September 1902 when Meyerhold was twenty-eight years old. His experimental and pedagogical practices developed alongside his mainstream production work, notably through his work with Stanislavsky's Theatre Studio on Povarskaya Street, Moscow in 1905, then from 1906 until 1908 at Vera Komissarzhevskaya's Dramatic Theatre in St Petersburg, and in his own Studio on Borodinskaya Street, St Petersburg between 1913 and 1917. After the Bolshevik Revolution he developed a course on stage production in Petrograd (which, however, seems never to have operated meaningfully); then, in 1921 the Meyerhold Free Workshop was established in Moscow, and this was absorbed into the Meyerhold Theatre when that became a reality in 1923. From then until its liquidation in 1938, the Meyerhold Theatre school trained actors conscientiously and in significant numbers.

Meyerhold cared passionately about his pupils. Erast Garin, one of his star graduates, painted an unforgettable picture of the Master overseeing his students:

> He would appear in the doorway with a green military greatcoat flung carelessly over his shoulders. . . . The studio was never properly heated, but we were young, and involved in energetic exercises, so we didn't mind. Meyerhold sat by the round, tiled stove, smoking . . . and watching us as if he was studying each one of us.[3]

Meyerhold's own acting career began as a founder member of the Moscow Art Theatre. At that time, Stanislavsky had not even developed his 'round the table' method of analysing text, though his insistence that every stage action must be justified, or motivated, and that each character must have an 'objective' was already present in his work method. Meyerhold always held to these principles, even as he energetically rejected the Moscow Art Theatre's search for a life-like naturalism. The turn of the century was the period when Symbolism dominated avant-garde literature and art, especially in Russia, and Meyerhold sought a stylised means of staging the works of Symbolist dramatists. In 1906, however, his production of Alexander Blok's *The Fairground Booth* completely destroyed stage Symbolism. In the play, dreamy mystics and starry-eyed lovers confront the old theatrical masks, Harlequin, Columbine and Pierrot, and their spurious emotionalism is (literally) swept away by the theatrical games of the *commedia dell'arte*. Harlequin 'jumps through the window. The distance, visible through the window, turns out to have been painted on paper. The paper bursts. Harlequin flies head over heels into nothingness.' A few moments later, as the hitherto-agitated 'Author' joins the hands of Columbine and Pierrot, 'suddenly all the scenery rolls up, and flies away'.[4]

Figure 2.1 Biomechanics: The Stance on the Back.

This production signalled Meyerhold's rejection of mysticism in the theatre. From then on, as Erast Garin wrote later, Meyerhold's 'point of departure' became the 'liquidation of the awe-inspiring, shamanistic aura surrounding the art of the actor'.[5] It led to his discovery, through the *commedia dell'arte*, of the grotesque as an artistic principle, that is, the bringing together of matters, actions, ideas, which are not thought to naturally cohabit. At his Studio on Borodinskaya Street, under the pseudonym of 'Doctor Dapertutto', he experimented with the interplay of character and action as it had operated in various historical and exotic contexts, not only in Renaissance Italy, but also in eighteenth- and nineteenth-century France and in Shakespeare's England, in China, Japan and elsewhere. The work consciously combined actor training and experimental performance.

Meyerhold's ideas were drawn together and, in some senses, formalised in his syllabus for the course on stage production which he worked out with Leonid Vivien in Petrograd immediately after the 1917 revolution.[6] But his practice in the training of actors continued only when he moved to Moscow, first at his Free Workshop from 1921, and then at the school attached to his own theatre. As his system acquired a more integrated and theoretically justified basis, he gave it the typically Soviet, but not inappropriate, name of 'biomechanics', implying its connection with a technology of the body. Throughout the next two decades Meyerhold continued to adapt, refine, promulgate and demonstrate the biomechanical system, but in 1938 the Stalinist dictatorship closed his theatre. He was arrested the following year and judicially murdered in 1940, in gaol. Just at the time when Stanislavsky's ideas were receiving their greatest acclaim and support, both in Russia and in the USA, Meyerhold's career and work were wiped from the record, and his ideas consigned to oblivion. For fifteen years it was as if he had never existed. From 1955, when he was officially 'rehabilitated', his achievements were gradually rediscovered and made public again; at first cautiously through the Communist period, and then more expansively, so that by the end of the century his true position as one of the enduring colossi of the stage could again be legitimately argued.

From the time of his break with Stanislavsky (for whom, however, he retained the warmest admiration), Meyerhold's constant question was: what is 'theatrical' about the theatre? It was a question typical of its time, and may be compared with Kandinsky's contemporary search for the 'painterly' in painting, or the Russian Formalist critics' argument that it was the 'literariness' of literature that was its real strength and appeal. Stanislavsky's system was rooted in an earlier time, for it was designed to make stage action 'lifelike'. For Stanislavsky, 'theatricality' was a negative concept. Meyerhold, however, wanted a system which could cope with all styles (including naturalism, though he regarded this as something of an irrelevance; for him, Chekhov's appeal, for instance, did not lie in his 'truth to life'). The actor for the task which Meyerhold was to set – the ability to perform farce and tragedy, melodrama, pantomime and circus-style skits, to name but some of the genres he was interested in – needed a rigorous and long-lasting training: 'An actor must study as a violinist does, for seven to nine years. You can't make yourself into an actor in three to four years.'[7]

Beginning with the formulation that: 'Every art is the organisation of its own material', Meyerhold asserted that: 'In order to organise his material, the actor has to have a colossal reserve of technical resources.' The reason for this need was that the actor, unlike other artists, 'is at one and the same time the material and the organiser'.[8] This was formulated algebraically by Meyerhold as:

$$N = A1 + A2$$

(where N = the actor; A1 = the organiser of the material; and A2 = the material). The actor must therefore be able to move and to think.

But what – or rather, how – is the actor to think? He is not to identify with the part, wondering what the character is feeling, or trying to identify his or her wants. Rather, the actor's brain is to decide on the physical formulation of the moment. Igor Ilyinsky, one of Meyerhold's most impressive actors, noted that: 'If the physical form is correct, the basis of the part, the speech intonations and the emotions, will be as well, because they are determined by the position of the body.'[9] Another of Meyerhold's protégés, the film director Sergei Eisenstein, concurred: 'The pulse of the emotion (its curve) is the result of spatial-plastic placing. It is excited as a result of the quality of the treatment and training of the material' (that is, the 'A2' of the actor).[10] Therefore, the actor's training was, for Meyerhold, devoted largely to an understanding of the body in space, or as he called it, 'scenic movement'. Following his work on *The Fairground Booth*, his scenic movement class focused most closely on the 'play' of the *commedia dell'arte*. 'It is not necessary [for the actor] to feel, only to play, to play', Meyerhold exclaimed in 1913.[11] The actor was thus to be seen as akin to the child when he or she is playing: for the child, the play is 'real', but it involves, initially, recreating the motion of the action, not seeking the Stanislavskian objective of the character in the 'play'. Understanding, which may include an understanding of feelings, becomes accessible to the child, but through the doing. Jonathan Pitches, one of the few British performers to have trained with a Russian biomechanics Master, and then to have put what he learned into practice, noted that 'to experience biomechanics practically is to understand it . . . I developed a sensitivity for detail. I noticed which foot was leading, where the actor's weight was situated, the rhythmic pattern of each action'.[12]

In his Studio in St Petersburg in the 1910s, Meyerhold experimented tirelessly and in great depth; first with the *commedia*, the strengths of which lay not only in 'play', but also in the traditional characters – Harlequin, Pantaloon, Columbine and the rest – 'masks' whose characterisations derived most significantly from their individualised movement and gesture patterns. The characters were literally masks: the performers wore masks over their faces, partly to focus attention on their characteristic movements, but also because masks eliminated passing or fleeting emotions, and because they fixed and expressed specific attitudes, or mental or spiritual states.

The investigation of *commedia dell'arte* led to further explorations of clowns, puppets and marionettes, as well as of other theatrical traditions from both Europe and the Far East. These in turn led to a bewildering and eclectic array of exercises and other practical acting work, from which much of interest and importance emerged. For instance, the relationship between the stage and the proscenium or forestage was examined; the oriental concept of 'self-admiration' (a kind of self-watching or monitoring) was introduced; and actors found a fulfilling excitement in emitting a cry or shout at moments of intensity. Costume was explored as a decorative ornament rather than a utilitarian necessity, and the hat as something to be doffed, not just worn. A prop – a tambourine, for example, or a flower – acquired significance when it became an extension of the hand (which itself was an extension of the arm, and thus an extension of the whole body: the resonance of the body as a whole being important); and stage furniture, such as the screen, was used in various ways. Entrances and exits were also playfully explored. All of these made an unsurpassed range of technical acting devices available to the Meyerholdian performer, not to be used merely for the recreation of past theatrical styles from which they were derived, but now as weapons in her or his armoury for contemporary stage compositions.

Meyerhold's 'scenic movement' covered all these experiments at this stage of his career (immediately before the Bolshevik Revolution), and created a grotesque 'polyphony' on the stage. But the exercises may be said to have had their focus in concepts of rhythm – spatial rhythm as much as temporal rhythm. His student actors improvised prolifically to develop physical agility and physical responsiveness to others on the stage (spatial rhythm), and then what he called 'musicality' (temporal rhythm). Thus, actors might be asked to hum whilst they moved, or they might treat speech and dialogue as musical scores. These concerns with rhythm found their confluence in the pause or 'silhouette', the expressive moment when the movement was spatially and/or temporarily broken.

Many surviving photographs of Meyerhold's productions show a picture-like composition, the theatrical equivalent of the still frame from a moving film, where the dynamic of the scene is reflected in the bodily postures of the performers, and their interrelationship in space. It was something not unlike Brecht's 'gestic interruption', but more self-referential, initially at least having more to do with the onward movement of the scene than with the socio-political structures in the outside world to which it might be referring. Meyerhold told Gladkov two decades later that: 'The swifter the text, the more distinct the breaks must be, the transitions from one segment to another, from one rhythm to another. Otherwise the motivation is lost, the living breath of meaning vanishes.'[13]

In his work at the Borodinskaya Street Studio, he found that this concern with what might be called the 'through rhythm' could be most easily explored in the improvised pantomimes he occasionally presented and with which he frequently worked. The specific learning cycle which he developed at the studio began with exercises. These were often developed into 'études', whose purpose was mainly to do with developing the actor, and then further expanded to become self-contained pantomimes suitable for public consumption. Such were most of the items in the presentations by his students.[14] Other examples were the traditional Chinese 'black comedy' improvisation, when actors pretend it is a dark night and creep furtively about on the brilliantly illuminated stage; and the three-minute version of *Antony and Cleopatra* which they showed to the visiting Italian Futurist, Filippo Marinetti.

By the time of the Free Meyerhold Workshop, and the establishment of his own school attached to the Meyerhold Theatre in Moscow, the 'polyphony' and the almost endless variety of explorations were becoming more focused and integrated. A new social awareness was also apparent in the work, and Meyerhold's students were now expected to have a sense of social responsibility which would inform their work. Thus, in Meyerhold's thinking about characterisation, instead of relying on the old traditional masks, he now developed the concept of the 'emploi' belonging to the 'set roles' of the actor, which extended the boundaries of the mask by relating it in new ways to what might be termed 'real life'.[15] At any given moment, Meyerhold's actors were asked to present a theatricalised 'mask' to the audience. But as the plot (or intrigue) developed, the character required a new mask. Their 'set role', and consequently their 'emploi' (what they did, or how they behaved), also changed.

As illustration, we might consider Hamlet. When he finds Claudius praying, his set role is that of the Revenger; but moments later, in his mother's bedroom, his mask is that of the disobedient child. Characterisation was, therefore, no longer simply a device of the pantomime, it was more like our experience of life, for, like Hamlet, we change: we behave as a child when with our parents, whatever our age; and – at least to some extent – we behave as a supplicant to our bank manager, as a 'good fellow' to our acquaintances in the pub, as a conscientious worker to our boss, and so on. The

Figure 2.2 Biomechanics: The Leap to the Chest.

actors' 'set role' changed through the production, so that instead of a consistent through-line, Meyerhold's creations were grotesque, paradoxical and associative. They theatricalised the action and were the agents for the expression of emotion. Thus they effectively became action-functions. The actor's 'emploi' – how she or he expressed the 'set role' – was therefore not quite psychological, nor was it a stylistic peculiarity of the production, though it owed something to both of these. Rather, it was the exposure of the driving force of the specific image at a particular point in the production, the theatricalisation both of the specific motive (the objective, in Stanislavsky's term) and of the state of the relationship.

This helped Meyerhold to develop the learning sequence from exercise–étude– pantomime as practised in the Borodinskaya Street Studio to exercise–étude–acting: in other words, this greater awareness and flexibility enabled the work to be utilised more easily for all sorts of acting work for the public stage. But it still depended primarily on Meyerhold's 'scenic movement', now called biomechanics, which Ilyinsky described powerfully and precisely. In biomechanics, he wrote, the actor

> seized his partner's body as it was stretched in the sun, threw it over his shoulder and carried it off. He dropped this body. He threw a discus and traced its imaginary course. He gave his partner a slap in the face, and received one back. He leaped on his partner's chest, and received him on his chest. He jumped onto his partner's shoulders, and his partner ran,

Figure 2.3 Biomechanics: The Stab with the Dagger.

carrying him. Certain exercises were very simple: to take the partner's hand and pull his arm, then repulse the partner, then seize him by the throat. . . . Although we sometimes gave demonstrations of these exercises, we did not need to transpose them literally to the stage: they served to give us the taste of conscious movement on the stage. The exercises combined the gymnastic, the plastic and the acrobatic; they developed in the students an exact 'eye'; they enabled them to calculate their movements, to make them meaningful and to coordinate them with their partners; and . . . they helped them to move more freely and with greater expressiveness in the stage space.[16]

The 'exact eye' is the 'self-admiration', or self-awareness, referred to above. In a theatre such as Meyerhold's, the actor needs to be extremely sensitive to what his body, his gestures, his movements are connoting. He needs a kind of in-built mirror.

Biomechanics is not arbitrary. It requires of the actor, and it trains: (1) balance (physical control); (2) rhythmic awareness, both spatial and temporal; and (3) responsiveness to the partner, to the audience, to other external stimuli, especially through the ability to observe, to listen and to react. It is worth pausing for a moment to consider these as they were experienced by Jonathan Pitches. His experience of the étude 'Throwing the Stone', for instance, was that it developed the solidity of the physical base by introducing falls, jumps, runs and exaggerated body positions and demanded the same movement away from the centre of gravity before finding this centre anew. The etude required a constant shifting of weight from left to right and, at one moment, from the lower body to the upper body. As the hieroglyphic body shape was adopted for the etude, one's balance was further tested, particularly by the jumps included in the exercise.

Pitches similarly found that the biomechanical exercises developed spatial awareness and the ensemble, noting particularly that the work,

> with its emphasis upon collective, collaborative action, insists that each element of the ensemble comes together with a shared point of intense concentration whilst retaining each person's uniquely individual stamp as a physical body on stage. There can be no progression until each person has found the appropriate rhythm and mastered the skills within each action. The ensemble is in effect bound by a common cause which breeds a humility in relation to the work.[17]

These are large claims, but by examining a few of Meyerhold's exercises and études in detail, and relating them to performance, it may be that we shall be able thoroughly to justify them.

Perhaps the first and simplest of the exercises is that with the stick, a straight piece of broom handle or dowel about a metre long. Stand with the legs about 30 centimetres apart, the knees slightly bent, the stick held three-quarters of the way down in one hand. Bend the knees to obtain momentum, and rise, and as you rise, toss the stick easily up so that it arcs over. Keep your eye on the other end of the stick, and catch it, letting it fall into your hand. Do not grab at it. Repeat. Continue to repeat each exercise many times. Now toss the stick so that it arcs twice and you catch the same end as you threw. Toss it so that it arcs once and catch it in the other hand. Toss it so that it arcs twice. Three times. Four times. Always bend the knees and toss as you straighten them. The exercise should be performed in as relaxed a manner as possible: easily, lightly.

Now hold the stick in the middle, vertical to the ground. Toss it from one hand to the other. Hold it horizontally, with the back of your hand upwards. Bend the knees, straighten them, and as you straighten them lift your hand and open your fingers so that the stick flies out. Bring your hand down, catch the stick, the back of your hand still upwards. Repeat, letting go with one hand, catching with the other. Pass the stick from one hand to the other under one leg; then under the other. Pass it behind your back.

Place the stick in the palm of the open hand. Toss it up. Catch it, without closing the hand. Catch it on the other palm, without closing the hand. When the stick is in the air, turn the hand over, 'bat' it up again with the back of the hand or the back of the wrist. Catch it on the open palm. Place the stick on the index and middle finger. Balance it. Push up with the index finger, 'catch' the stick between the middle and fourth finger. Push up with the middle finger, 'catch' it between the fourth and little finger. Continue, involving the index finger again, till you can twirl the stick.

Balance the stick on the palm of the hand so that it is perfectly still. Balance it on the back of the hand. Balance it on one finger. On the wrist. The elbow. The shoulder. Balance it on the foot, the knee, the back of the neck, the forehead. Keep the eye on

Figure 2.4 Biomechanics in action: D.E. (1924).

Source: from the collection of Robert Leach.

the end of the stick. The aim is for it to be absolutely still at all times. The number of stick exercises is enormous: these few simple beginnings will give some idea of the richness of the work. It is also useful to work in pairs, tossing the stick in various ways from one to another. Make sure your feet form a solid base, and concentrate on making the stick feel soft and light: never grab it, let it land in the hand. The stick is an indication of your own balance and co-ordination, especially when you balance it. Any movement in the stick indicates that you have not found your centre of gravity.

The remaining biomechanics exercises and études are more complex, and more strict, but each is carefully calculated to produce the kind of effect described here. The first exercise is the Dactyl, a sequence of moves designed to put the student-actor into a state of physical and mental readiness. A 'dactyl' is a verse foot, comprising of long beat, followed by two short beats. This is mirrored in the exercise.

THE DACTYL

Stance: stand firm, alert, but relaxed, feet about 30 centimetres apart, arms loose at sides, head up, facing front. There are no pauses in the exercise, the whole movement flows through the seven points isolated here. The tempo of the exercise may vary, but initially at least it is quite slow and relaxed, flowing from point to point until movement 4 below, when the movement speeds up and points 4–6 are performed with a degree of taut intensity.

1 Both arms swing in a wide arc from in front of the body backwards, knees bend, torso leans forward, head forward.
2 Both arms remain straight as they swing forward and up high, the knees straighten, the feet remain firm on the ground.
3 The arms are brought straight down in front of the chest with bent elbows, the torso inclines forward, the head begins to bend.
4 As the hands reach a point about level with the groin, they clap energetically.
5 Immediately after the clap, the body partially straightens again, the elbows bend, the hands are drawn up towards the chest, the head lifts.
6 Immediately the body bends again, the head lowers, the elbows straighten and the hands drop, clapping energetically again at about the level of the groin. The effect is of two quick, strong claps closely following one another.
7 Relax to starting stance.

This preparatory exercise is performed by student-actors before, and often at the end of, other exercises. It requires them to stretch the spine and bend it, to 'open' and 'close', and to be physically alert and responsive. Erast Garin noted that the movement of the hands 'transfers itself into the torso, imparting elasticity to the whole body'.[18]

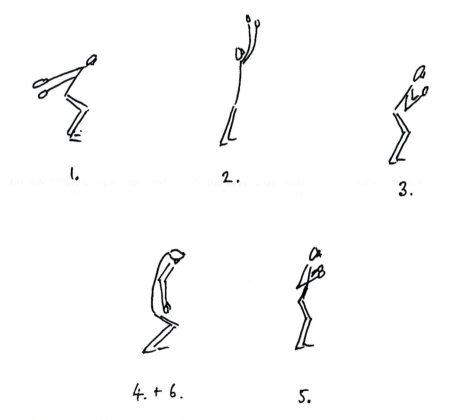

Figure 2.5 Meyerhold's exercise: The Dactyl.

There are other exercises, which lead on to études, and then into performance, including 'Pushing the Kneeling Partner with the Foot', 'Throwing the Stone', the 'Stab with the Dagger' and 'Shooting from the Bow', all of which are preserved on contemporary film from the 1920s in what are clearly Meyerhold's authorised versions. Others include the 'Leap on the Chest', the 'Slap in the Face', 'Dropping the Weight', the 'Leap on to the Partner's Back', and more. Meyerhold himself did not codify a specific series, and used them more or less as the situation seemed to demand. Modern practitioners such as Alexei Levinsky often argue that only five of the exercises are really essential for a biomechanical training: 'Throwing the Stone', the 'Slap in the Face', the 'Leap on the Chest', 'Shooting from the Bow' and the 'Stab with the Dagger'.

However that may be, it is interesting that a comparison between Levinsky performing, say, 'Shooting from the Bow'[19] and the same exercise performed by Meyerhold's actor in the 1920s reveals Levinsky's considerably more complex structure. The exercise itself is described in detail below, but an analysis of Levinsky's performance of it shows that he has twenty-eight discrete units, each segmented from the others by a pause. The earlier version recorded under Meyerhold's supervision includes only eighteen distinct movement units, and several of these run together with no pause between them. Moreover, Levinsky's performance gives an impression of deliberation, each move being considered and measured, and actually performed in almost the same tempo throughout. Meyerhold's actor changes tempo frequently, some of the actions being performed *presto*, others clearly *largo*.

This is not pointed out in order to detract from Levinsky's work; on the contrary, it shows that the exercises are capable of great personal variation as between one performer and another; as well as how the exercises have proved capable of development. Levinsky learned from Mikhail Kustov, who himself joined the Meyerhold Theatre's school around 1930. His version of this exercise is therefore likely to be later and more 'developed' than the earlier version.

The exercise of the 'Leap on the Chest' was one which allowed Meyerhold to delight his own students. In its simplest version, it is precisely what its name implies: one student-actor stands firms, one foot in front of the other, braced ready to catch the second student-actor. The second then runs straight at the first, and leaps up, placing his knees on the catcher's chest, and binding one arm round his neck, whilst the first actor wraps his arm (or arms) round the back of the leaper's knees. If the student-actor who is to perform the leap concentrates on leaping up, and not on his catcher, the exercise is quite easy.

It is then developed into an étude, which was what Meyerhold showed off. Based on the 'Stab with the Dagger', it was a miniature melodrama, which shows how Meyerhold was keen to theatricalise everything the students did. Erast Garin recalled:

> He chose a student who was strongly built, and showed him how to hold himself firmly, gripping the table behind him, and imparting 'give' to his body. Then he [Meyerhold] acted a pantomime of creeping up to the student, when he leaped upon his chest, his right knee against the student's ribs. With his right hand he then drew out an imaginary dagger from his belt, stabbed his partner in the neck, and leaped down. The wounded figure slumped to the floor, while the attacker straightened up.[20]

The exercise was transferred into performance precisely as a leap on to the chest in Meyerhold's 1922 production of *The Magnanimous Cuckold* by Fernand Crommelynck, when the Cooper rushed through a door and leaped on to the unsuspecting Bruno's chest. More interestingly, perhaps, a version of the étude was performed in Eisenstein's 1947 short dance *The Last Conversation*, performed by members of the Bolshoi Ballet. This dance was perhaps the film-maker's last creative work, and was based on the final act of Bizet's *Carmen*. In it, the faithless heroine was murdered in a danced, almost dreamlike sequence which ended when she was stabbed. Eisenstein did not simply reproduce the étude, however, but made his own version of it, and this at a time when Meyerhold's name was obliterated in the USSR and when any mention of him was dangerous. He created a piece which seemed on one level almost like his leave-taking, his regretful but desperately necessary breaking-away from his Master, with its unexpectedly moving finale. The choreography was a dynamic testimony to the enduring power and versatility of Meyerhold's creation.[21]

The exercise of 'Shooting from the Bow' is one of the best known in bio-mechanics, but it is much less easily transferred to the stage than the 'Leap on the Chest'. Student-actors at Meyerhold's school in the 1920s first learned a simplified version of the exercise:

> The left hand mimes carrying a bow, the left shoulder leading. When the student sees the target, his body stops, with the weight equally disposed between both feet. The right hand moves back in an arc to take the imaginary arrow from a quiver on the back. The movement of the hand is conveyed to the body as a whole, and the weight is shifted to the back leg. The hand finds the arrow, and brings it to the bow. The weight shifts again to the front leg. The arrow is aimed. The imaginary bow is drawn back, the weight shifting again to the back foot. The arrow is loosed, and the exercise is completed with a leap and a cry.[22]

Later, they discovered the full version (which, however, was shorter than Alexei Levinsky's as noted above). The exercise was preceded and concluded with the 'Dactyl'.

SHOOTING FROM THE BOW

Stance: as Dactyl (see above).

1   Slow swivel to left on right toe and left heel, arms by sides.
2   Bend and straighten knees, rapidly flick left hand to left shoulder, completely bending left arm, then extend the arm downwards and point with the finger (at imaginary bow on ground).

Pause.

3   Slowly bend knees, keep torso vertical, arms by sides.
4   Left hand moves rapidly to the floor (to pick up imaginary bow), takes the weight of torso which is now parallel to ground; right arm extended vertically, legs bent, weight on left leg.

Pause.

5   Return to position 3.
6   Slowly stand, weight on both feet, arms by sides, spine straight.
7   Slowly bend left arm so hand touches left shoulder, then extend left arm, hand vertically upwards, weight on right foot.

Pause.

8   Right arm makes a big arc parallel with the ground to draw imaginary arrow from belt at left hip, left arm bends to shoulder, weight is transferred to left foot, torso swivels left.
9   Right arm is raised to vertical above head, left arm extended, hand upwards, torso leans left, head half down, weight on left foot, right foot on toes, right leg bent, left leg straight.
10 Right arm rapidly bends, touches right hip, and extends vertically upwards again, torso bends left to be parallel with ground, left arm remains thrust out.

Pause.

11 Rapidly shift weight to right foot as right arm arcs back to horizontal, torso is brought back to vertical, head up, left arm still thrust out.

Pause.

12 Slowly, left arm is bent, hand nearly to shoulder, as right arm is brought in big arc over head to beside left arm, weight shifted to left foot.
13 Right arm 'draws bow', left arm extends horizontally, weight on left foot still.
14 Return to position 12.
15 Rapidly swivel torso to right and down, weight on right foot, both arms vertically down (as if 'firing' bow at right foot), torso bent over to right, head down.

Pause.

16 Rapidly swivel the torso to left and up, both arms raised, head up, weight on left foot, back arched.

Pause.

17 Bend knees, then rapidly straighten them and leap, left foot then right, pulling right arm down rapidly to vertical, whilst stretching neck and spine upwards; at end, weight equal, both feet firm on ground after leap.
18 Slowly bring left arm to side, face front, as at start of exercise. Stand.

This exercise led into the étude 'The Hunt', in which the hunter shot the bow at a wild animal. The actual hunt could take various forms, depending on the individuals performing it and the animal being hunted. Meyerhold was used to taking his students to the zoo for an afternoon to study the animals, which were then used as models for this étude. As 'Shooting from the Bow' is itself, at least in its most

2.

3.

4.

7.

8.

9.

10.

11.

12.

13.

15.

16.

17.

Figure 2.6 Meyerhold's exercise: Shooting from the Bow.

extended form, almost an étude, so 'The Hunt' is almost a pantomime: it is certainly instructive to watch good students perform it, since, at an advanced level, it does allow for the improvisation associated with the public presentations of the Borodinskaya Street Studio days. But after the Revolution, in Moscow it informed several production sequences, including the spectacular chase of Tarelkin by the police in The Death of Tarelkin, for which Eisenstein was the assistant director in 1922. Most notable, perhaps, was the adaptation of 'The Hunt' in the fourth episode of The World Turned Upside Down by Sergei Tretyakov, first performed in 1923, in which Erast Garin played the cook, whom he made into a sort of clown:

> In a white jacket and hat, and with a large knife in my hand, I had to chase a live cockerel which was to be put into the pot. I had to stumble and the cockerel flew out of my grasp. (It was secured by a long black string, since nobody completely trusted the way the cockerel might develop its part.) Then the chase began, full of comic improvisation. Once, before a packed house, I could see Meyerhold on the front row at the right hand side of

the stage. The audience was enjoying the chase. The cockerel stopped, blinded by the stage lights, and looked round. I jerked the string so as to get hold of it, but it flapped its wings madly, broke away from my grip and flew off towards the audience. The string had broken. Shame, misery. . . . Suddenly Meyerhold leaped from his chair like a cannonball from a cannon, a look of grim determination on his face. He caught the cockerel in mid-air, and tucked it under his arm. Then, with some difficulty but as nonchalantly as a stage attendant, he walked through the audience to the stage, and handed the cockerel up to me. I put it under my arm and exited hastily to wild applause![23]

Amusing, even exhilarating, as this is, it only indicates part of the true value of biomechanics for the actor, which Jonathan Pitches hinted at in his assessment:

At the beginning of the process there was no conceivable link between the workshops and the rehearsals on Gogol's text – the work on the etude merely acting as a diversion from the real matter in hand. It was my belief that as the pressure built on the schedule we would be forced pragmatically to lose the 'luxury' of the biomechanical training in order to devote all our time to the blocking of the text. But this scenario did not play itself out. As the language of the etude began to establish itself the biomechanics became progressively invaluable. The rewards of the training in terms of concentration, ensemble discipline, rhythmic under-standing and gestural expressivity were too great to be lost. We had no choice but to continue with the two hour workshop right up to the week of performance, a total of four months.[24]

It is clear from such an evaluation that Meyerhold's biomechanics do indeed uncover what is 'theatrical' in the theatre, and how it can be true to itself. The Russian critic Nikolai Pesochinsky observed how it may in fact transcend Stanislavsky's system: 'In the power of the [biomechanically trained] actor, there resides not only the imitation of ordinary life, but also the way towards its subconscious image-association, the embodiment of the metaphor.'[25] For Pitches, his biomechanical work showed how the training enabled the actor to 'maximise the theatrical potential of every moment in performance as the physical quality of the body itself is defamiliarised and estranged onstage via an approximation of the Meyerholdian grotesque'.[26] Because it has seemed strange in an age dominated by the naturalistic acting styles associated with Stanislavsky, Strasberg and their followers, the virtually limitless potential of biomechanics has long been obscured. Perhaps it will become apparent again in the new millennium.

Notes

1   Gladkov, Aleksandr (1997) *Meyerhold Speaks, Meyerhold Rehearses*, Amsterdam: Harwood Academic Publishers, p. 104.
2   The most significant works in English about Meyerhold are: Braun, Edward (1995) *Meyerhold: a Revolution in Theatre*, London: Methuen; Hoover, Marjorie (1974) *Meyerhold – The Art of Conscious Theater*, Boston, MA: University of Massachusetts Press; Leach, Robert (1989) *Vsevolod Meyerhold*, Cambridge: Cambridge University Press; Rudnitsky, Konstantin (1981) *Meyerhold the Director*, Ann Arbor: Ardis.

3   Garin, Erast (1974) *S Meierkhol'dom*, Moscow: Iskusstvo, p. 34.
4   Reeve, F.D. (ed. and trans.) (1973) *Twentieth Century Russian Plays*, New York: Norton, pp. 174, 175.
5   Garin, Erast, op. cit., p. 30.
6   See Leach, Robert, op. cit., pp. 50–51, where the basic syllabus is reproduced.
7   Gladkov, Aleksandr, op. cit., p. 108.
8   Meyerhold, Vsevolod, Biomechanics course notes, 1921–22, quoted in Titova, G.V. (1995) *Tvorcheskii teatr i teatral'nyi konstrukivism*, St Petersburg: MKR, p. 198.
9   Ilyinsky, Igor (1961) *Sam o sebe*, Moscow: Iskusstvo, p. 154.
10   Eisenstein, S.M., Notes from a lecture by V.E. Meyerhold, 1921–22, quoted in Bushueva, Svetlana (ed.) (1992) *Russkoe akterskoe iskusstvo XX veka*, St Petersburg: Russian Institute of History of the Arts, p. 141.
11   Verigina, Vera, in Valenti, M.A. (ed.) (1967) *Vstrechi s Meierkhol'dom*, Moscow: VTO, p. 57.
12   Pitches, Jonathan (1997) 'The Actor's Perspective', in Shrubsall, Anthony and Pitches, Jonathan, 'Two Perspectives on the Phenomenon of Biomechanics in Contemporary Performance', *Studies in Theatre Production* 16, December, p. 101.
13   Gladkov, Aleksandr, op. cit., p. 104.
14   An example was the presentation on 12 February 1915, the programme of which is reproduced in Leach, Robert, op. cit., pp. 48–49.
15   Meyerhold's list of 'set roles' for the 1922 biomechanics class is published in Leach, Robert, op. cit., p. 75.
16   Ilyinsky, Igor, op. cit., p. 155.
17   Pitches, Jonathan, op. cit., pp. 105, 119.
18   Garin, Erast, op. cit., p. 35.
19   Levinsky's work may be seen on Arts Archive, the Third Archive, video number 10, *Meyerhold's Biomechanics: A Workshop*, Arts Documentation Unit, Exeter, 1997.
20   Garin, Erast, op. cit., p. 36.
21   The short ballet *The Last Conversation* was reconstructed by Sally Banes, and the performance recorded by her on video, available from the Department of Theatre and Dance Studies at the University of Wisconsin-Madison, USA.
22   Garin, Erast, op. cit., p. 36.
23   Valenti, M.A., op. cit., p. 310.
24   Pitches, Jonathan, op. cit., p. 103.
25   Bushueva, Svetlana, op. cit., p. 104.
26   Pitches, Jonathan, op. cit., p. 125.

Bibliography

Benedetti, Jean (1988) *Stanislavsky: A Biography*, London: Methuen.
Bergen, Ronald (1997) *Sergei Eisenstein: A Life in Conflict*, London: Little, Brown.
Braun, Edward (ed.) (1969) *Meyerhold on Theatre*, London: Eyre Methuen.
—— (1995) *Meyerhold: a Revolution in Theatre*, London: Methuen.
Bushueva, S.K. (1992) *Russkoe akterskoe iskusstvo XX veka*, St Petersburg: Ministerstvo Kul'tury Rossii.
Eisenstein, Sergei (1985) *Immoral Memories*, London: Peter Owen.
Garin, Erast (1974) *S Meierkhol'dom*, Moscow: Iskusstvo.
Gladkov, Aleksandr (1997) *Meyerhold Speaks, Meyerhold Rehearses*, Amsterdam: Harwood.
Gourfinkel, Nina (1963) *Vsevolod Meyerhold – Le théâtre théâtral*, Paris: Gallimard.
Hoover, Marjorie (1974) *Meyerhold – The Art of Conscious Theater*, Boston, MA: University of Massachusetts Press.
Ilyinsky, Igor (1961) *Sam o sebe*, Moscow: Iskusstvo.
Kleberg, Lars (1993) *Theatre as Action*, London: Macmillan.
Leach, Robert (1989) *Vsevolod Meyerhold*, Cambridge: Cambridge University Press.
—— (1994) *Revolutionary Theatre*, London: Routledge.
—— (2003) *Stanislavsky and Meyerhold*, Bern: Peter Lang AG.
Meyerhold, V.E. (1968) *Stat'i, pis'ma, rechi, besedy*, 2 vols, Moscow: Iskusstvo.
—— (1976) *Perepiska 1896–1939*, Moscow: Iskusstvo.

Mikhailova, Alla *et al* (1995) *Meierkhol'd i khudozhniki*, Moscow: Galart.

Pesochinsky, Nikolai V. *et al* (1997) *Meierkhol'd v Russkoi teatral'noi kritike*, Moscow: Artist, Rezhisser, Teatr.

Picon-Vallin, Beatrice (1990) *Meyerhold*, Paris: CNRS.

Pitches, Jonathan (2003) *Vsevolod Meyerhold*, London: Routledge.

Rudnitsky, Konstantin (1981) *Meyerhold the Director*, Ann Arbor: Ardis.

Schmidt, Paul (ed.) (1980) *Meyerhold at Work*, Austin, TX: University of Texas Press.

Sherel', A.A. (1992) *Meierkhol'dovskii sbornik*, 2 vols, Moscow: Komissiya po tvorcheskomu naslediya V.E.Meierkhol'da.

Sitkovetska, M.M. (1993) *Meierkhol'd repetiruet*, 2 vols, Moscow: Artist, Rezhisser, Teatr.

Titova, G.B. (1995) *Tvorcheskii teatr i teatral'nyi konstuktivizm*, St Petersburg: Ministerstvo Kul'tury Rossii.

Valenti, M.A. (ed.) (1967) *Vstrechi s Meierkhol'dom*, Moscow: VTO.

van Gyseghem, Andre (1943) *Theatre in Soviet Russia*, London: Faber and Faber.

Zolotnitskii, David (1976) *Zori teatral'nogo oktyabrya*, Leningrad: Iskusstvo.

Chapter 3

John Rudlin

JACQUES COPEAU: THE QUEST
FOR SINCERITY

THE CONTEXT

JACQUES COPEAU ENTERED PROFESSIONAL theatre as a practitioner relatively late in life: he was thirty-two years old when he first became involved in directing his own adaptation of Dostoevski's *The Brothers Karamazov*, and it was not until two years later that he finally relinquished a promising literary career for a hazardous theatrical one. In 1913, with the help of friends from the *Nouvelle Revue Français* (of which he was a founder and the first editor), he set up the Théâtre du Vieux Colombier on the left bank of the Seine. The building had previously been a variety hall called l'Athénée St-Germain. Copeau not only renamed it – with deliberate simplicity – after the street in which it sat, but also stripped out its tawdry hangings and gilded plaster-work, and eventually even its proscenium arch.

This *mise à nu* was typical of his approach to all aspects of French theatre as he found it, and he had observed more of it than most, having spent eight years as a drama critic for several Parisian magazines. In review after review he had pointed out the detrimental effects of the star system and its basis in commercial exploitation. Such a critique had been of little consequence, however, and he considered it was now time for remedial action. He called his self-appointed task 'Dramatic Renovation'. As in the restoration of a work of art, he intended a peeling away of layer upon layer of over-painting so as to reveal, say, a Molière underneath, unembellished and in its original colours:

> It is often said that I intend to break with tradition. The exact opposite is
> true. I am seeking to bring works closer to the 'true tradition' by freeing
> them from the contributions loaded on them for three centuries by the
> official actors [of the Comédie-Française]. The important tradition is
> the original one.[1]

Copeau was in a sense, therefore, a pre-modern post-modernist. He did not believe in '-isms', or artistic movements and cultural revolutions, but in a renewable, rediscoverable entity, the medium of theatre. It was not that he had an antiquarian interest in the old, but that he considered the theatre had fallen into such disrepair that it could no longer offer a solid platform on which new works could be presented. His literary collaborators, many of whom were uncertain whether to write novels or plays, were hopeful that he would provide them with a radical but elementary outlet for their essays in various theatrical genres. Copeau is, indeed, often instanced as the champion of respect for the text in the production process. Some of his early *mises en scène* seemed, in fact, to be little more than dramatic readings: but rather that, in his view, than actors offering phoney emotions and nineteenth-century tricks-of-the-trade, the whole gamut of what he called *cabotinage*:

> a disease that is not only endemic to the theatre. It's the malady of insincerity, or rather of falseness. He who suffers from it ceases to be authentic, to be human. He is discredited, unnatural. . . . I am not only speaking of the 'so-called stars', of those phenomena, those poor monsters whose deformities are too obvious to require description. I am speaking of all actors, of the most unimportant of them and of his [or her] slightest gesture, of the total mechanisation of the person, of the absolute lack of profound intelligence and true spirituality.[2]

It was to prove, however, a deal easier to strip encrustations off walls than off actors. He chose his company with care, and took the actors away into the countryside, to his family house, Le Limon, near the tiny village of La Ferté-sous-Jarre in Seine et Marne to 'de-urbanise', as he called it. There they rehearsed in the open air, with daily warm-ups based on 'rhythmical exercises' together with sight-reading and sports such as swimming, fencing and ball games. In this natural environment he sought a natural simplicity and spontaneity from his performers consisting of authenticity of gesture to impulse, well-spoken text and a sense of collective playfulness leading to a unity of dramatic purpose. By the end of their first season together, this preparatory work had undoubtedly paid off: Paris was queuing to get into the Vieux Colombier production of *Twelfth Night*. In 1917, with Parisian theatres closed for the duration of the war, Copeau reflected:

> Why did I succeed, in the eight months from October 19th 1913 to May 1914, in that Paris which is said to be blasé, in forcing on an evergrowing audience a repertoire made up entirely of French and foreign classical masterpieces and of the boldest plays of the present generation? It was because I was surrounded by fellow-workers, men and women, whose pure souls and minds remained unsullied.[3]

Regrettably, they did not remain so for much longer: some never returned from the war, some proved to have concealed their true nature, and others left the company. Six years later, in 1923, Copeau remarked to his assistant, Michel Saint-Denis, after rehearsal:

> Did you see them today? I always know in advance what they are going to do. They cannot get out of themselves; they love only themselves. They reduce everything to the level of their habits, their clichés, their affectations. They do not invent anything. It is all sheer imitation of imitation.[4]

Figure 3.1 Copeau: gymnastics class in the garden at Le Limon.
Source: Photo from the Marie-Hélène Dasté collection.

Nevertheless, Copeau was never antipathetic to actors: in fact he became one himself, copying the practice of his acknowledged masters – Molière, Stanislavsky and Antoine – so that he was able to perceive the performer's difficulties from the inside out as well as, directorially, from the outside in. He described the underlying problem of acting as 'the freezing of the blood':

> The actor tells his arm 'Come on, now, arm, go out and make the gesture', but the arm remains wooden. The 'blood' doesn't flow; the muscles don't move; the body fights within itself; it's a terrifying thing. To someone on the outside this sounds like verbalisation or poetry. But we know, because we have often felt what it means to stand on the stage, we know that what you are doing is not what you mean to do, that you meant to move your arm differently and you meant to come over to the audience with ease and warmth, and instead you're standing there like a stick.[5]

Yet even worse than such paralysis, in Copeau's view, was the over-facility of an actor such as David Garrick, who on a visit to Paris once sat in a drawing room and, for the amusement of friends, including Denis Diderot, let his face run through a catalogue of emotions without, seemingly, feeling anything himself. In a preface to an edition of Diderot's *Paradoxe sur le Comédien*, Copeau wrote:

> the actor . . . applies his monstrous sincerity to being what he is not – not to expressing what he does not feel, but to feeling the make-believe.
> What upsets Hamlet the philosopher, as much as his other hellish

apparitions, is the diverting of natural faculties in the human being to a fantastic use.

The actor takes the risk of losing his . . . soul . . . which, having been too often upset by acting, too often carried away and offended by imaginary passions, contorted by artificial habits, feels irrelevant before reality. The whole being of the actor carries the stigmata of a strange relationship with the human world. When he returns among us, he looks as if he were coming from another world.

An actor's profession tends to pervert him. It's the consequence of an instinct which pushes a man to abandon himself and live a pretence. And consequently it is a profession that people despise; they find it dangerous, immoral, and they condemn it for its mystery. This pharisaical attitude, which has not been eliminated in even the most tolerant societies, reflects a profound idea. That is, that the actor is doing something forbidden: he is playing with his humanness and making sport of it.[6]

Copeau continually demanded personal sincerity from his actors as an antidote to the *cabotinage* which continued to dominate the boulevards and the Comedié Française (whose Conservatoire, incidentally, offered the only available actor training in France before the opening of the Vieux Colombier School). He sometimes stayed behind after rehearsal to watch the carpenters working on stage. What they did seemed purposeful, rhythmical, incidentally sincere. Whereas the actions of the actors in rehearsal had been unnatural and forced – lacking in a sure tradition of craftsmanship.

Between 1917 and 1919 Copeau was able to reassemble some of his company in New York. After the Great War, he reopened the Vieux Colombier in Paris in 1920, but with some reluctance. By this time he was only too aware that he had compromised his quest for theatrical renovation by putting, as the French say, the cart before the oxen. What was needed was not remedial work with established actors during rehearsals, but preliminary work in an attached school where the problem of sincerity could be addressed before the protective devices of *cabotinage* became ingrained: a separate place in which to educate, rather than train (or retrain), actors from the earliest possible age. Such performers would then be free of the egotism required by the star system and would have their allegiance to an ensemble emergent from their common apprenticeship. Copeau called this unity of spirit and commonalty of technique '*Choeur*', which translates roughly as both 'choir' and 'chorus'. In order to get on with the business of 'dramatic renovation', however, he had had to give the opening of the Vieux Colombier Theatre precedence over its School.

In 1915, whilst the Vieux Colombier was closed, he had visited Edward Gordon Craig in his school in Venice (also shut for the duration of the war). He noted:

In founding a school, Craig does not feel the same need as I do, does not pursue the same goal. He does not even pursue any immediate goal. He is not a theatre director. He is not trying to form a company of actors to fulfil the requirements of a repertoire. The actor does not interest him [but only] his theory of the 'Über-Marionette'.[7]

Craig told him that he had refused the directorship of the Théâtre des Arts in Paris unless the building could be closed to the public for ten to fifteen years whilst he prepared pupils for a renewed art of the theatre:

You will ask how it is that I did not follow Craig's advice and open a School before opening a Theatre. I did not do it because I was not able to do it, because I had neither the authority nor the means to do so. If, in October 1913, I had proposed the founding of a School, no-one would have listened to me. . . . Craig was being logical. If I had been so, I should have remained in oblivion. I was deeply convinced that it was imperative to exist first of all. We had to familiarise the public with our utopian ideas. We had to give proof of what a company of actors, mostly novices, could give in a year's work in common, under direction. . . . So, it is true that I started by making a concession to life's demands. But it was through caution, not ignorance. . . . The idea of the School and the idea of the Theatre are one and the same; they were conceived together and described as such in my *Attempt at Dramatic Renovation*.[8]

The Vieux Colombier School proper opened in December 1921 after an initial try-out period between December 1920 and June 1921, and a number of short-lived experiments previous to that, in both France and America. The director was the novelist and playwright Jules Romains, and the principal teacher was Copeau's *aide*, *confidante* and *amante*, Suzanne Bing, who was, up to that point, a leading actress with the company. Copeau himself was rarely seen at the School, except for giving a semi-public lecture course, but was able to monitor progress via his association with Bing. In 1922 he took over the directorship of the School himself, but was still prevented by a punishing production and performance schedule from being more than an occasional presence. Although the School had three divisions, it was the 'apprentice group' which more and more dominated his horizon. It consisted initially of a group of six pupils,[9] of both sexes, from fourteen to twenty years old, apprenticed for a minimum of three years. At the end of that time the intention was for a new, even younger group to be initiated. The key course was 'Dramatic Instinct', taken by Suzanne Bing. Copeau's only brief to her was to follow her own instinct, with the proviso that the students spoke no dialogue before the third year. At the end of 1923 he summed up the project so far:

> The first year is particularly concerned with the acquisition of fundamental concepts; the second with a common general and vocational cultural development; the third concentrates on specific abilities and individual excellence; performance work is undertaken for the first time.
>
> The teaching is based on *education of the body* (musical, gymnastic, acrobatic, dancing, games of strength and skill), with a progressive initiation into *craft skills* (drawing, modelling, decorative art, costume and props), *singing*, both choral and solo, *exercises in dramatic expression* (mask-work, physical games, physiognomy, mimicry), then to *improvisation* (plastique and with dialogue), to *elocution, diction and declamation*, to *general education* and to *dramatic theory* (laws of dramatic expression, study of the great epochs, scenic arts and crafts).
>
> Ultimately, *free play* gives way to small-scale productions for which people are left entirely to their own devices, as creators and workers. Working and living communally, not excluding specialisation according to individual capabilities, has rapidly made a real little company . . . with healthy ideals, a solid professional working basis, a remarkable *esprit de corps* and self-sufficiency.[10]

Here is an example of how one of the 'small-scale productions' emerged. As a development of the 'Follow My Leader' game, masked students would take the expressive focus in turn, with the rest of the masks responding sympathetically – though not necessarily reduplicating what the lead mask was doing. Often no theme would be given and intuitive discoveries made through initially abstract improvisation led to simple situations, such as that of village women in a wash-house gossiping whilst working. One such involved the gathering of a crowd to welcome home a ship. The quality of this piece, among others, intensified Copeau's dilemma over his future priority – to devote his time to the school or the company:

> A group of pupils come to the front of the stage. They produce, despite their masked faces, a vision of a strand and of fisher-folk peering out upon a stormy sea. Their bodies create not alone their own emotion, but by a subtle fugue the heave of the water. A rowboat comes up. It is created by two actors in a rhythmic unison of propulsion. They leave their boat and mount the stairs to the apron. They have news of the drowning of a comrade: the news transfigures the group. The scene shifts to what is an interior of a fisher cottage. The wife and children await the master. The friends come in with the tragic tidings.[11]

What was to be the future of this little group? In a year's time, some might have been subsumed into the Vieux Colombier company, others would have had to make their own way. Little by little the intensity of their collective experience would have been dispersed and diluted and Copeau would have had to continue in rehearsal his daily struggle with the 'problem of the actor'. On 15 May 1924, two weeks after the first semi-public presentation of the work of the apprentice actors from the School, Jacques Copeau did a remarkable thing, for which he has often been castigated and rarely sufficiently lauded: he closed the Vieux Colombier which had seemed by now to be a success established *en permanence*. He himself now acted instinctively and with no forward planning:

> persuaded that our compromises with the times would produce nothing fertile, tired of standing still and having rejected the 'boulevard' theatre since 1913, we resolved to reject the so-called 'avant-garde' theatre, which is already infected by counterfeits and lies. At the end of 1924, we decided to risk everything. We wanted this 'renovation' that we had tried for so long to define and to understand, to at least mean something for ourselves. We started over again. We turned backwards in order to check what we knew, learn what we did not know, experiment with what we vaguely felt, no longer proceeding without our sense of vocation, doing something that was not true, but building, moderately but purely.[12]

By September of that year he was established in the Château de Morteuil, 10 kilometres from Beaune in the heart of Burgundy, with the apprentice group, together with four young professional actors from the company and their families, plus two more performers living nearby, one technician, and a poet.

The 'château' was merely a large, imposing farm house situated in a damp hollow. It was filthy, had no electricity and the stoves did not work. Copeau himself was mentally and physically exhausted, suffering the first effects of an undiagnosed and debilitating disease. But there he was, with his furniture, his library, his own (extended) family, the contents of the Vieux Colombier costume store, and an excited coterie of dramatic voyagers ready to discover a new world of theatrical initiative, 'exactly like old man Noah on his ark, surrounded by a crowd of young faces quizzing my feeble looks'.[13]

On 4 November Le Patron, as he was universally known, brought them all together for an introductory talk. Someone noted down what he said:

> He explained why he had come and that he had abandoned everything in order to do so. He said he regarded it as his last chance in life and that we should realise the responsibility that placed us under; our sense of that responsibility would show itself in a perfectionist attitude to work and a dignified life style. He laid great emphasis on the morality of the artist and the discipline needed to aspire to it. He had not obliged anyone to come: we were all volunteers and would have to accept poverty as a condition of discipleship. There would be no question of erasing our personalities, rather of disciplining, managing and conserving our individuality. We would need respect for others, discretion and deference; above all, sincerity, charity, intelligence and good humour. He himself was not infallible, but he would never do anything knowing it to be unjust. We would never bore him. His powers were all coming back to him. He went on to explain how these general principles would be worked out in practical detail in the rules for the school and for the house. He could only work if these rules were observed, since freedom would only come from regulation and observance.[14]

It is worth pausing to appreciate the courageous admixing of family and working lives, the proposed *kibbutzim-style* attempt to live, work and play *ensemble*. The high moral tone, however, reflected Copeau's own recent re-embracing of the Catholic faith at a practically Jansenist level. Unfortunately, his personal spiritual crisis was still deepening, the château was damp and unhealthy and the funds expected to underpin the enterprise did not materialise. At the moment of nadir, five months later in February 1925, Copeau dissolved the community. Nevertheless, a few of the actors proposed to stay on at their own expense and, together with those members of the apprentice group that were part of Copeau's own extended family, to form a troupe that would perform in the villages and towns of Burgundy. It was, however, to be a training company and not a school that occasionally performed. Nevertheless, Le Patron became gradually drawn into its work and took over the reins in June of that year, acting, directing and providing texts, whilst Suzanne Bing and others such as Jean Dasté were again largely responsible for the training programme. There were happier times and happier climes as the company, now named Les Copiaus after the local dialect pronunciation of Le Patron's name, moved from the misty hollow to a large house on a sunny hillside in the nearby village of Pernand-Vergelesses. The renewed spirit of the Copiaus, he wrote, stemmed from their education in the 'dramatic instinct', which continued to be based on

> a conscientious examination of the principles of their craft and on a personal investigation of the elements of dramatic creation. Their teachers guide them towards those innermost discoveries that are necessary to the possession of any technique. Their sense of discipline consists of avoiding nothing, of never pretending, of never expressing or even thinking of

anything that they cannot personally and authentically think and express. They apply themselves to finding principles within themselves, to implanting in their bodies, hearts and minds a direct experience of the laws of theatre and the feeling for their necessity. Thus, they are brought back to a naïve state that is not an artificial or literary attitude, but is their natural position before a world of possibilities where nothing is corrupted by habits of imitation, nor perverted by an acquired virtuosity. . . . That is where they stand, and they aspire no further at the moment. Far from priding themselves on their sufficiency, they remain at the starting point. In my opinion this is a positive conquest.[15]

They played Molière farces, and adaptations by Copeau of Goldoni and Lope de Rueda. They also developed their own original pieces, increasingly depending on the new masks for *commedia dell'arte* which they had devised. Playing first at local fêtes and fairs, they gradually began to establish a national and international reputation. Perhaps their most typical piece was *L'Illusion*, since, although ostensibly written by Copeau after Corneille and Fernando de Rojas, it contained large amounts of material culled from improvisation. The text reveals the extent to which their performance style was interpenetrated by a 'naïve', albeit idealised, representation of their individual and collective lives. In the prologue, Copeau playing The Actor virtually as himself, ruminating on the 'freezing of the blood', was joined on stage by The Actress, played by Suzanne Bing:

ACTRESS: If we remain silent too long, if we remain too long in the contemplation of our thoughts, shall we retain the power of some day giving birth to the Illusion? I am only an actress. I don't care very much for reality. I don't like myself very much. I don't wish to be invaded by everything I am. My passions, my desires, my jealousy, my deceits: give me back Comedy so its fire will consume them and purify me.

(On this last line Maiène [Copeau's daughter, Marie-Hélène] enters.)

ACTOR: I was trying to invent something . . . a manner of acting, full of thwarted movements, of young faces, of love and music, and for you, a character overflowing with poetry which would make you love me as I love you. But I am haunted by nothing but sombre images . . .

(Maiène approaches the Actor.)

MAIÈNE: Good morning.
ACTOR: (Kissing her.) Good morning, my child.
MICHEL [Saint-Denis, Copeau's nephew]: (Entering.) Good morning.
ACTOR: Good morning, youth.
VILLARD [Jean Villard, former Vieux Colombier actor]: (Entering.) Are you ready, Actor? The young people are waiting.
ACTOR: What do these young people want of me? . . .
MAIÈNE: To be what we are.
ACTRESS: Actors who live by Comedy, free and poor, from morning to night, kneading the dough of their craft with their own hands.
ACTOR: My young companions, my young companions, are you going to give me back the courage necessary for forming a world each day out of nothing, and hanging it above reality, a world which falls apart even as it is being created? Will you have the strength, the constancy, the saintly humility?

> ... I had folded up my hope. My memories had faded away. Even the
> loveliest of them. ... Why do you come to make my head swim, like
> birds in a garden in the month of May?[16]

After the prologue the action began with a youth called Petit Pierre (a derivative of
the Pedrolino/Pierrot figure of the *commedia dell'arte*) joining the company to escape
the wrath of his old father. Once on stage he is able to join in because the drama
is improvised and there are no lines to learn. However, the father is in the audience –
is their only audience, in fact. He watches his son – in the part of Calixte – fall in love
with Melibée and win her (with supernatural assistance!). This all happens whilst
Melibée's father, Plébère, is away. When he returns, the spectator/father leaves and
the actors stop the play and argue as to the continuation of the plot. They decide that
Plébère should deal with Calixte in a traditionally heavy-handed manner; the illusion
is about to begin again when the father, who has not left after all, rushes on stage and
lectures Plébère about the undesirability of parental harshness. Father and son are
reconciled and go home. The actors pack up their effects, put them in their cart and
leave, singing the Copiaus' theme song.

The mood of the piece was almost whimsical, yet, in line with the desire not to
have actors express any sentiments they had not themselves experienced, Copeau
(Plébère) was making deliberate reference to the courtship of his own daughter,
Maïène (Calixte), by Jean Dasté (Petit Pierre). Was this incorporation of reality into
illusion the ultimate resolution of the quest for sincerity? Copeau called the piece
'pure theatre', neither a drama nor a comedy, but a theatre game. *The Times* of London
noted:

> You feel as you watch them that they are indeed a community *de famille et
> d'amitié* who are earnestly bent on re-discovering the childhood – or is it
> the second childhood? – of the theatre. An odd quest that would soon
> become tedious if pursued at length; but if we must have 'pure theatre',
> may it always come with the grace and polish of Pernand-Vergelesses.[17]

This astute appraisal presaged yet another severance in Copeau's career. The quest
was not 'pursued at length'; the underlying tension between his desire to have Les
Copiaus train for two-thirds of the year and their desire to perform as much as
possible, capitalising on their new-found acclaim, became too great. Rather than
compromise his vision of the Vieux Colombier School any further, he suddenly broke
with the company in June 1929. Led by Michel Saint-Denis, the Copiaus became La
Compagnie des Quinze and toured Europe with great success until the mid 1930s.
The last phase of Copeau's career as freelance director, playwright and man of letters
does not concern us here, since he undertook no further actor training.

THE TRAINING

Discovering dramatic principles within oneself, embracing the naïve without
intellectual reservation, developing an authenticity of gesture to emotional impulse –
how did Copeau attempt to unfreeze the blood of his apprentice actors without their
becoming insincere? Here are some notes on some of the methods used by him, and
by Suzanne Bing and others at his instigation.

Figure 3.2 Jacques Copeau as Plébère in L'Illusion.

Breath and text

Breathing, because it is an involuntary, essentially natural, life-sustaining activity, was for Copeau the *primum mobile* in his quest for gestural sincerity and vocal concord. The taking of voluntary control of the involuntary activity provided a resolution of the 'monstrous sincerity':

> Breathing controls everything.
> A voice which does not breathe becomes dull, collapses on itself and becomes sad. It flounders like someone drowning. It is dragged along by the text. It fails to dominate it and cannot articulate it either. It is breathing which ensures that our sensibility has the faculty to move in any direction. On it depends natural laughter and heartfelt emotion. From it comes nobility and authority, which give weight to one's presence. Inadequate breathing creates disorder. Vigorous breathing brings freedom.

Reading out loud requires perpetual *tours de force* of breathing. Above all, when a dramatic text demands constant switching from one tone to another, from one movement to another, from one character to another, to different ages and sexes.

One has continually to get a grip on oneself, to master one's own sincerity, change attitude and tonality, posture and rhythm, never let oneself get wrapped up in the text. The gymnastics, say, of the playwright.

Breathing makes lightness possible, which is one of the supreme virtues of the artist. That is to say that even in paroxysm one should not go to the end of one's powers: leave a little margin which allows the supposition that one could, if one had wanted, have gone further, that there is still a reservoir, a reserve. There is a sort of distinctiveness and reverence which is dictated by taste and made possible by lightness.

In this lightness there can be found a certain faculty of skimming over the text, a coming together of the eyes and of the mind in order to be always ahead of the tongue. A well-trained reader gives the impression of knowing the text by heart.

One does not know it by heart. That would be too easy. And it would be much less effective – one is saying by heart many things which one is understanding at that very moment, which one has just discovered and which are still fresh in one's mouth.[18]

During his first attempt at 'de-urbanisation' in the garden of Le Limon, Copeau, as we have seen, separated movement from text during the daily warm-up before rehearsal. Up to two hours were devoted to sight-reading out loud. Being himself a sought-after public reader, Copeau returned repeatedly to this exercise in his later schools. Often he would send two actors off with a non-dramatic work of literature, one to read and one to listen. This obliged the listener not only to listen with personal intent (and not just for their cues), but also to develop a critical faculty by which they learned from the other's mistakes. For the reader, the alertness and speed of reaction required, often with the eyes reading a line ahead of what was actually being vocalised, helped to break down habits of phrasing and inflection. And for both participants there was the slightly discomfiting knowledge that shortly it would be time to swap roles. The selection of suitable texts also extended the range of the participants' cultural awareness:

> Our graduated exercises in reading out loud, at first sight, pursue a double goal of increasing intellectual flexibility at the same time as per-fecting vocal articulation. In order to read well, whilst at the same time paying attention to diction and to the register of one's voice, one needs continual mental alertness, never to 'let oneself go', to understand quickly and to express oneself with precision. Thus actors have the possibility of avoiding their natural penchant for falling into ready-made inflexions, and also avoiding the difficulty they usually have, that of a slowness, a certain laziness in getting into the spirit of the text, something which obliges the director, during the first rehearsals, to pre-masticate all their dialogue for them . . .
>
> A good sight-reading, devoid of affectation, that is the open ground on which to build a healthy interpretation [of a role].[19]

Natural gymnastics

In referring to the interplay of mind and voice as 'gymnastic', Copeau was only too aware that the oral (and aural) training of sight-reading was the adduction of the literary man. A physical complement was needed. As a stop-gap at Le Limon, he tried to balance verbal exercises with physical ones. As noted above, daily rhythmical limbering was taken by one of the actors, Roger Karl, and sporting activities were encouraged. What Copeau ultimately sought, however, was not just a means of attaining a desirable level of fitness, balance, control and physical confidence, but a physical training which would be integral to the development of the actor as instrument. After a visit to Jacques Dalcroze in 1915, he tried to adopt the latter's system of eurythmics. But by 1921, after experimenting with three different teachers, he decided that it was 'another language, a speciality and consequently a deformation. [Eu]rhythmics leads to a personal idolatry of the body.'[20] Eventually the Vieux Colombier School adopted Georges Hébert's method of 'natural gymnastics', designed primarily to develop strength and flexibility for sporting rather than dramatic activities. However, thanks to monitor Jean Dorcy,[21] the method gradually became geared to the students' needs:

> At first these exercise sessions were poorly attended and quite limited. Dorcy finally complained that they were doing nothing but jumping, and did his best to expand the program. As class leader in the absence of M. Moine [Hébert's instructor], Dorcy made sure also that students did more than the exercises they did best. Some of these exercises were: marching, leaping over obstacles, balance-bars. Out-door work at St. Cloud once a week was more varied and rigorous, including jogging, high-jump contests, push-ups, throwing a medicine ball, obstacle courses, military endurance exercises, and even some trapeze work.[22]

When work began again in November 1923, it was largely Dorcy who worked with the group. All noted improved agility and flexibility and balance, acquiring a 'relaxed tonality through work with solid obstacles'.[23] Later, in Burgundy, it was Jean Dasté who took over the role of monitor; later still Dasté's own scion, Jacques Lecoq, used the Hébert method in his school in Paris: 'pull, push, climb, walk, run, jump, lift, carry, attack, defend, swim. These actions trace a physical circuitry in sensitive bodies in which emotions are imprinted.'[24]

Lecoq himself came from a sporting background, and his is perhaps a larger claim for the potential of the method than Copeau would have believed possible. He would certainly have found such a development of it desirable.

Corporeal music

Music was a mystery to Copeau, which is perhaps why he continually sought to incorporate it in the training. Students at the Vieux Colombier School learned choral and solo singing, reading music and the basics of an individual instrument. However, Copeau did not want any part of the instruction to be an island, a specialism. He intended music to be integrated with movement studies, primarily with the dance course given by Mlle Lamballe.[25] This class was begun in late November and was given somewhat sporadically. Mlle Lamballe worked with the students on classical ballet positions and exercises, as well as steps like the *pas de bourrée, saut du chat,* slides, *jetés,* and dances like the minuet and gavotte. It was Suzanne Bing, as usual, who took on the task of applying such dance concepts to dramatic expression. She often held her course in 'Musique Corporelle' just after ballet class, discussing and working with such concepts as time and duration, space, shape, force, speed, volume, intensity and weight.[26]

Bing began by focusing on breathing, and filling a particular duration with breath. Next she added movements, to be accomplished in the same duration. These simple exercises grew into movements on beats, with more complex assignments given to fill time sequences with improvised dialogue or mimed action. She then had the students analyse and explore the relationships between emotional quality of a gesture and its time of preparation – first with breathing, then movement, using various parts of the body, stressing imagination, continuity and unity of direction. This method of developing a gesture was then continued in ensemble movement and in movement sequences. Later they played 'Follow my Leader' in order to become instinctive at performing actions together within the same time sequence.

One of Bing's exercises was to begin an action and then interrupt it with a brief movement. The students then worked to juxtapose two different tempos – the arms keeping the beat whilst the feet walked in a circle on the measure, accompanying themselves with the voice instead of music. Examples of everyday phenomena were found to illustrate different tempos: a sewing machine as quick, percussive, a lift as sustained. Early in the New Year rhythms were introduced based on regular intervals as exemplified in drawing, poetry and prose, architecture and music. The group clapped different rhythms, imitating each other, then putting poly-rhythms together. Clapping was then replaced by simple verbal exclamation – 'Ah!' for example. Subsequently they played musical charades, using rhythms whose musical qualities were simple and clear – then afterwards they had to guess what the music was. They discussed the effects of quality, duration, silence, and made up rhythmic examples to illustrate each.

Group compositions were performed in silence, then with accompanying piano music – an addition which highlighted plastic rather than the dramatic qualities. These were followed by a study of dynamics – visualising loudness and softness in space, for example. Eventually these exercises were used in the creation of dances. Exercises in 'taking possession of space' were also an important element, to which was added expansion in sound and the exploration of shapes – individually and in a group. Later they did exercises related to obedience to a particular rhythm, standing in a circle and using a ball thrown in patterns to reinforce the concept. Then came study of spoken phrases and the analysis of differing meanings conveyed through the use of pause. In application they worked with three different types of phrases: spoken, in movement and musical – discussing the different means of differentiating between phrases, accents, silence, contrasts. For movement phrasing, elements to use might be: changes in direction, weight, duration, level, using different parts of the body. A complex exercise in the use of space exploring phrases and sentences was performed with three groups: the first ran and stopped in position; the second group took a complementary position; the third group completed the figure. They then tried the exercise with their eyes closed.

Thus Bing utilised the study of a particular style of movement – ballet – to help students discover more general characteristics of style that they could apply to their own work. Using an approach somewhat reminiscent of Laban and modern dance exploration, Bing stressed both analysis and play. Work was often facilitated by music on the piano, accompanying exercises such as the mirror game or the miming of opening a door. The students discovered the difference between choreographed movement to music, or dance, and that which is performed with an internal rhythm and no music, i.e. corporeal mime. Music gave their movements greater purity and abstraction, but often blurred the dramatic sense. Bing was sometimes bothered by the students' inability to concentrate on pure movement and their insistence on using anecdotal material. They sometimes lost sight of an objective she had proposed, or did not experiment enough with abstract concepts. She noted, incidentally, that Copeau's occasional presence seemed to paralyse the students – a freezing of the blood again![27]

Neutrality

'*The point of departure of an expression*. The state of repose, of calm, of relaxation or decontraction, of silence or simplicity.'

> To start from silence and calm. That is the first point. An actor must know how to be silent, to listen, respond, keep still, begin a gesture, develop it, return to stillness and silence, with all the tones and half tones that those actions imply.[28]

Such a state of neutrality should not be construed as being negative, it has nothing to do with being neutered. It means simply 'Putting oneself in a state of readiness' (*Décontraction préalable*).

Much more is known today about relaxation than in the 1920s, and to offer a résumé of Copeau's practice would be of academic interest only. Were he working today, I am personally convinced that he would borrow from the disciplines of Yoga and T'ai Chi, provided that they did not leave a stylistic imprint on the performer. Suffice, then, to say that from a state of maximum possible relaxation in the whole body (i.e. one in which phasic muscles receive no unnecessary support from voluntary ones), Copeau's students learned to isolate energy in different parts of themselves. That area was then encouraged to lead a particular expression.[29] The back, for example, was used to express astonishment, disquiet, grief-strickenness, anger, remorse, courageousness or the regaining of hopefulness. The face (as simply another part of the body) was used to express subtle gradations of emotion which the rest of the apprentice group tried to guess by name. This exercise was not meant to emulate Garrick's party tricks – the return to the neutral state between expressions was considered crucial to the honest development of the next intention. After one such session in silent improvisation Copeau concluded that:

> There are two kinds of manifestations in an actor's playing: discontinuous manifestations that seem intentional, phoney, theatrical, and continuous manifestations that give an impression of modesty and internal sincerity, of real life and power. Continuity and slow pace are conditions of powerful and sincere playing.[30]

Slow motion was henceforward incorporated in the training. As usual, it was Bing who developed the detail of the exercise. After the state of decontraction (which is physical), she proposed mental states: pre-formation of the expressive idea; suspense,

i.e. not immediately giving in to the impulse; then attack, i.e. a complete commitment of the body to the pre-formation; then the return to the neutral state.

As an aid to the discovery of the neutral state, the neutral mask has been
developed by Jean Dasté, Jacques Lecoq and others from Copeau's use of the 'noble'
mask, outlined below. I have sometimes had students approach me to 'borrow some
of those neutral masks for the show we're doing'. The whole point of such masks is
that they are not expressive and have no performative validity. They afford a tool with
which to deepen an understanding of the neutral state, which in itself is only a
foundation and no longer visible as part of the expressive edifice of performance. The
absence of such a foundation is precisely why Copeau wanted a school attached to his
theatre, but separate from it.

The noble mask

Copeau became aware of the potential of the mask, both in actor training and,
ultimately, in performance, during his visit to Craig. It made its appearance in his
work almost by accident – whilst rehearsing a scene at the Vieux Colombier he
despaired of an actress who found herself repeatedly physically blocked during a
scene and unable to move – a literal freezing of the blood. Copeau took his hand-
kerchief and covered her face, noting that her body was immediately released as an
expressive instrument. It was her face which had been making all the effort. This
experiment was immediately put to work in the School, using stockings as well as
pieces of cloth. Jean Dasté later noted:

> When the face is masked or hidden, one is less timid, feels freer, more
> daring and insincerity is quickly apparent. . . . The mask demands both a
> simplification and an extension of gestures; something forces you to go
> to the limit of the feeling being expressed.[31]

An invaluable tool had been discovered to aid the work on neutrality. Eventually the
students made their own 'noble' masks based on maquettes of their own faces,
modelled in clay to remove individual characteristics and regularise the features.
Copeau called them 'noble' after the expressionless masks worn by the aristocracy up
till the eighteenth century when wishing to pass incognito in the street. In order to
enhance rather than interfere with the neutral state, a ritual was developed for putting
on the mask:[32]

(a)   Well seated in the middle of the chair, not leaning against the back of the seat.
      Legs spaced to ensure perfect balance. Feet flat on the ground.
(b)   Stretch the left arm horizontally forward, shoulder high; it holds the mask,
      hanging by its elastic. The right hand also stretches out, thumb holding the
      chin, index and second finger seizing the opening of the mouth.
(c)   Stretch out the elastic over the top of the head and put the mask on the
      forehead.
(d)   Lower the mask over the face.
(e)   Simultaneously inhale, close the eyes and shoe the mask.

> In all this, only the arms and hands are active. They carry out the small move-
> ments necessary to fasten the mask on the face, arrange the hair, verify the

proper adjustment of the elastic, so that the mask will cling well and hold without slackness.[33]

(f)   Simultaneously, breathe and place forearms and hands on the thighs. The arms, as well as the elbows, touch the torso, fingers not quite reaching the knees.

(g)   Open the eyes, inhale, then simultaneously close the eyes, exhale and bend the head forward. While bending the head, the back becomes slightly rounded. In this phase, arm, hands, torso, and head are completely relaxed.

(h)   It is here, in this position, that the clearing of the mind occurs. Repeat mentally or utter, if this helps, during the necessary time (2, 5, 10, 25 seconds): 'I am not thinking of anything, I am not thinking of anything. . . .' If, through nervousness, or because the heart was beating too strongly, the 'I am not thinking of anything' is ineffective, concentrate on the blackish grey, steel, saffron, blue, or other shade found inside the eye, and extend it indefinitely in thought: almost always, this shade blots out conscious thought.

(i)   Simultaneously, inhale and sit upright, then exhale and open your eyes.

Now the masked actor, sufficiently recollected, can be inhabited by characters, objects, thoughts; he is ready to perform dramatically.

When the actor is not seated but standing, nothing changes; however (see h), the back should not be rounded, for the weight of the head would draw the torso forward.

All these phases are for beginners. Later, the technique may be altered. But . . . it should never be neglected.[34]

Once 'in' the noble mask, students were given initially very simple transactions to explore, simultaneously and without reference to each other. Words or phrases were called out and the students, after pre-forming and suspending the impulse, would let the mask 'attack', moving in slow motion to an intuitively felt physical position which expressed this word or phrase. They then held that position for a brief moment to confirm the impression before returning to a decontracted, neutral stance.

The first exercises were composed of sets of tasks dealing with the exploration of the five senses. Then the students were asked to let the mask handle imaginary objects, making them as concrete and specific as possible by exploring weight, texture, shape and function. Next, they had to experience certain physical sensations such as fatigue, heat and cold. Then they were asked to explore actively the five senses more fully, followed by an exercise in which they were deprived of one sense, such as being deaf. Next came simple physical actions such as throwing, lifting and pulling objects. Finally they were required to give bodily expression to some simple emotions.

The second set of exercises involved making combinations from the first set. For example, a simple emotion was combined with a simple physical activity, or an exploration of one of the senses was paired with the handling of an imaginary object. In a third set of exercises, the students were asked to physically represent inanimate objects. Following this came the final and most difficult exercises: the embodiment of moral and abstract ideas such as 'glory' or 'strength'.[35]

From these silent exercises the students went on to non-verbal sound explorations in the mask. The voice was used 'not in speaking or in singing but in a sort of primitive gamut of autopoetic sounds. . . . The voice, at the beginning, is a kind of arabesque like the castanets of the classic Spanish dance.'[36] These sounds were

Figure 3.3 Copeau's production of *Les Fourberies de Scapin*, Place Saint-Sulpice, Paris (1922) with Georges Vitray as Scapin and Suzanne Bing as Hyacinthe.

Source: Photo from the Marie-Hélène Dasté collection.

later developed into 'grummelots' – elements of gibberish language which have all the phrasing and inflection of real speech, but do not turn a physical improvisation into a word-driven one.

Copeau perceived spontaneity as another key to collective creativity. Working in this case without allowing time for premeditation, he would call out a word such as 'Paris!', 'Storm!', 'Goal!', etc. The (unmasked) students 'immediately, without an instant of reflection, had to react by one or more gestures, by a state of being, by a sequence of movements, etc.'.[37]

Play and games

Such exercises in spontaneity bring me to the last area of Copeau's pedagogical practice that there is space to consider, which is arguably one that should have been discussed first, since without it the spirit of élan and freedom of expression which enlightened the work of the apprentice group cannot be understood. In the first draft prospectus for the School he wrote:

> It is through play, in which children imitate more or less consciously all human activities and sentiments, which is for them a natural path towards artistic expression and for us a living repertoire of reactions of the most authentic kind – it is through play that we wish to construct, not a system, but an educational experience. We seek to develop the child, without deforming him or her, through the means which the child provides, towards which he or she senses the greatest inclination, through play, in playing, in games which are imperceptibly disciplined and exalted.

Since he was unable to take children from as early an age as he would have liked, when the play instinct was still naturally present, he compromised by working with adolescents and tried to reopen for them the door to the enchanted garden. Again, it was Suzanne Bing to whom he handed the key. During the Vieux Colombier's stay in New York, from 1917 to 1919, she had taught at The Children's School, which embraced the latest educational theories to do with freedom of choice and creative expression for children of primary-school age. There she used, in particular, games based on animal mimicry, and she later took the same classes in the Vieux Colombier School without making any adjustment for the greater age of the pupils. Today there are any number of books on the use of dramatic games in the classroom and else-where, right up to their political and therapeutic use in the work of Augusto Boal. In the face of such sophistication, any listing here of the actual exercises used by Bing would seem simplistic. The important thing to note is that Copeau sought to gain nothing from play *a priori* except those things which belong to it naturally.

> We observe the children at play. They teach us. Learn everything from children. Impose nothing on them. Take nothing away from them. Help them in their development without their being aware of it. All this is difficult to describe because it is still in a state of experimentation, nothing dogmatic. Inspired from life and human contact. Full of promise. Labour of patience already begun. Aim for making the actor not only the medium, but the source of all dramatic inspiration.[38]

He said that in 1917. Throughout the period of the Vieux Colombier School and of the Copiaus, he created a culture where imaginative play informed the work and did, as he had promised, lead to 'small-scale productions for which people are left entirely to their own devices, as creators and workers'.[39]

As much as he believed in *laisser jouer*, however, he could not bring himself to let it happen without absenting himself altogether. Bing could do it for him, but in the end he let her go too. In 1929 she, and the Copiaus, were indeed left to their own, separate, devices. Copeau took his ball and stayed at home. He had always maintained that his work was provisional and preparatory: prophetic, one might say, rather than messianic. It may be that the future came too close, or that he had a temperamental preference for disillusion and preferred to leave it to others to claim the domain which he had helped to discover.

Of his actors, Charles Dullin and Louis Jouvet went on to become the most influential French directors of the inter-war years. Of his pupils, Jean Dasté carried the banner of decentralisation in his work as director of the Comédie de St Etienne, whilst Michel Saint-Denis continued the pedagogy, founding the London Theatre Studio and the Old Vic School, the National Theatre School of Canada and the Drama Division of the Juillard School, New York. Following another star, Etienne Decroux became the father of modern corporeal mime. Copeau's real legacy, however, has been to put the playfulness back into plays and the quest for sincerity back into playing them. This quest has been disseminated latterly throughout the world via countless of his and Suzanne Bing's drama exercises and their derivatives.

Notes

1   From 'Comment mettre Molière en scène', interview in *Lecture pour tous*, January 1922; translated in *Copeau, Texts on Theatre* (1990), edited and translated by John Rudlin and Norman Paul, London: Routledge, p. 145.

2   From an address to the Washington Square Players, New York, 20 April 1917, Rudlin and Paul, op. cit., p. 253.

3   *Vanity Fair*, April 1917, p. 49.

4   Michel Saint-Denis (1982) *Training for the Theatre*, New York: Theatre Arts, London: Heinemann, p. 31.

5   Lee Strasberg (1965) *Strasberg at the Actors Studio*, ed. Robert H. Hethmon, New York: Viking Press (quoted in T. Cole and H.K. Chinoy (eds) (1970) *Actors on Acting*, New York: Crown, p. 624.

6   From *Réflexions d'un comédien sur le Paradoxe de Diderot*, Plon, 1929, translated in Rudlin and Paul, op. cit., pp. 72–73.

7   From 'L'Ecole du Vieux Colombier', unpublished notebook, translated in Rudlin and Paul, op. cit., p. 21.

8   From an unpublished notebook 'L'École du Vieux Colombier No. 2', 1915–20, translated in Rudlin and Paul, op. cit., p. 28. 'An Attempt at Dramatic Renovation' is the correct English translation of Copeau's 1913 manifesto for Le Vieux Colombier, 'Un Essai de Rénovation Dramatique'.

9   In 1922–23 the number went up to twelve; it then shrank again to nine in 1923–24.

10 From: 'L'Ecole du Vieux Colombier', in the Vieux Colombier programme for *La Locandiera*, January 1924, translated in Rudlin and Paul, op. cit., pp. 46–47.

11 Waldo Frank (1925) 'Copeau Begins Again', *Theatre Arts Magazine*, IX (September), pp. 585–90.

12 From an open letter to the Swiss press, May 1928, translated in Rudlin and Paul, op. cit., pp. 168–70.

13 Copeau (1931) *Souvenirs du Vieux Colombier*, Nouvelles Editions Latines, Paris, p. 106.

14 These notes are taken from *Le Journal de Bord des Copiaus* (1974), Paris: Gontard, pp. 45–46.

15 Letter to the Swiss press, op. cit.

16 Translated from the manuscript in the *Fonds Copeau* of the Bibliothèque de l'Arsenal, Paris, in Rudlin and Paul, op. cit., pp. 172–76.

17 30 November 1928.

18 Copeau, quoted in 'Copeau l'Eveilleur', ed. Pavis and Thomasseau (1995) *Buffoneries* 34: 15–16, no source given.

19 From Copeau's first plan for the Vieux Colombier School, 1916.

20 Undated notes in Copeau's Journal, translated in Rudlin and Paul, op. cit., p. 67.

21 Jean Dorcy, later to found the Danse et Culture School, whose pupils included Marcel Marceau, was an actor in his mid-twenties, attached to another division of the Vieux Colombier School.

22 Barbara Anne Kusler (1974) 'Jacques Copeau's Theatre School, 1920–29', Doctoral thesis, University of Wisconsin, p. 133.

23 Livre de bord, quoted Kusler, op. cit., p. 144.

24 Jacques Lecoq (1997) *Le Corps Poétique*, Paris: Actes Sud, p. 82.

25 Lucienne Lavalle, of the Opera Ballet Company, was first in her class in 1923. She danced such roles as Coppelia, the cat in *Sleeping Beauty*. In Paris and on tour she was especially cited for her technique in *Romeo and Juliet*. She later taught at the Paris Opera.

26 This weekly class lasted from November 1921 to June 1922.

27 For this section I am indebted to Barbara Anne Kusler, op. cit., pp. 132–33. She in turn relies on the class notes taken by Bing and Marie-Hélène Copeau, which are not available to me at the time of writing.

28 *Notes sur le Métier d'un Comédien*, notes taken from the diary and writings of Jacques Copeau by Marie-Hélène Dasté (Paris: Michel Brient, 1955, p. 47), translated in John Rudlin (1986) *Jacques Copeau*, Cambridge, p. 46.

29 This study of 'isolations' was later greatly to be developed by Copeau's pupil Etienne Decroux.

30 Rudlin, op. cit.

31   Jean Dasté, from an article for the programme of the *Cahiers de la Maison de la Culture de Grenoble*, 3 November 1945, translated Rudlin and Paul, op. cit., p. 236.
32   The French word used was '*chausser*', meaning to put on a shoe. This has no single equivalent in English and the usually adopted translation of 'shoeing the mask', to my mind conjures up images of horses' hooves and farriers.
33   A conflation of notes by Jean Dorcy and Jan Doat, as suggested by Sears Eldredge (1975) 'Masks: Their Use and Effectiveness in Actor Training Programs', Doctoral thesis, University of Michigan, 1975, p. 179.
34   Jean Dorcy (1975) *The Mime*, trans. Speller and Marceau, London: White Lion, pp. 108–9.
35   *Précis* from Jan Doat (1944) *L'Expression Corporelle du Comédien*, Paris: Bordas, pp. 53–55.
36   Waldo Frank (1925) 'Copeau Begins Again', *Theatre Arts Magazine*, IX (September), pp. 585–90.
37   Letter from Marie-Hélène Dasté to Barbara Anne Kusler, December 1973.
38   From Copeau's notes for his third lecture (given in French) at The Little Theatre, New York, 'L'Ecole du Vieux Colombier', 19 March 1917, translated in Rudlin and Paul, op. cit., p. 12.
39   See note 10.

Bibliography

Borgal, Clément (1960) *Jacques Copeau*, Paris: l'Arche.
Doisy, Marcel (1954) *Jaques Copeau ou l'Absolu dans l'Art*, Paris: Le Cercle du Livre.
Evans, Mark (2006) *Jacques Copeau*, London and New York: Routledge.
Frank, Waldo (1918) *The Art of the Vieux Colombier*, Paris, New York: Editions de la NRF; reprinted in his *Salvos*, New York: Boni and Liveright, 1924.
Kurtz, Maurice (1950) *Jacques Copeau, Biographie d'un Théâtre*, Paris: Nagel.
Lerminier, Georges (1953) *Jacques Copeau, le Réformateur*, Paris: PLF.
Levaux, Léopold (1933) *Jacques Copeau*, Louvain–Paris: Rex.
Paul, Norman H. (1979) *Bibliographie Jacques Copeau*, Société des Belles Lettres, Université de Beaune.
Pavis, Patrice and Thomasseau, Jean-Marie (eds) (1995) 'Copeau l'Eveilleur', *Buffoneries* 34: 15–16.
Rudlin, John (1986) *Jacques Copeau*, Cambridge: Cambridge University Press.

Anthologies, catalogues

Jacques Copeau et le Vieux Colombier (1963) Catalogue for exhibition at Bibliothèque Nationale.
Bing, S., Copeau, J. and Chancerel, L. (1974) *Le Journal de bord des Copiaus*, ed. Denis Gontard, Paris.
Cabanis, A. (ed.) (1976) *Registres II. Molière*, Paris: Gallimard.
Dasté, Marie-Hélène and Maistre Saint-Denis, Suzanne (eds) (1979) *Registres I. Appels*, Paris: Gallimard.
—— (1979) *Registres III. Les Registres du Vieux Colombier I*, Paris: Gallimard.
—— (1984) *Registres IV. Les Registres du Vieux Colombier II, America*, Paris: Gallimard.
—— (1993) *Registres V. Les Registres du Vieux Colombier III, 1919–1924*, Paris: Gallimard.
Rudlin, John and Paul, Norman H. (eds and trans) (1990) *Jacques Copeau, Texts on Theatre*, London and New York: Routledge.

Chapter 4

Franc Chamberlain

MICHAEL CHEKHOV ON THE TECHNIQUE OF ACTING: 'WAS DON QUIXOTE TRUE TO LIFE?'

THE CONTEXT

A S AN OUTSTANDING ACTOR and author of one of the best actor training manuals ever published in the European tradition,[1] Michael Chekhov (1891–1955) is one of the key figures in twentieth-century theatre. His ability to transform himself onstage was celebrated by some of the major directors of the century, including Stanislavsky, Vakhtangov, Reinhardt, and Meyerhold: whilst his practical advice continues to inspire actors through his writings and through teachers and schools in Russia, Lithuania, Holland, Germany, Great Britain, Australia, the USA and elsewhere.

The nephew of the playwright Anton Chekhov, Michael Chekhov was only seven years old when Nemirovich-Danchenko and Stanislavsky formed the Moscow Art Theatre (MAT) in 1898, including his uncle's play *The Seagull* in their first season. In a diary entry written in the same year, Vsevolod Meyerhold recorded a conversation between some of the MAT actors and Anton Chekhov. Bemused to hear of plans to introduce countryside noises offstage in *The Seagull* in order to make the environment more 'realistic', the playwright laughed, asserting that the theatre was art and that the additions were superfluous.[2] Stanislavsky's approach, at this time, was to attempt to create as detailed an imitation of life onstage as possible.

By contrast, Meyerhold, inspired by the symbolist plays and theories of Maeterlinck and Bryusov, was interested in the idea of a stylised theatre which emphasised 'atmosphere' or 'mood' over naturalistic detail. Atmosphere, for Meyerhold, was generated by the actors and, despite his reservations regarding Stanislavsky's concern for naturalistic production values, he felt that the MAT actors had managed to evoke the appropriate mood of *The Seagull*. The importance of the actor as a creative artist was picked up by Bryusov, who argued that it was the theatre's task to assist the actor in manifesting this creativity in a way that would be understood by the audience. Working with these symbolist influences for a decade, Meyerhold attempted several productions of Maeterlinck, searching for a technique which would use movement as 'plastic music' in order to construct an 'external depiction of an inner experience'.[3]

The search for a new approach to acting which would emphasise the creativity of the actor was being undertaken across Europe. Even Craig, whose polemical attack on actors is well known, argued that actors should 'create . . . a new form of acting' in order to revitalise their art.[4] Stanislavsky had always aimed to break the fixed habits of actors and to develop acting as a creative art. His failures to stage Maeterlinck in 1904 and 1908, however, together with his resistance to the proposed solutions of Meyerhold and Craig, led him to explore new directions by setting up the experimental First Studio under Sulerzhitsky in 1912.

The themes of atmosphere, actors' creativity, physicalisation of inner experience, and the question of style, which were to become important elements in Michael Chekhov's method, can be seen to have been part of the theatrical milieu for over a decade – well before 1912, when he joined the MAT. As part of the First Studio, Chekhov developed his skills under the tutelage of Sulerzhitsky, who instructed the actors in the basic elements of Stanislavsky's method: relaxation, concentration, naïveté, imagination, communication and affective memory. Chekhov was eventually to reject Stanislavsky's emphasis on memory but the other aspects of the Studio's work were to find a place in his own method, although somewhat transformed.

Between 1912 and 1918 Chekhov developed his reputation as a talented actor in a number of roles, despite occasional conflicts with Stanislavsky and some of the other members of the company. A part of the problem appears to have been the expression of his creativity as an actor. In one of his earliest roles at the MAT, in *Le malade imaginaire*, Stanislavsky criticised Chekhov for having too much fun with the role, and on another occasion Stanislavsky held him up before the rest of the company as 'the ulcer of our theatre'.[5] It was in Boleslavsky's production of *The Wreck of 'The Good Hope'* (1913), however, that Chekhov first attracted critical attention when he transformed the minor role of Kobe from a stereotypical 'idiot fisherman' into a 'sincere and morbid seeker of the truth'.[6] When his interpretation of the role was challenged on the grounds that it was not what the playwright had intended, Chekhov asserted his creative individuality by claiming that he had found the 'true' character by going beyond both text and author.

By 1919, despite his success at the Studio, Chekhov's life was falling apart. He was drinking heavily, and within the space of two years his wife had left him and taken their daughter away, his cousin Vladimir Chekhov had committed suicide and his mother had died. He was unable to act, and on one occasion left the stage in the middle of a performance. Interpreting his extreme state as a spiritual crisis, Chekhov began to investigate the anthroposophy or spiritual science of Rudolf Steiner, which was attracting the interest of a number of Russian artists, including Andrei Bely and Wassily Kandinsky. Steiner, like Kierkegaard and others before him, drew a distinction between the everyday self, with which we normally identify, and the higher ego which is our more authentic and creative self. Anthroposophy enabled Chekhov to gain a distance on his personal troubles and to put them in a different perspective, from which he saw himself as a 'drunken egotist'.[7] He began an intense study of Steiner's teachings as a means of liberation from his self-indulgent and self-destructive tendencies. Steiner's theories were to form the basis of Chekhov's personal belief and would have a significant impact on his theory of the actor.

It is after 1918 that Chekhov comes out most strongly against Stanislavsky's use of personal experience and emotion, arguing that this, in effect, binds the actor to the habits of the everyday self, which was not the way to liberate the actor's creativity. Furthermore, Chekhov argued that the emphasis should be on the character's feelings, not the actor's – not 'how would I feel?' but 'what does the character feel?' –

and that this would enable the actor to transform into the character, rather than reducing the character to the personality of the actor. Chekhov gives a very good example of what he means by this. In a scene where a character's child is ill, the Stanislavskian actor will focus on the child and see 'only the things seen by the character residing within him'.[8] The Chekhovian actor, on the other hand, will focus on the character and observe how the character responds to the child. Chekhov believed that Steiner's higher ego, which he interpreted as the 'artist in us that stands behind all of our creative processes',[9] was the key to this approach. Chekhov eventually identified four ways in which a sensitivity to this higher ego would help the actor's work: (1) it was the source of the actor's 'creative individuality', which explained why different actors played the same role differently, and which helped the actor to go beyond the text; (2) it was possessed of an ethical sense which enabled the actor to feel the conflict between 'good' and 'evil' in the play; (3) it enabled a sensitivity to the audience's perspective on the play in performance; and (4) it brought a sense of detachment, compassion, and humour into the actor's work by conferring freedom from the 'narrow, selfish ego'.[10]

Chekhov also drew on Steiner's explorations into movement and speech through eurythmy and his theories of speech as invisible gesture, and both found their way into his system.[11] Once the work of Steiner was added to the influences from the Moscow Art Theatre and his own reflections on the actor's art, Chekhov began to construct a coherent system of training that was distinct from Stanislavsky's. Between 1918 and 1921 he ran workshops in his flat in Moscow to explore the possibilities opened up by his new interests, although these experiments were only popular with a minority, and financial difficulties led to the closure of the workshop. Chekhov's recovery from his illness led to his blossoming as an actor from 1921 to 1927. His performance of a number of major roles, both at the First Studio (which became the Second Moscow Art Theatre in 1924) and at the MAT, confirmed his exceptional talent.

During his time at the First Studio, Chekhov built a strong friendship with Evgeny Vakhtangov, who was initially very taken by Stanislavsky's notion of emotion memory, but who eventually argued for a combination of Stanislavsky and Meyerhold's thinking, which he called 'fantastic realism'. Vakhtangov felt that Stanislavsky was too attached to naturalism and missed the significance of theatricality in the theatre, whilst Meyerhold's fascination with stylised physicality had led him to ignore the importance of feelings – it was necessary to combine both approaches to create a theatre which was both 'live' and 'theatrical'.[12] One of Chekhov's major acting triumphs was when he appeared in the leading roles in Vakhtangov's production of Strindberg's Erik XIV at the First Studio in 1921.

Erik XIV tells the story of a weak and deranged sixteenth-century Swedish king who imprisons and murders the nobility, is deposed in a rebellion led by his brothers, and after marrying his mistress attempts to flee the country. Strindberg saw Erik as a Swedish Hamlet, and Chekhov's Erik XIV was full of internal conflict, revealed through sharp contrasts in physical and vocal dynamics. In his search for a physical means to represent the weakness of the character, Chekhov was inspired by Vakhtangov, who visualised Erik trapped within a circle from which he constantly tried to escape. Stretching out his hands beyond the circle in hope, Erik would find nothing, and leave his hands dangling in misery. Chekhov felt that the essence of Erik's character was expressed in Vakhtangov's gesture, and claimed that from that moment he had no difficulty in playing the character with all of the appropriate nuances throughout the whole of the play.[13] This condensation of the essence of the

Figure 4.1 Chekhov in the title role of Strindberg's *Erik XIV* (1922) directed by Vakhtangov and performed by the Moscow Arts Theatre.

Source: Dartington Hall Trust Archive.

character into a single full-body gesture is the prototype of Chekhov's psychological gesture, and he reports another example from his work with Stanislavsky on Gogol's *The Government Inspector* at the MAT in the same year.

Chekhov describes a rehearsal with Stanislavsky where the director is giving him suggestions for playing Khlestakov. He 'suddenly made a lightning-quick movement with his arms and hands, as if throwing them up and at the same time vibrating with his fingers, elbows, and even his shoulders'.[14] Once again, Chekhov understood the whole of the role from this condensation. What both of these incidents show is that the idea of expressing the essence of the role in a gesture was familiar to Stanislavsky and Vakhtangov, and that the idea was not Chekhov's as such. Nonetheless he was the one who developed the idea of the psychological gesture and made it an important aspect of his training as an intuitive, rather than an analytical, approach to character.

In contrast to the brooding melancholy of Erik, Chekhov's Khlestakov in *The Government Inspector* was light and mischievous. Critics were stunned by the scene in which Khlestakov improvised fantastic lies in the Mayor's house, because Chekhov would play it differently each night. Opening to the higher ego involved a means of accessing the creativity and spontaneity that Stanislavsky had been searching for, and provided an alternative approach to his creative state of mind. The problem for Chekhov was that when creative energy was unleashed, the actor was inclined to overstep necessary boundaries, and there was a need to develop a way of ensuring that the limits of the performance were respected.[15] By the time of the performance, Chekhov was able to keep the basic shape of the scene, but earlier in rehearsals he had got so carried away improvising with an apple that he lost contact with the objective of the scene and the other actors before Stanislavsky called a halt. The ability to improvise within set limits was another aspect of the performer which Chekhov wanted to develop through his teaching.[16]

Vakhtangov died in 1922, and Chekhov was offered the directorship of the First Studio, which became the second MAT in 1924. He continued to act as well as to teach and direct, and in the 1924–25 season he directed and performed the title role in a critically acclaimed production of Hamlet. Despite the acclaim Chekhov received for Hamlet, however, there was concern that the second MAT was not producing revolutionary plays. By 1927 Stalin's clampdown on experiments in the arts was beginning, and Chekhov was accused of being a mystic and a 'sick' actor who would spread corruption. Anthroposophy was banned in the Soviet Union and Chekhov was warned that he was about to be arrested. Chekhov left Russia in 1928 and his work was discredited in the Soviet Union. It was not returned to the official curriculum until after 1969 (although teachers such as Maria Knebel managed to pass on some of the work).

Accepting an invitation from Max Reinhardt, Chekhov moved to Berlin in 1928. During the same period he continued his studies in anthroposophy, and directed the Habima in Twelfth Night. Chekhov was unhappy with Reinhardt's theatre, but had a strong experience of his higher ego in the role of Skid in Artists, when he saw the character as if he were viewing it from the perspective of the audience or the other actors. Skid was indicating to Chekhov how he should sit, move and speak.[17] Meeting Stanislavsky in Vienna soon after the performance in 1929, Chekhov insisted on the importance of the imagination and criticised Stanislavsky's emphasis on emotional recall as being dangerous.[18] In a lecture during 1941 he repeated his criticism and argued for the importance of a divided consciousness:

> When we are possessed by the part and almost kill our partners and break
> chairs, etc., then we are not free and it is not art but hysterics. At one time
> in Russia we thought that if we were acting we must forget everything
> else. Of course, it was wrong. Then some of our actors came to the point
> where they discovered that real acting was when we could act and be
> filled with feelings, and yet be able to make jokes with our partners – two
> consciousnesses.[19]

By the time Chekhov gave this lecture, however, Stanislavsky had already acknow-ledged the significance of the actor's dual consciousness in his writings, although this was not to appear in English until 1946, eight years after Stanislavsky's death.[20] Despite his ongoing criticism of the emotion memory approach, Chekhov did acknowledge in his 1955 classes that Stanislavsky had only used it as a rehearsal device and did not intend for it to be used on the stage.[21]

In 1931 Chekhov moved to Paris where, together with Georgette Boner, he set up another studio but encountered a number of difficulties. Chekhov had hoped that he would find support for his work from the large Russian émigré community in Paris, but in this he was disappointed. He staged an adaptation of Tolstoy's fairy tale The Castle Awakens, working with eurythmy and other ideas from Steiner, but the pro-duction was a commercial failure. In 1932 and 1933 he worked at the state theatres in the still independent Latvia and Lithuania, but a heart attack whilst he was directing

Wagner's *Parsifal* in Riga suspended his work. By the time he recovered the political situation had deteriorated and he was once again on the move, returning to Paris.

In 1934–35 Chekhov put together a company of exiled Russian actors for a short tour of the USA with seven plays and an evening of stage adaptations of Anton Chekhov stories. He also gave a lecture-demonstration to the Group Theatre at the invitation of Stella Adler. In this lecture-demonstration, Chekhov suggested that when approaching a character the actor must first identify the archetype on which the character is based. He also outlined his theory of centres and the imaginary body, and considered the notion of personal atmosphere.[22]

It was in New York that Chekhov met Beatrice Straight and Deirdre Hurst du Prey, who invited him to the experimental community at Dartington Hall in Devon. Chekhov accepted the invitation and the Chekhov Theatre Studio was established at Dartington in 1936. The arrangement was ideal for Chekhov because there were no commercial pressures and he was free to develop his system of training. Chekhov planned a three-year course which would include the development of concentration and imagination, eurythmy, voice and speech (drawing on Steiner), and musical composition. Folk tales were to be studied as a means of freeing the imagination, and students would start with short scenes and improvisations, gradually building to longer and more difficult pieces. By this time the main components of his system were in place: imagination and concentration, higher ego, atmospheres and qualities, centres, imaginary bodies, radiation and style. Chekhov also added what came to be known as the 'Four Brothers', a series of linked exercises that focused on feelings of ease (to replace Stanislavsky's relaxation), form, beauty and the whole.

Chekhov was in an enviable position, but the outbreak of war with Germany in 1939 caused him to move once again – this time to Ridgefield in Connecticut – taking a number of his students with him. Unfortunately there was more financial pressure on Chekhov in Connecticut than there had been in Devon, and he was forced to stage performances too early. Initial productions, such as *The Possessed* (1939) were not well received[23] but the Chekhov Studio production of *Twelfth Night* attracted positive reviews on Broadway in 1941. It was during this period that Chekhov began to formulate his ideas on the psychological gesture which had been in the process of gestation since the 1920s. Inevitably, war once again interrupted his work and in 1942 the Studio was forced to close because of the draft. In 1943 Chekhov moved to Los Angeles and began a film career in Hollywood which included an Oscar nomination for his role in Hitchcock's *Spellbound* in 1945. His film career was interrupted by a heart attack during filming in 1948, and ended after a second heart attack in 1954. Whilst in Los Angeles Chekhov continued to teach, and included Jack Palance, Mala Powers, Marilyn Monroe and Anthony Quinn among his students. After a career constantly interrupted by personal, financial and political difficulties, Michael Chekhov died of a heart attack in Los Angeles in 1955 at the age of sixty-four.

THEORY AND PRACTICE

In 1942 Chekhov completed his manual for the actor entitled *To the Actor*, but it was not until 1953 that it was published in a seriously modified form.[24] In 1991 a new edition entitled *On the Technique of Acting* restored Chekhov's original manuscript and, in 2002, the 1953 version was republished with additional material on the Psychological Gesture taken from the 1946 Russian-language version.[25] Over a hundred of Chekhov's exercises have been published, covering all of the main aspects of the

Figure 4.2 Chekhov in the Dartington Studio with students. *Photographer: Fritz Henle.*
Source: Dartington Hall Trust Archive, courtesy of the Fritz Henle Estate.

technique. This catalogue is not exhaustive, however, as Chekhov was inventing new exercises until his death, and the basic principles of the technique will allow as many variations and creations as there are creative individualities. The following material offers a 'taster' of Chekhov's work, focusing on a small number of key elements and exercises.

Imagination and concentration

Chekhov's fascination with the imagination stayed with him throughout his life. He felt that any artist needed to be able to work in a disciplined way with the images that appeared in hypnagogic and dream states, as well as those that appeared in response to engaging with an artwork. What fascinated Chekhov about hypnagogic images was that they transformed themselves independently of any conscious intervention from the individual. The task for the actor is to become an active participant in the process of imagination rather than just a passive dreamer, to bring the world of the imagination on to the stage and give it life. In order to do this, the actor – according to Chekhov – has to develop a feeling for artistic construction, and this can be done by studying 'great works' of the past and imaginatively altering certain aspects of them. How would it be if Mona Lisa's smile was a little broader? If Hamlet had killed Claudius whilst he was at prayer? By asking such questions, the actor begins to develop a sense of the rules of composition, and this understanding will help in making appropriate choices. At the same time this questioning assists in developing an awareness of the 'flexibility of images'. By imagining fairy-tale or dreamlike transformations (a frog into a prince, a flamingo into an elephant) and by paying close attention to the stages of the transformation, the actor will develop both concentration and a facility for working with images. The actor also has to be able to let go of the images, to allow them to sink into the subconscious, and to welcome the changes in them when they return transformed. By recognising and accepting the independence of the world of the imagination, the actor begins to soften the boundaries of the everyday self and 'confront the Higher Ego'.[26] This takes the actor away from the Stanislavskian 'true to life approach'. As Chekhov pointed out: 'what if the character's psychology and inner life are not true to life? Was Don Quixote true to life?'[27]

The actor has eventually to begin to embody these images and, in addition to a well-developed and flexible imagination, Chekhov required the actor to have a body which was sensitive to inner impulses, noting that 'every actor, to a greater or lesser degree, suffers from some of [the] body's resistance'.[28] Chekhov proposes a number of useful exercises for increasing the body's flexibility and responsiveness, but he notes that the exercises in concentration, atmosphere and imagination also assist in this process of sensitisation.

Atmosphere

Although Meyerhold and Bryusov discussed the importance of atmosphere at the beginning of the century, Michael Chekhov developed the idea in theory and practice more extensively than anyone else, and it became one of the major elements in his technique.

An atmosphere can be considered as the dominant tone or mood of, among other things, a place, a relationship, or an artwork. An old ruined castle, for example, has a different atmosphere from a busy casualty department, and each atmosphere will have a different effect on individuals in contact with it. Chekhov used the example of walking along and arriving at the crowded scene of a street accident; we will be aware of the atmosphere before we realise exactly what has happened. Each individual in the scene will have their own response to the situation, but there will be a dominant atmosphere which is experienced as a whole and as an external phenomenon. In this sense Chekhov considered atmospheres to be 'objective'.

A more orthodox Stanislavskian approach would involve the actor focusing on their own emotional response to a previously experienced street accident or analogous circumstance. Even in Stanislavsky's later period, when he was working on his method of physical actions as a less direct approach to the actor's emotions, the question for the actor would have been: 'What would I do if I were in this situation?'[29] Chekhov's emphasis is on the evocation of the overall tone of the situation, and he considered atmospheres to be the equivalent of musical keys. A sensitivity to atmospheres and the ability to create them onstage is a key skill for the Chekhovian actor, and one which forges a connection between actor and audience.

Chekhov encouraged actors to practise creating atmospheres in their imagination by reading through scenes from plays, getting a sense of the overall atmosphere and then imagining the characters acting and speaking in tune with it. Rather than doing this just once, Chekhov proposes that the exercise is repeated until the inner performance is satisfactory, and then suggests that the atmosphere is altered. The following exercise focuses on emotional atmospheres, and is Chekhov's alternative to Stanislavsky's affective memory work.

Exercise 1

Imagine the air around you . . . filled with the Atmosphere that you have chosen. It is no more difficult than imagining the air filled with light, dust, fragrance, smoke, mist, and so on. You must not ask yourself, 'How can the air be filled with fear or joy, tenderness or horror?' You must try it practically. Your first effort will show immediately how simple it is. What you have to learn is how to sustain the imaginary Atmosphere that now envelops you. Your main aid will be a developed Concentration. . . . In this exercise you do not need to imagine any special circumstances or events to justify the Atmosphere. It will only distract your attention and make the exercise unnecessarily complicated. Do it as simply as described above.

After a certain period of time, when you feel sure of being able to imagine and sustain the Atmosphere around you, proceed to the next step. Try to relate the reaction inside you to that of the imaginary Atmosphere outside. Do not force yourself to feel anything, simply realize the reaction, which will appear of itself if the first part of the exercise has been carefully and patiently done. The whole value of this exercise will be lost if you impatiently impose the reaction upon yourself, instead of letting it grow freely. In the beginning the exercise may take time, but very soon you will see that the process of creating the Atmosphere and reacting to it is almost instantaneous. Gradually the Atmosphere will penetrate deeper and deeper into the realm of your emotions.[30]

The next phase is to speak and move in harmony with the atmosphere and to begin to radiate the 'inner life' stimulated by the atmosphere back into the space, thereby setting up a kind of feedback loop which amplifies both the atmosphere and the inner response.

Once actors develop a basic facility in creating atmospheres they can explore transforming them and breaking them. According to Chekhov, two strong atmospheres cannot exist in the same space; one will always be dominant. If a group of clowns surrounded by an atmosphere of playfulness were to chance upon the street accident mentioned above, one of the two atmospheres would have to change.

The Four Brothers

A group of exercises known as The Four Brothers is significant because it focuses on qualities which pertain to all other work in the Chekhov technique. They are the feelings of ease, of the whole, of form and of beauty. The feeling of ease involves performing any action with a sense of lightness and ease, no matter how 'heavy' the situation or subject matter. This replaces Stanislavsky's exercises in relaxation, and

Figure 4.3 'Lightness' exercises by Chekhov Theatre Players in the Dartington Hall Gardens (1936). *Photographer:* Fritz Henle.

Source: Dartington Hall Trust Archive, courtesy of the Fritz Henle Estate.

Chekhov considered it to be a crucial aspect of art as well as being connected to humour.[31] The feeling of the whole requires an awareness that every action, every piece of stage business, every speech, has a beginning, middle and end which needs to be clearly defined, however subtly. The feeling of form develops an ability to perceive one's own actions from an aesthetic viewpoint, to become aware of the shapes made in space and their appropriateness. The feeling of beauty is an inner sense which involves a feeling of deep satisfaction in the work and is to be distinguished from 'showing off'. Chekhov gives the example of someone profoundly engaged in a physical task flowing effortlessly. Each of these qualities fosters a sense of aesthetic distance in the work, encouraging the actor to take a view from outside rather than inside.

The psychological gesture

The psychological gesture (PG) is a means of expressing the entire character in condensed physical form through an intuitive grasp of the character's main desire. The PG was Chekhov's answer to an analytical approach to role which could offer keen insights but leave the actor without a means of embodying them. The PG is perhaps Chekhov's single most original contribution to twentieth-century actor training. Drawing on the work of Steiner, Chekhov notes that we often use gestural language when talking of psychological processes. For example we 'grow pensive', 'draw conclusions' or 'grasp ideas'. Chekhov considers that these phrases suggest that a 'tendency to produce such a gesture'[32] exists at these moments, and can stimulate us to make the physical gesture if necessary. The following exercise involves a focus not on language, however, but on an imaginative and intuitive search for the character's objective (in the Stanislavskian sense). Nonetheless, once the psychological gesture becomes invisible the character still speaks in accordance with it, and this makes the link to Steiner's idea that gesture disappears into speech:

Exercise 2

Imagine [any play] as we have described before, without choosing any part for yourself. Continue imagining until the events and characters of the play become a living performance for you. While doing so, fix your attention on moments which . . . seem significant or expressive to you. Concentrate on the character that appears central in the moment you have chosen. Ask this character to act before you in your Imagination and follow its action in all details. Simultaneously, try to 'see' *what* the character is aiming at, *what* is [the character's] wish, desire? In doing so, attempt to avoid reasoning, but rather seek to penetrate as clearly and as vividly as possible into the character's *what* by means of the image before your mind's eye. As soon as you begin to guess what the character is doing, try to find the most simple Psychological Gesture for it. Do it physically, looking at the same time at your image.

Improve the Psychological Gesture in its simplicity and expressiveness by exercising it. Do not ask your imaginative character to do the Psychological Gesture for you. It is useless. The character must only act in terms of the play. Hamlet, for instance, when the curtain is raised, can sit motionless in the throne room. This is your imagination. But Hamlet's Psychological Gesture might be a large, slow, heavy movement with both arms and hands, from above downward toward the earth. You may find this Gesture right for Hamlet's dark, depressed mood at this time of his life. And this Gesture is what you must do in reality, while you are watching your image. Then try to act and to speak like Hamlet, having now the Psychological Gesture only in the back of your mind as it were.

Do the Psychological Gesture and the acting alternately, until it becomes evident to you that behind each internal state or movement in acting is hidden a simple and expressive Psychological Gesture that is the essence of the acting. . . . The Psychological Gesture will appear before your mind's eye and, after being practised, will always remain with you as a kind of inspiration while you are acting.[33]

There is some confusion as to whether or not the PG should be visible to the audience; in this example it is suggested that it should be invisible. Earlier in the same chapter, however, Chekhov uses the term to refer to 'visible (actual) gestures as well as to invisible (potential) gestures'.[34] Either way, the PG has an effect on the actor's inner life.

In addition to a PG being found for the role as a whole, Chekhov also suggested using the PG to work on separate moments of the role, individual scenes, speeches, and a score of atmospheres.[35]

INTO PRODUCTION

Chekhov argued for a plurality of theatrical styles, and the variety of work he engaged in – from Moscow to Hollywood – indicates the range to which he thought his technique could be applied. Each project will require its own 'special technique', but will keep to the basic principles of the 'general technique'.

The most readily available material on Chekhov as director is on his production with the Actors Lab in *The Government Inspector* in 1946, published in Charles Leonard's *Michael Chekhov's To the Director and Playwright*. This material is not particularly helpful in developing an understanding of Chekhov's directorial approach, and part of the problem is that Chekhov was working with actors who were not trained in his system, and whom he did not have time to train. Nor is it clear whether the chapter in *To The Actor* on the 'Composition of the Performance', which uses *King Lear* as its example, has any direct connection to Chekhov's production. In fact this is unlikely, as he comments that Shakespeare's plays should be shortened and restructured in order to give them a 'driving force' appropriate to the times, but chooses not to indicate how this would be done.[36] The material in Leonard and in *To the Actor* does, however, illustrate Chekhov's ideas on how a text should be examined for its main and auxiliary climaxes.

In this material, Chekhov suggested that a piece should have a threefold structure in which a conflict is generated, unfolds and concludes, with the main qualities of the opening being transformed into their opposite by the end. Each of the three major sections will contain a moment of maximum tension or climax and will also have a number of moments of lesser tension (auxiliary climaxes). Chekhov believed that these climaxes should be discovered through the 'artistic intuition' developed in the training.

A clear sense of the form of these key moments and the rhythmic ebb and flow of energy is important for the composition of any performance. Outside of the climaxes and auxiliary climaxes there are smaller moments of significance, known as 'accents'. These are lines or actions which provide impulses for transformations, or clarify past or future occurrences. A further element in the structure of a piece is the use of repetition. Any aspect of a production might repeat and either recur unchanged or transformed, and each kind of repetition has different effects on the spectator's perception.

This emphasis on the structure has a more abstract and analytical flavour than most of Chekhov's work and, whilst offering some useful guidelines, it seems as something of an afterthought to his main body of theory. The chapter entitled 'The Four Stages of the Creative Process', which appeared for the first time in the 1991 edition of Chekhov's manual, offers a clearer sense of the relationship between training and production. Unlike the material on *The Government Inspector* or *King Lear*, there is no reference to any specific production or text, but a description of Chekhov's ideal process. The first key to this process is that actors and director should have trained in the technique and be able to share a working language.

Chekhov claims that an understanding of the four stages will free the actor 'from the slavery of accidents, personal moods, disappointments, and nervous impatience',[37] and thus generate a sense of 'assurance'. He argues for the importance of the basic pattern but does not dictate what must happen at any moment: 'the rehearsals can at any time take any course that may be required to further the work'.[38]

The first stage of the production process involves the actors reading the text and beginning to get a sense of the general atmosphere of the play. Chekhov described this stage as 'musical', and likened it to the act of listening to a distant piece of music and gradually being able to pick out its different aspects. At this point, even though the play has been cast, it is important for the actors to pay attention to the entire work, and not focus solely on their own character. In addition to the general atmosphere, the actors need to get a sense of the style, the 'dynamic of good and evil' and the social significance of the piece. This work is done in the actor's imagination, and Chekhov indicates that the 'more conscientious' the actors have been in practising the method the 'more successful'[39] their results will be. Entering into the general atmosphere of the play, the actors should read it again and again, allowing various images to arise without interference. Chekhov suggests that the actors keep a 'diary' of this part of the process, noting down the visions which attract them most in words and images. As this stage progresses the actors will become more focused on their specific characters but still keep a sense of the whole.

The second stage involves the conscious elaboration of images and the beginning of the working conversation between director and cast. Now that the actors have familiarised themselves with the text and have allowed their imaginations to engage with it, they are ready for a mutual exchange of visions with the director. The director has overall responsibility, but it is important that the creativity of all parties is respected. Chekhov recognised the director as a creative artist but never abandoned the importance of the actor's creativity. It is during this period that the cast show the psychological gestures for their characters, and may begin to move and speak with them. Different scenes in the play are explored for different points of view: ease, form, style, atmosphere and so on.

During the first two stages material and ideas are generated and a working relationship is developed. The third and longest stage is that of incorporation, when the work starts to become more embodied. For Chekhov the 'best way to proceed' at this stage is

> to create a series of Incorporations of the characters with short moments from the play. The director may ask [the] actors such questions as the following: What do the arms, the hands, the shoulders, the feet of your character look like at such and such moments? How does the character walk, sit, or run in other moments? How does it enter, exit, listen, look? How does it react to different impressions received from other characters? How does it behave when enveloped in a certain Atmosphere?[40]

The actors perform their answers for the director, who offers feedback and other suggestions as the exploration develops. This dialogic approach is helped in Chekhov's model by the requirement that the director has been trained in the technique and understands the processes of acting. Chekhov suggests at one point that the 'best way' for the director to communicate what is required is to act it. If the actors have been appropriately trained, Chekhov believed they would 'grasp the essence' and would 'not need to copy their director outwardly'.[41]

The third phase is the rehearsal stage proper and involves the repetition of scenes and the development of the performance score. Chekhov suggests that different segments of the play are explored with different 'grounds', by which he means that the sequences should be explored whilst emphasising different aspects of the technique.

Figure 4.4 Chekhov as Malvolio in Shakespeare's *Twelfth Night* performed by the Moscow Art Theatre.

Source: Dartington Hall Trust Archive.

The fourth and final stage commences towards the end of the rehearsal process and is the phase of inspiration and divided consciousness. At this point in his description Chekhov leaves behind questions of text, ensemble and actor–director relationships, and focuses primarily on the individual actor. If the actor has worked through the process conscientiously, then it is at this point that the actor can stand back from the character and admire it as an aesthetic object. Chekhov quotes Rudolf Steiner at this point in a brief passage that makes clear the relationship between the theories of the two men: 'The actor must not be possessed by his role. He must stand facing it so that his part becomes objective. He experiences it as his own creation.'[42]

Chekhov's recipe for the creative process, together with the great detail and wealth of exercises offered in his writings, offers a practical and experimental approach that demystifies the art of acting. For Chekhov the last thing an actor should worry about is talent:

> The actor should never worry about . . . talent, but rather about . . . lack of technique . . . lack of training, and . . . lack of understanding of the creative process. The talent will flourish immediately of itself as soon as the artist chisels away all the extraneous matter.[43]

Acknowledgements

The 3rd Michael Chekhov International Workshop at Emerson College, Sussex, in 1994 was such a rich experience for me that I cannot possibly thank by name all of those who helped me. I benefited greatly from the generosity of former Chekhov students by participating in workshops, having my own work audited, listening to anecdotes and memories and through conversation. I am indebted to Mala Powers, Jack Colvin, Deirdre Hurst du Prey, Mary-Lou Taylor, Hurd Hadfield, Ford Rainey, Joanna Merlin, Paul Rogers and Daphne Field. At the same event Professors Andrei Kirillov and Marina Ivanova were stimulating in debate and possessed a tremendous depth of knowledge concerning Chekhov's life and work in Russia. I hope that the demands of this task have not led me into any unforgivable errors.

In addition, I am grateful to Joanna Merlin, Sarah Kane, Jonathan Pitches, Martin Sharp, Andrew White and Jerri Daboo for offering comments and suggestions during the process of revision.

Specified excerpts from *On the Technique of Acting* by Michael Chekhov.
Copyright © 1991 by Mala Powers
Reprinted by permission of HarperCollins Publishers, Inc.

Notes

1   Whilst this is a personal view it is one supported by practitioners as diverse as Richard Hornby and Eugenio Barba. See also Simon Callow's foreword to the recent edition of *To the Actor*, Chekhov (2002) pp. xi–xxiv. Interest in Chekhov's work has grown significantly since the first version of this essay was published in 2000 and there is now more access to primary and secondary materials, as well as to the practice itself. I have, however, chosen not to make any significant changes to this essay.
2   Vsevolod Meyerhold (1969) 'The Naturalistic Theatre and the Theatre of Mood' in Braun (ed.) (1969) *Meyerhold on Theatre*, p. 30.
3   Vsevolod Meyerhold (1969) 'The Naturalistic Theatre and the Theatre of Mood' in Braun (ed.) (1969) *Meyerhold on Theatre*, p. 30.
4   Craig (2009) *On the Art of the Theatre*, p. 30.
5   Reported by Chekhov biographer Professor Marina Ivanova at the 3rd Michael Chekhov International Workshop (MCIW), Emerson College, 1994.
6   Gordon (1987), p. 119.
7   Gordon (1987), p. 124.
8   Michael Chekhov 'The Teachings of the Great Russian Directors' in Leonard (1984), p. 51.
9   Chekhov (1991) *On the Technique of Acting*, p. 16.
10 Chekhov (1991) *On the Technique of Acting*, p. 24.
11 Eurythmy, not to be confused with Dalcroze's Eurhythmics, has been described as the 'difficult task of interpreting speech in movement' (Raffe et al., 1974, p. 14). This does not mean that the text is interpreted through movement but is based on the idea that sounds themselves have fundamentally physical qualities. Whilst eurythmy is a dance form in its own right, Steiner considered that the actor's task was to internalise these movements so that the gesture is 'taken back into the word' and alters the quality of the speech. The combination of these ideas with the Stanislavskian 'objective' led to Chekhov's technique of the 'psychological gesture'.
12 Vakhtangov (1922) 'Fantastic Realism', in Cole and Chinoy (1963), pp. 185–91.
13 Chekhov (1991) *On the Technique of Acting*, p. 89.
14 Chekhov (1991) *On the Technique of Acting*, p. 89.
15 Chekhov (2002) *To The Actor*, p. 88. This idea is missing from the section on Creative Individuality in *On the Technique of Acting*.
16 Deirdre Hurst du Prey (1983) 'Working with Chekhov', *The Drama Review*, 27(3): 89.

17   Gordon (1987), p. 148.
18   Gordon (1987), p. 149.
19   Chekhov (1985) *Lessons for the Professional Actor*, p. 102.
20   Stanislavsky refers to the experience in positive terms in *Building a Character* (1979), p. 21, although the book was written after Chekhov discussed his experience with Stanislavsky. Although Chekhov appears to experience divided consciousness for the first time in the role of Skid, it is a well-discussed phenomenon in Western actor training since Diderot. Coquelin's version of the idea was very much part of the debate on the actor's art during the first part of the century and was also explicitly referred to by Irving and Meyerhold. See also Chapter Eight of Hornby's (1992) *The End of Acting*; Copeau 'An Actor's Thoughts on Diderot's Paradoxe' in Rudlin and Paul (eds) (1990) *Copeau: Texts on Theatre*, pp. 72–78; and Leach (1997) 'When He Touches Your Heart . . . – The Revolutionary Theatre of Vsevolod Meyerhold and the Development of Michael Chekhov', *Contemporary Theatre Review*, 7(Part 1): 67–83.
21   Powers (2004) *Michael Chekhov: On Theatre and the Art of Acting*.
22   Gordon (1987), pp. 155–59. Powers (2004) *Michael Chekhov: On Theatre and the Art of Acting*.
23   See my discussion of the critical reception of *The Possessed* in Chamberlain (2004), pp. 83–104.
24   Chekhov's 1942 text was rejected by publishers. Chekhov felt that his written English was to blame and translated the work into Russian. He then re-translated the work into English only to suffer rejection once again. In 1952, Chekhov gave Charles Leonard permission to edit the manuscript in any way he saw fit, and Leonard's reduced version of *To the Actor* was published in English in 1953. It is through Leonard's version that Chekhov's work became widely known. A special issue of TDR devoted to Chekhov in 1983 followed by the publication in 1985 of Deirdre Hurst du Prey's transcription of Chekhov's 1941 classes *Lessons for the Professional Actor* sparked a renewed interest in Chekhov's work. In 1991 Mala Powers (ex-student of Chekhov and executrix of the Chekhov estate) re-edited the 1942 manuscript and it was published by HarperCollins as *On the Technique of Acting*.
25   This additional material was translated with a commentary Andrei Malaev-Babel and is included as an appendix to the main text. Chekhov (2002) *To the Actor* pp. 183–215.
26   Chekhov (1991) *On the Technique of Acting*, p. 15. See my discussion of the critical reception of *The Possessed* in Chamberlain (2004), pp. 83–104.
27   Chekhov in Leonard, 1984, p. 38.
28   Chekhov (2002) *To The Actor*, p. 2.
29   Benedetti (1988) *Stanislavski: A Biography*, p. 338.
30   Chekhov (1991) *On the Technique of Acting*, pp. 32–33; see also Chekhov (2002) *To the Actor*, p.56.
31   Chekhov (1991) *On the Technique of Acting*, p. 48; see also Chekhov (2002) *To the Actor*, pp. 13–14.
32   Chekhov (1991) *On the Technique of Acting*, p. 59.
33   Chekhov (1991) *On the Technique of Acting*, pp. 64–65.
34   Chekhov (1991) *On the Technique of Acting*, p. 60.
35   See Chekhov (2002) *To the Actor* pp. 186–208.
36   Chekhov (2002) *To The Actor*, p. 93.
37   Chekhov (1991) *On the Technique of Acting*, p. 146.
38   Chekhov (1991) *On the Technique of Acting*, p. 151.
39   Chekhov (1991) *On the Technique of Acting*, p. 147.
40   Chekhov (1991) *On the Technique of Acting*, p. 151.
41   Chekhov (1991) *On the Technique of Acting*, p. 154.
42   Chekhov (1991) *On the Technique of Acting*, p. 155.
43   Chekhov (1991) *On the Technique of Acting*, p. 155.

Bibliography

Ashperger, Cynthia (2008) *The Rhythm of Space and the Sound of Time: Michael Chekhov's Acting Technique in the 21st Century*, New York/Amsterdam: Editions Rodopi.
Barba, Eugenio (1995) *The Paper Canoe: A Guide to Theatre Anthropology*, London: Routledge.

Benedetti, Jean (1988) Stanislavski: A Biography, London: Methuen.

Black, Lendley (1987) Mikhail Chekhov as Actor, Director, and Teacher, Ann Arbor, MI: UMI Research Press.

Braun, Edward (ed.) (1969) Meyerhold on Theatre, London: Eyre Methuen.

Bridgmont, Peter (1992) Liberation of the Actor, London: Temple Lodge.

Chamberlain, Franc (2004) Michael Chekhov, London: Routledge.

Chekhov, Michael (1985) Lessons for the Professional Actor, New York: PAJ Books.

—— (1988) 'The Golden Age of the Russian Theatre', Alarums and Excursions 2, Los Angeles.

—— (1991) On the Technique of Acting, New York: Harper Perennial.

—— (2000) Lessons for Teachers of his Acting Techinque, (transcribed and ed. Deirdre Hurst du Prey), Ottawa: Dovehouse.

—— (2002) To the Actor, London: Routledge.

—— (2005) The Path of the Actor, ed. Andrei Kirillov and Bella Merlin, London: Routledge.

—— and Gromov, Viktor (1995) 'The Castle Awakens', trans. from the German Mel Gordon, Performing Arts Journal, 17 (1): 113–20.

Cole, Toby and Chinoy, Helen Krich (eds) (1963) Directors on Directing: A Source Book of the Modern Theatre, New York: Bobbs-Merrill Company.

Craig, E.G. (2009) On the Art of the Theatre, London: Routledge.

Daboo, Jerri (2007) 'Michael Chekhov and the Embodied Imagination: Higher Self and Non-Self', Studies in Theatre and Performance, 27 (3): 261–73.

Gordon, Mel (1987) The Stanislavsky Technique: Russia. A Workbook for Actors, New York: Applause Books.

—— (1995) 'The Castle Awakens: Mikhail Chekhov's 1931 Occult Fantasy', Performing Arts Journal, 17 (1): 110–12.

Green, Michael (1986) The Russian Symbolist Theatre: An Anthology of Plays and Critical Texts, Ann Arbor, MI: Ardis.

Hornby, Richard (1992) The End of Acting: A Radical View, New York: Applause.

Innes, Christopher (1998) Edward Gordon Craig: A Vision of the Theatre, Amsterdam: Harwood Academic Press.

Kirillov, Andrei (1994) 'Michael Chekhov – Problems of Study', Eye of the World 1, St Petersburg.

—— (2006) 'Michael Chekhov and the Search for the "Ideal" Theatre', New Theatre Quarterly, 22 (3): 227–34.

Leach, Robert (1997) 'When He Touches Your Heart . . . – The Revolutionary Theatre of Vsevolod Meyerhold and the Development of Michael Chekhov', Contemporary Theatre Review, 7 (1): 67–83.

Leonard, Charles (1984) Michael Chekhov's To the Director and Playwright, New York: Limelight Editions.

Marowitz, Charles (2004) The Other Chekhov: A Biography of Michael Chekhov, the Legendary Actor, Director and Theorist, New York: Applause Books.

Meerzon, Yana (2005) The Path of a Character: Michael Chekhov's Inspired Acting and Theatre Semiotics, Frankfurt-am-Main: Peter Lang.

Meyer, Michael (1987) Strindberg, Oxford: Oxford University Press.

Nietzsche, Friedrich (1993) The Birth of Tragedy, London: Penguin Classics.

Pitches, Jonathan (2006) Science and the Stanislavsky Tradition of Acting, London: Routledge.

—— (2007) 'Towards a Platonic Paradigm of Performer Training: Michael Chekhov and Anatoly Vasiliev', Contemporary Theatre Review, 17 (1): 28–40.

Raffe, Marjorie, Harwood, Cecil and Lundgren, Marguerite (1974) Eurythmy and the Impulse of Dance, London: Rudolf Steiner Press.

Rudlin, John and Paul, Norman H. (eds) (1990) Copeau: Texts on Theatre, London: Routledge.

Schopenhauer, Arthur (1966) The World As Will and Representation, Vol. 2, trans. E.F.J. Payne, New York: Dover.

Senelick, Laurence (1981) Russian Dramatic Theory from Pushkin to the Symbolists, Austin, TX: University of Texas Press.

Stanislavski, Constantin (1979) Building a Character, London: Eyre Methuen.

Steiner, Rudolf (1960) Speech and Drama, London: Rudolf Steiner Press.

—— (1964) Knowledge of the Higher Worlds and its Attainment, California: Health Research.

—— (1987) Secrets of the Threshold, London: Rudolf Steiner Press.

Vakhtangov, Eugene (1922) 'Fantastic Realism', in Cole and Chinoy (eds) *Directors on Directing: A Source Book of the Modern Theatre*, New York: Bobbs-Merrill Company, pp. 185–91.
Zarrilli, Phillip B. (ed.) (1995) *Acting (Re)Considered*, London: Routledge.
Zinder, David (2002) *Body – Voice – Imagination: A Training for the Actor*, New York, NY: Theatre Arts/Routledge

Journal

The Drama Review (1983), 27 (3), is an issue devoted to Michael Chekhov's career and legacy.

Video

Mason, Felicity (1993) *The Training Sessions of Michael Chekhov*, Exeter: Arts Documentation Unit.
Merlin, Joanna (2000) *Michael Chekhov's Psychological Gesture*, Exeter: Arts Documentation Unit.
Michael Chekhov Association (2007) *Master Classes in the Michael Chekhov Technique* (3 DVDs), London: Routledge.
Sharp, Martin (2002) *Michael Chekhov: The Dartington Years*, Hove: Palomino Films.

Audio

Grove, Eddy (1992) *The Nature and Significance of Michael Chekhov's Contribution to the Theory and Technique of Acting*, New York: Eddy Grove.
Powers, Mala (2004) *Michael Chekhov: On Theatre and the Art of Acting – A Guide to Discovery with Exercises* (4CDs), New York: Applause.

Websites

The Michael Chekhov Association (MICHA): In the US: www.michaelchekhov.org; in the UK: www.michaelchekhov.org.uk
The Michael Chekhov Studio: www.themichaelchekhovstudio.org
The Michael Chekhov Acting Studio: www.michaelchekhovactingstudio.com
Lisa Dalton's Michael Chekhov Connection: www.chekhov.net
Daniele Legler's: www.chekhovactorstraining.com
Michael Chekhov Europe: www.michaelchekhoveurope.eu/

Chapter 5

Jane Baldwin

MICHEL SAINT-DENIS: TRAINING THE COMPLETE ACTOR

CONTEXT

MICHEL SAINT-DENIS (1897–1971) fell in love with a dream of theatre as a boy in his early teens and remained faithful to that ideal until his death. Except for his military service during the First and Second World Wars, Saint-Denis's entire life was bound up in his multifaceted work as a theatre practitioner. Today he is best remembered for his contribution to theatre training through his schools and his two books, *Theatre: The Rediscovery of Style* and *Training for the Theatre*. Saint-Denis's approach to training differed from that of his contemporaries; it aimed to develop practitioners in each discipline: acting, directing, design, playwriting, and stage management. His schools functioned as embryonic theatre companies. Part of his legacy is the widespread acceptance of this educational paradigm.

Saint-Denis's professional life was characterised by constant beginnings; he frequently remarked that his career had been divided into five-year periods. Circumstances – war, economics, sickness – forced him to move on before fulfilling his intentions. But there was a positive side to recurrent change: each time he created another institution, he added to the knowledge acquired from his previous experiences. It kept his work fresh.

Two major strands of early twentieth-century acting discoveries were at the core of his teaching: the first, a physical approach in which the body is trained to become a fully expressive instrument and the second, a more internal approach that might be termed realistic characterisation. Together, they offered the student a holistic model. His major influences were his uncle, Jacques Copeau and, to a certain extent, Konstantin Stanislavsky. Underlying Saint-Denis's teaching was the all-embracing but equivocal notion of style. For Saint-Denis's acting students, style denoted the acquisition of the physical, vocal, intellectual, imaginative, and emotional skills that would enable them to tackle all types of drama.

Saint-Denis's career began in 1920 with his apprenticeship at Jacques Copeau's Paris art theatre, the Vieux-Colombier (Saint-Denis, Unpublished diary notes, undated). Starting as general secretary, he proceeded to rehearsal assistant and then stage manager. In 1922, he made his acting début as Curio in a revival of Copeau's *Twelfth Night*, and the following year, he staged *Amahl ou la lettre du roi* with students of the Vieux-Colombier School. These years with Copeau were critical for Saint-Denis's artistic development. His uncle imbued Saint-Denis with an ideal of theatre, taught him the craft of theatre by example, and shared with him his ideas, goals, doubts, and the results of his explorations. Saint-Denis learned from Copeau the importance of training and borrowed freely from his concepts, which he augmented, clarified, and, to a degree, systematised. During the early days of his independent career in France, Saint-Denis clung quite closely to Copeau's practice, while trying to develop it further, as in his work with improvisation, for instance. Later, in London, where he spent most of his professional life (1935–52), he gained more intellectual and artistic freedom: 'because there, I knew, I would be totally alone, a million miles from my friends, a million miles from my master Copeau' (Saint-Denis, Diary notes). He explored pedagogically and professionally a repertoire that differed from Copeau's, trained students for a professional theatre that he hoped to reform, not recreate, and worked with the best actors in England in pursuit of excellence.

The Copiaus

During Saint-Denis's next career phase (1924–29), he became an actor, teacher, writer, and director of the Copiaus, a Burgundy-based troupe composed of Copeau's disciples. They included actors Suzanne Bing, Auguste Boverio, and Jean Villard as well as students who would make a name in French theatre: Marie-Hélène Copeau, her future husband Jean Dasté, Étienne Decroux, Jean Dorcy, and Aman Maistre. Although the vision initiating the Burgundy experiment had been Copeau's, he proved himself an unreliable and ambivalent leader. Saint-Denis stepped in and filled the void and this experience laid the foundations of his career as a director and educator. The Copiaus's common goal was the renewal of the theatre through what Saint-Denis called the 'rediscovery of style' in acting, dramaturgy, and scenography. They proposed to restore theatre to the central place it once held by stripping away the accretions of habit to uncover and learn from its practice during its most signifi-cant eras: ancient Greece, the Middle Ages, the popular theatre of Renaissance Italy, Elizabethan and Jacobean England, and seventeenth-century France. Their means were research and practice, their inspiration in large part the *commedia dell'arte*, since they also aspired to revivify popular theatre.

Classes were formal and informal; individuals skilled in specific domains taught them to the others. Coursework consisted mainly of gymnastics, movement, music, mime, mask work, mask modelling, and improvisation, the latter taught by Saint-Denis. They trained both autonomously and collaboratively. An actor might conceive a character and develop it privately before bringing it to the group for suggestions and criticism. At other times, a performer or performers generated an idea for a group improvisation that all researched and rehearsed. Again, the group critiqued and supported the individual members. This close collaboration resulted in a strong ensemble.

Improvisation had two principal concentrations: the development of characters – particularly masked and comic ones – and themes, which might evolve into plays. Themes were broad, even universal, at some times farcical, at others filled with pathos. Characters, on the other hand, were infused with regional traits that their Burgundian audiences would readily identify. In all cases, the company was

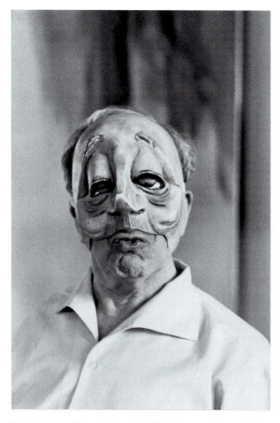

Figure 5.1 Saint-Denis giving a mask workshop at Juilliard retreat (1968) *Photographer*: Robert Gold.

searching for ways to represent its subject, relying on mime, rhythm, sound, and music. In lieu of words, they sometimes used an invented language called *grummelotage*, communicated through tones and inflectional patterns. During the Copiaus's existence, the performers generated seven original productions, which grew out of theatre games, improvisations, and continuing research.[1] Over time, Saint-Denis began adding dialogue to the scenarios, on occasion writing with Jean Villard, an actor, singer, and musician. Their more polished productions toured the villages and towns of eastern France, and went on to Switzerland, Belgium, Luxembourg, and Holland.

The genesis of the 1928 *Danse de la ville et des champs*, one of their most fully realised productions, exemplifies their methods. It began life a year earlier as an exercise called *Le Printemps*, a piece which had a few public showings in the Burgundy countryside. Pleased with the results, the company decided to develop it into a full-length work. Jean Villard composed the music, orchestrated for flute, accordion, and percussive instruments. Saint-Denis wrote the minimal text, praised for its poetic quality (Vincent, 1928). Designed to appeal to their local following, the plot was deliberately simple and naïve, pitting the wholesome charms of rustic life against the seductions of the city. It follows the adventures of a young Burgundian peasant who, having exchanged the country for the town, is disillusioned and returns to home and sweetheart. In keeping with the Copiaus's anti-naturalistic aesthetic, François, the symbolically named protagonist, was a type, not a psychologically developed character. Like the other performers, he was masked and his acting grew out of physical expression.

In contrast with the clichéd storyline, the *mise en scène* was innovative and inventive. In this sound and movement piece, the actors were living scenery, 'signs in action,' according to director and playwright Léon Chancerel (Chancerel 1930). The cast of nine played the many characters and provided the physical environment. On a bare stage, through gesture and 'oscillating bodies' (ibid.), two groups, one left, one right, created the illusion of nature's cycle: beginning with aborning vegetation, trees, for example, bursting forth from the earth – an exercise well known by later generations of acting students, but generally executed in the abstract.[2] Birdsong, wind, storms, thunder were devised by the performers. The city was represented as an industrial machine, made up of intertwined actors as gears, levers, and other moving parts (another exercise familiar to contemporary students). As before, the Copiaus produced the soundscape, now bells, sirens, horns, and rhythmic pounding. Performed in the context of a play by a troupe committed to creating meaning through movement and, to the greatest extent possible, sound without words, these 'exercises' were stunning in their originality and theatrical truthfulness. At its best, *La Danse de la ville et des champs* recalled the 'Noh, liturgical drama, the celebration of a sacred rite' (ibid.).

Despite their success, the Copiaus, especially Saint-Denis, grew dissatisfied with these creations. Although the Copiaus remained wedded to movement theatre, richer, fuller, better shaped texts than Saint-Denis could furnish might bring the collective to a higher level of expression.

In the spring of 1929, the Copiaus dissolved for various reasons: Copeau's apathy and sometimes antipathy towards the company he had inspired; Saint-Denis's belief that they had reached the limits of possibilities in Burgundy; and the conflicting ambitions of the actors. Invaluable for Saint-Denis, the Burgundy experience was influential in setting the model for his future schools. Among the ideas he took and adapted were the use of gymnastics, improvisation, and mask as training tools, the importance of working as an ensemble, ongoing research, and an integrated approach.

The Compagnie des Quinze

A year later, in Paris, Saint-Denis assembled the fifteen best of the Copiaus to form the Compagnie des Quinze. He invested his dreams in the new company, hoping to combine a laboratory theatre of professional performers with a training programme for talented students. Like the Copiaus, it continued to investigate collective creation, but now working with a writer, André Obey.

Together, they developed six plays, which ranged across epochs and theatrical styles: *Noé* (1931), *Le Viol de Lucrèce* (1931), *La Bataille de la Marne* (1931), *Loire* (1932), *Vénus et Adonis* (1932), and *Don Juan* (1934). Some, like *La Bataille de la Marne* and *Loire*, were drawn from early improvisations; others were prompted by ideas that Saint-Denis had contemplated since their Copiaus days. The source for *Noé* (Noah) was the medieval mystery play; *Le Viol de Lucrèce* owed its inspiration to Shakespeare's poem and the Japanese Noh; *Vénus et Adonis*, also taken from a Shakespearean poem, was farcical. *La Bataille de la Marne* was based on a historical First World War event; *Loire* was an original allegorical poetic work, which transcended time; *Don Juan* looked back to Molière and the Baroque Spanish playwright Tirso de Molina.

Each of these productions helped Saint-Denis to formulate his views on style, which he continued to refine and develop throughout his career. In working with

Obey, he began to consider the playwright, rather than the actor, as the principal creative figure in the theatre. Consequently, he came to believe that the responsibility of all the other practitioners – director, actors, designers – was to serve the text, which holds the key to the play's style. Although all of Obey's plays were lyrical and movement based, the fact that they explored various eras and genres called for different approaches. Saint-Denis's actors explored the play's context as fully as possible. They researched the customs, behaviour, physicality, art, music, and clothing of the culture and brought the results into the rehearsal hall.

Obey's presence altered the group's working methods to a degree, largely because of a power shift. In spite of the Quinze's egalitarian ethos, the dramatist became a second authority figure. Nonetheless, improvisation remained a dominant element in the rehearsal hall, characters continued to grow out of corporeal exercises, masks were employed, the choral aspect of the productions was still important. But with an author writing text, the chorus's words took on more significance. The ancient Greek choral leader was revived, in the form of the modern narrator, resulting in long monologues for one or two actors, while the rest of the chorus mainly used mime and sound.

Obey and Saint-Denis carried forward the Copiaus's symbolist tradition,[3] as can be seen from *La Bataille de la Marne*.[4] Based on Obey's and Saint-Denis's personal experiences as soldiers in the First World War as well as the previous Copiaus exercise, it shows two worlds. The first, the France of the war with its fighting men and suffering civilians; the second, a spiritual and eternal France, symbolised by two characters, the narrators. France – depicted as always as a beautiful woman, here, the masked Marie-Hélène Dasté – afflicted by her losses, rallies the troops, comforts the sick and dying, and consoles the peasant women, who, having stayed behind to work the fields, are fleeing the invaders. The Messenger (played sans mask by Auguste Boverio) represents figures of French tradition – a courtier, soldier, and peasant – denoted by the three different cloaks he wears. His role has a double function: to describe the war, mimed by the choruses of men and women, and to interact with France as her servitor.

Saint-Denis's *mise en scène* was considered remarkable for its ability to portray the horrors of war, complete with battles, invasions, and mass emigrations, using the simplest of props, scenery, and effects, and a cast of fifteen. The scenic design presented a colourless world; greyish-brown hangings masked the stage walls; the stark platform was sharply raked, allowing the actors to play on numerous planes. Shifting offstage sound effects and music – a Bach chorale for the Germans and the marching song 'Auprès de ma blonde' for the French – and gunfire brought the war closer. For several critics, including the former director André Antoine, this mimed, dance-like, and spoken poetic drama evoked Aeschylus's *The Persians* (Antoine undated); others found that its stylised quality augmented its emotional authenticity (Marshall 1957: 64).

Despite (or because of) the novel discoveries made by the Quinze, the company was unable to attract a large Paris audience. Maintaining the company was a continual financial struggle. Perhaps the biggest obstacle to economic stability was generating new productions: Obey was unable to supply enough new material; other dramatists they worked with never wrote more than one text for them. Productions premiered in Paris and then went on the road, travelling regularly for short stays to cities in eastern France, Belgium, Switzerland, once to Spain, and, most often, to London. Outside Paris, the Quinze's performances were widely acclaimed, nowhere as much as London. Saint-Denis met young and forward-looking British theatre practitioners attracted to his avant-garde theatricalist approach. They were deeply impressed by the combination of movement theatre, strong ensemble, and sincerity of acting, a package previously unknown to them. Saint-Denis's difficult decision to change his base of operations from France to England was made easier by the Quinze's problems: constant touring, insufficient funds, and defections by the actors. He accepted Tyrone Guthrie's proposal to back a theatre school in London, where Saint-Denis could institute his ideas on training and affect the direction of the English theatre.[5]

THE SCHOOLS

The transfer to London changed the course of Saint-Denis's professional life. He ceased to act. And although his aspirations remained unwavering – to build and run a theatrical organisation in which an experimental company would operate in tandem with a 'non-conforming' theatre school – more often than not the school became the primary institution. Even as he continued to direct, in some cases, ground-breaking productions, his reputation as a master teacher brought him international notice. Saint-Denis was to found five drama schools dedicated to a comprehensive training in all facets of the theatre: The London Theatre Studio, the Old Vic School, Strasbourg's École supérieure d'art dramatique, the National Theatre School of Canada, and the Juilliard Drama Division. He designed the training programme for actors at the Royal Shakespeare Company, which he ran from 1962 to 1965. He also acted as curricular adviser to other institutions.

The London Theatre Studio

Thus, in 1938, when Saint-Denis founded the London Theatre Studio (LTS), he brought to it all he had learned as a director of a collective for over ten years. The LTS functioned in much the same way as the Copiaus and the Quinze; it was a collaborative enterprise with an authority figure at its head. As the first of Saint-Denis's formal schools, it had more of a spirit of experimentation than the later ones. Ideas were tried out, most accepted, some abandoned. For example, a section for professional actors interested in acquiring new skills or refining existing ones attracted sixteen professionals, including Laurence Olivier and Alec Guinness. Although their presence added another level of intensity to the young students' work, the section ultimately proved impractical.

If not his most polished school, the LTS is of particular interest because it was there that Saint-Denis formulated his ideas for a training institute, adjusting his previous pedagogical experience for cultural differences. He spent six months devising the curriculum, working with George Devine,[6] whom he met in London, and the actor Marius Goring,[7] who had joined the Quinze in its last days. As members of a close-knit circle of emerging theatre reformers, Devine and Goring were conscious of the specific shortcomings of the British theatre. With the exception of Suria Magito,[8] recruited in Paris, faculty members were drawn from these connections.

As part of his preparation for designing the LTS curriculum, Saint-Denis went to the theatre. In the 1930s it was conservative, largely untouched by the innovations

that had taken place on the Continent. The West End mounted frivolous fare performed in an outmoded style that Saint-Denis disdained. While there were a few
courageous art theatres, most floundered and failed; the prominent exception was the
Old Vic Theatre, home of the British classics, especially Shakespeare. It was there,
watching actors of the calibre of Peggy Ashcroft, Edith Evans, John Gielgud, Charles
Laughton, and Laurence Olivier that Saint-Denis began to understand the art and the
problems of playing Shakespeare. An inveterate fan of the leading English music-hall
entertainers, Saint-Denis realised that the parallels between their routines and the
comic improvisatory characters of the Copiaus could be exploited to train students
and give faculty and students a common language for physical comedy. In the
summer of 1936 he directed John Gielgud in an English production of Obey's
Noah. Notwithstanding the play's favourable reviews, Saint-Denis felt the actors'
performances lacked the vigour, inventiveness, and corporeal capabilities of the
Quinze's version. These deficiencies confirmed his opinion that he 'had something to
contribute to the English theatre' (Saint-Denis 1982: 43).

Saint-Denis assembled a talented faculty of practitioners who shared his organic
and integrated approach to acting. At the LTS, students gained technical tools before
utilising them as a whole in plays. They acquired a certain proficiency in movement
before working on difficult texts, trained in poetry in advance of doing Shakespeare,
and took speech classes before undertaking roles. This was a radical departure from
the piecemeal methods of standard British drama schools. His faculty cooperated
closely, so that each area of instruction related to the others. If, for example, students
were working on a Shakespearean play in their interpretation class, their movement
teacher focused on Elizabethan dance; the theatre history teacher discussed the
playhouses, dramas, and culture of the period; the music teacher instructed them in
its songs. Difficulties encountered in one course might be addressed and remedied
in a second. The same spirit of coordination mandated frequent faculty meetings to
discuss each student's progress, problems, and ways of improving instruction. In its
final year, each cohort came to fruition as a company and performed for the public.
Saint-Denis's later schools stressed group identity even more through the symbolic
numbering of each class.[9]

The LTS, like all Saint-Denis's schools, had programmes for designers, technicians,
stage managers, and directors. (At the LTS, the directing section remained rudimentary.) These students attended non-technique classes such as theatre history and
textual study. Integration of coursework reached its height in production when the
year's students participated in every phase. Actors sewed costumes, constructed sets,
and worked as assistant stage managers under the supervision of the faculty; technical
students played small roles or were supernumeraries.

In the acting programme, students took rigorous movement courses, and studied
both spoken and silent improvisation, character (or comic) and tragic (or neutral)
mask, music and singing. Saint-Denis was the first to introduce mask as a standard
course in a drama school committed to training professional actors. Character and
tragic mask, considered discrete disciplines, were taught by Saint-Denis (tragic) and
George Devine (character). Devine learned his mask skills from Saint-Denis. Tragic
mask, initially psychologically stressful for many, required longer training. By contrast, the more accessible character mask tended to free up students, sometimes
almost immediately. Improvisations took numerous forms, from simple tasks for
the individual, to more complex exercises – both solo and partnered – to fully
fledged group scenarios performed for audiences. Saint-Denis also taught silent basic
improvisation and advanced spoken group improvisation. Through the practice of

improvisation and mask, students learned that spontaneity and technique were not mutually exclusive.

While the LTS had multiple goals, the overriding objective was 'to serve the contemporary theatre' (Saint-Denis 1982: 47) through raising the standards of the text-based professional theatre; hence the emphasis on the interpretation of existing dramatic literature. Vocal study, consisting of voice production, diction, and speech, became as important as movement. The three disciplines (voice, speech, movement) taught by different instructors, while overlapping with each other, were kept distinct, in line with the Saint-Denis philosophy.

Stanislavsky

Concentration on dramaturgy affected Saint-Denis's views on style, leading him into new areas as an educator and a director. He incorporated a personalised version of Stanislavsky's discoveries, which he had scrutinised in 1922 when the Moscow Art Theatre brought *The Cherry Orchard*, *The Lower Depths*, and *The Brothers Karamazov* to Paris. He had met and spoken with Stanislavsky at the time. In 1936, the inaugural year of the LTS, Elizabeth Hapgood's translation of *An Actor Prepares* was published. Armed with this material, he began exploring realism, which he carefully distinguished from naturalism. Saint-Denis associated naturalism with the nineteenth-century 'directorial excesses' of André Antoine, whom Saint-Denis faulted for his emphasis on overly explicit detail and a repertory mainly composed of 'superficial, factual little plays' (Baldwin 2003: 120). For him, realism, as exemplified by Chekhov's works, probed beneath the outer wrappings to 'express the nature of things, the meaning of human life, what happens behind and below appearances' (Saint-Denis 2008: 51). Like Saint-Denis, Stanislavsky used improvisation as an instructional instrument. However, Saint-Denis objected to improvisations where actors extemporise upon a scene, since he believed it diminished the importance of the text. Moreover, Saint-Denis felt that Stanislavsky's improvisational work was too realistic and internal, lacking sufficient detachment. While he recognised that an actor trained in the psychological technique of Stanislavsky acquires 'a practical knowledge of the means to . . . liberate his own subconscious forces' (Saint-Denis 1959: 26), the actor 'must find a balance between contemporary subjective truth and the objective qualities which the text brings to him' (Saint-Denis 2008: 114). This balance between opposing values was key to his teaching. Without subjectivity, a performance is cold and distant; without objectivity, the actor loses both control and awareness of the audience.

Saint-Denis believed that only a thorough grounding in classical theatre gave actors the tools for all other styles that they would encounter. An ongoing question was how to apply Stanislavsky's theories not only to realism, but to the classics, since Saint-Denis intended to develop practitioners capable of performing 'the classical plays of all times and all nations' (Forsyth undated). The answer was ultimately found in the assimilation of Stanislavsky's physical actions throughout the curriculum, an 'outside-in' approach more compatible with Saint-Denis's convictions and teaching methods.[10] The actor finds the physical actions in the text, continues to explore them in silent études, and ultimately incorporates them into the text.[11]

The interpreter and the improviser

Despite Saint-Denis's dictum that the playwright is the principal creator in the theatre, he divided actors into two categories: the interpreter and the improviser. The improviser was the rarer, a performer most often found in the music hall, vaudeville, or the circus who works without a written text, combining the imaginative abilities of the playwright with the interpretive talents of the actor. While few acting students will achieve this degree of inventiveness, Saint-Denis endeavoured to stimulate the student's originality 'by making him pass through the experiences of the actor/creator' (Saint-Denis 2008: 114).

THE OTHER SCHOOLS

The Second World War brought the LTS to a close. However, in 1947 Laurence Olivier, artistic director of the Old Vic Theatre, invited Saint-Denis to develop an institute of which the Old Vic School would be a part.[12] The principal pedagogical changes Saint-Denis made were the addition of a touring children's company composed of the most promising graduates, a playwright to work on collective creation with the students, a directing programme, and the inclusion of three new faculty members, Litz Pisk in movement, Jani Strasser in voice, and Marion (Mamie) Watson in speech (*l'expression parlée*). Strasser's use of singing as the point of departure for speech adhered to Saint-Denis's beliefs about the role of the choral ensemble in the theatre. Where Strasser utilised physical exercises in conjunction with vocalising to free the voice, Pisk employed vocal exercises in combination with movement. She began by introducing spontaneous sounds, gradually inserted words, and eventually text.

The Old Vic School was closed in 1952 by its Board of Governors, despite its remarkable achievements. At the root of the problems were internecine feuding, rivalries, and conflicting ambitions among the administrators and Board members.[13] Saint-Denis was left without a job. He accepted an offer to participate in France's post-war theatrical decentralisation by developing Strasbourg's École supérieure d'art dramatique and taking charge of its regional theatre. For this school, Saint-Denis adjusted the emphasis of the repertory from English to French. Restoration comedy was replaced by Molière; modern dramas included Giraudoux and Anouilh. Shakespeare, who has no French equivalent, was taught in translation. At Strasbourg, for the first time he was able to increase the training from two years to three. He remained in Strasbourg from 1952 until 1957, when he fell victim to a stroke.

After a partial recovery, he was commissioned by the Rockefeller Foundation to establish the Juilliard Drama Division, for which he engaged the faculty, supervised the design of the facilities, and wrote the curriculum. Since this school was to produce a new kind of actor for the classical repertory employed at the emerging regional theatres, an alternative to the usual training in the American Method was needed. The Division was ten years in the making, during which time Saint-Denis's health deteriorated further. When the Division opened in 1968, Saint-Denis taught for a semester before being incapacitated by another stroke. His wife, Suria, acted in a supervisory role to ensure the school followed Saint-Denis's curriculum. Cultural amendments included instituting a four-year degree-granting programme to conform to American practice.

In the late 1950s, Canadian officials and theatre practitioners also turned to Saint-Denis for leadership in developing the bilingual National Theatre School. His expertise in French and English theatre was invaluable in setting up a drama school, divided into two sections by language, housed under one roof. After three years of intensive preparation, during which Saint-Denis split his time between Montreal and New York, the National Theatre School opened in 1960. The cultural differences that divide Canada are at work here. The English side tends to be more conservative, language based, and wedded to the English classics. At the same time, a US influence permeates the training. The French side is more inventive, movement based, and committed to the development of Québécois culture. Other disparities include the three-year English programme as opposed to the four-year French one. Saint-Denis's theory had flexibility, it could be modified and still remain faithful to its foundation.

EXERCISES

For Saint-Denis, the essence of acting was transformation, although he recognised that actors have to start from the self – the rationale for individualising the training. Once the student-actor has developed a few movement skills and a certain measure of confidence, the mask is an ideal learning tool. It transforms, but does not hide. It will help the student's 'concentration, diminish his self-consciousness, strengthen his inner feelings and lead him to develop his physical powers of outward dramatic expression' (Saint-Denis 2008: 176). Both character and neutral mask emphasise clarity of intention, of action, of feeling. The full-face neutral mask, in particular, deprives actors of their normal modes of expressiveness, the face and voice, forcing them to communicate using only the body.

   That there are parallels with the practice of Étienne Decroux and Jacques Lecoq is natural, given that the Copiaus's discoveries are at the root of all three artists' approaches. Decroux was a member of the Copiaus in their first phase; Lecoq was a disciple of Jean Dasté, a Copiau and member of the Quinze. Of the two, it was Lecoq whose training shared the greater similarity with Saint-Denis's, particularly in the areas of neutral and character mask. But Lecoq extended the work, perhaps most notably with the addition of the larval mask and the red nose. Larval masks are large, full faced, and abstract, with only the suggestion of human features. Their lack of specificity leads student-actors into more experimental areas. Red noses, the simplest of masks, leave actors most exposed in order to explore the clownesque in them-selves. The purpose of Saint-Denis's training differed. No longer a 'specialist', he sought to create the complete professional actor. Thus, at his schools, mask training was and is by necessity shorter, a means to an end, not the end in itself. Theatre companies developed by the disciples of Saint-Denis and Lecoq further illustrate the differences between their teaching. The Manchester Royal Exchange in England was founded by former Old Vic students whose objectives were to alter the traditional audience–performer relationship by eliminating the formal barriers between them, to create a regional theatre, and to produce plays whose values were 'universal and enduring' (Fraser 1998: 43). In practice, that meant an arena theatre where the actor is the main focus, a repertory that emphasises the classics, and a workshop to encourage new playwrights. By contrast, Lecoq's former students developed com-panies such as the Theatre de Complicité in England and the Dell'Arte in the US that are movement based and create devised theatre pieces. It is ironic that, despite Saint-Denis's involvement with devised theatre, none of his students founded a theatre of that type.

Neutral mask

The neutral mask has its origins in ancient Greek tragedy, one reason why this type of mask work is associated with tragic themes.[14] At the London Theatre Studio, following Saint-Denis's specifications, the design faculty Motley[15] developed eight flesh-coloured masks – four female, four male – archetypes of four stages of human development: childhood, adolescence, maturity, and old age. These were the prototypes for masks still used in the Saint-Denis schools. Features are represented, emotions are not. It is the actor's task to fill the mask, to bring life and feeling to it. If the actor animating the mask is convincing and explicit, it will seem to take on its own facial expressions. Its purpose is threefold: to eradicate cliché mannerisms; to train students to develop and release creative impulses; and to teach them to work on classical or what Saint-Denis called 'big style' roles. By its nature, the neutral mask brings the actor into contact with high emotional moments. It demands large movements; subtle gestures will not read.

In order to lessen or even eliminate self-consciousness (rather than self-awareness), Saint-Denis insisted that it be confronted. Students were as 'naked as possible' (Saint-Denis 2008: 91) in their improvisation and mask classes. At the LTS and the Old Vic School, male and female students wore identical, unbecoming, one-piece practice costumes, resembling an old-fashioned bathing suit. Today's students, less modest about their bodies, wear leotards and tights. But the outfit's function is still to strip away all but the essence, to make students aware of the line of the body, its relationship to space and storytelling possibilities. The actor's question is: How can I use my body to communicate?

Neutral masks, although they excite, call for an almost ritual calm. Movement must be deliberate; the slightest turn of the head matters. The student begins by selecting one of the eight masks, gazing at it for a long while, and finally putting it on and raising and lowering the head. She or he is beginning to inhabit and be inhabited by the mask. The student, prohibited from looking in the mirror while wearing the neutral mask, guards the memory of its appearance. The justification is that if actors see themselves in the neutral mask, they may be overwhelmed by its depersonalising qualities and impose a characterisation based on the external vision rather than acting what they feel. The age demarcated by the mask influences the kind of movement the actor employs as much as does the situation, parallel to character and plot in a play.

The first exercises are simple tasks assigned by the teacher. For example, a student wearing the female mask of maturity might enter reading a letter.[16] Even an exercise like this can become emotionally charged. The second time she performs it, the student discovers it contains bad news. What is the news? The death of a parent, perhaps? How does the actor give an account of what the letter evokes in what was called the 'zone of silence'? Using gesture and movement, she must connect the audience to her emotional reaction, which needs to stem from an inner truth, not just be demonstrated. To use the language of the Method, 'indicating' is unacceptable. At the same time, the intimate psychological realism required by the Method is useless behind the mask. The paradox of the neutral mask is its power to immerse the actor in a subjective world while forcing him or her to relate objectively to the spectators. Through questioning, the teacher pushes the students to explore more profoundly.

How might that same improvisation be performed by an actor wearing the male mask of childhood? How might the gestures, walk and tempo be affected? A second student attempts it; the change of mask requires a change in approach.

In the next stage, the teacher suggests more complex exercises with several actions. As the students' imaginations develop, they assume responsibility for inventing exercises, études, and eventually scenarios with longer, more elaborate stories. In the last phase of the work, students create and rehearse two-person improvisations, ideally with a number of transformations.

Scenarios and even études are drawn from primitive fears, myths, day dreams, fairy tales. The mask characters become archetypes: a grieving mother, a young lover, a crone, a king, a betrayed child. An étude might consist of a dream in which the mask of youth encounters a monster. It could be broken into three actions: the attack, the fight, and the ending, in which the boy either defeats or is defeated. In another, a very old woman struggles to get out of bed. The actress chooses to play the discovery of her difficulty, fear, the struggle to rise, and resignation. The teacher encourages the students to make their transitions distinct.

A typical two-person scenario is built around a meeting after a long absence, for instance, of past lovers or former enemies. As homework, the actors experiment with various dramatic possibilities and bring the results to class for comment. Another quintessential scenario is the prison escape of two men. Trying to elude capture, one falls and is wounded. Does the second help or abandon him? Scenarios with masks of different ages offer other potentialities. More inventive students conceive scenarios where they use several masks to represent the passing of time.

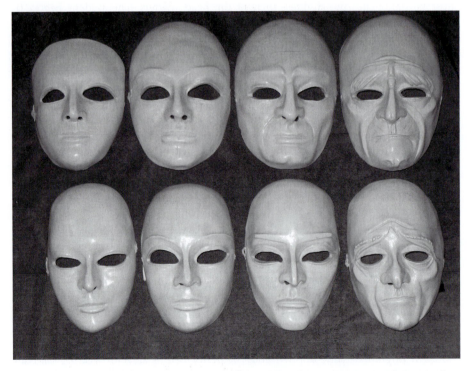

Figure 5.2 Neutral or 'noble' masks: Four male (top) and four female (bottom). Left to right: four stages of life – childhood, youth, maturity and old age. *Photographer:* Lawrence Baldwin.

Character mask

Character mask, inspired by the *commedia dell'arte*, focuses on physical comedy and farcical characters. Where neutral mask impels students toward legendary archetypes, character mask leads them toward contemporary stereotypes which are firmly attached to quotidian reality. As in neutral mask, the student individualises the types through imagination, talent, and acquired technique. At the LTS, Motley also designed Halloween-like half masks; the twenty-four masks that were later developed are less grotesque. In contrast with the neutral mask class, character mask students make use of props, costumes, and a few simple set pieces. They fabricate their own dialogue for their comic improvisations. While the aim of both classes is to liberate the student-actor, results are more quickly attained in character mask. Neutral mask is ascetic and ritualistic; character mask is sensual and bawdy, one explanation for its greater accessibility.

The lighter tone of the class notwithstanding, the student is expected to approach the comedic work with the same seriousness of purpose demanded by the neutral mask. Class begins with selecting a mask; the student may experiment with several before finding an appropriate one. Next come costume pieces and props. Once dressed, the masked students engage with the mirror, allowing their image to suggest a character. Experience had shown Saint-Denis that, far from being overwhelmed by their reflection in a comic mask, students generated more ingenious characters. Conceivably, the half-mask produces a different reaction because the students' faces are still recognisable to them.

Subsequently, students walk around the classroom, simultaneously experimenting with vocal sounds, trying out their identity. How does this character stand, walk, sit, speak? It is not yet time to respond to one another. Both character and neutral mask require the actor to return to the 'basics' of acting. Who are you? Where are you? What are you doing? As in the early stages of the neutral mask, the instructor supplies the circumstances. However, here the circumstances may change during the course of the improvisation, requiring quick adjustments (a useful pedagogical strategy for character mask, which uses a faster tempo). Students are cautioned that movement precedes speaking and never to talk for the sake of talking. Whilst movement and gesture are more restricted in character mask than in neutral, their role is more important than the verbal aspect.

As the shell of a character materialises, the instructor poses questions, as, for instance: 'Where do you live? What do you do for a living?' The actor answers as the character being constructed. Saint-Denis claimed that 'farce is usually concerned with the common people' (Saint-Denis 2008: 182), and more often than not its characters come from the bottom of the social hierarchy. The students' characters are usually failures in the game of life – a vagrant, a downtrodden alcoholic, an abandoned, impoverished mother, a spoiled brat, etc. Their status as outsiders grants the characters licence to lampoon a society that despises them.

Because of the occasions for conflict, three is the optimal number of actors for an early character mask improvisation. Character supersedes plots. The improvisations are set in mundane situations: three people find themselves thrown together in a dentist's office or in line at a supermarket or bus stop. When proficiency is gained and the improvisations are on their way to becoming fully fledged scenarios, more students participate. The work is more autonomous as they develop what is a collectively devised creation reminiscent of the Copiaus days.

PRODUCTION

The Three Sisters

It is notable that, after his collective creation period, Saint-Denis developed new techniques through pedagogical research, especially in his British training programmes. Once his involvement with teaching became dominant, his professional directorial output started to decline. The schools took the place of the laboratory theatre that he continued to yearn for. His first directing encounters with the Greeks, Shakespeare, and Chekhov were at the London Theatre Studio. Professional productions such as *Macbeth* (1937) and *Electra* (1951) grew out of these earlier efforts. Having developed the productions, Saint-Denis studied them further in his classes. This symbiosis between the professional and the academic enriched both sides of his working life.

At the end of their course of study, the LTS students presented their work to a paying public for a two-week period. The shows, composed of several pieces representative of the theatrical styles studied, were directed by Saint-Denis and other faculty members. The LTS's first public presentation in 1937[17] was made up of scenes from *Macbeth*; *The Fair*, a short commedia-like farce; *Judith*, a creation drawn from the biblical legend; and the first act of *The Three Sisters*, the latter directed by Saint-Denis. These performances were reviewed by newspaper critics and attended by prominent members of the theatre community. Thus, John Gielgud saw *The Three Sisters* and invited Saint-Denis to direct it, as part of a season of four plays.

This marked Saint-Denis's professional début as a director of a realistic play. It was the first time he had directed professionally without masks. In *Macbeth*, Banquo and the witches wore literal masks, while Olivier, in the title role, wore stylised make-up; the same mélange held true for *The Witch of Edmonton*. But Saint-Denis was not without resources for his venture into realism: he brought to *The Three Sisters* his

Figure 5.3 Saint-Denis's production of Chekhov's *Three Sisters*, for John Gielgud's season at The Queen's Theatre, London (1938).

Source: Michel Saint-Denis website.

preparation for the LTS end-of-term show, his study of Stanislavsky's *An Actor Prepares*, and his vivid memory of Stanislavsky's production of *The Cherry Orchard*, whose 'passionate search for truth' (Saint-Denis 1952: 928) had deeply impressed him. Saint-Denis also had an extraordinary cast: John Gielgud played Vershinin; Michael Redgrave, Tusenbach; Glen Byam Shaw, Solyony; Gwen Frangcon-Davies, Olga; Carol Goodner, Marsha; Peggy Ashcroft, Irina; George Devine, Andrey; Leon Quartermaine, Kulygin; Angela Baddeley, Natasha; and Alec Guinness, Feodotik. A few LTS students played minor parts. The majority of the actors had worked together previously, and several had acted under Saint-Denis, paving the way for the strong ensemble.

The Three Sisters was the fifth play Saint-Denis mounted in England[18] and, thanks to Gielgud, the first to have a generous rehearsal period. The two months that Saint-Denis deemed necessary – unheard of in English professional theatre in the 1930s – were worrisome to the cast, who wondered how they would spend all that time. So much of Saint-Denis's practice has become standard for text-based directors that it is difficult to appreciate how radical his process seemed. Certain aspects were fixed, regardless of the play's style. The first week or two were spent on table work, with an exegesis of the script by Saint-Denis, followed by consecutive read-throughs with accompanying discussion. (Usually, a realistic play received more time at the table.) The actors' task was to familiarise themselves with the text and its language, rhythms, meaning, and context.

The deliberate pace continued as director and actors delved into individual scenes, working on mood, atmosphere, relationships, moving towards characterisation. Saint-Denis restrained his actors from making definitive choices too early, encouraging them to experiment. He then blocked the play, deviating somewhat from his previous practice. Despite Saint-Denis's reputation for beginning rehearsals with 'every move and piece of business prepared beforehand on paper' (Hayman 1971: 112), he allowed more leeway for a realistic play, since the staging was less intricate, less formal (though certainly not without form). Consequently, he organised an outline of entrances, exits, and key moments, and added details during rehearsals (Saint-Denis, 'Way to Conduct Rehearsals'). He joined his actors on stage while developing the remaining blocking, explaining the motivations for each move, creating the feeling that the director was part of the ensemble. The actors became accustomed to 'living in the setting, as if in the intimacy of their home' (ibid.) – especially important for *The Three Sisters*, in which the characters' relationship and feelings toward home are a focal point. Indeed, the Prozorov's apartment was analogous to a character. Critics commented on a moment early in the play when the actors disappeared into an inner room, leaving the stage to five armchairs, which 'seemed to breathe' (Agate 1939: 72–73), so infused with life was the production. Another instance – perhaps influenced by Stanislavsky's techniques, but also reminiscent of *La Bataille de la Marne* – was the hovering presence of offstage life that reached the audience 'in audible murmurs through the walls, in the doorbells and sleighs and military orders and the shouts of carnival roisterers' (Marshall 1938), which reflected the moods of the onstage characters.

Saint-Denis incorporated improvisation into the rehearsals in the form of exercises corresponding to Stanislavsky's use of sense memory. Many of these involved mood and atmosphere. For example, the company spent hours inventing and rehearsing particulars to reveal the effects of the seasons on the characters. These effects did not go unnoticed by the critics: 'we had never been more moved in the fall of leaf', remarked J.C. Trewin (Trewin 1960: 119). Peggy Ashcroft remembered Frangcon-Davies clapping her hands to swat mosquitoes. Although this was a novel approach to working up a role for most, if not all of the actors, they found it stimulating (Gielgud 1963: 91).

Saint-Denis captured the comedy as well as the pathos of Chekhov, whose plays were frequently regarded as unrelieved melancholy. Michael Redgrave, who had also read Stanislavsky and was endeavouring to apply his precepts to Tusenbach, had difficulty finding the comedy. It was only when Saint-Denis pointed out that he was trying to make sense of the lines, instead of throwing them away, that Redgrave began to find the key to playing Tusenbach. Although the actor and director serve the text, for Chekhov (the master of subtext) Saint-Denis insisted that the lines should not be played too earnestly or the result would be mawkishness and/or tedium. As the actors honed their characterisations, rehearsals intensified, reaching what Saint-Denis called 'a hothouse effect' (Saint-Denis, 'Way to Conduct Rehearsals'). Now ready and less dependent on the director, they started run-throughs, finally putting aside their scripts. The last rehearsals before the tech and dress were spent on rhythm, tempo, and 'lightness of mood' (ibid.) In other words, avoiding longueurs and overacting.

Saint-Denis did not discard his overall concepts of directing, but adapted them. He considered *mise en scène* as 'a kind of choreography, where the language must have its own measure to correspond with the measure of the movement in the three dimensions of space, if the interpretation of the play is to come to a concrete expression . . .' (Saint-Denis 1949). Saint-Denis's *mise en scène* for *Three Sisters* paid the same careful attention to body placement and movement as did his productions for the Quinze, the difference being that here the physical work is subtler, more 'natural'. *Three Sisters* had the unselfish 'teamwork' that the Quinze was noted for, despite its cast of stars. The acting was praised for its 'tenderness . . . so exquisite that it is like the passing of light', attaining the poetic qualities that Saint-Denis uncovered beneath the realistic surface of Chekhov. As for Gielgud, he judged it 'stunning', recollecting that 'everybody said that it was the best Chekhovian production that has ever been done in this country' (Brandreth 1984: 71).

Notes

1 Their other productions were principally Jacques Copeau's adaptations of medieval and renaissance works, although they also prepared an occasional French classic.
2 This imagistic acting exercise is often used as a warm-up to relax, focus, and stretch the body, as the instructor talks the students through it. The student starts in a crouched position as a seed, and slowly moves through the tree's stages of life until its maturity, where it reacts to the sun, wind, and rain.
3 While the Copiaus and the Quinze did not embrace every element of the symbolist movement, they were symbolists in their rejection of naturalism in favour of an investigation of the internal or 'spiritual' world. Their productions explored archetypes, images, and symbols.
4 The 1914 battle of the Marne marked a turning point for the French army. Fearing the invasion of Paris, the military authorities ordered Parisian taxi drivers to transport thousands of troops to the front in their cabs.
5 Guthrie's gift of £1,300 as a start-up fund was followed up by contributions from others.
6 George Devine, then an actor, would later become a director and found the English Stage Company at the Royal Court, known as a 'writers' theatre'.
7 Marius Goring, a classical actor in his early career, later appeared in film and television.
8 Magito was a Russian movement specialist and dancer who had built her career in Paris. Her theatrical values corresponded to Saint-Denis's. She married Saint-Denis in 1960.

9   The début class at the Old Vic was Group One; the second, Group Two, etc. As a school
      matured, this classification also fostered a sense of connection with past, present, and future.
      For instance, Juilliard's entering class in September of 2008 was Group Forty-one, the age of
      the Drama Division.
10   Pierre Lefèvre, interview with author, 13 January 1989. Lefèvre was a disciple and confidant
      of Saint-Denis who taught mask in every one of Saint-Denis's schools. He also ran the
      Strasbourg School after Saint-Denis's departure.
11   See Carnicke in Chapter 1.
12   In its entirety, the Old Vic Centre, as it was to be called, would include the School, an
      experimental theatre with Saint-Denis at its head, and the Young Vic, the children's theatre.
      The experimental theatre never came into being.
13   The history surrounding this event is treated in detail in both my book *Michel Saint-Denis and the
      Shaping of the Modern Actor* and Irving Wardle's *The Theatres of George Devine*, London: Eyre Methuen,
      1978.
14   Lefèvre, interview with author, 13 January 1989. Jacques Lecoq discusses tragedy in a related
      way in *Le Corps Poétique* (Actes Sud, 1997), 135–45.
15   Motley was a successful trio of female designers of the mid-twentieth century: Margaret
      Harris, Sophie Harris, and Elizabeth Montgomery.
16   The mask creates the character's gender, although in Saint-Denis's lifetime it would have
      been unlikely that a male student would employ a female mask and vice versa.
17   Although the London Theatre Studio was a two-year programme, the coursework of the
      entering class was cut short, since the school's opening was delayed.
18   The first two, produced in 1935, were translations of Quinze productions, *Noah* and *Sowers of
      the Grain*. The year 1936 saw *The Witch of Edmonton* with Edith Evans, and 1937, *Macbeth* with
      Laurence Olivier, both at the Old Vic Theatre and incorporating mask work.

Bibliography

Agate, James (1939) *The Amazing Theatre*, London: George C. Harrap & Co., Ltd.

Antoine, André (undated) *L'Information*.

Aykroyd, Phyllis (1935) *The Dramatic Art of La Compagnie des Quinze*, London: Eric Partridge.

Baldwin, Jane (2003) *Michel Saint-Denis and the Shaping of the Modern Actor*, Westport, CT: Greenwood
      Press.

Brandreth, Gyles (1984) *John Gielgud: A Celebration*, Boston: Little & Brown Co.

Chancerel, Léon (1930) article in *Jeux, Tréteaux, et Personnages*, 15 October.

Delpit, Louise (1939) 'Les Dernières épigones de Jacques Copeau', *Smith College Studies in Modern
      Languages*, 21: 44–63.

Forsyth, James (undated) 'The Old Vic Theatre School', filmstrip, British Council.

Fraser, Davis (1998) *Words and Pictures: The Royal Exchange Theatre Company*, Manchester: Royal
      Exchange Theatre Company Ltd.

Gielgud, John (1963) *Stage Directions*, London: Heinemann.

Gontard, Denis (ed.) (1974) *Le Journal de bord des Copiaus 1924–1929*, Paris: Éditions Seghers.

Hayman, Ronald (1971) *John Gielgud*, New York: Random House.

Kusler, Babara-Anne (1974) 'Jacques Copeau's Theatre School: L'École du Vieux-Colombier',
      dissertation, University of Wisconsin.

Lecoq, Jacques, Carasso J.G. and Lallias J.C. (1997) *Le Corps poétique: Un enseignement de la création
      théâtrale*, Actes Sud.

Marshall, Norman (1957) *The Producer and the Play*, London: Macdonald.

—— (1938) *News Chronicle*, 1 February.

Rudlin, John (1986) *Jacques Copeau*, London and New York: Cambridge University Press.

Saint-Denis, Michel (1949) 'Music in the Theatre', unpublished lecture notes at Bryanston
      Music School.

—— (1952) 'Naturalism in the Theatre', *The Listener*, 4 December.

—— (1959) 'Stanislavsky and the Teaching of Dramatic Art', *World Theatre*, 8, Spring: 23–29.

—— (1982) *Training for the Theatre*, ed. Suria Magito Saint-Denis, New York: Theatre Arts Books.

—— (2008) *Theatre: The Rediscovery of Style and Other Writings*, ed. Jane Baldwin, London and New York: Routledge.

—— (undated) Unpublished Diary Notes.

—— (undated) 'Way to Conduct Rehearsals of Plays of Different Styles', Lectures Notes, Old Vic School.

Trewin, J.C. (1960) *The Turbulent Thirties: A Further Decade of the Theatre*, London: Macdonald.

Vincent (1928) *Comoedia*, 18 June, Lausanne.

Chapter 6

Sharon Marie Carnicke

THE KNEBEL TECHNIQUE: ACTIVE ANALYSIS IN PRACTICE[1]

MARIA OSIPOVNA KNEBEL (1898–1985) is arguably the most important theatrical voice of Russia's Soviet era. She studied acting and directing with three major figures from the Moscow Art Theatre – its founders (Konstantin Stanislavsky and Vladimir Nemirovich-Danchenko), and the brilliant actor Michael Chekhov. By synthesising their work, she became a prism for all that was best in the famed company's tradition. As a director and teacher, Knebel jump-started the careers of prominent actors like Oleg Efremov (who founded the innovative Contemporary Theatre in 1957), bold new playwrights like Victor Rozov (who reinvigorated Russian drama in the 1960s), and imaginative directors like Anatoly Vasiliev (Russia's most internationally known contemporary director). Without a doubt, theatrical art would be the poorer without her. At the centenary of the Moscow Art Theatre, Vasiliev placed her legacy next to those left by Jerzy Grotowski and Yury Liubimov (Smeliansky 1999: 215).

During her career, Knebel championed Stanislavsky's last rehearsal technique, Active Analysis, through which actors embody a play by exploring its conflicting vectors of action and counteraction in improvisations (see Chapter 1 and Carnicke 2008). Close examination of the play's text also accompanies the improvisatory work. How do the playwright's words create dramatic style? Why do characters speak these words and not others? Answers to such questions inform improvisations; and improvisations, in turn, prompt new questions.

Knebel was perfectly positioned to make Stanislavsky's Active Analysis her mission. She had learned from Michael Chekhov to trust imaginative improvisation and from playwright Nemirovich-Danchenko to read plays as closely as others read poetry. As she explained, 'I understood that the method of Active Analysis strengthens the improvisatory nature of the actor, helps uncover the actor's individuality, and cleans the dust of time off literary works with wonderful images and characters in them' (Knebel 1967: 485). Thus, despite a Stalinist ban against it during the 1940s and 1950s, Active Analysis became her primary 'path in art' (ibid.). She used it to direct, taught it in her classes, and promoted it through her writings. In so doing, she not only kept Stanislavsky's last work alive, but also revitalised theatre in Russia.

Moreover, her efforts on behalf of Active Analysis best demonstrate how Stanis-lavsky's thinking can resonate in our postmodern world. Because Active Analysis, like vector analysis in physics, asks actors to map the dynamic forces of action conflicting with counteraction, theorist Patrice Pavis (2003) unknowingly supports its primary principle when he draws attention to performance as an art of 'vectorisation.'

To equate Knebel with the Moscow Art Theatre alone, however, would be to do her a disservice. In the 1930s she began directing in the shadow of the great theatricalist Vsevolod Meyerhold. In the 1950s, at Moscow's Central Children's Theatre, her ensemble of professional adult actors performed a wide repertory in various theatrical styles: classics by Shakespeare, Molière, and Griboedov, new plays on contemporary issues, traditionally scripted children's plays, and fairy tales devised entirely from the company's improvisations. For her, theatrical style was an expressive means, not an aesthetic programme. In the 1960s, when Russian director Adolf Shapiro enrolled in her class, he expected to find the 'psychological' method, usually associated with Stanislavsky. Instead of this 'insufficiently vivid [. . .], even boring' approach, Knebel's teaching 'unexpectedly took me prisoner for life' (Shapiro 1999: 133–35).

Despite Knebel's centrality in contemporary Russian theatre, little is known about her in the West. Several reasons may explain this relative obscurity. First, her directing career was ill timed. She began it when Soviet theatres employed teams of directors, called 'brigades,' to stage forgettable, propagandistic plays (Vladimirova 1991: 12); thus she was easy to miss in the long lists of names printed in the programmes. She then left directing at the very moment when Soviet audiences began to value the innovations of talented new directors (many of whom were her protégés). Second, she worked in a male-dominated profession where women's contributions were often undervalued. The press routinely ascribed her success

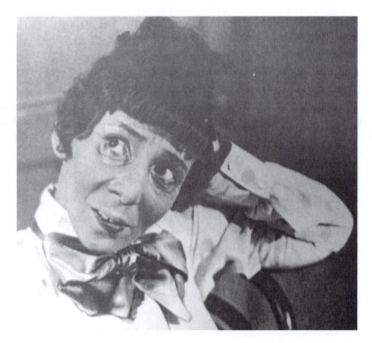

Figure 6.1 Knebel as Charlotta in Chekhov's *The Cherry Orchard* performed by the Moscow Art Theatre.

to the talents of her actors and designers. 'Being a woman director is not easy,' Knebel admits (1976: 248). In fact, she understates the context of hostility she faced on a daily basis. When the Moscow Art Theatre director Vasily Sakhnovsky proclaims that 'women who direct are not women,' he gives the majority opinion (Liadov 1998: 31). Third, unlike teachers in the West, who brand their pedagogy with their own names (i.e. the Strasberg, Adler, Meisner and Chubbuck techniques), Soviet teachers called whatever they taught the 'Stanislavsky System.' This cultural expectation, coupled with Knebel's dedication to Active Analysis, effectively masked her own innovations in actor training.

This chapter establishes Knebel's rightful place in theatre history by distinguishing her unique contributions from those of her teachers. Below, I explore the difficult cultural context in which she worked, sketch the tenets of her teaching, and describe two of her directorial successes.

A SOVIET LIFE IN THE THEATRE

Knebel forged her personal and artistic integrity from her country's rich culture and against its stormy political history. She called her childhood in Tsarist Russia 'happy, bourgeois' (Liadov 1998: 60); it had helped her to become an intelligent and well-educated person who brought the 'aroma of culture' into every room she entered (Shapiro 1999: 135). In her subsequent life as a Soviet citizen she encountered political suppression of her ideals; and by finding canny ways to evade attack, she developed an indomitable will and an independent heart. Knebel survived, said one colleague, because of her 'sober idealism' (Liadov 1998: 9).

Maria Knebel was born in Moscow on 19 May 1898 to a Jewish family who cultivated her love of literature and art. Her father, Iosif Nikolaevich Knebel, had arrived there as a penniless immigrant from Galicia, and by the time of her birth he had become Russia's preeminent publisher of art and children's books. The family's friends included many artists, scholars, and writers, among them the famed novelist Leo Tolstoy. No wonder she seemed to her later Soviet students like living history! 'She lived when Anton Pavlovich Chekhov lived,' said one (Kheifets 2001: 155).

Every Sunday, Maria's father took his three children to the Tretyakovsky Gallery, a treasure trove of Russian art, where they played a guessing game that he had invented. They would choose a painting and together imagine a story that would end with the image before them. Close observation was the only rule. In their stories, the children had to take account of all the observable details in the people's poses, the depicted landscapes, and the painter's choice of colours, brush strokes, and composition (Knebel 1967: 12–13). From her father's game, Knebel acquired a keen visual imagination that would later infuse her directing and teaching.

From the age of nineteen, when she began acting, until her death at eighty-seven on 1 June 1985, her career spanned all but six years of the complete history of the Soviet Union. Nearly seven decades of political turbulence, set in motion by Russia's governmental experiment in communism, impacted every phase of her adult life.

In 1917, the year of the Bolshevik revolution, Maria was a young adult choosing a profession. With a sharp, analytical mind and exceptional strategic skills in chess, she planned to study mathematics. While she was passionately attracted to acting, her father had discouraged her. She was too shy in demeanour and too short in stature; moreover, he added, she lacked the necessary good looks. One evening, however, a classmate took her to visit an acting studio recently opened in the home of the well-known actor Michael Chekhov. Having suffered a mental breakdown, he had decided to try his hand at teaching. Chekhov was so impressed with Knebel's abilities that he urged her to join. When she told him that she had decided against acting because of her looks, Chekhov assured her that she could find good character roles (Knebel 1967: 56). Thus, she studied with him from 1918 until 1921, when he returned to the stage. He taught her creative ways to develop her imagination through theatrical improvisations.

Knebel then enrolled in the school run by the Second Studio of the Moscow Art Theatre, where she placed Chekhov's imaginative training into the disciplined and logically sequenced System that Stanislavsky had by that time developed (Knebel 1967: 144). In May 1922, while still a student, she premiered as one of Stanislavsky's sons in the Moscow Art Theatre production of Henrik Ibsen's *An Enemy of the People*. In December, she became a member of the Second Studio's professional company, and her father now joined in applauding her choice of career (Knebel 1967: 154). Two years later, when the Second Studio was incorporated into its parent company, she joined the Moscow Art Theatre, where she performed until 1950. True to Michael Chekhov's prediction, she excelled in character roles, among them: the madwoman in Alexander Ostrovsky's *The Storm*, a dwarf in Johann Schiller's *The Robbers* (a non-speaking role which she herself had devised), Charlotta in Anton Chekhov's *The Cherry Orchard*, and the childish 'Sniffles' in Maurice Maeterlinck's *The Bluebird*.

During these decades, Knebel saw the Bolshevik Revolution of 1917 turn into a bitter civil war between the Tsarist forces and the communists. The family found themselves cold and hungry, making bread from potato peelings and reusing old coffee grounds (Knebel 1967: 27) when Iosif Knebel's publishing company was confiscated by the state. Maria now returned to the Tretyakovsky Gallery to earn extra money as a guide (Liadov 1998: 80).

Following Lenin's death in 1924, Joseph Stalin forcibly industrialised the largely agrarian nation through a series of Five Year Plans. In 1929, under the first of these, her family's apartment was requisitioned for communal use. Suddenly, Maria and her new husband found themselves living in one room, when strangers had been assigned living spaces in what had once been her family's private dwelling. No doubt, her divorce in 1932 resulted from these cramped and far from private living conditions (Liadov 1998: 81).

Far worse than this, however, was the bloody, ideological war that Stalin waged against the citizens of his country. He exiled, imprisoned, or executed anyone who seemed unwilling to accept his policies. The scope of his terror can best be expressed through a single statistic: on 12 December 1938 Stalin signed execution orders for 3,167 people (Ermolaev 1997: 51).

Knebel keenly felt the price of integrity in the Soviet Union. In 1928, an arrest warrant was issued for her first acting teacher, whose spiritual beliefs had been made illegal. After Michael Chekhov fled Russia, even the mention of his name became prohibited by the Soviet censors. Yet, Knebel would sometimes disappear from the classroom with trusted students in order to tell them about him in secrecy. By 1938, the Soviet propaganda machine had also turned her second mentor, Stanislavsky, into a false but unassailable theatrical icon of Socialist Realism. She saw his holistic System bled of its multi-dimensionality (see Chapter 1 and Carnicke 2008). Yet Knebel continued to use the System's full complexity, even when she could not name it. By the 1960s, she fought back, calling what had passed for the System under Stalinism a gross 'vulgarization' of her mentor's actual work (Knebel 1971: 109).

Stalin's terror invaded her family, too, when her brother Nikolai was deemed an enemy of the people during the 1940 anti-Semitic campaign. He was arrested in front of his mother and two sisters (Liadov 1998: 88–90). The branding of Maria's brother as an enemy meant that she too became dangerous company. 'In the corridors of the Moscow Art Theatre people would avoid meeting her, so that they would not be obliged to say hello,' recalled a former student (Liadov 1998: 100).

In 1950, Knebel herself became a casualty of Stalinist policy on the arts when she was abruptly fired by the Moscow Art Theatre's newly appointed Artistic Director, Mikhail Nikolaevich Kedrov (1893–1972). At the end of the 1949 season, an administrator had told Knebel that Kedrov would work only with those who considered themselves his 'students' (Knebel 1967: 477). Since she was Kedrov's age and had virtually the same theatrical experience as him, she thought the statement a joke. When she arrived at the theatre for the 1950 season, however, she found that her salary had been suspended and that all the plays in which she regularly performed, including The Cherry Orchard, had been pulled from the repertory. Kedrov's move against Knebel seemed consonant with the Art Theatre's pervasive anti-feminism and the Soviet Union's anti-Semitism, but Kedrov was also responding to Stalin's policies on the arts. To understand her dismissal as political, however, one must look more deeply at Knebel's developing artistic vision.

By the early 1930s, character roles were proving too limiting, and so, in her off hours, Knebel began directing at small experimental theatres in Moscow. In 1934, a group from Vsevolod Meyerhold's Theatre of the Revolution arranged for her first production at the Electric Energy Institute. From 1935 to 1941 she also worked at the Ermolova Studio Theatre, often co-directing with leading members of Meyerhold's company. This work gave her a facility with many different theatrical styles. It also prepared her to accept and generously encourage a full range of artistic tastes in her later students.

By 1936 she was juggling commitments as an actor at the Moscow Art Theatre and as a director at the Ermolova, when Stanislavsky unexpectedly summoned her to his home. At that time he was living in virtual isolation from the rest of the world, confined both by illness and Stalin's desire to keep the old man's theatrical experiments out of the public eye (see Chapter 1 and Carnicke 2008). Stanislavsky was allowed, however, to work with a select number of actors at his home. He invited Knebel to assist him in this work. Thus, she joined his Opera-Dramatic Studio, where she encountered Active Analysis. Taken with it from the first, she immediately began to apply it to her directing. As she did so, she consulted closely with Stanislavsky. For two years, he regularly reviewed her directorial notes and pushed her toward bolder and bolder usage of his latest technique (Knebel 1967: 264–84).

At first, she used Active Analysis only in conjunction with more traditional methods, but in 1940 she co-directed Shakespeare's As You Like It at the Ermolova using Active Analysis from conception through performance. Her co-director was Nikolai Khmelev, whom she considered among the best of the Moscow Art Theatre's actors (Knebel 1966: 140). They divided their work, as was customary at that time: she assisted the actors in their creation of characters and he staged the play. At first sceptical about her new rehearsal process, Khmelev was won over when he saw the results (Knebel 1967: 345). In 1942 she brought Active Analysis onto the main stage of the Moscow Art Theatre when Nemirovich-Danchenko asked her to co-direct with him. With her 1954 doctoral dissertation on Active Analysis she became its definitive spokesperson. By the end of the twentieth century, Knebel had come to be seen in Russia as the most clear-sighted witness to Stanislavsky's last experimental work.

Kedrov too had assisted at the Opera-Dramatic Studio, and with Stanislavsky's death in 1938, Kedrov proclaimed himself the old man's rightful heir by staging for public performance one of the last house projects, Molière's *Tartuffe*. When Kedrov was later appointed as the Moscow Art Theatre's new artistic director, Knebel's parity in experience and her advocacy of Active Analysis threatened his claim.

Not only was she telling a radically different story than he about what exactly had happened in the Studio, but her version was out of step with Soviet ideology on two counts. First, 'action' conflicting with 'counteraction' lies at the heart of Active Analysis. Yet, post Second World War policies on the arts had made conflict itself politically subversive. Soviet artists were enjoined to depict their society as having successfully transcended class conflicts. Critics, playwrights, and directors reacted with the 'theory of conflictlessness,' which proposed that in the Soviet Union's allegedly perfect society conflict had become irrelevant. Only competition between the better and the best was appropriate for dramatic works (see Bown 1998: 221–301). Second, Active Analysis depends on the close interplay of mind, body, and spirit in performance. In other words, Active Analysis embraces the whole of Stanislavsky's psychophysical technique. Knebel taught actors to use every aspect of their artistic beings, from soul to finger tips, as they embodied the playwright's words. Not only did this approach defy atheistic Marxist philosophy by embracing spiritual dimensions in art, but Knebel's term for the rehearsal process stressed the actor's holistic usage of body through 'action' and mind through 'analysis.'

In Kedrov's politically correct version, Stanislavsky had finally arrived at a scientifically accurate approach to acting, which de-emphasised conflict and stressed the logical sequence of physical actions. This version suited communist teleology and Marxist materialism. His story, therefore, better accommodated the tenor of the times. Kedrov also provided an *imprimatur* for his version, calling it the 'Method of Physical Actions'.[2]

Knebel's abrupt firing from the Moscow Art Theatre did not mean her abandonment of Active Analysis. She vowed to keep 'the secret cult of knowledge' alive (Knebel 1968: 46); and she found a haven for it in children's theatre. By the 1940s theatre for young audiences had become an established Soviet institution, fully subsidised and professionally staffed with well-trained adult actors and directors. These theatres could sometimes escape the bounds of strict Socialist Realism by staging fantasies in theatricalist styles, because their audiences were children who expected fairy tales. As Russian theatre scholar Anatoly Smeliansky observes, during the darkest of times 'the artistic flame [. . .] was kept alive in various theatrical catacombs,' not the least of which were children's theatres 'where, immediately after the death of Stalin, the revival of the Russian stage would begin' (1999: 5–6). Moscow's Central Children's Theatre fostered careers for many innovative theatrical directors, Knebel being chief among them.

She began directing at the Central Children's Theatre in 1950 and became its Artistic Director in 1955. Her usual rehearsal method was, of course, Active Analysis; and she used it to develop productions of unusual candour. She had rejected the romantic notion that children are tender and innocent beings. 'I strove to speak with children through the language of great art,' she writes, 'without the babbling condescension that could be heard loudly in other children's theatres during those years in which the "theory of conflictlessness" was blossoming' (Knebel 1967: 484). Knebel staged classics (such as Griboedov's *Woe from Wit* in 1951 and Molière's *Bourgeois Gentilhomme* in 1954), dramatic adaptations of novels (including Gogol's *Dead Souls* in 1952 and Dickens' *Oliver Twist* in 1956), fairy tales (like *The Little Humpbacked*

Horse in 1952 and *The Magic Blossom* in 1958), and contemporary plays on current issues (like Pogodin's controversial treatment of Nikita Khrushchev's agricultural reforms in *We Three Went to the Virgin Lands* in 1955).

Her consistently high artistic standards also led her to employ outstanding actors, innovative directors, and bold young playwrights. A roster of those she hired reads like a who's who of Soviet theatrical talent in the latter half of the twentieth century. No wonder Knebel's seemingly modest children's enterprise became one of the most popular theatres in Moscow. In 1958, this body of work earned her the title of National Artist of the Russian Republic of the USSR.

As Stalin's terror abated and Khrushchev began a 'thaw' in the arts, Knebel turned to full-time teaching. She had taught part time since 1936, when assisting Stanislavsky meant teaching groups of actors under his supervision. In 1943, Nemirovich-Danchenko added her to the acting faculty of the newly created Studio-School of the Moscow Art Theatre. In 1948 she formed a nearly legendary teaching partnership with the like-minded director, Aleksei Dmitrievich Popov (1892–1961). She had first met Popov in 1934, when he had challenged her to try directing. Over the years, they co-directed a number of productions, co-taught a class at Russia's State Institute of Theatre Arts (GITIS), and shared passionate discussions about the aesthetics of theatre (Knebel 1967: 289–91). In 1961, Knebel left the Central Children's Theatre in order to accept the chairmanship of the directing programme at GITIS.

As she taught, she also wrote. By 1985 she had published six books and more than a hundred articles on her teachers and their pedagogy. During her last years, Mikhail Gorbachev's political reforms (known as *glasnost*) allowed her to risk something that she had long hoped to do – to bring the name and methods of her first teacher back to his homeland. She collected Michael Chekhov's writings from around the world to assemble the first-ever Russian-language edition of his works (1986). Sadly, she did not live to see this two-volume set appear in print.

The 'sober idealism' (Liadov 1998: 9) that had helped her survive as an actor and director from the 1930s through the 1950s also sustained her during her years as teacher and writer. In her sixties, when appointed chair of directing at GITIS, she joined the Communist Party for the first time. She needed this political credential for her new job because, as a colleague explains, 'A party membership was like a school child's corridor pass, like a legal residence permit, like proof of loyalty' (Liadov 1998: 55). As a writer, too, Knebel understood the stringency of Soviet censorship. Thus, without betraying her principles, she was careful to quote Marxist philosophy and use the rhetoric of Socialist Realism wherever she could in order to ensure that her divergent ideas got past the censor's eye.[3] She relied on her readers to read between the censored lines for dissident innuendos, a kind of reading that had become a normal part of Soviet culture (Carnicke 2008: Chapter 6). In her eighties, when Knebel received an award from the Red Army, she struggled (as she did in her writings), to find words that were both grateful and truthful. As she accepted her award, she thanked, not the Army, but her teachers (Liadov 1998: 8).

Just as Knebel kept writing until shortly before her death, so too did she continue to teach. Her students carried her up to her usual third-floor classroom at GITIS when she could no longer climb the stairs. Her lively spirit during these last years can be felt in an anecdote, told by director Leonid Kheifets, who was at that time her student. One day, he noticed a small tear in her sleeve and inadvertently remarked upon it. At the next class she responded by donning a stylish outfit and French perfume, mischievously eying him while telling her students that she had replenished her wardrobe. She was eighty-six at the time (Kheifets 2001: 156–57). Throughout her career, her generosity in supporting the individual talents and varying tastes of her students made her seem, even into her eighties, 'a contemporary person, never "old-fashioned" ' (Liadov 1998: 43).

THE KNEBEL TECHNIQUE

Knebel developed her own unique approach to theatre by synthesising theatrical principles she had encountered in the Moscow Art Theatre tradition.

From Michael Chekhov she learned that acting is deeply improvisatory and inseparable from the actor's imagination. He taught her that in any performance, however carefully scripted and blocked it may be, an actor can still retain an improvisatory approach toward the role, what she would call the actor's 'improvisatory state of mind.' During 1921–22, she observed him perform Khlestakov in Stanislavsky's production of Gogol's *The Inspector General*, and she noticed that Chekhov added something new and surprising at each performance without changing text or blocking. She concluded that Chekhov was 'a genius of improvisation' (Knebel 1995a: 28). 'One of the secrets of his art,' she observes, 'and, in fact, the most important principle behind creativity, is the actor's improvisatory state of mind in the role' (Knebel 1995b: 17). Moreover, she understood that this state of mind springs from the actor's imagination. In short, Chekhov taught Knebel not only to free her own imagination but to understand how an actor's fantasy can prompt creativity within the strictures of written texts and tightly directed productions.

At the Second Studio's School, Knebel placed Chekhov's lessons into Stanislavsky's disciplined training programme.[4] She now moved progressively, through preparatory exercises, into focused work on the creation of roles. Then, at the Opera-Dramatic Studio, Knebel learned directly from Stanislavsky how to bring her Chekhovian angle of vision to the rehearsal of texts through Active Analysis. She clearly saw that Stanislavsky had designed his last theatrical experiments 'to create for the actor an improvisatory state of mind and body within the rigid framework of first-class dramatic material' (Knebel 1967: 276). Given the synergy that she found between Chekhov's and Stanislavsky's insights on performance, is it any wonder that Knebel adopted Active Analysis as the centrepiece of her own practice?

Finally, from Nemirovich-Danchenko, whose theatrical sensibility sprang from playwriting, Knebel saw how close readings of great literature can enhance actors' imaginations. Moreover, she intuited an important link between the processes of acting and writing. Through Active Analysis she watched actors recapitulate the writing process as they rehearsed. By improvising the dynamic structures of actions and counteractions that undergird dramatic scenes, actors discover the need for dramatists' words; in effect, they write the play anew every time they perform. When Knebel tells actors that they 'draft' and 're-draft' their performances through their improvisations (Knebel 1971: 53), she encodes this deep insight in the language of her technique. While Danchenko and Stanislavsky had themselves become sadly estranged from each other (Carnicke 2008), their estrangement is healed through Knebel. 'In my own work,' she writes, 'I could not separate Stanislavsky and Nemirovich-Danchenko,' and 'over the years their teachings became more and more interconnected' (Knebel 1967: 485).

Knebel's synthesis of these influences made her a charismatic director and teacher in her own right. Undoubtedly we would have called her unique approach 'The Knebel Technique' had she lived in the West. But, as a Soviet citizen, it was expected that she should teach the officially sanctioned curriculum. Therefore, in Russia her name is unsurprisingly linked to Stanislavsky's. She herself contributed to this linkage by writing a great deal about him and scrupulously describing the specifics of his System. When the innovative director Anatoly Efros baldly states that, having studied the Stanislavsky System for years, 'I actually understood what this method was in practice only when I came into contact with Maria Osipovna Knebel' (Efros 1993: 139), he echoes the common Russian sentiment, even as he distinguishes her from other, less talented teachers.

Yet, 'The Knebel Technique' is not very difficult to find. One need look no farther than her book *The Poetry of Pedagogy* (1976), which is at once a useful manual and deeply personal. She had long resisted writing about her own methods, despite many requests for her to do so. In her view, teaching is as necessarily improvisatory as acting and therefore as mutable as mercury. When she finally conceded, she felt that she had to give more than practical information. Of course, she describes the progression of her curriculum, sets forth many different types of exercises, and demonstrates her use of Active Analysis, but she also depicts her students as they work and as they interact with her and with each other. We listen, as well, to her philosophical musings about theatre as an art and about the challenges of pursuing it as a profession. In short, she offers the kind of information that distinguishes her from other teachers. I base the following brief outline of her practice on this personalised book.

THE CURRICULUM

Knebel was most renowned for her work with directors, who, 'as a rule, "speak" to audiences not through themselves, but through actors' (Knebel' 1976: 50). Consequently, she believed that directors need 'to understand the actor and know the laws of acting, its nature, its complexities, etc.' (Knebel 1976: 53). Moreover, because 'directors need all the skills that actors need' (Knebel 1976: 56) her curriculum for directing serves actors as well.[5]

Part I: Fundamentals of acting

The first two years of Knebel's programme closely parallel exercises from the Stanislavsky System (see Chapter 1), with some notable interventions from Michael Chekhov and Vladimir Nemirovich-Danchenko.

1   She begins by interrogating Stanislavsky's notion of the 'super-superobjective' (or the 'super-supertask') because she believes that no theatrical work of value can be conducted without answering a single foundational question: 'Why stage this play today?' (Knebel 1976: 41).

2   She then spends significant time developing skills of 'observation' and 'concentration.' She focuses especially on how an actor's 'objects of attention' can be simultaneously 'outer' (material and physical) and 'inner' (mental, psychological, and spiritual). Moreover, as she teaches students to identify and attend to the many points of focus in any given scene, she also asks them to select from these many 'objects of attention' a single 'main object.' She takes this latter term from Nemirovich-Danchenko's notion that every scene has a 'main

object' that can be distinguished from the many secondary ones that also vie for an actor's attention during performance. By asking students to distinguish a 'main object,' Knebel helps them isolate what is most important in a given scene, and thus she trains them to tell dramatic stories cleanly and clearly (Knebel 1976: 350).

3   Her exercises on 'communication' depend upon the presumption that people send and receive invisible, but palpable rays of energy whenever they communicate with each other. Both Stanislavsky and Michael Chekhov had used this notion of 'radiation' to great effect. In fact, we know many of their exercises on rays because Knebel taught them. In addition, she also uses exercises in which the actor tosses a ball to her partner as she speaks, and the partner throws it back as he answers. The different ways in which the ball can be pitched make students physically aware of the dynamics of their interactions. She had learned this exercise from Michael Chekhov (Knebel 1976: 157–58).

4   Finally, she turns to issues of 'tempo-rhythm,' which she learned to value from Stanislavsky. The very medium of theatrical art, she observes, 'is composed of moments of differing durations and impacts.' Therefore, performance always juggles with 'the rhythms of time' (Knebel 1976: 102). In order to experience how changing perspectives on time can evoke different emotional sensations, she would ask students to perform simple activities (combing their hair, buttoning a coat, etc.) using different speeds and varying rhythms (Knebel 1976 103).

To these familiar exercises, Knebel adds unique emphases of her own. The two most prominent of these involve visual imagination and psychophysical sensibility.

1   'An entire stage of our work on visual attention involves the study of paintings,' she writes. 'I spare neither effort, nor time, piously believing that the study of visual arts is an indispensable condition of our profession' (Knebel 1976: 77). In short, she uses visual arts extensively to train acting skills. In fact, some of her exercises recall the game her father had invented at the Tretyakovsky Gallery. Consider the following examples.

- Visit a local museum, choose a painting to study, and observe it at length. In class, describe the painting in such detail that your classmates can visualise it along with you (Knebel 1976: 56). This exercise increases the power of observation, the ability to remember what has been observed, and the skill of conjuring up an absent object.
- Now turn the classroom into a virtual museum, perhaps the Louvre, by performing a group improvisation. Imaginatively place on the museum's walls all the paintings that you and your classmates have observed and shared with each other in class. As you walk through this museum, stopping to view the various paintings and to discuss them with each other, you will exercise your recall and your ability to recreate the imaginative work that you and your classmates have previously done (Knebel 1976: 165).
- Choose a portrait and observe the person's pose, or, as Knebel puts it, the 'mise en scène [blocking] of the body' (Knebel 1976: 81). Using your observations, speculate about the person's occupation, general psychology, and, more specifically, about the momentary mood and

physical state expressed in the portrait. In class, show the portrait by taking the pose into your own body (Knebel 1976: 80–82). This exercise develops the skill of characterisation in a number of ways. By understanding how a physical pose suggests an inner life, students interrogate Nemirovich-Danchenko's notion of a 'seed,' from which a dramatic role can grow. Knebel also cites as source Michael Chekhov, who taught that people's psychological 'centres' of gravity can be found in various areas of their physical bodies, and that actors can conjure up characters' 'imaginary bodies' and then step into these, as if into suits of clothes (Knebel 1976: 220–22).

- Go to the window and observe a passer-by with the same careful attention that you used earlier when you observed the portrait. Come back from the window and take the passer-by into your own body (Knebel 1976: 216–18). Notice that this exercise limits the amount of time during which observation can occur, and yet demands the same level of recall from the actor who recreates what has been observed.

When Knebel extends her classes beyond acting, into directing, she continues to use paintings to provoke students into using their visual imaginations richly. For example, she asks each young director to determine the story behind a complex painting, and then to stage a classroom improvisation which enacts the story. The exercise ends when the actors have recreated the image in the painting (Knebel 1976: 28).

2   Like Stanislavsky and Chekhov, Knebel defines the actor's psychophysical technique as the holistic use of body, mind, and soul. But in so doing, she zeroes in on the intrinsic complexity of acting in ways that go beyond her mentors' teachings. She sees true value in the artist's embrace of complexity, and often criticises 'contemporary theatre practice' for its propensity to over-simplify. 'Sometimes [. . .] we dismiss that which is complex,' she writes; and such dismissal brings distortion. 'By being reduced to the simplistic, that which is complex loses its true scope' (Knebel 1995a: 22). She pointedly blames this reductive process on the banning of Chekhov's spiritual ideas about acting and on the Sovietisation of Stanislavsky's System. In her classes she nurtures holistic practice by making it crystal clear that every exercise demands from actors more than one skill.

- When teaching Nemirovich-Danchenko's approach to 'inner monologue' (in which students are asked to create the specific thoughts that provoke their characters' speech) Knebel asks students to connect their characters' thoughts to a host of dramatic matters: 'the given circumstances' of the play, the character's physical state during the thought process, the scene's 'tempo-rhythm,' etc. 'A person's train of thought,' she notes, 'always depends upon a whole series of issues, each in its turn influencing physicality and behaviour' (Knebel 1976: 149).
- Do something simple (sew on a button, set a table, comb your hair, etc.), and use this activity to mask a specific attitude toward your partner (anger, disdain, a desire to manipulate, a desire to avoid, etc.). While one partner performs the activity, the other watches and listens intently. As the actors notice the many thoughts that arise naturally from their work (some that assist and some that hinder their efforts), each experiences the formation of a continuous and complex inner monologue. This exercise

allows actors to establish the connection between attention and inner monologue, and thereby also understand how an apparently simple task prompts a complex state of interaction (Knebel 1976: 126–27).

- Knebel introduces beginning students to Stanislavsky's complex technique of 'adaptation,' whereby actors use specific mental and physical adjustments in the role to communicate an action or personality trait more clearly to their partners and spectators (Carnicke 2008: 213). In doing so, she goes against the prevalent wisdom of her peers, who regularly taught this notion to advanced students only. 'Must students in a first course think about this concept?' Knebel asks and then answers, 'Yes, absolutely. Because one must grasp the complexity of Stanislavsky's System from the first' (Knebel 1976: 118).

Part II: Active Analysis for actors and directors

In the last two years of Knebel's curriculum, students apply acting fundamentals to the Active Analysis of plays (see Chapter 1 and Carnicke 2008: chapter 10). Through this discrete technique, Knebel teaches the various ways in which art reflects and reshapes life. She cautions actors and directors alike against assuming that art bears a simple relationship to reality.

> Theatrical art does not simply copy life; art creates its own forms, its own lines, colours and thoughts. [. . .] The talented person, who takes life in, does not copy life in art, but unfailingly forges it anew in the crucible of his or her own thoughts, feelings, sufferings, and dreams.
>
> (Knebel 1976: 209–10).

Moreover, by using Active Analysis on a variety of dramatic genres and styles, she demonstrates the potential richness of dramatic forms.

At this stage of training, Knebel insists that her students remain unconcerned with how they might fit into *a priori* professional expectations. In her classes, for example, casting proceeds without regard to type. Men can play women, and women men; and anyone can play any age or type, as long as they can respond to their roles. Knebel asks only that they explore how performance shapes human experience, communicates thoughts, and tells stories. This avowedly non-professional approach kept her students from accepting as given the prevalent theatrical norms. No wonder so many of them broke new artistic ground!

In these last two years of training, the curriculum for actors and directors begins to diverge. Actors now create roles by actively analysing excerpts from a wide variety of plays, as they learn to create a range of characters in collaboration with their partners. In contrast, directors work on complete plays, in order to learn how to tell full stories. While previously directors learned acting so that they would understand the primary medium of their work, they now use their performance skills to assist actors. Like musical conductors, 'who hear each separate instrument in the orchestra and know how to align each with the whole' (Knebel 1976: 53), directors now learn to 'stand at a distance from the work being created by each separate actor, and watch as if in the audience' (Knebel 1976: 50).

In practice, Active Analysis consists of two interrelated processes. The first entails an objective 'examination of the facts' of the play. Included in this process are historical research and close readings of each scene for its dynamic structure. In this last item lies the true heart of Active Analysis; actors determine how a scene's main 'event' is created by the collision of an impelling 'action' and a resisting 'counter-action.' Knebel warns, however, that this determination must take into account more than story and 'given circumstances'; it must also pay strict attention to how characters speak, what style of language the playwright uses, and how specific words in the text can prompt the imagination (Knebel 1976: 332–36). Furthermore, objective examination does not mean that students dismiss their subjective reactions; rather they begin to strike a balance between objectivity and their personal passions. 'In point of fact,' Knebel observes, 'the very sense behind this technique is that every director brings to the process what is most precious and interesting to him or her as an artist' (Knebel 1976: 310).

The second process involves 'études' (French for 'studies,' or, in more common theatrical language, 'improvisations'), through which actors test their discoveries and hypotheses about the play. Before memorising a scene the actors improvise its dynamic structure of 'action' and 'counteraction' in order to see whether the 'event' that they expect will indeed occur. In their 'études' they sometimes paraphrase, sometimes perform silently, and sometimes use fragments of text that they remember. If their improvisation does not result in the appropriate 'event' they re-examine the facts and try another 'étude.' When the 'event' does occur, they further refine it through a re-examination of the facts. They repeat this oscillation between text and improvisation until the playwright's words, rhythms, images, and style emerge from their work. Knebel notes that études 'teach actors to be bold, to use specific actions, and to welcome sudden and unexpected reactions. The very method speaks to the actor's improvisatory state of being in performance' (Knebel 1976: 344).

Taken together, the two inseparable processes of Active Analysis tap the holistic nature of acting. As actors move from reading to improvising, and from improvising back to reading, they use their minds and bodies, emotions and spirits. Only when they understand the dynamics of a scene intellectually, physically, and emotionally do they memorise the text. At this point, however, actors often find that the text is already inside them.

In Active Analysis, directors look for the overall shape of the play by identifying how its various 'events' differ from each other in intensity and importance. In other words, they examine how a play tells its story. They define the event which 'incites' the story; they distinguish 'main events' from 'secondary' ones; they determine how various characters might interpret the same events differently, thus choosing different 'actions' under the same 'given circumstances.' As Knebel says, the 'chain of events' becomes a 'magnet, which draws out of the play its complexity and perspectives' (Knebel 1976: 303).

Her curriculum concludes with the staging of a new play, performed before its author and the entire GITIS faculty.

ACTIVE ANALYSIS IN PRODUCTION

The Magic Blossom

With few exceptions, Knebel had directed all her productions using Active Analysis, and at the Central Children's Theatre she also experimented with using her preferred

Figure 6.2 Knebel's production of *The Magic Blossom* at the Central Children's Theatre, Moscow.

technique to write new plays. For her 1952 production of *The Little Humpbacked Horse*, based on Pyotr Ershov's 1834 fairy tale poem, she used the company's études to assist playwright P.G. Malierevsky in fashioning his dramatic adaptation (Knebel 1967: 500–508). In 1958, Knebel went even further with the dramatisation of a Chinese fairy tale, *The Magic Blossom*, for which she had no formal text at all. 'If Active Analysis had been able to help us as directors and actors with analysing classical works and Soviet plays, and if for *The Little Humpbacked Horse* it had helped not only us but also the playwright to refine conflicts and psychological developments,' she reasoned, then why not 'in this instance, use it to create the entire play?' (Knebel 1967: 508).

    After each rehearsal, Knebel and her assistant director would record dialogue that had emerged from that day's improvisations. In addition, Knebel hired a specialist in Chinese theatrical dance to inform the company's work. As the cast learned the new physical vocabulary, they incorporated its style into their études. 'As we got to the essence of the fairy tale,' she observed, 'we tried bolder and more varied forms of expression' (Knebel 1967: 509). The resulting production employed a unique inter-weaving of language, dance, and pantomime. As critic Pavel Markov wrote, 'Theatrical stylisation had become fairy tale reality' (Vladimirova 1991: 133).

The Cherry Orchard

Knebel's 1965 staging of Anton Chekhov's classic play is among her most notable productions. The play itself had come to mean a great deal to her; so much so that, despite her retirement from directing four years earlier, she could not resist the invitation from her late co-teacher's son, Andrey Popov, to revisit it at the Theatre of the Soviet Army. Moreover, when the Abbey Theatre in Dublin invited her to direct in

1968 (an occasion that allowed her to travel abroad for the first and only time), she chose to re-create her 1965 production with the Irish actors (Knebel 1969).

Important memories coalesced around this play. First, at the age of ten, she wept after viewing Stanislavsky's famed production at the Moscow Art Theatre. An usher, who had worked there since the production's premiere in 1904, consoled her: 'There's no need to cry! Anton Pavlovich called his play a comedy' (Knebel 1967: 207–8). But, Knebel recalls that, 'These weren't tears of sadness. The presence of art had stirred my soul even as a child' (Ryzhova 1967: 64).

Second, in 1934, as a member of the Art Theatre's company, Knebel took advantage of an unusual custom whereby actors could initiate auditions for roles they wished to play in the current repertoire by preparing a scene for the company's co-founders. She decided to audition for Charlotta. But finding a discrete scene from *The Cherry Orchard* proved impossible, since the eccentric governess is so fully inter-woven into the fabric of the play. Knebel prepared instead the 'seed' of Charlotta's character and, at the audition, performed a magic show. Stanislavsky was so taken with Knebel's work that he stepped into the audition as Gaev (his role in the play), asking Charlotta questions about her life and debating with her about the politics that informed the play. Suddenly, Gaev invited Charlotta to play his favourite game of billiards (Knebel 1967: 261). The audition ended when the game was finished. Knebel won the role and played Charlotta 'incomparably' (Rozov 1977: 60) for nearly twenty years, until her wrenching dismissal from the company. Indeed, her final appearance at the Moscow Art Theatre was as Charlotta. 'I can still recall [Stanislavsky's] production not only in my mind but in my muscles,' she wrote in the 1960s (Knebel 1967: 569).

In revisiting *The Cherry Orchard*, however, she did not want to recreate the familiar production. She wanted to speak to her contemporaries about a process of renewal that she recognised in the play:

> Chekhov understood very well what it means to lose that which you infinitely love. [. . .] Each of us has lost and will lose our own 'cherry orchard.' Each of us will try to hold on to it. And in the moment

Figure 6.3 Knebel at GITIS.

[of loss ...] it seems to us that we have lost everything. But that is precisely when we can find ahead of us a life that is a thousand times richer than what we have lost.

(Knebel 1967: 570)

Dismissal from the Moscow Art Theatre was her 'cherry orchard'; and only by turning her back on her first company could she find her own voice as an artist at the Central Children's Theatre. In her autobiography (written at about the same time that she was staging *The Cherry Orchard*), she describes her experience in just this way:

Very slowly and gradually did I come to realize that what was most important and dear to me were not the walls of the Moscow Art Theatre, but what I had taken from within them. Having lost my home, I found it within myself. . . . And only after understanding that with all my soul, with all my being, did I feel free and able to work.

(Knebel 1967: 484)

With the help of her designer (Yury Pimenov), Knebel used her autobiographical insight to break away from an illusionist set, replacing the trees of the orchard and the walls of the house with a kaleidoscope of projected images that suggested both the play's locales and the Chekhovian literary landscape (Loehlin 2007: 149).

Knebel also positioned the widow and landowner, Lyubov Ranevskaya, as the production's centrifugal force. Russian theatre critic Konstantin Rudnitsky saw Ranevskaya as a 'noble, pure, strong and wilful woman, admirable, to be sure, but not without her flaws' (Rudnitskii 1974: 143). Through this characterisation, Knebel seems to describe herself. Not only had she, too, lost a home, but she, too, was a complex woman. As theatre historian Zoia Vladimirova writes, 'For all Knebel's generosity of soul, one can't say that she was a gentle angel. She could be sharp and sarcastic, unflagging in her convictions.' But, to her credit, she did not blame her enemies. She simply moved on, because she 'understood that it is stupid to bear a grudge, to nurse it, if one can overcome it, especially when one can create something equally dear to the offended and the offender' (Vladmirova 1991: 20). In short, Knebel invested her production of *The Cherry Orchard* with this complex sensibility and offered through the play optimistic advice about dealing with life's difficulties.

CONCLUSION

It is time for the West to discover Russia's most important theatrical voice since Stanislavsky.

Not only does Maria Knebel serve as an admirable model of a theatrical artist who remained true to her calling in tough times, but, as an eye-witness to major theatrical developments from the turn of the twentieth century to the century's end she can teach us much that is still unknown about the history of the globally famous Moscow Art Theatre tradition. Through her, actors and directors can see clearly how Michael Chekhov did not so much depart from Stanislavsky as build upon his teacher's holistic approach to theatre. Moreover, through Knebel we learn that Stanislavsky shared with Michael Chekhov a deeply held belief in the transcendent power of theatre, a belief that, like Chekhov's, was actively quashed by the Soviets.

Through Knebel, we can also learn much about the efficacy of Nemirovich-Danchenko's overlooked work with actors. While he and Stanislavsky are famous for their differences in artistic taste and personal proclivities, Knebel demonstrates how key aspects of the Stanislavsky System (like the inner monologue) began with Nemirovich-Danchenko.

Yet, what most resonates for me in the Knebel Technique is how easily I see the actors in my own classes adapt it to the conditions in which they work. Her perspective on art's complex relationship with reality allows artists of different stripes to use her tools for a diversity of theatrical styles. The innovative, non-traditional casting that she used in her classes offers a model for breaking down gender and racial typecasting. And most importantly, her teachings on Active Analysis offer many valuable and flexible tools to actors and directors who must now work across different performance media (stage, film, television, and internet). Whatever artistic style we might prefer and in whatever venue we might choose to work, Knebel reminds us that acting is a vital and important art form that should be protected and treasured into the twenty-first century.

Notes

1 Research was sponsored in part by the American Society for Theatre Research, the US National Endowment for the Humanities, and the Fund for Advancing Scholarship in the Humanities and Social Sciences (University of Southern California).
2 Kedrov cites unpublished manuscripts as his source for the term, in 'To Preserve the Legacy of Stanislavsky Means to Develop It' (1956). The manuscripts were then published in *Teatr* (September 1950, No. 11, 48–52) as K.S. Stanislavskii, 'O fizicheskikh deistviiakh: iz neo-publikovannykh materialov' ['On Physical Actions: From Unpublished Materials']. In 1961, Elizabeth Reynolds Hapgood translated some of these for Constantin Stanislavski, *Creating a Role* (New York: Theatre Arts Books). See Chapter 1 above for more on the distinction between The Method of Physical Actions and Active Analysis.
3 In his abridged French edition of Knebel's writings (Knebel 2006), Anatoly Vasiliev cuts Knebel's concessions to Soviet censorship.
4 When Knebel studied with Chekhov, he had not yet developed a systematic approach for actor training. He would only do so after he emigrated from Russia.
5 After the fall of the Soviet Union, GITIS was renamed the Russian Academy of Theatre Arts (RATI), but the curriculum that Knebel developed there (including the close link between actor and director training) is still taught there.

Bibliography

I use Library of Congress transliteration in the references and bibliography, but anglicise Russian names in the chapter's text. All translations are my own, unless otherwise specified.

Bown, Matthew Cullern (1998) 'Conflictlessness', in *Socialist Realist Painting*, New Haven: Yale University Press: 221–301.
Carnicke, Sharon Marie (2008) *Stanislavsky in Focus: An Acting Master for the Twenty-First Century*, second edition, London: Routledge.
Efros, Anatolii (1993) *Repetitsiia – liubov' moia* [*Rehearsals – My Passion*], Moscow: Panos.
Ermolaev, Herman (1997) *Censorship in Soviet Literature: 1917–1991*, New York: Rowman and Littlefield Publishers, Inc.
Kedrov, M.N. (1956) 'Khranit' nasledie Stanislavskogo – eto znachit razvivat' ego' ['To Preserve the Legacy of Stanislavsky Means to Develop It'], *Ezhegodnik MKhAT-a: 1951–1952* [*The Year-book of The Moscow Art Theatre: 1951–2*], Moscow: MKhAT: 99–116.

Kheifets, Leonid (2001) *Prizvanie* [*My Calling*], Moscow: GITIS.

Knebel, M.O. (1954) *Slovo O Tvorchestve Aktera* [*The Word in the Actor's Creativity*] Moscow: VTO. This edition was republished by GITIS in Moscow in 2009.

—— (1995a) 'Mikhail Chekhov ob iskusstve aktera' ['Michael Chekhov about the Actor's Art'], in M.A. Chekhov, *Literaturnoe nasledie* [*Literary Heritage*], ed. M.O Knebel', Vol. II, second edition, Moscow: Iskusstvo: 5–30.

—— (1995b) 'O Mikhaile Chekhove i ego tvorcheskom nasledii' ['About Michael Chekhov and his Artistic Heritage'], in M.A. Chekhov, *Literaturnoe nasledie* [*Literary Heritage*], ed. M.O Knebel', Vol. I, second edition, Moscow: Iskusstvo: 9–33.

—— (1966) *Shkola Rezhissury Nemirovicha-Danchenko* [*The Directing School of Nemirovich-Danchenko*], Moscow: Iskusstvo.

—— (1967) *Vsia Zhizn'* [*All of Life*], Moscow: VTO.

—— (1968) 'Vysokaia prostota' ['Superior Simplicity'], *Teatr*, 9: 46–49.

—— (1969) 'Vyshnevyi sad v Irlandii' ['The Cherry Orchard in Ireland'], *Teatr*, 5: 158–66.

—— (1971) *O Tom, Chto Mne Kazhetsia Osobenno Vazhnym* [*That Which Seems Most Important to Me*], Moscow: Iskusstvo.

—— (1976) *Poeziia Pedagogiki* [*The Poetry of Pedagogy*], Moscow: VTO.

—— (2006) *L'Analyse-Action* [*Active Analysis*], ed. Anatoli Vassiliev, Paris: Actes Sud-Papiers.

Liadov, V. I. (ed.) (1998) *O M. O. Knebel'* [*About M. O. Knebel*], Moscow: no publisher.

Loehlin, James N. (2007) *Chekhov: The Cherry Orchard*, Cambridge: Cambridge University Press.

Pavis, Patrice (2003) *Analysing Performance*, trans. David Williams, Ann Arbor: University of Michigan Press.

Rozov, Viktor (1977) 'Rezhisser, kotorogo ia liubliu' ['A Director Whom I Love'], *Avrora* [*Aurora*], 1: 60–66.

Rudnitskii, K. (1974) *Spektakli raznykh let* [*Productions from Various Years*], Moscow: Iskusstvo.

Ryzhova, Valentina Fedorovna (1967) *Put' k spektakliu* [*The Path toward Productions*], Moscow: Iskusstvo: 56–92.

Shapiro, Adol'f (1999) *Kak zakryvalsia zanaves* [*How the Curtain Opens*], Moscow: Novoe literaturnoe obozrenie.

Smeliansky, Anatoly (1999) *The Russian Theatre After Stalin*, trans. Patrick Miles, Cambridge: Cambridge University Press.

Vladimirova, Z.V. (1991) *M. O. Knebel'*, Moscow: Iskusstvo.

Chapter 7

Peter Thomson

BRECHT AND ACTOR TRAINING: ON WHOSE BEHALF DO WE ACT?

CONTEXT

BRECHT WAS SIXTEEN YEARS old and living in his parents' home in Augsburg when the Archduke Franz Ferdinand was assassinated in remote Sarajevo. He was twenty when the war that was the consequence of that untidy assassination ended. The blustering, posturing adolescent of 1914 was, by 1918, an angry young man. Anger is something that must always come into the reckoning when Brecht's theatrical career is under scrutiny. Anger at the way things are provides the impetus for political or social campaigning, and Brecht's approach to acting cannot properly be divorced from his campaign to change the world. That campaign found its eventual rationale in Marxism, but it began with the impulse to contradict. Given the conventional Christian upbringing of a bourgeois provincial in traditionally Protestant Augsburg, Brecht responded with confrontational pragmatism:

> What business have they got putting that stuff about Truth in the catechism
> If one's not allowed to say what is?
>
> (Brecht 1976b: 16)

These are the concluding lines of a poem written shortly after his twentieth birthday and obliquely addressed to his mother – worried about his dirty linen and dirtier language. It was time for Brecht to get away from Augsburg into the headier atmosphere of Bavaria's cultural capital, Munich. In the months following the signing of the Armistice on 11 November 1918, he travelled regularly between Augsburg and Munich, where he was trying to establish a literary foothold. It was a period of extraordinary political turmoil in Bavaria, and Brecht was caught up in it.

The King of Bavaria had abdicated a day before the German Kaiser, and a revolution designed to sever the link between Bavaria and Prussia (Munich and Berlin) had established a new government, led by a socialist intellectual, Kurt Eisner. Eisner's admirable attempts to inaugurate a new order in Bavaria were thwarted by reactionary nationalists, on the one hand, and left-wing revolutionaries, on the other. He was too radical; he was not radical enough. On 21 February 1919, shortly after making a speech at the reconstituted Second International in Berne, Eisner was shot dead by a young aristocrat. In illogical revenge, his deputy was shot and severely wounded by a communist worker at the opening session of the Bavarian parliament. In the chaos that followed, Munich was briefly in the hands of a socialist soviet, but the soviet was ousted by the better-programmed communist faction. Predictably, the threat of communism galvanised the powers of the battered German nation into counter-revolutionary action. The army moved against Munich, and by the beginning of May the Bavarian political adventure was over. The decisive military advance began in Augsburg.

Brecht's published correspondence is largely silent about these events, though he is known to have been an active supporter of Eisner's social democrats, and may have been a fellow-traveller with the soviet. The most abiding outcome was a lifelong scepticism about acts of quixotic heroism, a scepticism which ran alongside his animosity towards the grandiose human aspirations of German expressionism. Ernst Toller, prominent among expressionist playwrights, was one of the leaders of the Munich soviet. In his autobiographical retrospect on political history, he writes of the ordinary Bavarians who wanted peace, but found themselves suddenly invested with power: 'Would they learn to keep their power?' (Toller 1934: 133). They did not, and the failure helped to guide Brecht towards the mature conviction that an effective revolution, political or theatrical, must be achieved through reason and scientific principle. Quite unlike Toller in most ways, Brecht shared with him a curiosity about what they considered a moral paradox. Toller expressed it in this way: 'Men could be good with so little trouble, yet they delight in evil' (Toller 1934: 26). Brecht wrote a short poem about it:

> On my wall hangs a Japanese carving
> The mask of an evil demon, decorated with gold lacquer.
> Sympathetically I observe
> The swollen veins of the forehead, indicating
> What a strain it is to be evil.
> (Brecht 1976b: 383)

Given what we know of their respective lives, most people would be more surprised to find Brecht in heaven than to find Toller there. But the fundamental question addressed in the work of both men is the one Toller remembers asking himself after the death of an uncle: 'what is a good man?' (Toller 1934: 8). Was Galileo good? Is Grusha? Or Shen Te? Or dumb Kattrin? Or the Young Comrade in *The Measures Taken*? How good? Good how? From early in his life Brecht developed a habit of provocation. At its political centre was a determination to take nothing for granted. We cannot, after all, hope to change what we unknowingly assume to be unchangeable. To develop a capacity to be surprised by the familiar might be a staging post on the road to Brechtian goodness. It is certainly a staging post on the road to Brechtian acting. We should recognise, in the context of this chapter and this book, that there is a difference between being good at acting and being a good actor. Whatever is exclusively of the theatre is of no interest to Brecht and little benefit to humanity. For Brecht, the world, like the disputed land in the opening scene of *The Caucasian Chalk Circle*, should belong to those who are good for it. In his own moral system, goodness could not be divided from efficacy.

Brecht entered the German theatre as a writer, and became a practitioner primarily in order to intervene in the production of his own plays. He had no training, nor was there any tradition of actor training in Germany. The simplified view of the style of acting he would have encountered, hectically delivered by Martin Esslin, is that it sought to produce 'the maximum impression of emotional intensity by indulgence in hysterical outbursts and paroxysms of uncontrolled roaring and inarticulate anguish' (Esslin 1970: 88). Clearly carried away, Esslin goes on to write of 'orgies of vocal excess and apoplectic breast beating'. He has in mind the excesses of the court theatres of old Germany, which lingered in the celebrated performances of pre-war luminaries, and which had again come into service in the ecstatic rhetoric of the new expressionist drama.

But this declamatory grand manner was by no means the only model available to the young Brecht. Although Otto Brahm, the outstanding exponent of naturalism in Germany, had died in 1912, the impact of his advocacy of true-to-life acting did not die with him. Brecht's early loyalty to the naturalistic drama of Gerhart Hauptmann was fed by a visceral response to witnessed productions of his plays. One of his earliest published letters, dated 10 November 1914, commends Hauptmann's 'art of exalting everyday happenings to spiritual heights' and proposes Zola as a model because 'the soul of the people has not yet been explored' (Brecht 1990: 20).

Quite as influential on the development of Brecht's ideas of performance was the generally cool, presentational style of cabaret, which had already been released into drama through the work of Frank Wedekind. Wedekind himself combined the writing of plays with performing in cabaret right up to his untimely death in March 1918. Brecht was in the Munich bar where Wedekind made one of what turned out to be his last appearances, and his own sporadic cabaret performances honoured Wedekind by imitation, as well as sharpening his sense of an audience. Esslin's emphatically partial account serves his argument that Brecht's approach to acting was a legitimate response to German histrionics, but of limited relevance elsewhere. It ignores the range of Brecht's theatrical experience in a country with an uncommonly rich artistic tradition.

Before making his first attempt to direct professional actors, he had observed Max Reinhardt and other Berlin directors at work in rehearsal. This was in November 1921, when Reinhardt was preparing Strindberg's *A Dream Play*, characteristically in search of its musical orchestration. The outcome was highly artificial, but certainly not an occasion of 'apoplectic breast beating'. Brecht was already too opinionated and too censorious to share Reinhardt's sheer appetite for theatre, nor had he yet developed his admiration for the craft of the actor. That became clear in the spring of 1922, when he was invited to direct his friend Arnolt Bronnen's *Vatermord* (Patricide) for the newly formed Junge Bühne in Berlin, and was so scathing about the quality of the acting that one actress was reduced to tears, the veteran Heinrich George walked out, and Brecht was replaced by the more tactful Berthold Viertel. It may be that he returned to Munich a wiser man, able to contribute to, but not dictate, the conduct of rehearsals for the first of his plays to be performed: *Drums in the Night* (Munich, September 1922), *In the Jungle* (Munich, May 1923), and *Baal* (Leipzig, December 1923).

The year 1923 was one of soaring inflation in Germany, and discontent in Munich had an ominously Nazi fringe. The opening of *In the Jungle* provided a pretext for nationalist protesters to release tear-gas in the auditorium of the Munich Kammerspiele. The play was dropped from the repertoire and the dramaturg, Jacob Geis, was sacked. Such glimpses of power served as a drug to one of Brecht's fellow residents in Munich. On 8 November 1923, supported by the legendary hero Field Marshal Ludendorff, Adolf Hitler attempted to take over the city. Brecht was probably attending rehearsals of *Baal* in Leipzig at the time, and he, like all too many of his countrymen, found Hitler slightly comic for a while. His own political attention, particularly after his meeting with the activist Helene Weigel in the autumn of 1923, was turning towards Karl Marx. Before long he would embark on a full-scale programme of Marxist self-education, in open contradiction of the increasingly fascist atmosphere in Munich. In September 1924 he abandoned Bavaria for Berlin, but not before bidding a significant farewell to the Munich Kammerspiele by directing *The Life of Edward II of England*.

Brecht admired the narrative drive and psychological sparseness of Christopher Marlowe's original, and the adaptation he prepared with Lion Feuchtwanger accommodates his own peculiarly visceral poetic voice. He was at ease with the text, happy to change it, and, perhaps for the first time, able to work confidently with actors. Bernhard Reich recalls his determination that the soldiers should hang Gaveston with authority: 'Brecht . . . insisted relentlessly that they repeat the hanging, but to do it like experts. The audience had to get pleasure from seeing them put the noose round the fellow's neck' (Völker 1979: 72). The outcome, in the words of the contemporary dramatic critic Herbert Ihering, was innovatory: 'The actors had to account for what they did. He insisted that they keep their gestures simple. He made them speak clearly, coolly. No emotional faking was tolerated. By these means the objective, epic style was established' (Völker 1979: 72).

Brecht remained active in the Berlin theatre until Hitler's rise to power forced him into exile in late February 1933, but his activity was always governed by the pressure to produce. Ideologies of performance were in inevitable conflict with the exigency of opening nights, and, in a country lurching towards fascism, his priorities were more consistently political than aesthetic. The formulations that give Brecht right of access to a book on actor training were almost all the result of the enforced idleness of exile, and the practice that tested the theory was confined to the last years of his life with the Berliner Ensemble. The sequence of collaborations with Kurt Weill is of critical importance in the history of music theatre, but it added comparatively little to the discoveries about acting that Brecht had made during the rehearsals for *Edward II*. A Brechtian actor will know how to sustain the poise of one who might at any moment sing, but Brecht had not yet devised a rehearsal system to serve his purposes. His aim, both with Weill and in his *Lehrstück* project, was to reach a new audience, the traditionally disempowered but now alert workers of post-war Germany. The loss of access to this audience was one of the bitterest consequences of his exile.

The exile lasted more than fifteen years and included prolonged residences in Denmark, Sweden, Finland and the United States. A stranger to every language, Brecht was constantly frustrated in his attempts to gain access to theatres. His ideas about acting found expression in the plays he wrote, sporadically in his journal and conversations with fellow-exiles and friends, through encounters with active theatre groups, and in theoretical writings of which the most carefully wrought were *The Messingkauf Dialogues* (written 1937–40) and *A Short Organum for the Theatre* (completed in 1948). It is from these, and from the recorded practice of the company he founded in East Berlin in 1949, that conclusions about his approach to actor training have been most reliably drawn.

We should note, however, that Brecht was a compulsive articulator. Much of what he wrote and subsequently published was a response to immediate circumstances.

Given his taste for contradiction and his advocacy of dialectics, we should not be surprised by evident inconsistencies. There is no static, once-and-for-all manifesto. The measure of Brecht's truth is efficacy: what may be thought or half-thought expressed through what is done. In that respect, the determining document is not the *Messingkauf* nor even the *Short Organum*, but *Theaterarbeit* (1952). This volume, 'an exceedingly mixed bag of essays, notes and fragments by many hands' (Willett 1964: 239), was something new in the history of theatre: an attempt to record for posterity the processes of a theatre company during its first two years of operation. The many rehearsal photographs speak, not singly but cumulatively, about acting even to those who cannot read German. *Theaterarbeit* testifies to theory's need of a practice.

EXERCISES

It is a prerequisite of Brechtian actor training that the trainee should be open to a study of history, including the history of the present. The tendency of historical enquiry is almost inevitably towards astonishment in the enquirer. We discover details that compel us to reassess the causes of events we had previously taken for granted. When Brecht advised his actors to note for later recall their first impressions of a play, or of their part in a play, it was because he knew how rehearsal may iron flat the seams of surprise. When trainee directors at the Berliner Ensemble were invited to watch rehearsals and write down whatever they disagreed with, it was to keep alive a recognition that there is more than one way of doing the same thing. Actors who are no longer surprised by the behaviour of the characters they play are not Brechtian actors. For Brecht, this is less a matter of psychology than of history. The fact that Galileo recanted does not make his recantation historically inevitable. The fact that life expectancy has increased does not ensure better care of the aged. Brecht's consistent project, both as writer and as practitioner, was to destabilise facts and interrogate the necessary. Significantly, he came to credit actors with sufficient curiosity to collaborate in the project. It was this that struck Peter Brook most forcibly when he visited the Berliner Ensemble:

> What Brecht introduced was the idea of the intelligent actor, capable of judging the value of his contribution. There were and still are many actors who pride themselves on knowing nothing about politics and who treat the theatre as an ivory tower. For Brecht such an actor is not worthy of his place in adult company: an actor in a community that supports a theatre must be as much involved in the outside world as in his own craft.
>
> (Brook 1972: 85–86)

The Brechtian actor's training begins with observation of the outside world. This was what Brecht chose to stress in his poetic 'Speech to Danish Working-Class Actors on the Art of Observation':

> In order to observe
> One must learn how to compare. In order to compare
> One must have observed. By means of observation
> Knowledge is generated; on the other hand knowledge is needed
> For observation.
>
> (Brecht 1976b: 233–38)

Figure 7.1 Brecht directing Regine Lutz in Heinrich Von Kleist's The Broken Jug.

Source: Photo Hainer Hill by permission of the Bertolt Brecht Archive.

The paradoxical circularity is typical of Brecht's thinking about acting. The answer to a question is another question; the end of interrogation is interrogation. But actors cannot question what they do not notice. They must see the obvious clearly enough to mistrust it.

The question mark is Brecht's starting-point for observation. His famous essay on 'The Street Scene' (Willett 1964: 121–28) asks what an actor may learn from the way in which an onlooker describes a street accident. But this onlooker is an exemplary actor in the everyday theatre of the street, concerned not only with *what* happened but with why and how. If we watch and listen to him carefully we will understand that the accident need not have happened. We will have our own questions about human interaction under the current dispensation. Among Brecht's papers there is an undated list containing a skeletal scheme of twenty-four exercises for acting schools (Willett 1964: 129). 'The street accident' is the twenty-second, and it is enigmatically glossed, 'Laying down limits of justifiable imitation'.

Brecht did not want the exercise to be used indiscriminately. It is about more than observation; critically approached, as part of the present-historical, it lays bare the functioning of society; uncritically approached, its imitation is unjustifiable. The deaths of Swiss Cheese and Kattrin in *Mother Courage* are, after all, street accidents, and they need to be accounted for as well as imitated. The first four exercises on Brecht's list, though cunningly interrogative in their way, call more straightforwardly for observation:

1   Conjuring tricks, including attitude of spectators.
2   For women: folding and putting away linen. Same for men.
3   For men: varying attitudes of smokers. Same for women.
4   Cat playing with a hank of thread.

We ask of the conjuror, how did you do that, but why are some spectators amazed and others dismissive? Do women and men do things differently? Why? Is doing things with linen a female thing? Who determines that? How can an activity as common as smoking betray the social class of the smoker? What do people play with? How do we know, when playing with a cat, that the cat is not playing with us? The observation of society ends with a question mark, too.

Almost all of Brecht's proposed exercises involve actors working together, and there is nothing surprising about that. The questions arising from observation are asked on behalf of society as a whole. The image is of interdependence. This is a point spelt out clearly in the *Short Organum*:

> the learning process must be co-ordinated so that the actor learns as the other actors are learning and develops his character as they are developing theirs. For the smallest social unit is not the single person but two people. In life too we develop one another.
>
> (Willett 1964: 197)

The social heart of an episode, which Brecht would have called its *Gestus*, is dependent on the disposition of all the characters on stage. During the Berliner Ensemble's interactive rehearsals, the actors were expected to ask where their characters stood and how they (the actors) stood towards their characters. Such questions require close attention to the totality of a text and its dramaturgy. Brecht's awareness of this is expressed in his 'Notes on Stanislavski': 'Stanislavski when directing is first of all an actor. When I direct I am first of all a playwright' (Brecht 1964: 165). Most of the exercises he used with the Ensemble were directly related to the play in rehearsal, but not necessarily to the play as it would be performed. If the actors were to work on the audience in such a way as to rob the familiar of its inconspicuousness, it might help if the familiar text could be made conspicuous to the actors.

It was in this spirit that Brecht recommended to Giorgio Strehler the rehearsal of tragic scenes for comic effect (Mitter 1992: 57). By contradicting a text, the actors might gain new insights into it. Such contradiction is not designed to open access to what Stanislavsky termed a subtext, but to surround a text with a metatext linking it to the world outside, the world that is in need of transformation. The several practice pieces for actors that Brecht wrote in 1939 with Swedish students in mind (Brecht 1976a: 339–55) are anachronistic mistreatments of the classics, which highlight the plight of an underclass disregarded in *Macbeth*, *Hamlet*, and *Romeo and Juliet*. They call attention to what is missing from the plays but present in the social order, and they invite actors to develop a critical attitude to the characters they are playing. Thus the actors become, in the language of metaphor, double agents, sometimes self-employed and sometimes employed by the character.

The metaphor is Joseph Chaikin's. He uses it to describe the performances of the man he considers the definitive Brechtian actor, Ekkehard Schall: 'I never believe he is the character by name. Nor do I believe that he is "playing himself". He performs like a double agent who has infiltrated the two worlds' (Chaikin 1991: 16). This double agency is effectively tested in one of Brecht's so-called 'exercises in temperament': 'Situation: two women calmly folding linen. They feign a wild and jealous quarrel for the benefit of their husbands; the husbands are in the next room' (Willett 1964: 129).

The manifest disparity between the orderliness of the action and the disorderliness of the speaking makes demands on the control of the actors and, at the same time, makes unusually conspicuous the commonplace activities of folding and quarrelling. Such contradictory juxtapositions are the typical ammunition of *Verfremdung*. They make strange what we might otherwise scarcely notice. A Brechtian actor must be alert to the social significance of every kind of human transaction, even the most mundane. 'I don't act emotions', explained Schall, 'I present them as ways of behaviour' (Honneger and Schechter 1986: 35).

There is a danger of distortion here. Despite what has often been said, sometimes by himself, the mature Brecht rejected neither emotion nor psychological enquiry. Angelika Hurwicz, a leading member of the Ensemble, denies that Brecht was 'hostile to drama exercises aimed at ensuring the truth to life and the warmth of the presentation of the role; in fact, he regards them as a pre-requisite' (Witt 1974: 132). In a sequel to the linen-folding exercise, for example, Brecht proposes that the game 'turn serious' (Willett 1964: 129). His departure from Stanislavskian methods was not total, but graduated. In the first stage of rehearsal actors should become acquainted with their characters, the second phase is one of empathy, 'and then there is a third phase in which you try to see the character from the outside, from the standpoint of society' (Brecht 1964: 159).

It is to the transition from the second to the third phase that the third-person exercises belong. There is an indicative journal entry, written as the opening night of the Berliner Ensemble's *Mother Courage* approached:

> I put in 10 minutes epic rehearsal for the first time in the eleventh scene.
> gerda müller and dunskus as peasants are deciding that they cannot do

anything against the catholics. I ask them to add 'said the man', 'said the woman' after each speech. suddenly the scene became clear and müller found a realistic attitude.

(Brecht 1993: 405)

This is an exercise designed not to obstruct emotional engagement, but to show that the actor's emotion does not need to coincide with that of the character. The notion of double agency is at its most complex here, but the actor's eye is on the audience. The actor both presents and scrutinises the behaviour of the character in such a way as to invite the audience's interrogation. If it is circumstance, not human necessity, that governs behaviour, actors and audience should combine to change the circumstance.

It is generally true that a Stanislavskian actor will locate in character the explanation for behaviour, whilst the Brechtian actor will look for it in circumstance. The aim of rehearsal exercises will not have been to embed action in individual psychology, but to place it in the social transactions of the group. The outcome for the audience should not be psychoanalysis but moral debate. The metaphor for a final set of exercises is that of multiple doors. You will go through only one, but you could go through any. The task is to make your choice in such a way as to indicate to the onlookers that there are other choices you could have made:

> Whatever [the actor] doesn't do must be contained and conserved in what he does. In this way every sentence and every gesture signifies a decision; the character remains under observation and is tested. The technical term for this procedure is 'fixing the "not . . . but" '.
>
> (Willett 1964: 137)

Brecht provides no list of 'not . . . but' exercises, knowing that they can be readily devised and appropriated according to context. He does, however, describe the practice, as, for example, in Helene Weigel's final moments as Mother Courage: 'Even in paying for the burial, Weigel gave one last hint of Courage's character. She fished a few coins out of her leather bag, put one back and gave the peasants the rest' (Brecht 1972: 383). If an actor can learn how to show that the choice made was not the only available choice, the audience may be encouraged to choose for change. The aim of the 'not . . . but' exercises is to train actors to ask why not as well as why, but Brechtian actors have always a design on the audience.

PRODUCTION

John Fuegi has calculated that, before the opening of *The Caucasian Chalk Circle* on 7 October 1954, the actors of the Berliner Ensemble had rehearsed for 600 hours (Fuegi 1987: 161). It is an over-literal calculation, but it speaks appropriately of the slow pace of rehearsal once the company was fully established. Given time, Brecht explored all the elements I have mentioned:

1   Contradiction as a route to a metatext.
2   The identification of goodness with efficacy.
3   The presentational style of the actor who may at any moment sing.
4   The priority of narrative and circumstance over character.

5   The approach through history, including the historicisation of the present.
6   Observation sharpened by interrogation.
7   The ensemble working together to deliver the social *Gestus*.
8   The double agency of actor and character.
9   Speaking in the third person (sometimes augmented by speaking the stage directions).
10   Fixing the 'not . . . but'.

Brecht's major productions with the Berliner Ensemble, *Mother Courage* (1949) and *The Caucasian Chalk Circle* (1954), have been described in some detail by, respectively, Peter Thomson (Thomson 1997) and John Fuegi (Fuegi 1987). It is more appropriate here to set out the broader terms within which he went about making theatre.

Alone amongst the practitioners featured in this book, Brecht was a major playwright. He was also a poet, a wordsmith. Language mattered intensely to him, both the sound of the meaning and the meaning of the sound. He was quite as likely, in rehearsal, to join an actor in interrogating a sentence as in questioning a gesture. Either way, the goal of the interrogation was efficacy. An archival fragment provides a list of what he might ask of a sentence:

1   Who is the sentence of use to?
2   Who does it claim to be of use to?
3   What does it call for?
4   What practical action corresponds to it?
5   What sort of sentences result from it? What sort of sentences support it?
6   In what situation is it spoken? By whom?

(Willett 1964: 106)

The solemnity is misleading. The atmosphere at Brecht's rehearsals was normally relaxed, even expansive. His policy was to remain silent in order to provoke the actors into making suggestions, though he was typically capable of mischievous intervention. Hans Bunge remembers Brecht the director saying of Brecht the playwright, 'One cannot always be guided by what *he* says' (Fuegi 1987: 148). Changes might be made to the text if the actors came up with a preferred alternative, although the changes were sometimes obliterated in the published version. The Ensemble was incorporated in the creation of a play, not subjugated to the revival of a text, and Brecht expected the creation to be definitive. To whom will the play be of use? What practical action corresponds to it? These are metatextual matters, and only the performance can resolve them. What Shomit Mitter has called 'the tussle between text and commentary that is the hallmark of the Brechtian theatre' (Mitter 1992: 46) is fought out on the stage.

The image of struggle is entirely appropriate to any consideration of Brecht. His creative energy was always charged by disagreement. The early play *Baal* was provoked by the urge to counter the heroic vision of Hanns Johst's *Der Einsame* (The Loner), and the impulse to write counter-plays (*Gegenstücke*) remained with him. Not surprisingly, then, Brecht's work with actors displays aspects of a counter-practice (*Gegenpraktik*). Persuaded that traditional styles of performance, like the established dramatic repertoire, reinforced the social *status quo* by rendering the audience passive, Brecht set about changing both.

There is no reason to doubt his belief that whatever could be made visible could also be mastered, and it was certainly his conviction that Stanislavskian performances in Aristotelian drama disempowered the audience. The concept of *Gestus* became a counter to pathos, and it is a pity for those who would like to systematise Brechtian practice that Brecht himself used the word so loosely. Among the many attempts to define it on Brecht's behalf, one of the simplest is Mitter's. *Gestus*, he suggests, is 'a compound term which intrinsically harnesses both content and opinion' (Mitter 1992: 48).

The problem with this formulation is that it implicitly sells short the integral contribution of the actors. Meg Mumford, in an extended study of *Gestus* from the actor's perspective, has proposed it as the essential counter to Stanislavsky. For her, *Gestus* is 'the aesthetic gestural presentation of the economic and socio-ideological construction of human identity and interaction', something which 'finds ultimate expression in the corporeal and intellectual work of the performer' (Mumford 1997: xviii). However complex the understanding, there is no escaping the fact that *Gestus* is the key concept in Brechtian actor training and the defining quality of a truly Brechtian performance. Before semiotics became a recognised focus of theatrical criticism or performance theory, *Gestus* guided the productions of the Berliner Ensemble. In socio-political terms at least, it remains the most sophisticated application of semiotic principles to the preparation of actors. Carl Weber, who worked with Brecht in Berlin, recalls its relevance to individual actors:

> The *Gestus* was to be mainly determined by the social position and history of a character, and Brecht instructed his actors to develop it by careful attention to all the contradictions to be discovered in the actions and verbal text of the role ... this may sound quite abstract, but it was achieved during rehearsal in a most practical, even playful manner.
>
> (Thomson and Sacks 1994: 182)

It was the business of rehearsal to anatomise what was said and done by each individual actor, however small the part. In this respect, *Gestus* is diagnosis applied to social history. The object, when it comes to production, is to present a narrative with such clarity that the audience can read not only the behaviour of the characters, but also the provenance of that behaviour and its application to their own lives. 'The actor in Brecht's theatre', says Mumford, 'does not focus on an individual's inner life but on their *Gestus*' (Mumford 1997: 156). In his notes on particular productions, Brecht frequently records how actors embodied the *Gestus*. In the fourth scene of *Mother Courage*, for instance, after singing 'The Song of the Great Capitulation', Weigel both displayed and contradicted Courage's depravity:

> Weigel's face in this scene shows a glimmer of wisdom and even of nobility, and that is good. Because the depravity is not so much that of her person as of her class, and because she herself at least rises above it somewhat by showing that she understands this weakness and that it even makes her angry.
>
> (Brecht 1972: 362)

The Brechtian actor represents more than the self of the character. It was Brecht's contention that *Gestus*, when properly applied, would enable an audience to understand both the story of a play and its implications even if it were separated from the actors by a soundproof glass wall. To some extent, certainly, he was a pictorial director, concerned to paint meaning through costume, properties and the grouping of actors. Archive photographs, particularly of *The Mother* but sometimes even of *Mother Courage*, encapsulate the context of struggle with the starkness of Käthe Kollwitz's woodcuts.

The relationship of director, designer and actors at the Berliner Ensemble was a significant innovation. It has been finely described by Christopher Baugh (Thomson and Sacks 1994: 235–53), and is not centrally the business of this chapter. But it is important that actors should be able to visualise themselves as part of a scene, and both Caspar Neher and Karl von Appen were vital contributory members of Brecht's production team. The absence of Neher during the rehearsals of *Mother Courage* was a source of anxiety. It was Neher who originated the custom of sketching scenes in advance of their rehearsal. The disposition of the characters on the stage and the placing of the attention in performance, sketched out in suggestive sequence, became a subject of enquiry. During rehearsal these sketches could be tested, contradicted, reaffirmed. The quest was always for the *Gestus* that carried the scene closer to reality. At the still centre of every mobile episode in a Berliner Ensemble production there was always a signifying tableau. It is important to recognise, though, that the spirit of contradiction operated even here. Despite the image of the soundproof glass wall, the priority of the visual was constantly contradicted by detailed attention to the words. We can never afford to forget that Brecht was a writer. Attempting a third-person summary of his unique achievement in the prose work *Me-Ti*, he wrote:

> He made use of a type of language which was at the same time stylized and natural. He achieved this by paying attention to the attitudes underlying sentences: he only incorporated attitudes into sentences and always saw that the attitudes were visible through the sentences. To this kind of language he gave the name 'gestic', since it was just an expression of people's gestures.
>
> (Morley 1977: 120)

As a shorthand guide to Brechtian acting, it would be difficult to improve on 'paying attention to the attitudes underlying sentences' and 'an expression of people's gestures'.

Bibliography

Brecht, B. (1964) 'Notes on Stanislavski', *Tulane Drama Review*, 9 (2): 157–66.
—— (1972) *Collected Plays*, vol. 5, New York: Vintage Books.
—— (1976a) *Collected Plays*, vol. 6, New York: Vintage Books.
—— (1976b) *Poems 1913–1956*, London: Eyre Methuen.
—— (1990) *Letters 1913–1956*, New York: Routledge.
—— (1993) *Journals 1934–1955*, London: Methuen.
Brecht, B. *et al.* (1952) *Theaterarbeit*, Dresden: Dresdner Verlag.
Brook, P. (1972) *The Empty Space*, Harmondsworth: Penguin Books.
Chaikin, J. (1991) *The Presence of the Actor*, New York: Theatre Communications Group.
Esslin, M. (1970) *Brief Chronicles*, London: Temple Smith.
Fuegi, J. (1987) *Bertolt Brecht: Chaos According to Plan*, Cambridge: Cambridge University Press.
Honneger, G. and Schechter, J. (1986) 'An interview with Ekkehard Schall', *Theater*, Spring: 31–43.
Mitter, S. (1992) *Systems of Rehearsal*, London: Routledge.
Morley, M. (1977) *A Student's Guide to Brecht*, London: Heinemann.

Mumford, M. (1997) 'Showing the *Gestus*: a Study of Acting in Brecht's Theatre', unpublished
    PhD thesis, Bristol: University of Bristol.
Thomson, P. (1997) *Mother Courage and Her Children*, Cambridge: Cambridge University Press.
Thomson, P. and Sacks, G. (eds) (1994) *The Cambridge Companion to Brecht*, Cambridge: Cambridge
    University Press.
Toller, E. (1934) *I Was a German*, London: John Lane.
Völker, K. (1979) *Brecht: a Biography*, London: Marion Boyars.
Willett, J. (1964) *Brecht on Theatre*, London: Methuen.
Witt, H. (ed.) (1974) *Brecht as They Knew Him*, London: Lawrence and Wishart.

Chapter 8

Clive Barker

JOAN LITTLEWOOD

CONTEXT

ALTHOUGH JOAN LITTLEWOOD HAS refrained from producing works of theory, as many other directors have done, that does not mean that there is no theory behind her work. Angela Hurwicz, when asked if Brecht had spoken much about theory during rehearsals, said not at all.[1] Kurt Jooss was once asked how much theory Laban referred to in rehearsals. He said none.[2] Whatever is set out in print is only relevant if it refers directly to what happens on the stage, which is the sole place of arbitration. Peter Brook has written a great deal on his views of theatre, but it contains a large proportion of rhetoric. This can be, and often has been, inspiring for the reader, but it does not always give any clear inkling as to how Brook works in rehearsal.[3] To discover that, it is probably more valuable to refer to the testimony and anecdotes of his actors.

The evidence for Littlewood's theory lies in snippets of statements in interviews and manifestos and in the memories and anecdotes of the actors who have worked with her; although these documents, which include this chapter, have to be questioned carefully, and seen as both idiosyncratic and subjective.[4] What anyone sees and how they interpret it depends on what attitudes they bring to the work and what resources they have to contextualise it. The student handbook for London's East 15 Acting School, which was founded by a former company member, Margaret Walker (Bury), refers to Theatre Workshop as 'substantially challenging notions of repertoire, theatre propriety, actor/audience relationships and the social basis of their audience'. East 15 was founded 'to ensure the retention of the *working method* . . . which was never set down, codified or systematised' (my italics).

Littlewood herself has denied the existence of any method or way of working to a system.[5] If things are not set down, they nevertheless rub off. The unfortunate result of Littlewood's reluctance to set down her working methods and their theoretical backing has been that she has been accused of being a dilettante who somehow managed to hit the right button on some occasions – which is a long way from the truth. Throughout the early periods of the company, each performance was charted in long and detailed analytical notes posted the next day. There was nothing hit or miss about these notes. The slightest lapse of concentration, a failure to sustain, or the presence of cliché was noticed with what seemed an eagle eye which never relaxed.[6] Actors who have spent any time working with her are, in my experience, never in doubt as to what she intended – a clear demonstration of a shared aesthetic and technique. Richard Harris is on record as saying he learned more from one afternoon with Littlewood than in all the other time he spent at drama school.[7] I find no contradiction in Littlewood's refusal to set out her theoretical positions. There has clearly always been a deep mistrust of the word over the action. 'We know what they say but what are they doing?'[8] could be applied to the whole business of creating theatre as well as analysing a single unit in a play.

In one of the few direct statements that Littlewood has made about her view of theatre she said:

> I do not believe in the supremacy of the director, designer, actor or even the writer. It is through collaboration that this knockabout art of theatre survives and kicks. . . . No one mind or imagination can foresee what a play will become until all the physical and intellectual stimuli which are crystallized in the poetry of the author, have been understood by a company, and then tried out in terms of mime, discussion and the precise music of grammar; words and movement allied and integrated.[9]

This sublime piece of theatre rhetoric merits consideration for the questions it raises about the process of making theatre, Littlewood's problems with the theatre establishment, and for the clues it offers to clarify the way she worked. Paramount is the insistence on the power of the ensemble, a group of artists with different talents, skills and minds, working and playing in a cooperative, rather than authoritarian, mode or synthetic manner.

She has consistently declined to accept a dictatorial approach, dismissing with contempt the 'genius' director, sitting in his or her study with a model of the set and some toy soldiers, working out the choreography and stage pictures of the proposed production: directing the actors, from day one of rehearsal, to carry out his or her preconceived instructions. Theatre based on such an approach results in seventeen people illustrating one person's imagination. How much more powerful to have eighteen people's imaginations working in concert! Further to this concept, she characterised the work of Theatre Workshop as a jazz combo against the classical orchestra, which was the model of established theatre practice. The quotation above is based on the understanding that it is harder to create great jazz than to play in a symphony orchestra, requiring much rigorous investigation of form, structure and style, and greater instrumental flexibility and virtuosity. The British theatre has consistently looked suspiciously at anyone who takes theatre that seriously and who appears to have faith in imagination over methodical drilling. The late Kenneth Tynan, the most influential critic at the time of Littlewood's work, once said to me that his feeling was that British directors were afraid of actors. That could never be said of Joan Littlewood.

Figure 8.1 Littlewood directing Fanny Carby in a rehearsal of *They Might Be Giants* by James Goldman (1961).

Source: The Theatre Workshop Archive.

BACKGROUND

Theatre Workshop was preceded by a sequence of other companies assembled in the 1930s by Joan Littlewood and Ewan MacColl.[10] The major feature of these companies was social commitment, often overtly political. Theatrically they consistently drew upon the rich experimentation that was taking place on the Continent in the 1920s and 1930s, which hardly touched the British theatre at that time. A large part of this book is given over to artists who were influential in the New Movement in the theatre, which also extended to include the United States.[11] The influences they absorbed came through personal contact and through voracious study.

   Along with the new staging and lighting techniques, they took in the concepts of the ensemble, as the creative instrument of making theatre, and the concept of the research theatre company. Companies such as those led by Copeau, Stanislavsky and Meyerhold consistently researched the history of theatre practice from whatever sources were obtainable and through practical recreations and experimentation. The later Littlewood/MacColl companies in the 1930s, up to and into the war, mounted a systematic research of the history of theatre performance. Each actor was allocated a period or style, being expected to produce papers and lectures, to communicate his or her understanding to the others. All this apart from the personal research of Littlewood and MacColl.[12]

   They were searching for an aesthetic, a philosophy of theatre, and gradually it began to emerge, basing itself on:

1   An awareness of the social issues of the time, and in that sense, a political theatre.
2   A theatrical language that working people could understand, but that was capable of reflecting, when necessary, ideas, either simple or involved, in a poetic form.
3   An expressive and flexible form of movement, and a high standard of skill and technique in acting.
4   A high level of technical sound and light into the production.[13]

Some of the major features that were absorbed and were continued through the work of Theatre Workshop consisted of a combination of both Stanislavskian techniques, to create the inner truth of the characters, and those derived from the work of Rudolf Laban, to structure the expressive techniques of performance.[14] Added to this was the use of lighting in a dramatic way. With light directed to play on textured scenic units, often three-dimensional, it was possible to paint the stage to create atmosphere and mood, and to restructure the overall space into specific isolated, or related, areas of action. This was in contradiction to the majority of British theatre practice, which relied on painted two-dimensional flats, lit with bland, smooth illumination. The tendency in the 1950s and 1960s was towards smooth multi-lantern settings. Theatre Workshop used lanterns sparsely, in settings in which shadows and darkness were as important as lit areas. The settings employed levels and ramps, often built from scaffolding, and frequently opened the wings and flies of the stage to create auxiliary playing spaces. The aim was to utilise setting with the principal intention of projecting the actors into a variety of forms of relationship with the audience. This also involved a running battle with the confining and defining effect of the proscenium arch. These features were constituent parts of a major conceptual leap into style, a subject which obsessed many practitioners and theorists from around 1900, united against the dead hand of naturalism.

Two aspects of this debate and experimentation mark out Littlewood and MacColl's search. Much of the experimentation of the early twentieth century was concerned with finding forms and structures in the past theatres which would offer clues to the establishment of popular theatre, accessible to a much wider audience. When Littlewood and MacColl began Theatre Workshop in 1946, their manifesto contained a recognition that all the great theatres of the past – Shakespeare, Molière and others – had enjoyed an audience of mixed classes and contained a large pro-portion of the working population, as well as thieves, rogues and the unemployed. All had combined song and dance within the dramatic action. Theatre Workshop wanted a way of performing the classics which made them accessible to a wide range of audiences, and put an end to elitist notions of theatre.[15]

The second feature of the experimentation which characterised the work of Theatre Workshop was the definition of style as the means through which the essence of a play was communicated to an audience.[16] Richard Findlater, writing in 1953, characterised the style of the British theatre as 'polite naturalism', and regretted that the theatre at that time showed no sign that its major innovators and world figures had ever existed.[17] The work of Theatre Workshop has never been charac-terised by polite naturalism or by consistent style, either overall or within the scenes and units of a play.

This is what makes the 'knockabout art' of theatre require such detailed and rigorous testing to make it survive and kick, as in the quotation earlier. One small but striking example is the inclusion of Chinese theatre techniques in the

Figure 8.2 Henry Chapman's *You Won't Always Be On Top*.
Source: Photo by V.J. Spinner by permission of The Theatre Workshop Archive.

sixteenth-century play *Arden of Faversham*. Act II, scenes ii and iii, take place by a river as the villains Black Will and Shakebag attempt to ambush and murder Thomas Arden. Because the ambush takes place at night the plan fails, and the villains are thwarted. Clearly, in the Elizabethan theatre these scenes were played in broad daylight and a lot of the comedy arose out of the visible actors playing as though in the dark. Modern staging techniques make this stylised acting unnecessary and a lot of the fun is lost in modern recreations.

Amalgamating scenes from two Peking Operas, 'The Fight in the Dark' from *The Inn at the Cross-roads* and the set piece of *Crossing the Autumn River*, Littlewood staged the scenes in two (non-existent) boats in the middle of the river. In the great theatres of the past, actors were required to undertake the double transformations of space and character. The presence of the stage designer tended to take the first of these away from the actor. The designer transforms the actual space of the stage into the virtual space of the setting and in front of this the actor creates character. This division restricts the use of the actor's imagination and physical techniques. Littlewood's restoration of the transformation of space to the actor reached its apotheosis in *Oh, What a Lovely War!*

PREPARATION

Given such an approach, where each play is assessed for its intrinsic theatrical properties and values, even to the extent that productions were characterised by montages of scenes in differing styles, no two productions were ever approached in the same way. What was common was an opening period in which the text was worked over and tried out to reveal the secrets of its theatricality. Dense, classic texts were given a long time for analysis. Contemporary plays were often experimented with in terms of lines and passages of dialogue spoken by a succession of different actors and pairings to discover timing and qualities of irony or social *gests*. In all cases, the social background was explored at the same time. Actors brought books and other research materials to rehearsal and the insights these gave were incorporated into the discussions.[18]

Often these insights provided the stimulus to move the play into the active, exploratory stage. The early stages of Brendan Behan's *The Quare Fellow* were filled with the actors walking round the roof of the theatre for long periods, the prisoners trying to communicate by talking out of the corners of their mouths, the warders trying to catch them doing it. *The Hostage* began with stories and songs that Behan told the company, and continued after he had left with recordings made of him holding court and developing a party atmosphere. The final text of *Oh, What a Lovely War!*, insofar as anything was ever final, grew out of the actors' own research being shaped in rehearsals.[19]

The use of games and improvisations in the early stages of rehearsal was not a simple matter, and served many functions in shaping the production. It could supply the text on occasions, or animate it as lines and dialogue were fed into the structure of the activity. The usual actor's task of learning lines was not much in evidence in Theatre Workshop – they were learned collectively during the rehearsals.[20] Action and dialogue were integrated and one informed the other. The prompter, so necessary in most theatres, was not in evidence at Theatre Workshop. If text, movement and action were integrated, the possibility of an actor 'drying' was barely conceivable and, if this happened, it was considered axiomatic that the other actors in the scene would be able to improvise from their own integrated understanding, to carry the scene forward without difficulty.

Probably the clearest example of the importance of the games and improvisations in Littlewood's work with actors comes from a production of Büchner's *Danton's Death*, which was never actually mounted.[21] The play was written in 1835, but was not performed until the early years of the twentieth century, and the writer made little concession to its possible staging. There are scenes of the revolutionary mob teeming through the streets of Paris. In the early stages of rehearsal, a square was drawn on the floor and the actors played a children's game called 'The Raft of the *Medusa*'. The *Medusa* was a ship which sank near the equator with inadequate boat and raft capacity to save those on board. In order to live, survivors struggled to push the weakest overboard to the sharks.

In the game, all players crowd into the square and then push and pull until only one person – the winner – is left in the square. Those who touch the ground outside the square are out. This game was played for many days before Littlewood began to introduce new rules. These, first, indicated the time that the raft had been in the sea. Five days on the equator, ten days, two weeks, etc. At each stage the energy with which the actions were played declined, and the movement slowed down and lightened. Then a copy of the painting of *The Raft of the Medusa* by the Romantic painter Géricault was brought in and the actors were told to play the game in the style of Géricault. Finally, the square was dispensed with and the actors moved into the streets and the style of the playing was established. Out of a simple game, a complex solution involving period style evolved, through which to play the street scenes.

Figure 8.3 Littlewood's production of *The Hostage* by Brendan Behan at the Théâtre des Nations Festival, Paris.

Source: Clive Barker collection.

The games and improvisations became a laboratory through which Littlewood was able to explore such qualities as time, weight, direction and flow – the qualities through which Laban characterised all movements. It was also the process through which the rhythmic patterns of the performance were established. The abiding memory I have of the productions I saw and took part in is of complex interweavings of the individual actor's rhythms into the jazz ensemble to which I drew attention earlier. It was this rhythmic ensemble playing that carried the flow of the production and, again, made the presence of a prompter irrelevant.

REHEARSAL TECHNIQUES

A large part of the usefulness of working this way lies with the particular faculties which Littlewood brings to rehearsal. Apart from the quality and direction of her own research and her experience, she has the ability to think on her feet very fast, much faster than any of the actors. In rehearsal she was always able to change and develop the direction of improvisations, which took the pressure off the actors and propelled them into cognitive situations at a speed and with such imagination that the actor was not able to see where the rehearsal was going until it got there. This required a particular type of actor, naive and trusting, and accounts for many who were unable to respond to her direction and left early.

Littlewood has particular anathemas, expressed in the Theatre Workshop time as 'Old Vic Acting', although no one could ever remember her going within miles of that institution, and 'past tense acting'. By the former she intended criticism of the conservatoire-trained actor.[22] It is common in some theatres to place no great value on the ensemble company, for the actor to work out his or her character and actions independent of the rest of the company and to rely on the director to choreograph the parts into a seeming whole. This process is one of preconception. It is all worked out in advance, very often incorporating mannerism, devices and effects which have 'worked' in other situations in the past, and then repeated in rehearsal and performance. To some degree it is a defence mechanism to save actors from the disruptive interference of poor directors. It is known as 'doing your homework', and British actors have been for a long time very good at taking responsibility for their own performances in this way.

For someone who works in an ensemble, jazz-like manner, this way of working is characterised by intractable actors. Rehearsals are reduced to synthetic, factory-like procedures. The moves are worked on, then each actor constructs a simplistic, cause-and-effect line to explain what he or she is going to do, often regardless of the others, but usually with a nod towards agreement. Then the lines are learned and in the later rehearsals the actors polish what has been set by marking through the moves and action until the final rehearsals when the actors 'let it go'. The production is then fixed and the intention is that this fixity should be repeated at each subsequent performance.

There is little or no room in this process to explore alternatives or to develop new approaches to a scene. All performances are kept within a controlled 'normal' limit. There is no room for an actor to explore the extremities of the character's psychology, pathology or creativity. Since the purpose of performance is to repeat identically the past reality of the fixed production, everything happening in the present has to be ignored. If the wall falls down, ignore it. If there is a disturbance in the auditorium, carry on regardless. Reality lies in remembering, recovering and repeating the past. It produces 'past tense acting'. This is characterised by an insensitivity to space, a slight but significant retarding of the pelvis, which alters the balance of the body and allows the mind to predominate over the physical sensations of the body, and by an absence of direct eye contact between the actors, each enclosed in their own world.

This is the antithesis of the Theatre Workshop process. It should be clear by now that productions were not conceived on synthetic lines, but holistically. There was no question of adding A to B, but of constantly challenging, changing and developing A. In this the work of Littlewood has affinity with that of Meyerhold, of whom it was said that every rehearsal looked like a performance and every performance like a rehearsal. At no point did a Theatre Workshop production ever become set.

There was no room in Theatre Workshop for an actor who tried out pre-conceived effects, or for someone who tried out the actor's defensive and evasive device of claiming 'I don't feel it'. This brought a response on at least one occasion of: 'You're not here to fucking feel, you're here to fucking do.'[23] Experienced actors working this way reached levels of performance they could not reach elsewhere. Willing novices were preferable to the conservatoire-trained actors. The lore of Theatre Workshop ran that to join the company you should never audition but should take a job in the bar or as the boiler man.

The process of creating an ensemble and inhibiting preconceived intentions and actions went along with the process of breaking the actor down. It was not simply a question that some actors pre-planned what they were going to do and some did not, but that all actors to some extent set limits to the exploration and delay setting sail on an uncharted sea. This process is complicated, relies upon trust and self-confidence in giving up the conscious control which the actor often inhibits.[24] The intuitive actions of the subconscious are overridden in favour of conscious control, which inevitably results in the production of clichés.

Sometimes a drastic process of breaking down personality defences is necessary to allow the actor the flexibility to choose alternative ways of acting. Sexually unsure and inexperienced, and coming from a society rootedly homophobic, I was made by Littlewood to get up on stage and display femininity. I hated doing this, but as with other things it broke through my defensive inhibitions. The superb performance of the actor playing Edward II for Theatre Workshop was achieved, through great pain, by having him confront his latent homosexuality, at a time when no great sympathy or tolerance could be expected from society at large.

Often the process resulted in continual repetition of actions through a use of the *via negativa*. Seemingly endless repetition of units of action was met with a categorical rejection. Anyone who has worked with Littlewood will wince at the memory of going over single lines time and time again, each actor in turn speaking the line until the valid intonation, phasing and emphasis emerged. Units were run over endlessly until all the actor could think was: 'I have no idea what to do. I've run out of every idea I have. Oh, shit.' At this point, devoid of conscious intention, the actor would enter the stage and simply do it. This was almost invariably correct and accepted without comment.[25]

In addition to the processes outlined above, Littlewood at times has resorted to a German technique known by the French term of the *siffleuse*, the whistler. Each actor is allocated a prompter who moves behind him or her, speaking the lines half a line before the actor as a conscious prompt. The actor is not only free to explore the situation, free of having to remember the lines, but learns the text in the functional, communicative manner in which it is delivered by the prompter, close to how the line should be spoken. The use of the *siffleuse* reinstates a process close to the inter-active relationship of mind and speech, which is natural to us. The use of the *via negativa* and the functional intervention of the *siffleuse* remove self-imposed and textural pressures which interfere with the action of the subconscious.

The work of the director who acts as a coach and trainer of an ensemble is more often concerned with removing obstacles to authenticity than adding to, or refining, what the actor preconceives. Directing is conceived as steering rather than ordering.[26] It should be noted that the company carried out training during the rehearsal period. The purpose, beyond that of simply keeping the instrument tuned, was, first, to condition the actor to work instinctively, and also to establish a language, largely based on Stanislavsky and Laban, through which to communicate as the process of fine-tuning in the rehearsals began.

LATER REHEARSALS

One of the particular talents which Littlewood possesses is her ability to analyse a text in terms of work effort. I have known her put up a detailed rehearsal schedule at the beginning of the week, for the whole week, and not be more than twenty minutes out at the end. In this she sensed that certain units presented problems on which much of the later action depended. This may be related to Brecht's concept of the nodal points which pull together the previous action and from which future action flows. Her perception of these has always been a matter of judgement not accessible to analysis but singularly successful.

Rehearsals generally continued along the lines I have indicated above. Key units were worked on to explore intention and motivation. Changes were explored in terms of the Laban movement efforts being used by the actor(s). One frequent solution to problems was for the actor to sing or dance the unit, to physicalise, by extension, the line or movement. Units were often conceived in terms of another concept which springs from Laban – that of dance mime. Working actions are gradually extended in size and accentuated rhythm to transform the action into dance. A counter-process would bring the dance back down to the ground working action.

In *Oh, What a Lovely War!*, there is a scene in which soldiers portray the burial of the dead, although, as always with that play, the action is portrayed very much in the Chinese theatre fashion without any scenic attempt to represent a real graveyard with real corpses. As the action proceeds, the music comes up underneath it and the movement is gradually extended into song and dance, with shovels taking the place of skeletal partners. The result is 'The Bells of Hell Go Ting-a-ling-a-ling'. At the end, the music fades and the movement returns to the more realistic, mimetic representation it began with. This is not a unique use of this technique, which appears in several Laurel and Hardy films.[27] It was, though, particularly poignant, and it is characteristic of Littlewood's refusal to stay within naturalistic techniques and, rather, evidence of her use of a wide range of stylised techniques.

Rehearsals explored counterpoint. Actors were made aware of what they brought on stage with them. Where the text made the given circumstances, the intention and the emotional mood quite clear, actors were asked to complement, or even contradict, this with other information. There was a constant use of other actors to offer, through their attitudes and movement, alternative views and interpretations of the main action. The stage became peopled with characters, each with a distinct, coherent and continuous life of their own, replete with values, hopes, ambitions, fears and judgements.

There were never any spear-carriers or supernumeraries on the stage.[28] In opposition to the synthetic, linear approach to making theatre, Theatre Workshop created a theatre rich in texture, in which every corner of the stage was alive and active. In this way it was possible to see a production over and over again and always find something new. In the sense that there were so many human beings playing out their lives in concert, no performance could ever be remotely the same in detail, but each was always bedded down in a common understanding, purpose and rhythmic technique. This interdependence and co-ordination made for a lack of self-consciousness. If the purpose of playing is not to make things happen but to let things happen, as Littlewood believes, this technique constantly strove for that state. The late Harry H. Corbett, who could stand as the epitome of the Theatre Workshop actor, said to me once that his ambition was to give one performance in which he had only one motivation, the one which took him out of the wings and onto the stage. From that point, he wanted to play only off of his reaction to the other actors. In a theatrical world where so many stages are littered with actions and questions to which no one responds, Theatre Workshop approached that ideal. In spite of poor physical and financial resources, but also in the sense of 'poor theatre' (which Grotowski and Barba use to mark out a total utilisation of the actor's resources), Theatre Workshop was a rich, multi-textured theatre.[29]

The guiding principles behind this way of working are, first, that everything should come from the actor, since only the actor appears on the stage, and, second, that what the actor does on stage is determined by what has been done in rehearsal.

On stage the actor can only play. This is true of all actors, but not all actors have prepared to the same extent and in the same ways. In conversation, Littlewood once said that any actor should be able, at the dress rehearsal, to take a direction to enter through a different door from the one which had been rehearsed. If they could not, they should not be in the theatre. But if they had not explored the material of the performance in rehearsal, there was no way they could act in any meaningful way.

There is one caveat to this. At a certain point in time, the pressure of the opening night and the consequent presence of an audience make it inevitable that, if the actors have not at that point caught the full scale of the performance, the director must supply direction to pull the production together. In fact, working in this way leaves a mass of loose ends and a lack of overall consistency. At this point the director must head for home. In the synthetic theatre, the director begins to head for home from day one of the rehearsal period. It is in the character of Littlewood that she could delay this moment until very late: three days or so before the opening night. There has been criticism of this. Actors who have not understood these processes have complained that in the end she did what she wanted with the production, regardless of what went before. Critics have noted and praised the composition of significant groupings and images in the production. There is no contradiction here. To hold back from dictatorially directing the production until such a late date depends upon a confidence in being able to pull things technically into a coherent shape, and Littlewood's early training and talent for painting facilitated her ability to rapidly choreograph stage action. However, without the complex processes which led up to that point, there would have been nothing to pull together or choreograph.

PERFORMANCE

If one quality characterised Theatre Workshop performances it was high energy. There are two kinds of performance energy. One is seen when the performer goes out to 'sell' the show, blasting energy regardless of the quality, or even the nature, of the material. This was always strongly discouraged by Littlewood, who often gave instructions in terms of, 'Don't go out there to succeed, you will only fail. Go out there prepared to fail and you might succeed.' To do this involves trusting the material you have been working with, the preparation you have made during the rehearsal and, of course, the other actors. To do this involves a high level of risk and Theatre Workshop was always a theatre which encouraged risk. 'Efficiency is death' was an injunction often given.

The energy which characterised Theatre Workshop was an internal energy which sprang from engagement with the processes followed during rehearsals. This will always gain a greater response from an audience than the externally applied kick energy, which often pushes the audience back from engagement with the play. In working on the units of action, there was a continuous overlap. Before one unit ended, the next had already begun. In many lines of dialogue there was a point at which the thought could be grasped without the full line being delivered. That point was the trigger to spark off the next action and the dialogue overlapped. Actors began their actions and reactions before they had a line to speak.

This gave a continuous flow of action, which heightened the concentration and stimulated energy in the actors and kept the audience continuously engaged. Actors were never allowed to become cosy, which often happens in ensembles. The actors become 'pally': personal relationships begin to stray onto the stage and soften

Figure 8.4 Littlewood's production of Brendan Behan's *The Quare Fellow*.
Source: Photo by V.J. Spinner by permission of The Theatre Workshop Archive.

the conflicts. Kent Baker recalls a note from Littlewood saying, 'All the actors love you and they ought to hate you'. Theatre Workshop was not a comfortable place to be and actors were often fed false opinions, slander and lies to disturb their complacency. It was the only place, said Howard Goorney, where you could stay a week and write a book on your experiences.

Notes

1   She is also said to have heard the term *Verfremdung* once in her time with the Berliner Ensemble. See Margaret Eddershaw (1994) 'Actors in Brecht', in Thomson and Sacks (eds), *The Cambridge Companion to Brecht*, Cambridge: Cambridge University Press.

2   Jooss says this in the course of an interview with John Hodgson, issued on video by the Department of Drama, University of Hull.

3   See Graham Ley (1993) 'The Rhetoric of Theory: the Role of Metaphor in Brook's *The Empty Space*', *New Theatre Quarterly* 35 (August): 246.

4   The author of this chapter worked with Joan Littlewood, as stage-manager, technical director and actor, for various periods, adding up to between three and four years, from 1955 to 1973. When no formal teaching programme exists, it is easy to credit where the learning process began but very difficult to disentangle, after a period of years, the origins of your development from what you have learned since from your own experiences.

5   What has united Littlewood with Ewan MacColl, in my experience, has been a mixture of great generosity in playing down their genius and an almost paranoiac resentment at not being given enough credit for it. Such blanket denials should be taken with a pinch of salt.

Both sides of the dialectic can be seen in their autobiographies: *Joan's Story* (1994) London: Methuen and *Journeyman* (1990) London: Sidgwick and Jackson.

6   See H. Goorney (1981) *The Theatre Workshop Story*, London: Eyre Methuen, pp. 173–75. Most of what is expressed in this chapter is amplified greatly in this book.

7   Stated in BBC2 TV Programme on Littlewood, 1996.

8   Note dropped in conversation by Joan Littlewood.

9   Quoted in Charles Marowitz (1965) 'Littlewood Pays a Dividend', in *The Encore Reader*, London: Methuen University Paperbacks, p. 230. He gives no attribution for the original source.

10   The history of Theatre Workshop has three major sources: Joan Littlewood (1994) *Joan's Story*, London: Methuen; Howard Goorney's *The Theatre Workshop Story*, quoted earlier; Ewan MacColl (1990) *Journeyman*, London: Sidgwick and Jackson. The history of the earlier political theatre companies can be found in Goorney and MacColl (eds) (1986) *Agit-Prop to Theatre Workshop*, Manchester: Manchester University Press and Samuel, MacColl and Cosgrove (eds) (1985) *Theatres of the Left 1880–1935*, London: Routledge and Kegan Paul.

11   See Derek Paget (1995) 'Theatre Workshop, Moussinac and the European Connection', *New Theatre Quarterly* XI, Part 3 (43), August.

12   See quotation from Rosalie Williams in Goorney, *The Theatre Workshop Story*, p. 20.

13   See Goorney, p. 8.

14   See Rudolf Laban (1960) *The Mastery of Movement*, London: Macdonald and Evans; Rudolf Laban (1975) *Modern Educational Dance*, London: Macdonald and Evans; also Jean Newlove (1993) *Laban for Actors and Dancers*, London: Nick Hern Books.

15   See Goorney, pp. 41–42.

16   I am indebted to Albert Hunt, who first formulated this recognition of Theatre Workshop.

17   See Richard Findlater (1953) *The Unholy Trade*, London: Gollancz, p. 81.

18   The research for *The Dutch Courtesan* was an education in the nature of the Elizabethan underworld.

19   See Derek Paget (1990) 'Oh, What a Lovely War!: The Texts and Their Context', *New Theatre Quarterly* VI, Part 3 (23), August: 244.

20   Brian Murphy, in conversation, said he was thrown into panic when he left Theatre Workshop and went to work in repertory. He realised he would have to learn lines in isolation, which he had never done before.

21   During the rehearsals it was learned that Theatre 69 was planning to open the same play at an earlier date. The production was, therefore, cancelled, although there is a strong suspicion that no production was ever really intended and the work on the play was only ever intended as a training exercise.

22   It should be pointed out that the training of actors today is much more advanced than it was in the 1950s and 1960s, when actors tended to be more stereotypical, mannered and self-possessed. The irony is that around the time Littlewood gave up directing, actors were beginning to emerge who were much more adaptable to her way of working. Today, she would have no problems in finding the actors she would want.

23   In this she is in line with the process, stated as an aphorism by the French director, Louis Jouvet: the text; the action; the emotions.

24   Keith Johnstone's (1981) book, *Impro*, London: Methuen, categorises the many means that actors employ to prevent themselves from being creative.

25   During the rehearsals for *The Hostage*, I was obviously pleased with myself and was becoming self-possessed. One day I arrived at the theatre earlier in the morning, passed Littlewood on the stairs and said, 'Good morning, Joan'. She stopped, glared at me and issued the damning judgment: 'You're nothing but a fucking broomstick, with fucking bananas for fucking fingers.' She moved on. I entered the rehearsal in a state of nervous shock but I was prepared to give her what she wanted.

26   In the video interview quoted in note 2, Jooss qualifies his statement that Laban never discussed the theory behind his work, by describing a dance rehearsal in which Laban rejects every move made until – Jooss asserts – a 'space' exists inside the dancer. 'Whatever' fills that space will be 'authentic'. Only that human being can make that action. Whether Littlewood adopted this directly from Laban, whom she knew well, I cannot say – but something of this order characterised the Theatre Workshop rehearsals.

27   The use of this technique exists in many areas of popular comedy. See Morecambe and Wise prepare breakfast to the music of 'The Stripper'.

28   The texture of the performances, achieved through counterpoint, contradiction and inter-woven story lines was carried out by a group of actors, known collectively as 'the slag'. I am very happy to have spent several years as a member of that group.
29   See Goorney, p. 175.

Bibliography

Bradby, D. and Williams, D. (1988) *Directors' Theatre*, Basingstoke: Macmillan.

Goorney, Howard (1981) *The Theatre Workshop Story*, London: Eyre Methuen.

Goorney, H. and MacColl, E. (eds) (1986) *Agit-Prop to Theatre Workshop*, Manchester: Manchester University Press.

Laban, Rudolf (1960) *The Mastery of Movement*, London: Macdonald and Evans.

—— (1975) *Modern Educational Dance*, third edition, London: Macdonald and Evans.

Leach, Robert (2006) *Theatre Workshop: Joan Littlewood and the Making of Modern British Theatre*, Exeter: University of Exeter Press.

Littlewood, Joan (1994) *Joan's Story*, London: Methuen.

MacColl, Ewan (1990) *Journeyman*, London: Sidgwick and Jackson.

MacColl, Ewan (2008) *Plays 1*, London: Methuen.

Marowitz, C., Milne, T. and Hale, O. (eds) (1965) *The Encore Reader*, London: Methuen.

Newlove, Jean (1993) *Laban for Actors and Dancers*, London: Nick Hern Books.

Paget, Derek (1990) '*Oh What a Lovely War!*: The Texts and Their Context', *New Theatre Quarterly*, VI, Part 3, 23, August: 244–60.

—— (1993) 'The Rhetoric of Theory: The Role of Metaphor in Brook's *The Empty Space*', *New Theatre Quarterly*, 35, August: 246–54.

—— (1995) 'Theatre Workshop, Moussinac and the European Connection', *New Theatre Quarterly*, XI, Part 3, 43, August: 211–24.

Samuel, R., MacColl, E. and Cosgrove, S. (eds) (1985) *Theatres of the Left 1880–1935*, London: Routledge and Kegan Paul.

Thomson, P. and Sacks, G. (eds) (1994) *The Cambridge Companion to Brecht*, Cambridge: Cambridge University Press.

Chapter 9

David Krasner

STRASBERG, ADLER AND MEISNER: METHOD ACTING

METHOD ACTING IS ONE of the most popular and controversial approaches to acting in the United States. According to Harold Clurman, the 'Method', as it is commonly called, is 'an abbreviation of the term "Stanislavsky Method" '. The 'Method' itself, Clurman adds, is a 'means of training actors as well as a technique for the use of actors in their work on parts' (1994: 369). Like Stanislavsky's System, Method acting codifies acting exercises, rehearsal techniques and working procedures, with the intention of helping actors achieve greater persuasiveness, feeling and depth. The Method combines Stanislavsky's techniques and the work of his pupil Eugene Vakhtangov for the purpose of understanding and effectively performing a role.

Although there are many instructors, directors and actors who have contributed to its development, three Method acting teachers are recognised as having set the standard of its success: Lee Strasberg (1901–82), Stella Adler (1901–92), and Sanford Meisner (1905–97).[1] Whilst they collaborated together in the Group Theatre during the 1930s, each emphasised different aspects of the Method. My objective here will be first to present an overview of the Method, and then to consider the theories, exercises and contributions of these three Method acting instructors. In addition, I will pay close attention to the differences of the three teachers – Strasberg's emphasis on the psychological, Adler's on the sociological, and Meisner's on the behavioural – demonstrating the diversity of Method training. Moreover, because the three teachers were interested in process rather than result – in teaching acting as a craft rather than promoting commercial productions – they tended to emphasise pedagogy over directing.[2] With this in mind, I will concentrate on theories and exercises of the Method, rather than particular productions.[3] First, a thumbnail sketch of the Method's history and theory.

INTRODUCTION TO THE METHOD

The American Method began in the United States at the American Laboratory Theatre, where from 1923 to 1926 acting classes taught by Stanislavsky's émigré students Richard Boleslavsky and Maria Ouspenskaya introduced American actors to a new performing technique.[4] These classes, supplemented by the Moscow Art Theatre's visits to the United States in 1923 and 1924, introduced American actors to a new way of working that created a distinct 'Method'. The Method, like Stanislavsky's System, wanted to see both human beings as having depth, and the actor as a complex psychological being who generated layers of meaning in performance which lie beyond easy comprehension. Boleslavsky's and Ouspenskaya's students Harold Clurman and Lee Strasberg, along with Cheryl Crawford, met in 1925 at the Theatre Guild, where their association led to the Group Theatre (1931–40).[5] The Group consolidated around a collection of actors dedicated to producing new American plays, and performing them in a style derived from Stanislavsky's System. Moreover, the Group was committed to theatre that stressed social protest, moral and ethical concerns and political activism. Hence, 'Method acting' emerged as a technique that drew from Stanislavsky's emphasis on the craft of acting, and accentuated working on a role that called upon the actor to build from his or her personal life and political ideals.

Method acting was the Group's sole approach to rehearsals and plays. It evolved from the ensemble techniques and collective rehearsal procedures developed by Group actors, providing the company with a practical and theoretical grounding that differed considerably from the acting systems in the American theatre at the time. Stanislavsky's and Vakhtangov's work on the actor's 'inner life' was part of the Group's working procedures. Instead of the star system, ensemble work was emphasised; instead of relying on inspiration alone, Group actors were trained to evoke specific emotions and actions; instead of mannerisms, Group actors developed an unassuming natural stage presence; and instead of grandiose theatricality, Group actors stressed real behaviour in performance. Group actor and teacher Robert Lewis explains that real behaviour on stage must be 'really experienced, but artistically controlled, and correctly used for the particular character portrayed, the complete circumstances of the scene, and the chosen style of the author and play being performed' (1958: 99). For the Group, 'indicating' emotions and feelings were replaced by actual 'felt' experiences; inspiration and craft 'were not mutually exclusive' (Smith 1990: 38); and actors would experience their roles by observing and living the lives of their characters. As Stella Adler explained, the 'Group Theatre contributed a standard of acting that transformed the American theatre' (1976: 512).

Teachers of the Method were influenced by their collaboration at the American Laboratory Theatre, the Group Theatre and the Yiddish Theater.[6] During the 1950s and 1960s, Strasberg (at the Actors Studio),[7] Adler (at the Stella Adler Conservatory), and Meisner (at the Neighborhood Playhouse) advanced their own versions of the Method, each claiming to be the rightful descendants of Stanislavsky's System, and each using various stages of Stanislavsky's and Vakhtangov's work to underscore their approach. Whilst the three diverged on some matters of emphasis, they more or less agreed on ten principles essential to Method acting:

1   The actor must justify every word, action and relationship on stage. The actor moves and speaks spontaneously, but everything is thought out during rehearsals to ensure the maximum emphasis on *motivation*.

2   In finding the character's motivation, actors search for *objectives*, *actions* and *intentions*. Actors discover the character's *super-objective*, or '*spine*', that motivates all the actions on stage.

3   The character's super-objective must have *urgency*: every action and objective must have an immediacy ('how badly do you want the objective, and what consequences will occur if you do not attain it?'). This includes creating *obstacles* that prevent easy access to achieving the objective. The work on urgency must emerge from *relaxation*, *concentration* and the *creative selection* (choices) of objectives.

4   To support the objective, the actor creates *subtext*, or thought processes, that motivate the character's actions. Every word in a play has an underlying, non-verbal base which informs and supports the playwright's written word. The playwright's words serve as a surface blueprint; the subtext supplies the role's interior definition.

5   In finding the subtext of the role, the actor rejects generalisations, emphasising instead the specific *given circumstances* of the play, everything from period style and social fashion to the way a character behaves, lives and relates to other characters and situations.

6   In defining the given circumstances, actors behave *as* if they are living in the situation of the play. In doing so, the actor must bring his or her *imagination* into focus, *particularising* creative choices that will enhance the text and flesh out compelling ideas that lurk beneath the words.

7   An emphasis on *truthful behaviour*; feelings must never be 'indicated'. Rather, the actor works from his or her passions and emotions, which is often referred to in Method acting as working from the 'inside out'. Method acting director and former member of the Group Theatre, Elia Kazan, building on Vakhtangov's theories,[8] wrote that for Method actors, experience on the stage 'must be actual, not suggested by external imitation; the actor must be going through what the character he's playing is going through; the emotion must be real, not pretended; it must be happening, not indicated' (1988: 143).

8   To accomplish the experience of real feelings, the actor works *moment-to-moment* on *impulse*, talking and listening as if the events on stage are actually happening in the immediate present. In Method acting, characterisation is not fixed, but a fluid and spontaneous response to events on stage. Strasberg explains that

> the actor has to know what he is going to do when he goes on the stage, and yet has to permit himself to do it so that it seems to happen for the first time. This means that the body, the voice, every facet of expression, must follow the natural changes in impulse; even though the actor repeats, the strength of the impulses may well change from day to day.
>
> (1965: 167)

9   Rehearsals require *improvising* on the dramatic text – gibberish (Strasberg), paraphrasing (Adler), or repetition exercises (Meisner) – encouraging the actor's personal interpretation and investment, thereby freeing the actor from a dependency on words.

10   Finally, the actor *personalises* the role, i.e. draws from the self, from his or her emotional, psychological or imaginative reality, bringing into view aspects of one's memories, life experiences and observations that correlate with the role.

This final element has drawn criticism from Robert Brustein, who complains that the Method actor, reflecting their interest in the self, 'usually purveys a single character from role to role, one that is recognisably close to his own personality'. For Brustein, this 'subjective, autobiographical approach to performance is reflected in the most prominent American acting method, where the current jargon includes phrases like "personalisation" and "private moment", signifying techniques with which to investigate one's own psychic history' (1973: 1). What Brustein fails to realise is that the self is neither static nor fixed, but evolving – in other words, human beings reinvent themselves continuously. The self changes by entering into new relationships, and the actor must bring new ideas to each successive characterisation. Moreover, the self is never to the exclusion of the study of character; investing personal experiences with textual analysis and observations of life are not necessarily contradictory working procedures. Brustein's view of the Method is a common albeit misleading opinion present in much academic writing on the subject.[9] In what follows, I hope not only to avoid such errors, but to define the three principal approaches to Method acting that illuminate its diversity and wide-ranging applicability. The three approaches described here were products of the Group Theatre experience, but each drew on specific facets.

LEE STRASBERG

Truth and emotion: using the self in public

The human being who acts is the human being who lives.

(Strasberg 1965: 78)

Figure 9.1 Lee Strasberg directing a scene during class at The Actors Studio.
Source: Photo © Leonard McCombe/Time Life Pictures/Getty Images.

Lee Strasberg was the founding member of the Group Theatre. He later withdrew from the Group in 1937, continuing his career as a teacher and director. In 1949 he assumed the Directorship of the Actors Studio. Although not a founder of the Studio, he eventually became identified with the school. The term Method Acting itself is most closely associated with Strasberg and the Actors Studio.

Lee Strasberg developed a number of approaches to acting, but three aspects of his work stand out: relaxation, concentration and affective memory. For Strasberg, the fundamental effect of the actor must be directed towards the 'training of his internal skills' through a process of 'relaxation and concentration' (1987: 116). This dual process of relaxation and concentration leads performers to personalisation, what Strasberg student Kim Stanley explains as finding 'things in yourself that you can use' (quoted in Gussow 1982).

Strasberg's theory of the Method is predicated on 'procedure, not a series of rules to be applied specifically' (Hull 1985: 18). For Strasberg, there is no one way into a role; each presents its own problems to be studied and solved. But above all, Strasberg described an actor as one who 'can create out of himself' (1965: 81). To do this, the performer must 'appeal to the unconscious and the subconscious'. Arriving at the state of creativity requires the 'presence of something that stirs the actor subconsciously' (1965: 82). Strasberg defines the main feature of his teaching:

> Let's say the actor learns to relax and concentrate. He learns to arouse his imagination, which is his belief in the reality and logic of what he is doing; but then we find that the actor's expression of these things is weak. Often we see things going on inside that can't come out – the face contracts, the eyes contract – the emotion isn't let through. The actor feels at times like crying but he can't cry, he can't uncurl the muscles to permit the tears to flow. Such strong conditioning has been created against the expression of emotion. I would say that I have experimented with the whole problem of freeing the expression of the actor.
>
> (1964: 123)

For Strasberg, freeing the expression begins with relaxation and concentration. David Garfield observes that to facilitate relaxation, 'Strasberg has the actor sit in a chair and proceed to find a position in which, if he had to, he could fall asleep' (1980: 169). The actor must relax before an audience, something not easy to do. Of particular importance is the relaxation of the jaw, an area of much concern for Feldenkrais practitioners.[10] As feelings of relaxation increase and emotions stir, Garfield explains that the actor 'opens his throat and permits a sound from deep in the chest to come out, to make sure the emotion is not blocked' (1980: 168). The actor continues to emit sounds that help release tension and free creative expression.

In developing concentration, Strasberg emphasises a series of sense-memory exercises. Sense-memory is the stimulation of the senses (tactile, taste, olfactory, auditory and visual). The actor recalls important events in their life, and then tries to remember only the sensual facets: touch, taste, sight, etc. The ability to recall senses stimulates the body rather than the mind, giving the actor greater visceral awareness and experience.

In sense-memory exercises, the actor begins by handling imaginary objects. Actors recreate drinking coffee, shaving or other daily activities.[11] The point is not merely to mime the activity, but to find the psychological motivation underlying the experience. Garfield is clear on this: 'the ultimate range of imaginary objects that a performer must create on stage is enormous. It may include physical objects, overall sensations, mental or fantasy objects, situations, events, relationships, and other characters.' If the actor is to fulfil the obligations of the role, Garfield asserts, 'he must be well grounded in the simplest sense-memory work' (1980: 170). By 'grounded' Garfield means that the actor does not merely create an object, but invests in the object a personal history. For example, if an actor holds a glass, the glass is not merely an object, but a gift from a lover or friend. The actor recalls how the lover offered the glass as a gift, and in so doing, the actor remembers, through the senses, the time of day, the weather, the colour of the shoes of the lover, and so on.

In Strasberg's private moment, the actor lives out their 'private moments' before a classroom audience. Private moment is the literal performance of an activity that one does in private. According to Doug Moston, it was developed by Strasberg in 1956 and 1957 'to aid actors in creating the ability to behave in a truly private fashion while being observed by an audience' (1993: 93). In being private in public, the actor frees inhibitions. Foster Hirsch explains that because private moment is an exercise rather than a performance, it 'releases the actor from any obligation to a text or . . . to an audience' (1984: 136). Working from private experience, the actor is free, as Strasberg puts it, 'to sit before us, to smell an aroma, and not to do anything physical, but to focus only on what you're doing with your concentration' (quoted in Hirsch 1984: 137). Private moments also allow the actor to experience feelings that, owing to inhibitions, they would otherwise not share. Strasberg uses an example of an actress whose voice was monotonous. In doing her private moment, he discovered that she enjoyed playing music when alone and would dance with 'abandon'. He then had the actress play the music she liked, and dance wildly on stage. He describes the experience:

> It would make your hair stand up. You would never have thought that this girl had this degree of response and expression. We made her do it, and it worked and from that moment on her voice and action changed. We got through some kind of block by making use of the Private Moment.
>
> (1964: 125)

Strasberg's most controversial exercise is affective memory, developed by combining Stanislavsky's early work on Pavlovian training,[12] Vakhtangov's work on performative emotions,[13] and the work of psychologist Théodule Ribot.[14] Its purpose is to release emotions on stage. Strasberg states:

> The basic idea of affective memory is not emotional recall but that the actor's emotion on the stage should never be really real. It always should be only *remembered* emotion. An emotion that happens right now spontaneously is out of control – you don't know what's going to happen from it, and the actor can't always maintain and repeat it. Remembered emotion is something that the actor can create and repeat: without that the thing is hectic.
>
> (1964: 132)

For Strasberg, affective memory 'is the basic element of the actor's reality' (1964: 131). In particular, it draws out the emotions from the past that are ingrained in one's mind and body, rather than what Strasberg identifies as the merely 'literal', or indicated, interpretation from the text (1964: 131; 1965: 112). Edward Easty explains that by

having a 'repertoire' of emotional experiences, the actor can call forth, at
the proper time, the desire[s] one needed for the character. The broader
his 'repertoire', the greater the resources for creativeness and the greater
the number of roles he will be able to act.

(1981: 45–46)

Although it usually begins as an attempt to evoke emotions appropriate to the circumstances of the play, the emotion may appear in a somewhat different fashion,
since, as Strasberg explains, 'the emotional value of the experience may have
changed'. However, 'by attempting a lot of affective memories, the actor gradually
obtains a stock of memories that are permanent and become easier to invoke as
he continues to use them' (1965: 111). Robert Lewis maintains that in affective
memory, emotions derived from the events you are calling up are 'likely to be
different [i.e. they will change] in quality or quantity or both when you repeat the
exercise' (1980: 126). This is to be not only expected but welcomed; since your
feelings towards the event have evolved, your emotions will evolve accordingly. In
fact, they will subtly change each time you perform the exercises. The significance
lies in the fact that the actor becomes emotionally available, prepared to respond
instantly and expressively with feelings and passions.

   In affective memory, the actor is completely relaxed. Then, the performer tries to
recall, as Lewis describes it, 'some event in your past which you think might stir up
some feeling usable for the problem in your scene, preferably from your distant past'
(1980: 126). The operative word here is 'problem', since the performer is having
difficulty in coming to terms with feelings required for the scene. The actor is not
trying to force emotions; rather, they recall the event by remembering all the
sensations that occurred at the time: smells, taste, sights, sounds and tactile sensations.
The actor relies on sense memory to trigger the emotion.

   Wendy Smith provides a detailed explanation of affective memory. The actor
concentrates on an incident from their own life that produced the desired emotion.
However:

> The actor [does not] try to recall the feeling directly, but rather to re-
> experience the sensory impressions surrounding it; the size of the room it
> happened in, the colour of the walls, the fabric on the furniture, the time
> of day, how the people there were dressed, what they looked like, and so
> on. Then the actor went over the exact sequence of events, concentrating
> on re-creating as precisely as possible the physical reality of the moment.
> When done properly with a strong a situation, the exercise almost invari-
> ably brought the emotion flooding back to the present. The actor could
> then play the scene with the appropriate feeling.
>
> (1990: 38)

Strasberg explains that an 'actor who masters the technique of using the affective
memory begins to be more alive in the present' (quoted in Hirsch 1984: 141).

   Affective memory is simply one way of calling up the passions that help the actor
play a role. It is not, as Colin Counsell would have it, effective merely for 'sad' or
unhappy events (1996: 58). Rather, it is one way to evoke all feelings correlative to the
events in the scene. Nor is it demanded that every Method actor perform an affective
memory; in many instances, uninhibited actors at the Actors Studio were dissuaded
from making use of it. Moreover, the feelings evoked during an episode of affective

memory may surprise the actor (you may laugh when you thought you would cry), and that is significant – the performer has created a true, original and spontaneous sense or feeling in response to scenic events.

Strasberg insists that work on emotions must not be at the expense of actions or characterisation. Work on affective memory is not designed for film (though it can be used there), but for theatre, where the need to return to the emotion is required of the actor several times a week. As he says, in order to repeat a performance, 'you have to have emotional memory. If you don't, then you repeat only the externals of it' (1976: 549).

Strasberg pursued a stage reality that brought forth feelings from the actor. Critics of affective memory seldom understand its purpose: it is an exercise to be used in practice and rehearsal. In other words, it is a *rehearsal technique* that allows the actor to find the emotional triggers that set off appropriate feelings. Richard Hornby suggests that Method actors tend 'to lag behind the play, where quick, drastic ebb and flow of action is common' (1992: 183). But once the actor has incorporated the memory that evokes the emotion, feelings become part of the ebb and flow in a natural way. Like Diderot, Strasberg was interested in enabling the actor to repeat performances with uniform emotional intensity, and not 'dry up' after one or two rehearsals or shows. Strasberg sums up the exercise's purpose in the following:

> Affective memory is the basic material for reliving on the stage, and therefore for the creation of a real experience on the stage. What the actor repeats in performance after performance is not just the words and movements he practiced in rehearsal, but the memory of emotion. He reaches this emotion through the memory of thought and sensation.
>
> (1987: 113)

David Garfield asserts that affective memory 'is by no means an indulgence of Strasberg's. It is an absolute necessity to his concept of acting as the creation of real experience in response to imaginary stimuli' (1980: 175). Its purpose, Garfield adds, is 'to create whatever reality in whatever "style" the actor, the director, or the play calls for' (1980: 181). Along similar lines, Steve Vineberg enjoins us to consider that the 'aim of all Method teachers, whatever their means, is to produce genuine emotion on the stage, but Strasberg's actors have been accused of displaying emotionalism, as a result of his prodding and pushing at their feelings'. Whilst Strasberg's emphasis on feelings resulted in making his classroom appear more like group therapy than performance, Vineberg is correct to point out that he was no fanatic. Strasberg, Vineberg says, 'often took tension as a sign of emotional excessiveness, and his relaxation exercises fought against it' (1991: 109).[15]

Despite Strasberg's continuing significance as a teacher of Stanislavsky's principles and a pioneer of his own acting theories, he remains largely misunderstood. Robert Gordon's study of acting, to cite just one of many anti-Strasberg examples, condemns Strasberg for betraying a 'faithful version of Stanislavsky's system' (Gordon 2006: 4). Gordon claims that Strasberg's method has 'little similarity with Stanislavsky's search to discover the "natural laws" of artistic creation' (77). This line of thinking has prevailed in the history of acting analysis (see Hornby, Brustein, Counsell, Harrop, and others); it is, however, inaccurate. Strasberg's contributions to acting are multifaceted and closely aligned with Stanislavsky. In his superb essay on Stanislavsky and Strasberg, Marc Gordon clarifies the intricate relationship between them and provides evidence of their similarities, offering one of several examples: for Strasberg, he says, 'emotions have a conditioning factor; the key is finding the trigger. Stanislavski, too, discovered that actors could arouse or evoke certain emotions with the proper inducement' (in Krasner 2000: 53). Strasberg followed Stanislavsky in the pursuit of an emotional 'trigger', or 'inducement', what Stanislavsky called 'decoys'. Decoys, Stanislavsky said, 'are precisely those stimuli to Emotional Memory and recurrent feelings which . . . lure them out'. The actor 'must know which stimulates what, what the right bait is to get the bite. You have to be a gardener, so to speak, of your own heart' (2008: 225).

Strasberg's highly important and oft-overlooked 1941 essay 'Acting and the Training of the Actor' traces the history of actor training, calling attention to the modern aspects of mind, body and emotional development along with the following remarks: 'The actor to appear alive and real must really think on the stage; he must not only make believe he thinks, he must really be doing something' (1941: 142). Real behaviour means real thinking and doing in relation to the scene and its given circumstances. Like Viola Spolin, Strasberg seeks to eliminate the actor's desire for audience approval which gets in the way of truthful behaviour relative to the role. Strasberg additionally emphasises training the body's sensory apparatus (not just the emotions), in making objects visceral and exciting. Thus the work in acting class must consist of the actor 'training himself to make these imaginary objects or stimuli real to himself as they would be in life, so that they will awaken the proper sensory, emotional, and motor response' (1941: 143–44). Strasberg emphasises animal exercises in developing character work – 'we can't just be ourselves', he says (1941: 154) – and actions. He says: 'In making use of "action," three steps are necessary: (1) action, what are you doing; (2) motivation, why are you doing it; (3) adjustment, under what circumstances. The last decides the form in which the action is carried out' (1941: 161).

Strasberg never denied the importance of voice, physicality or script analysis. But for him, the actor must purge the sense of 'performing' and find believability:

> It is difficult to realise how much the sense of 'I'm doing, I'm acting' can commandeer the mind. It is difficult to realise how strong and animal-like the adherence to a verbal pattern or convention can be. It is difficult for the actor to perceive how ferociously the cliché holds on to him.
>
> (1965: 212)

The emphasis on emotion and credible behaviour was, for Strasberg, a process of required actor training.

STELLA ADLER

Imagination, given circumstances and physical action

> Your life is one millionth of what you know. Your talent is your imagination. The rest is lice.
>
> (Hirsch 1984: 214)

Stella Adler was the youngest daughter of the Yiddish actors Jacob and Sarah Adler. As a child star on the Yiddish stage, she learned her craft from the ground up. She was one of the original members of the Group Theatre, and in 1934 she and her then husband, Harold Clurman, went to Paris where they met Stanislavsky and probed

Figure 9.2 Stella Adler giving direction to acting students at the Stella Adler Conservatory.
Source: Photo © Marianne Barcellona/Time Life Pictures/Getty Images.

deeply into his teaching. From 1934 onwards she broke with Strasberg on the fundamental precepts of the Method. Although she continued to appear on stage, by the 1950s she became one of America's leading acting teachers.

Adler emphasises a play's given circumstances, the actor's imagination and physical actions. She quotes Stanislavsky to the effect that the 'truth in art is the truth of your circumstances' (1988: 31). She acknowledges the importance of drawing on oneself in a role; but the source of inspiration is not purely psychology or past experiences (as in Strasberg), but the actor's imagination as they relate to the given circumstances of the play. Adler writes:

> The playwright gives you the play, the idea, the style, the conflict, the character, etc. The background life of the character will be made up of the social, cultural, political, historical, and geographical situation in which the author places him. The character must be understood within the framework of the character's own time and situation. Through the proper use of craft, the actor will see the differences of social, historical, and cultural environment between himself and the character. Through his craft he will be able to translate these difficulties and use them to arrive at the character.
>
> (1964: 149)

Imagination, Adler claims, can be touched upon 'as a source for the actor's craft' (1964: 143). For her, 99 per cent of events on stage derive at least in part from the imagination, because on stage

> you will never have your own name and personality or be in your own house. Every person you talk to will have been written imaginatively by the playwright. Every circumstance you find yourself in will be in an

imaginary one. And so, every word, every action, must originate in the
actor's imagination.

(1988: 17)

Adler asks performers to concentrate on their creative imagination rather than their
conscious past. By doing so, they would be optimally effective in creating a past in
sympathy with the characters they portray. For Adler, the imagination is crucial to
classical performances as well as plays that are stylistically non-realistic. In order for
the actor to understand the life of a character within a period or stylised play, they
must read, observe paintings, study architecture and listen to music, becoming what
Paul Mann called an 'actor-anthropologist' (1964: 87).

Adler, however, rejects simplistic devices for finding character and inspiration.
The most important thing for the actor is to choose images that *evoke an inner feeling*.
Perfunctory choices may 'sound' correct analytically, but leave the actor devoid of
feeling. The actor may feel they are making the 'right' choice intellectually, but the
actual performance is dull and uninspired. The actor then may try to 'pump up'
emotions rather than make decisions that effectively touch the heart. If the role and its
context as written fail to inspire or move the actor emotionally, then the actor must
look elsewhere. For example, if the play takes place at a lakeside resort in Switzerland,
but the actor can find nothing moving or exciting about Swiss lakes, then, as Adler
says, 'put your lake in Morocco'. In this way, the actor may 'get away from the real
thing because the real thing will limit your acting and cripple you' (quoted in Flint
1992). In other words, if the actions, words or events of the play seem lifeless to the
actor, then the actor must create another set of circumstances that correspond to
the events of the play, but create excitement and passion internally.

Adler devises a number of exercises for developing the performer's personalisation of the role. For example, suppose an actor has to describe fruit in a grocery store.
As Adler would have it, the actor's task is to personalise the experience:

> I saw fantastic pears that were big but looked too expensive to buy. Then I
> saw those wonderful Malaga grapes, long and very sweet. There were also
> some of those big, blue grapes, and the baby ones, the little green ones.
> Those you can eat by the pound, and by the way, they're very cheap.
>
> (1988: 21)

Adler wants to bring out the actor's feelings and passions towards the subject, revealing the performer's creativity relative to the circumstances. She is also convinced that
paraphrasing the text is 'an essential feature of the actor's technique'. She explains
that paraphrasing 'is taking the author's ideas and putting them into the actor's
words, and thereby making them belong to the actor. Paraphrasing encourages you to
use your mind and your voice and gives you some power that equals the author's
power' (1988: 102). By paraphrasing, actors find in their imagination things that
move them to react, speak and move. She goes on to say: 'Some actors hold back and
do not react. Actors should consciously take things that will make them react. In your
choice is your talent. Acting is in everything but the cold words' (1988: 26).

Whilst Strasberg emphasised the realisation of the character from the material of
one's own personal life, Adler suggested that the actor's inspiration should come
from the world of the play itself. Hirsch notes that Adler 'urges students to explore the
given circumstances of the play rather than those of their private lives' (1984: 215).
Still, Adler did not completely abandon the inner belief of the actor's performance; as

she says, 'the whole aim of modern theatre is not to act, but to find the truth of the play within yourself, and to communicate that. If you play simply for the lines, you're dead' (quoted in Hirsch 1984: 216). The reality of place, where you are and why you are here, must contribute to the basic understanding of your motivation and justification as an actor.

Finding the correct physical actions for a scene also assists the actor in discovering the excitement of the role. For Adler, the 'actor must lose his dependency on the words and go to the actions of the play', because the actions 'come first and words second. Words come out of the actions' (1988: 115). The actor must find actions beneath words by developing the 'physicalisation of actions'. The method of physical action, which Adler borrowed from Stanislavsky's later work, draws from the active doing and performing of actual tasks. Moreover, the actor must build a repertoire consisting of a vocabulary of actions. As she claims, an action is something you do; it has an end; it is done within the given circumstances; and is justified (1988: 35). To find the right action, the actor looks for the play's 'ruling idea'. This ruling idea must appeal to the actor 'emotionally and intellectually'. Moreover, the actor 'must know how to make the [ruling idea] his own' (1988: 38). In other words, the actor must know how to personalise the material, playing the actions convincingly.

Adler also stressed justifying the things said and done on stage. She borrowed from Vakhtangov the idea of 'agitation from the essence', whereby the actor comes 'to realise the necessity of actions pointed out by the author – they become organic' (Vakhtangov 1955: 145). The actor seeks justification of the author's perspective, what Vakhtangov called 'scenic faith' (1955: 146–47). Adler offers some elaboration on Vakhtangov's ideas:

> The justification is not in the lines; it is in you. What you should choose as your justification should agitate you. As a result of the agitation you will experience the action and the emotion. If you choose a justification and experience nothing, you'll have to select something else that will awaken you. Your talent consists of how well you are able to shop for your justification. In your choice lies your talent.
>
> (1988: 48)

Though Adler and Strasberg differ in emphasis, they shared the belief in truthful behaviour, self-exploration (whether psychological or sociological) and respect for acting as art. For Strasberg, the essence of acting is psychological; resources abound in the actor's memory. For Adler, the essence of acting is sociological; actors draw from the given circumstances of the play. However, Ellen Burstyn, who studied with both, remarked: 'Stella stresses imagination and Lee stresses reality. You use Stella's imagination to get to Lee's reality. They are finally talking about the same thing' (quoted in Flint 1992). For Adler, the building blocks of acting are discovered in the imagination and are arranged according to the play's given circumstances and the exigencies of physical actions.

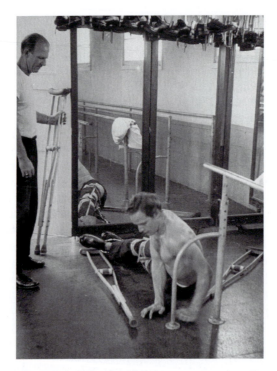

Figure 9.3 Marlon Brando practicing for his role as a paraplegic in the film *The Men*.
Source: Photo by Ed Clark/Time Life Pictures/Getty Images.

Figure 9.4 Marlon Brando stars in the film *A Streetcar Named Desire*, directed by Elia Kazan.
Source: Photo by Hulton Archive/Getty Images.

SANFORD MEISNER

Behaviour, relationships and the reality of doing

> The foundation of acting is the reality of doing.
>
> (Meisner and Longwell 1987: 16)

Sanford Meisner was a member and principal actor of the Group Theatre. In the mid 1930s he became disillusioned with the Group and the direction in which it was heading. In 1935 he joined the Neighborhood Playhouse, and the following year became its Director. From 1936 until the time of his death Meisner spearheaded the Neighborhood Playhouse, developing it into a significant school of actor training.

Acting for Meisner is in the doing; from this all other facets of the role emerge. In his classroom were posted signs which read: 'Act Before You Think', and 'An Ounce of Behavior Is Worth a Pound of Words'. Active behaviour is the raw material of Meisner's theory. He states:

> Let there be no question about what I'm saying here. If you do some-thing, you really do it! Did you walk up the steps to this classroom this morning? You didn't jump up? You didn't skip up, right? You didn't ballet pirouette? You really walked up those steps.
>
> (Meisner and Longwell 1987: 17)

Figure 9.5 Sanford Meisner.

Source: by permission of the Sanford Meisner Center.

Larry Silverberg elaborates on this theme, saying that for Meisner: 'if you read on stage, really read; if you eat, really eat; and if you want something (an objective), really want it, go after it, pursue it; don't stop until you have achieved it'. As Maria Ouspenskaya puts it, '*Really see*; instead of *acting*, seeing. Don't act, do' (1994: 3).

Meisner did not entirely reject use of emotional recall or substitution (replacing the play's events with your own), but he required that substitution must 'be done as *homework*' (1964: 145). Once inner feelings and physical tasks required by the director and the role are shaped during rehearsal, the actor plays spontaneously, all the while allowing subtle shifts in emphasis and focus. In other words, once the actor reaches the time to perform, what remains is the actual doing and reacting.

For Meisner, the play is merely a blueprint for the actor's interior life. He says:

> The text is like a canoe, and the river on which sits is the emotion. The text floats on the river. If the water of the river is turbulent, the words will come out like a canoe on a rough river. It all depends on the flow of the river which is your emotion. The text takes on the character of your emotion.
>
> (Meisner and Longwell 1987: 115)

Although for Meisner the point of doing resembled Adler's emphasis on physical actions, he departs from Adler in his introduction of the repetition exercise. As an exercise, repetition demands of actors that they verbalise what they perceive in another actor. In other words, one actor might begin by saying 'You're looking at me', and the other actor might reply, 'I'm looking at you'. The essence of the phrase ('looking at') is repeated about a dozen times; all the while each actor 'reads' the other actor's behaviour. Meisner explains that actors ought to observe behaviour, and in turn 'your instinct picks up the change in [the other actor's] behaviour and the [repetition] dialogue changes too' (Meisner and Longwell 1987: 29–30).

As actors gain confidence through repetition, their insight deepens with respect to the other member of the scene. In other words, rather than saying 'you're staring at me', they begin to address the feelings that lurk behind the stare. Such insight is then reflected in phrases such as 'you're angry with me', or 'you're laughing at me'. Actors no longer take 'inventory' of the other actor superficially, but observe the scene-partner's emotions, feelings and thoughts.

As actors gain more experience in the repetition exercises, they begin to improvise scenarios called 'The Knock on the Door'. The following is an example of a Meisner 'Knock on the Door' improvisation. Actor A is required to have an 'independent activity', which is a task that is real (no mime), urgent and particular. An independent activity is something that has a beginning, middle and end, and has to be done for compelling reasons. For instance, an independent activity can be stringing a guitar for an important audition. The actor is late; the guitar lacks strings. The actor intended to string the guitar, but his girlfriend was in an accident and he had to take her to the hospital. The element of urgency and lateness adds to his desperation and intensity.

Actor B enters the room ('knocking on the door') where actor A is completing his independent activity. Actor B has an 'objective' that relates to actor A. For instance, actor B imagines he is the father of actor A, and actor B does not want his son to leave medical school and be a musician. The father enters the room, and urgently tries to persuade the son to drop music and return to medical school.

In Meisner's version of this standard dramatic conflict, the actors do not discuss the given circumstances (though they must share an understanding of it). They do not talk about the story, but rather they use the repetition exercise only. In this way, the actors are compelled to deal with observed behaviour rather than dialogue and plot. This helps to foster ensemble interplay, or communion, rather than words. Since the scenario/plot is artificial (it is an acted father–son relationship), Meisner wants actors to place their focus on subtextual dialogue – the 'chemistry' between the actors and the 'reality' of the situation (human behaviour). If an actor is yelling, that is tangible, something everyone can hear and observe. The other actor reads the behaviour of yelling and reacts to it instinctively. Reading behaviour compels actors to focus on scene-partners rather than the artifice of the plot. As a result, actors react spontaneously, play as an ensemble, and 'read' behaviour as it happens organically.

In the repetition exercises, Meisner found an exercise that refined impulse. For Meisner, impulse is a response to internal or external stimuli. As the actor receives the stimuli, they then feed it to the imagination and personal associations. The actor responds by acting on the stimuli, creating an 'impulsive' behaviour that emerges truthfully and spontaneously from reactions rather than from pre-planned behaviour. This procedure must be performed without intellectual interference, without 'thinking' or 'dwelling' on the reaction. As Meisner put it, the exercise eliminates 'all that "head" work'; it takes away 'all the mental manipulations and get[s] to where the impulses come from' (Meisner and Longwell 1987: 36). Larry Silverberg explains that in Meisner's repetition exercise, the actor must not use the work as a kind of trick, but rather as an attempt to commune with another actor, to enable the actor to move 'towards your fully *being with* another human being'. The aim of repetition, Silverberg goes on to say, is in 'becoming fully available to your partner, authentically responsive in each moment' (1994: 42–43).

Many commentators have misunderstood the purpose of the repetition exercise. Michael Quinn, for instance, has argued that in Meisner's version of the Method, the 'actor is the central subject, and the Other is the character – not the audience, the acting partner, or the director'. Quinn maintains that for Meisner 'the problem addressed in his class is teaching actors to project themselves into an Other [character] that is already there, written in terms which are fixed into the fiction' (1995: 14).

But this is mistaken, since the repetition exercise builds on the relationship of the actor with the acting partner; the 'Other' is the scene-partner, not the character. In other words, for Meisner the creation of character is fluid and spontaneous. Rather than a 'fixed' characterisation, the performance is based on relationships, either to scene-partners or to the audience. Actors act on the relationship to the other actor, using the specifically observed behaviour of scene-partners, or, in the case of direct address to the audience, the spectators. If a scene-partner changes their behaviour, the actor must adjust their own behaviour to correspond to the different signals and stimuli. Meisner compels actors to work 'as if' they are the characters, but this does not imply fixity. Rather, the impulses received from the other actor, stimulated through repetition, take on a dynamic based on the continuing real-life examination of human give and take. Reacting can therefore be said to be the foundation of Meisner's repetition technique.

Meisner believes that action is not in the character or the plot of the play but in *relationships*. To this end he stresses the repetition exercise, because the exercise compels the actor to 'work off the partner'. In this way the partner allows the actor to create the role from the given material present on stage and in the life of another person, rather than a mental preconception of character. More than Strasberg and Adler, Meisner emphasises ensemble behaviour, creating a spontaneous exchange in a jazz-like atmosphere of action and reaction. Performing the actions for Meisner is therefore not 'fixed into the fiction', as Quinn would have it, but relational, dialogic and alive to immediate and spontaneous human communication and interaction.

William Worthen also errs when he notes that in 'Meisner's well known [repetition] exercise . . . the actors improvise a given situation using only a single word or phrase, repeated again and again' (1992: 61). Repetition does not emphasise a 'given situation' (as Adler would have it), but rather the *behaviour of the acting partner*, such as, *someone in a situation*. This is an important distinction, because Meisner's repetition exercise, as opposed to Adler's emphasis on circumstances, is intended to promote impulsive behaviour as a consequence of living relationships (the actual moment on stage), rather than merely the given situation.

In Meisner's work, 'an ounce of behaviour is worth a pound of words'. The repetition exercise is used to read behaviour from either the scene-partner or the spectators. In direct address, the actor's attention is not, as Worthen implies, 'diverted from the audience' (1992: 61); rather, the audience should be viewed as the scene-partner. In other words, in directly addressing the audience the actor uses the audience in much the same way as a stand-up comic does: gauging the laughter and responses of the spectators and responding according to the actor's impulses.

Meisner's repetition exercise helps to promote spontaneous reactions that became the trademark of his brand of the Method. As Richard Brestoff astutely observes: 'Meisner felt that the connection between actors was vital to the life of a scene, and that when that bond was broken, the acting lost its special quality and power' (1995: 129). Meisner's emphasis on truthful interaction between actors, Brestoff goes on to say, helps actors 'to respond genuinely to one another, and to live spontaneously, moment to moment, within imaginary circumstances' (1995: 137). Meisner's specific contribution to the Method is his emphasis on spontaneous communion between actors.

CONCLUSION: METHOD ACTING AS A TOOL

Whether emphasising psychology (Strasberg), sociology (Adler) or spontaneous behaviour (Meisner), Method actors search for the reality that must underlie a quality performance. The Method is neither singular in its outlook, nor mutually exclusive; one facet of the Method does not cancel out another. Affective memory, the play's given circumstances and repetition may function together; voice, speech and movement are integrated; and textual analysis is integral to working on a role. Method acting, when properly used, is holistic, enabling the actor to perform on several levels with conviction and confidence.

The American Method has evolved, yet many of its fundamental ideas are still actively employed. Founder and director of Chicago's Steppenwolf Theatre, Gary Sinise, elucidates what animates Method acting in a personal reflection:

> I try to keep them [the audience] leaning forward rather than leaning back because I feel those are the best experiences. The one that hits you in the guts will make you think about it, but a play that has you just thinking on an intellectual level won't necessarily hit you in the guts. The cardinal sin for me is boredom.

(qtd in Smith 1996: 10, 14)

Method acting explores the range of actorial possibilities within a dynamic of emotion – what Sinise calls 'in the guts'. It transcends the artifice of staged contrivances, offering actors opportunities to explore roles by calling on them to investigate their personal experience, imagination and behaviour.

Notes

1   Other acting teachers have had significant impact on the American Method school of acting, as, for example, Phoebe Brand, Uta Hagen, Robert Lewis, Paul Mann and Sonia Moore.

2   Strasberg's major directing works were *The House of Connelly*, *Men in White*, *Johnny Johnson*, and *The Case of Clyde Griffiths* in the 1930s, and *Three Sisters* in the 1960s. Meisner helped direct *Waiting for Lefty* in 1935. Still, Strasberg, Adler and Meisner, for the most part, did not stress directing, but teaching.

3   By and large, the teachers discussed here offered their schools as sanctuaries, places where actors could practise their craft, work on scenes and exercises, and perform in roles that they would not ordinarily be cast in. These safe harbours allowed actors a chance to escape the commercialism of show business. Method schools are not, as some have claimed, 'against' productions, but rather the Method offers places where actors can avoid the pressure of careerism and the business of selling their talent.

4   The American Laboratory Theatre was founded in June 1923 by Boleslavsky and several wealthy Americans who supplied the funds. Boleslavsky reached the United States in 1922, where he began a series of lectures at the Princess Theatre in New York that offered the philosophy of actor training from the Moscow Art Theatre (MAT). Miriam and Herbert Stockton, patrons of the arts, offered Boleslavsky an opportunity to direct a training school based on the principles of the MAT, and Boleslavsky enlisted the aid of his friend and colleague, Maria Ouspenskaya. The Lab opened at 139 MacDougal Street in 1923. See W. Smith (1990), pp. 14–15, for details.

5   The Theatre Guild began in 1915 as the Washington Square Players in New York. It presented one-act plays that were considered modern and unconventional. In 1919, the playwright Lawrence Langner restructured the Players into the Theatre Guild. During the 1920s the Guild became known for producing the Expressionist dramas of Ernst Toller, as well as plays by George Bernard Shaw, Elmer Rice, John Howard Lawson, and Sidney Howard. By the 1930s the Guild's younger members joined the Group Theatre, and the Guild eventually dissolved.

6   Whilst a study of Yiddish Theatre's influence on Strasberg, Adler and Meisner is outside the realm of this chapter, it is worth noting that all three were invested in the Yiddish Theatre. Yiddish Theatre's emphasis on melodrama, emotion and social commentary left indelible impressions on Strasberg, Adler, Meisner and the Group Theatre in general, and its significance has often been overlooked.

7   The Actors Studio was co-founded by Elia Kazan, Robert Lewis and Cheryl Crawford in 1947.

8   Vakhtangov referred to this feeling as 'agitation from the essence'; for Vakhtangov, it is necessary for the actor 'to live your own temperament on the stage and not the supposed temperament of the character. You must proceed from yourself and not from a conceived image; you must place yourself in the position of the situation of the character' (1955: 146).

9   As a method of study and training, the American Method approach has had a history of controversy and strife. On the one hand, it has a cadre of loyal supporters, and an admirable roster of first-class actors who claim the technique as their own. On the other hand, the Method has had its programmatic attackers. Some claim it is too heavily invested in emotion (Counsell, Harrop); others see its emphasis on psychology as destructive (Hornby, Richardson); and as a violation of the true teachings of Stanislavsky (Brustein, Hornby). Other critics claim that the Method is narrow in its vision, encouraging sloppy speech habits, poor diction, and avoiding movement training. It is accused of being anti-intellectual (Brustein 1958), opposed to the reading and criticism of dramatic texts (Hornby), dogmatic

in its approach (Richardson), and symbolic of mid-twentieth-century 'middlebrow culture' (Braudy, Conroy, Quinn).

10   See Feldenkrais (1972), pp. 68–69.

11   See Moston (1993), pp. 110–36, for an excellent discussion on sense memory.

12   Pavlov was the well-known turn-of-the-century behaviourist who experimented with canine response behaviour. After hearing a bell ring at feeding time, the dog in the experiment continued to salivate at the sound of a bell even after the food was removed. Pavlov thus concluded that all animals can condition their reactions based on physical cues.

13   Strasberg quotes Vakhtangov as saying that 'We never use real, that is, literal emotion in art, only affective memory emotion, only remembered emotion' (1965: 112).

14   Ribot was a French psychologist whose books, La Psychologie des Sentiments (1896) and Problèmes de Psychologie Affective (1910), influenced Stanislavsky.

15   Vineberg and Hornby offer two entirely different observations of Strasberg's portrayal of Hyman Roth in the film The Godfather, Part II. Vineberg finds the performance a superb and tightly controlled work where you 'can't find a moment of wasted emotion' (1991: 109), whilst Hornby finds Strasberg's performance 'unrevealing', lacking 'the emotional explosiveness of his finest students' (1992: 174).

Bibliography

Adler, S. (1964) 'Interview: The Reality of Doing', interview by P. Gray, Drama Review, 9 (1): 137–55.

—— (1976) 'Stella Adler', Educational Theatre Journal, 28 (4): 506–12.

—— (1988) The Technique of Acting, Toronto, Ont.: Bantam Books.

Boleslavski, R. (1933) Acting: The First Six Lessons, New York: Theatre Arts Books.

Braudy, L. (1996) 'No Body's Perfect: Method Acting and the 50s Culture', Michigan Quarterly Review, 35 (1): 191–215.

Brestoff, R. (1995) The Great Acting Teachers and Their Methods, Lyme, NH: Smith and Kraus.

Brustein, R. (1958) 'America's New Cultural Hero: Feelings Without Words', Commentary, 25: 123–29.

—— (1962) 'The Keynes of Times Square', The New Republic, 1 December: 28–30.

—— (1973) 'Are British Actors Better Than Ours?', New York Times, 15 April: 2.1, 30.

Clurman, H. (1950) The Fervent Years, New York: Alfred A. Knopf.

—— (1994) The Collected Works of Harold Clurman, ed. M. Loggia and G. Young, New York: Applause.

Conroy, M. (1993) 'Acting Out: Method Acting, the National Culture, and the Middlebrow Disposition in Cold War America', Criticism, 35 (2): 239–63.

Counsell, C. (1996) Signs of Performance: An Introduction to Twentieth-Century Theatre, London: Routledge.

Easty, E. (1981) On Method Acting, New York: Ivy Books.

Feldenkrais, M. (1972) Awareness Through Movement, New York: Harper and Row.

Flint, P. (1992) 'Obituary: Stella Adler', New York Times, 22 December: B10.

—— (1997) 'Obituary: Sanford Meisner', New York Times, 4 February: C25.

Garfield, D. (1980) A Player's Passion: The Story of the Actors Studio, New York: Macmillan.

Gordon, M. (2000) 'Salvaging Strasberg at the Fin de Siècle', in Method Acting Reconsidered, New York: St. Martin's Press, pp. 43–60.

Gordon, R. (2006) The Purpose of Playing: Modern Acting Theories in Perspective, Ann Arbor: University of Michigan Press.

Gussow, M. (1982) 'Obituary: Lee Strasberg', New York Times, 18 February: D20.

Harrop, J. (1992) Acting, London: Routledge.

Hirsch, F. (1984) A Method to Their Madness: The History of the Actors Studio, New York: W.W. Norton.

Hornby, R. (1992) The End of Acting: A Radical View, New York: Applause.

Hull, S. (1985) Strasberg's Method, Woodbridge, CT: Ox Bow.

Kazan, E. (1988) A Life, New York: Alfred A. Knopf.

Krasner, D. (ed.) (2000) Method Acting Reconsidered: Theory, Practice, Future, New York: St. Martin's Press.

Lewis, R. (1958) *Method – or Madness?*, New York: Samuel French.

—— (1980) *Advice to the Players*, New York: Theatre Communications Group.

Mann, P. (1964) 'Theory and Practice', interview by R. Schechner, *Drama Review*, 9 (2): 84–96.

Meisner, S. (1964) 'Interview: The Reality of Doing', interview by P. Gray, *Drama Review*, 9 (1): 136–55.

Meisner, S. and Longwell, D. (1987) *Meisner on Acting*, New York: Vintage.

Moston, D. (1993) *Coming to Terms with Acting*, New York: Drama Book.

Munk, E. (ed.) (1965) *Stanislavski and America*, New York: Hill and Wang.

Ouspenskaya, M. (1954) 'Notes on Acting', *American Repertory Theater*, 2 (2): 1–4.

Quinn, M. (1995) 'Self-Reliance and Ritual Renewal: Anti-theatrical Ideology in American Method Acting', *Journal of Dramatic Theory and Criticism*, 10 (1): 5–20.

Richardson, D. (1988) *Acting Without Agony: An Alternative to the Method*, Boston, MA: Allyn and Bacon.

Silverberg, L. (1994) *The Sanford Meisner Approach*, New York: Smith and Kraus.

Smith, S. (1996) 'Hooked for Life', *Playbill*, 96 (6): 10, 14.

Smith, W. (1990) *Real Life Drama: The Group Theatre and America, 1931–1940*, New York: Alfred A. Knopf.

Stanislavski, K. (2008) *An Actor's Work*, trans. J. Benedetti, London: Routledge.

Strasberg, L. (1941) 'Acting and the Training of the Actor', in J. Gassner (ed.), *Producing the Play*, New York: Dryden Press, pp. 128–62.

—— (1964) 'Working with Live Material', interview by R. Schechner, *Drama Review*, 9 (1): 117–35.

—— (1965) *Strasberg at the Actors Studio: Tape-Recorded Sessions*, ed. R. Hethmon, New York: Theatre Communications Group.

—— (1976) 'Lee Strasberg', *Educational Theatre Journal*, 28 (4): 544–52.

—— (1987) *A Dream of Passion: The Development of the Method*, New York: Plume.

Vakhtangov, E. (1955) 'Preparing for the Role', trans. B.E. Zakhava, in T. Cole (ed.), *Acting: A Handbook of the Stanislavski Method*, New York: Crown Paperback, pp. 141–51.

Vineberg, S. (1991) *Method Actors: Three Generations of an American Acting Style*, New York: Schirmer.

Worthen, W. (1992) *Modern Drama and the Rhetoric of Theater*, Berkeley, CA: University of California Press.

Chapter 10

Dorinda Hulton

JOSEPH CHAIKIN AND ASPECTS OF ACTOR TRAINING: POSSIBILITIES RENDERED PRESENT

An actor should strive to be alive to all that he can imagine possible.[1] Such an actor is generated by an impulse toward an inner unity, as well as by the most intimate contacts he makes outside himself. When we as actors are performing, we as persons are also present and the performance is a testimony of ourselves. Each role, each work, each performance changes us as persons. The actor doesn't start out with answers about living – but with wordless questions about experience. Later, as the actor advances through the progress of the work, the person is transformed. Through the working process which he himself guides, the actor recreates himself.
Nothing less.

(Chaikin 1972: 5, 6)

CHANGE AND TRANSFORMATION ARE at the heart of Joseph Chaikin's life and work. He began his theatre career as an actor and worked as actor, director, teacher, workshop leader and writer. This chapter is primarily concerned with his investigations and explorations into actor training with the seminal American group the Open Theater between 1963 and 1973.

CONTEXT

Chaikin was born in 1935 of Russian-Jewish parents in Brooklyn, New York and grew up in Des Moines, Iowa, where he attended Drake University. He dropped out before completing his degree, but was awarded an honorary doctorate in 1972. Kent State University awarded him the same degree in 1990.[2]

In 1954, at the age of nineteen, Chaikin moved from Iowa to New York City, studied philosophy, and co-founded a small theatre company, The Harlequin Players, in which he worked as both actor and director. The company lasted for two years and performed plays by writers such as O'Casey and Pirandello.

In 1957, Chaikin managed to get his first professional acting job with a summer stock company in Pennsylvania. The experience encapsulated an antithesis to the collaborative approach. Recalling it, he remembers the excitement of getting the job, and then being asked, on the morning of his arrival, to come up with a full-blown 'characterisation' in one day. At the end of the morning, the director threatened to replace him if he had not come up with something funnier by the afternoon. He didn't – and the director gave him till the following morning. After a sleepless night of 'funny walks' he finally came up with something the director found funnier. He kept the job. But the company of actors, he noted, 'were not friendly with one another', and in one week of rehearsal and two of performance, they played out various roles of 'betrayal and regret' (Kellman 1976: 18).

Between 1957 and 1959, Chaikin worked part time in offices in New York, was regularly sacked, waited on tables, and took a number of minor jobs in the professional theatre. During this time he also studied with different acting teachers, most of whom adhered rigidly to a form of actor training which was based on a selection of Stanislavsky's earlier perceptions and exercises. The approach was firmly rooted in the past, and although it was one which was to contribute significantly to the future development of acting in the cinema, the assertion that it was applicable by any actor, to any play, written in any period, within any style, was regarded with some scepticism by Chaikin. He rejected the dogmatism of the 'Method', and with it, the notion of working within predefined boundaries, preferring to believe that, had Stanislavsky been alive, he would 'still be exploring' (Chaikin 1972: 57, 58).

In 1959 Chaikin joined the Living Theatre, led by Judith Malina and Julian Beck. At the time the company was producing plays such as Pirandello's *Tonight We Improvise* and Paul Goodman's *The Young Disciple*, which included pre-verbal elements as part of its language.[3] Chaikin's first role with the Living Theatre was a small part in Goodman's *The Cave*, but he hoped it would lead to 'better' ones.

By 1962 he was playing the lead in Jack Gelber's *The Connection* on a European tour which made him feel, he says, 'very swelled, like a minor star', and whilst they were in Europe, the Becks asked him to play Galy Gay in Brecht's *Man is Man*. The play, written in 1924, presents the transformation of an Irish labourer into a human fighting machine. Back in New York, Chaikin remembers:

> it sounds like a fairy story, but it was in the playing of Galy Gay that I began to change. There I was, night after night, giving all my attention to pleasing, seducing, and getting applause from the audience, which is the very process wherein Galy Gay allows himself to be transformed from an innocent and good man into a thing, a machine – all because of flattery, one flattery after another.
>
> (Pasolli 1970: xiv)

In playing the role, Chaikin found himself moving towards a different kind of understanding of the possible relationships between actor, character, audience and play, and emerging out of this, a sense of theatre's power to effect change and transformation: transformation in the person of the actor within the process of acting, as well as Brecht's agenda for social change in the audience:

> it came mostly from considering the lines of the play, night after night after night. And saying them . . . the responsibility of coming out to the audience and talking directly to them – something I had never had to do

Figure 10.1 Joseph Chaikin with the Living Theatre in Brecht's *Man is Man*.
Photo: Karl Bissenger, 1962.

before – knowing that what I said to the audience I didn't believe, and
then coming to believe what I was saying.

(Chaikin 1972: 50, 51)

A related change was also occurring for Chaikin around this time. In the autumn
of 1961 Russia had resumed nuclear testing and the United States was 'considering
the resumption' of testing. Early in 1962 President Kennedy announced resumption,
and with other members of the company Chaikin became involved in the Women's
Strike for Peace. The rally took place in Times Square and Chaikin, with other
demonstrators, was attacked by police with night-sticks, arrested and jailed.
Rehearsals for *Man is Man* took place amid preparations for the second General Strike
for Peace, and a month after the play opened the Cold War heated to melt-down when
an American spy plane flying over Cuba was hit by a surface-to-air missile. Chaikin,
who had considered himself to be apolitical, recognised that the political aspect of
the Living Theatre, which he had previously thought of as being ridiculous, was, in
fact, very necessary (Tytell 1997: 176). He also had a 'real craving' to investigate
the processes of collaboration with, or between, actors, directors and writers – the
ensemble experience.

Nola Chilton, an acting teacher in New York at the time, had been experimenting
with ways of preparing actors to engage with the non-naturalistic imagery of the
absurdist playwrights. Chaikin was a member of this group, and when Chilton left for
Israel, in 1962, he and the others who had been working with her decided to continue.

In 1963, with these seventeen other young actors and four writers, Chaikin
co-founded the Open Theater. People came and went but the company functioned
for over ten years, in New York City, as a forum in which actors, writers, teachers,

directors, musicians, visual artists and intellectuals gathered and exchanged ideas and practices of theatre, and its relationship to society. R.D. Laing, the phenomenological psychologist, for example, talked with the company; and various critics – Gordon Rogoff, Richard Gilman and Susan Sontag – also attended sessions and talked with the group about different relationships between theatre theory, painting and the company's own experiments.[4] These experiments and investigations were part of a vigorous avant-garde movement which flourished in New York throughout the sixties, at a time of political and social upheaval in the country, as well as a redefinition of American identity – fractured and polarised by the war in Vietnam.[5]

The Open Theater was the first well-known American group to explore collaborative creation, and four major projects were undertaken in which the actor played a central role in generating and researching material for performance, with the writer or dramaturg contributing, shaping and editing material – rather than in the interpretation of already existing scripts. Chaikin was the director for each of these projects, and each was performed widely in varying contexts.

The group, however, began as a workshop – that is, a laboratory or research theatre rather than a production company – and central to its identity from the outset was a collective commitment towards exploring a new language for performance: one which was not based on naturalism or psychological motivation, but which was eclectic, inclusive and innovative, based on questions rather than answers, on imagined possibilities rather than given formulae.

Figure 10.2 (Left to right) Cynthia Harris, Shami Chaikin, Tina Shepard, Jim Barbosa, Ron Faber, Ralph Lee and Peter Maloney in *The Serpent* developed by the Open Theater between 1967 and 1969.

Photo: Freddie Tornberg.

Chaikin's book *The Presence of the Actor* was published in 1972. In it he questions a number of assumptions about acting and actor training, but gives no easy answers and certainly no formulae. It is a book full of dreams, hopes, wishes, challenges and provocations towards creativity.

The Presence of the Actor is a singular book: not chronologically arranged, with a non-linear structure and non-prescriptive tone which invites the reader to make connections between its disparate parts and to allow contradiction. It consists, Chaikin says, of notes written from several 'levels' of himself, and within it and in other writing he reaches often for metaphors or images, of 'space' and 'place', in order to communicate his ideas and perceptions. He speaks, for example, of territories, zones, spheres, abandonment, exile, occupation and habitation.

A key image is that of 'a house on fire'. Addressing the actor he suggests:

Imagine a burning house:

1   You live in the house which is on fire. Even your clothes are charred as you run from the burning house.
2   You are a neighbour whose house might also have caught fire.
3   You are a passer-by who witnessed the fire by seeing someone who ran from a building while his clothes were still burning.
4   You are a journalist sent to gather information on the house which is burning.
5   You are listening to a report on the radio, which is an account given by the journalist who covered the story of the burning house.

(Chaikin 1972: 9, 10)

Chaikin reaches for the image of a 'house', in my understanding, as a means of suggesting to the actor the different perspectives from which it is possible to respond within the processes of acting.[6] Inside the house is the 'living room', where each thing must confirm and validate each other thing; the 'attic', a place to store memories; and the 'cellar', a private place, a place to which no one else knows the passage. Outside the house are the witnesses to the 'fire', and outside it also, are the 'sky' and the 'stars'.[7]

Chaikin developed a number of exercises, with innumerable variations upon them, which provide a means of 'inhabiting' and journeying within and between such 'spaces' – and it is in the relationship between the 'inside' and the 'outside', as I understand it, that the 'wordless questions about experience' begin.

In *The Presence of the Actor*, however, Chaikin expresses a resistance towards describing exercises, and a resistance to 'recipe-books' that document exercises. His argument that they cannot be documented is based on a distinction between 'content' and 'structure'. The exercise is 'an agreed-upon structure', and whilst the structure can be explained, the content, which is associated with 'internal territory', is untranslatable. It is untranslatable because it is irretrievably located within particular people, at a particular time, in a particular place within a particular socio-political climate.

Chaikin's assertion here reads as a direct rejection of his own training with teachers of 'Method' acting, and the idea of its universal application. This approach, in which Chaikin had been a sceptical participant, was based on a number of Stanislavsky's earlier exercises, and transformed into a dogmatic code. Chaikin's perceptions of the main features of this code are listed here, as a means of indicating the kind of actor training that he was reacting *against*:

1   The principle of objectives, actions, and obstacles. This technique helps the
     actor draw from his character and circumstances (a) what his over-all objective
     in the play is, (b) what his dramatic action must be in order to achieve this
     objective, and (c) what obstacles stand in his way. That is, he learns to find the
     dramatic collision which is at the centre of every scene . . .

2   Sensory attention and emotional recall. Here concentration and relaxation are
     emphasised. The text is disregarded and the actor is urged to show only what he
     is feeling at the moment. Improvisations that seem like psychotherapy are freely
     used . . .

3   Logical analysis of the text. Every moment of the play is analyzed and scored
     in terms of the character, the situation, etc. And once the score is finished, it
     remains fixed, regardless of the actor you are playing with, the director, the
     audience, etc.

4   Inspiration. This [sic] teacher does not use direct criticism but 'inspires' the
     actor by giving him a kind of spiritual blood transfusion.

                                                        (Chaikin 1972: 43, 44)

None of these features addressed the idea of the creative actor who would collaborate
with writers and directors in the making of 'theatre events'. All (with the exception of
the fourth) assumed a text written by a playwright which was to be interpreted by
the actor.

    As an actor with the Living Theatre, Chaikin had become interested in Brecht's
idea of *verfremdungseffekt*, and his own perception of a confusion amongst American
actors at the time, between the notion of 'detachment' and that of 'not caring'. Like
Brecht, Chaikin cared. And he was interested, in his work with the Open Theater, in
the idea not only of actors who were able to collaborate in the making of 'theatre
events', but also of actors who cared about the whole theatre event they were engaged
in (Chaikin 1972: 38). 'My intention is to make images into theater events,
beginning simply with those which have meaning for myself and my collaborators;
and at the same time renouncing the theater of critics, box office, real estate, and the
conditioned public' (Chaikin 1972: 3).

    Chaikin and his collaborators had no system to realise this intention, and located
as their investigations were in personal and cultural histories, he was wary of the
application of external structures (in the form of exercises) within other contexts.

    All prepared systems fail. They fail when they are applied, except as a
    process which was significant, at some time, for some one or some
    group. Process is dynamic: it's the evolution that takes place during work.
    Systems are recorded as ground plans, not to be followed any more than
    rules of courtship can be followed. We can get clues from others, but our
    own culture and sensibility and aesthetic will lead us to a totally new kind
    of expression, unless we imitate both the process and the findings of
    another. The aesthetic remakes the system.[8]

                                                        (Chaikin 1972: 21)

Some of the exercises explored by the Open Theater were brought to the company
by other workshop members or visiting teachers, and many, as noted earlier, with
innumerable variations upon them, were developed by Chaikin. In the following
section of this chapter it is the intention to search for clues within three of these
structures, which may be seen as interrelated and which will, I hope, offer glimpses

movement can be repeated with clarity, and without alteration. An 'internal' image, or associative connection, recognised or discovered by the actor has, in effect, translated itself into abstract, dynamic, 'external' form – an image in sound and movement.

The actor, sustaining both the 'internal' image, and its 'external' form in sound and movement, moves towards another actor standing within the circle, or in the opposite line. For a few seconds both actors repeat the sound and movement, simultaneously – the first actor 'giving' the image and the second actor 'receiving' it. The second actor then moves out into the space and the process continues: the form of the sound and movement is allowed to alter – a new association surfaces in relation to the changing form – which in turn shapes the rhythm and dynamic of another sound and movement image – which in turn is given to another actor – received by that actor – and so on through the whole group – the last image potentially carrying traces of all previous forms.

The exercise may be further developed using a theme, which will feed a series of associations for the actors to work with. Within this development there is the complicating factor of the actor having to deal with a constantly changing set of 'internal' associations, at the same time as dealing with a different set of 'external' associations which have been given by another actor. Where stimulus and reaction begin and end is unclear, and whether stimulus or reaction is located within the 'inside' or the 'outside' of the actor is also unclear. This is an important point: within the process of change and transformation, there is essentially a flow or dialogue between the two. 'Don't let anyone tell you to go from the inside out – or the outside in. It's a circle' (Blumenthal 1981: 56).

A second important dialogue occurs within the 'sound and movement exercise'. This second dialogue, between body and mind, can be seen most clearly at the heart of the exercise – that is, within the process of change and transformation. During this process, when an actor takes the sound and movement out into the space, and allows it to alter, it is very clear when the actor 'pre-judges', mentally or physically, in one moment what will happen in the next. In such a case, the alignment between the person and the, as yet, inchoate image, within the process of transformation, is sensed not to be alive, moment to moment.

It is equally clear, however, when the actor allows a particular kind of shifting balance, or dialogue, between body and mind, in listening to and watching for the emerging form, the emerging image, and is able, moment to moment, to come into alignment with it. In such a case, there is a perceptible quality of 'presence', moment to moment within the process of change and transformation, this quality of 'presence' having more to do with the actor in operation with imagery rather than uniquely with the actor's 'self'. The image, in fact, becomes a 'possibility' rendered present.

> An exercise is a form usually repeated in order to develop one thing or another. . . . Some exercises are for bringing suppleness to the body or range to the voice. . . . Most exercises are practices in order to develop something other than the exercise itself. What then remains insufficiently exercised in many workshop situations is the doing of the act itself – that of performing in the present – the act of being itself.
>
> (Joseph Chaikin archives)

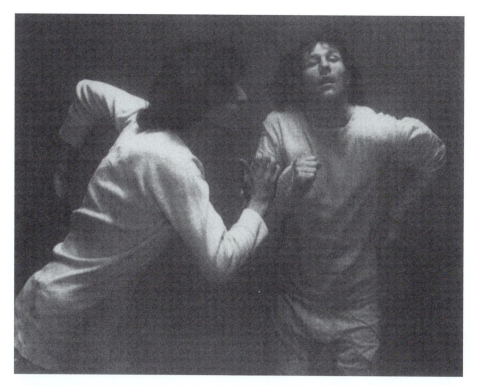

Figure 10.3 (Left to right) Paul Zimet and Raymond Barry in *Terminal* developed by the Open
Theater between 1969 and 1971.

Photo: Max Waldman.

There are, therefore, two interrelated dialogues which occur within the 'sound and
movement exercise': the first between the 'inside' and the 'outside', and the second
between the body and the mind. Both these dialogues inform the content and the
structure of the training as a whole.

I should note in passing that there is sometimes a polarity created between
exercises which invite somatic exploration and those which have their starting point
in 'thinking' or 'feeling'. In my understanding, within the 'sound and movement
exercise' it is not so much one dynamic, or the other, which is being exercised, but
a flow between the two. There is sometimes, also, an association made between
exercises which invite somatic exploration with a state of ignorance in the actor, and
a corresponding state of knowledge in the director. It is, of course, perfectly possible
for an actor to understand the reasoning behind 'an agreed-upon structure' which,
paradoxically, also invites somatic exploration. And certainly Chaikin, working
within a 'research theatre', understood conscious 'ignorance' to be an inspirational
point of departure for both actor and director.

Finally, two further factors mark Chaikin's innovatory structure. Both factors are
also connected centrally to the training as a whole, and Chaikin identifies them as
being the underlying principles of ensemble work: empathy and rhythm (Chaikin
1972: 59).

These two factors can be seen most clearly during the stage in the exercise when
the two actors are sharing the same sound and movement simultaneously. Apart from

the shared *gestalt*, within the sound and movement form, which is held between them at this time, there is both an empathetic and a rhythmic relationship. Thus, the intention within those moments is not simply to imitate the outward form of the other actor's sound and movement but to share the same inner rhythms and energy, that is, the same kinetic and psychic space.

Development – the chord exercise

The exploration of these principles of rhythm and empathy underwrote the development of innumerable variations of this exercise and others by Chaikin. As an example, I would like to include a brief outline of the 'chord' exercise.[13]

> The actors might begin standing in a circle, or lying on their backs with their heads inwards, a communal sound being gradually shared amongst them, beginning with the sounds of the breath – transforming into a hum – and then into a sung chord in which harmonies and counter-rhythms might develop. Movement might then be included, with each actor adjusting to the shape of the whole group.

This exercise, and others like it, invite the 'exiled emotions' of gentleness and sharing to determine the course of an improvisation, rather than a spirit of competition. The rhythms explored within it, their patterns, dynamic and intensity, are not imposed technically in order to shape the sound and/or movement. Rather, it is the intention that the actors listen carefully to the communal sound, or watch carefully the composite form which is being made, and allow their own energies both to feed and to respond to the contribution of others. The sounds and movements become more than the sum of their parts.

Both the 'sound and movement exercise' and the 'chord' have been included in training programmes by generations of companies interested in developing ensemble practices. They were also included in early programmes by the Open Theater (*as performance*), and in 1964 in *Mysteries and Smaller Pieces* by the Living Theatre. The performance quality of the two exercises, and others like them, however, is highly dependent on the relative skills of the participants, and an understanding of their dynamics and purpose. The 'chord' was adopted by demonstrators against the war in Vietnam, and became, in a way, a pacifist statement, a kind of emblem for the Open Theater itself.

PERFORMANCE

The programme note for the first performance by the Open Theater in 1963 contained the following:

> What you will see tonight is a phase of work of the Open Theater. This group of actors, musicians, playwrights and directors has come together out of a dissatisfaction with the established trend of the contemporary theatre. It is seeking a theatre for today. It is now exploring specific aspects of the stage, not as a production group, but as a group trying to find its own voice. Statable tenets of this workshop: (1) to create a

situation in which the actors can play together with a sensitivity to one another required of an ensemble, (2) to explore the specific powers that only the live theatre possesses, (3) to concentrate on a theatre of abstraction and illusion (as opposed to a theatre of behavioural or psychological motivation), (4) to discover ways in which the artist can find his expression without money as the determining factor.

(Open Theater archives 1963)

This performance and other early performances by the Open Theater consisted of collections of exercises, playlets, political sketches and improvisations in which, for example, sound and movement work, representative of 'inner' experience, was juxtaposed or elided with situational work indicating 'outer' behaviour. They were, in fact, mixed programmes whose structure and content questioned the distinction between process and product, acting and actuality.

Between 1963 and 1973, and subsequently in later collaborative projects, Chaikin continued to develop ways in which improvisatory exercises could be used both *as* performance and as a means of generating material for performance. Much of this exploration continued to be cross-fertilised by ideas, practices and skills which were brought to the company by other workshop members, directors and visiting teachers. Grotowski's visit in 1967, for example, resulted in the incorporation of an exercise known as the 'cat' – a sequence of movements adapted from Hatha Yoga which was used as a basis for physical and vocal improvisation. Moments uncovered

Figure 10.4 (Left to right) Tina Shepard, Paul Zimet and Jo Ann Schmidman in *The Mutation Show* developed by the Open Theater in 1971.

Photo: Howard Gans and Claude Furones.

within non-verbal exercises such as the 'cat', or the 'sound and movement exercise', were then selected, pared down and rhythmically scored, juxtaposed in relation to pieces of found text, and often further developed, edited and shaped by a writer, or dramaturg, with Chaikin as director.[14]

Jean-Claude van Itallie, a writer with the company between 1963 and 1973, noted that 'There was an emphasis in the work upon dream, myth, fantasy, poetry, ritual, and the confrontation of social issues.' The company was 'in short: a theatre committed to the imagination, the deep life of the time, and the true resources of the stage . . .' (Fundamentals of Open Theater, Open Theater archives).

I would like now to consider the process of generating material for performance, and to offer glimpses in relation to 'content', by outlining two further exercises developed by Chaikin. These exercises might be seen as developments of the sound and movement exercise, incorporating words.

Generating material for performance – the emblems exercise

Each actor took it in turn to tell a story, which might be either autobiographical or one discovered through research. The actors, as storytellers, could be as subjective as they wished in the telling of the stories and it was their aim to engage the workshop audience with the same points of contact as they, themselves, discovered. The tellings were made up of 'words, sounds, movements and silences', and once each story had been told, both the storyteller and the workshop audience tried to identify moments within it which might be chosen as 'emblems' for the story (Chaikin 1972: 116).

'Emblems', in fact, by nature of their economy – through a process of selection and reduction – provided a means by which imagery generated for performance could transcend its particular or autobiographical source.

In his notes from the summer of 1970 Chaikin gives an example of this process in relation to a story told by the actress Tina Shepard. At the time the company was beginning work on generating material for its new piece, Terminal, which took as one of its starting points the actors' responses to the themes of death and dying, and the way in which they perceived society to have constructed different ways of disguising these experiences. Shepard's story was about her mother, who was dying from cancer, and about the difficulty she felt in saying all the things she was expected to say – 'you look very well' or 'you look better'. Somewhere in the story was the line 'I see you' (said to her mother) 'but I don't see you dying' (said to the workshop audience). The story was much longer in the telling, but these two phrases and the particular gesture the actress used of 'hiding and revealing' were combined and selected as an 'emblem' for the story. This 'emblem' was, therefore, not so much a symbol which represented the whole story, as an image which was both expressive, and indicative, of an essential part within it (Chaikin 1972: 108, 109).

This same distinction would be applicable to the notion of an 'emblem' for a character, action or place. For example, a further means of generating 'character' developed by Chaikin was to discover the 'emblem' of a character in breath. In this process, the actor might start with a breathed sound into which is fed the sense of the energy, or inner rhythm, of the character at a particular moment within a story. This energy and rhythm would, then, be taken into the body, transforming itself into a gesture, a way of moving.

Chaikin's inspiration for the notion of 'emblems' derived from the ideograms of Chinese classical theatre, in which, through the use of specific gestures, characters are immediately recognisable to an audience familiar with the language of that form. The character of Death, for example, waves his arm each time he enters a scene – the wave of the arm not being, of course, in this instance, representative of 'character', in the way in which the term might be understood within naturalistic theatre (Pasolli 1970: 90, 91).

In defining an 'emblem' Chaikin said:

> The crown is emblematic of the king. The bars are emblematic of the prison. If an emblematic part of an action is played out, with the actor living in the action, there is a resonance beyond what there would be if the entire action were played out. The spectator completes the action from the part of it which is being performed. The emblem becomes a meeting point for the actor and the spectator.
>
> (Chaikin 1972: 113)

Figure 10.5 (Left to right) Tina Shepard, Shami Chaikin and Tom Lillard in *Nightwalk* developed by the Open Theater between 1972 and 1973.

Photo: Donald Cooper.

Generating material for performance – the jamming exercise

A related means of generating material for performance was explored through a development of the work on 'emblems', which came to be known as 'jamming'. As Chaikin noted in *The Presence of the Actor*, the term came from jazz, from the jam session.

In 'jamming', the actor improvised physically, vocally and verbally using the content, meaning and intention of an 'emblem' as a basis to work from and return to, 'travelling within the rhythms, going through and out of the phrasing, sometimes just using the gesture, sometimes reducing the whole thing to pure sound' (Chaikin 1972: 116).

Chaikin gives an example of 'jamming' by the actress Joyce Aaron whilst the company was working on *The Serpent*, a piece developed between 1967 and 1969. Exploration for this piece engaged the actors in addressing and questioning assumptions of innocence, guilt and responsibility, which were perceived as being part of a cultural inheritance from the book of Genesis. The words within the 'emblem' used by the actress were: 'What was given to me was impossible to work with.' In jamming, they became something like: 'What was – what was given – was given – what was given? – given to – was what? – to me? – what was given to me was given to me – was – was impo – was impossible . . .'

Chaikin described 'jamming' as a kind of 'contemplation' or 'extended study' of different associative senses within an 'emblem'. Certainly within the exploration the actor would sometimes need to 'rest and let the image move itself' in the mind. Within such a process, there is a dialogue between allowing the meanings within an 'emblem' to determine the development of the exploration, and consciously recognising and shaping that development (Chaikin 1972: 116, 117).

Process and production

The four major collaborative projects undertaken by the Open Theater directed by Chaikin were *The Serpent*, developed between 1967 and 1969 (with the writer Jean-Claude van Itallie); *Terminal* between 1969 and 1971 (with the writer Susan Yankowitz and co-director Roberta Sklar); *The Mutation Show* in 1971 (without a writer);[15] and *Nightwalk* between 1972 and 1973 (with dramaturg Mira Rafalowicz and contributing writers Jean-Claude van Itallie, Sam Shepard and Megan Terry).

All four 'theatre events' were performed widely in Europe, the Middle East, North Africa and America – in theatre spaces, colleges and prisons. Each was non-linear in structure and interwoven with musicality and humour. Each essentially explored a central theme from a number of different perspectives, and also, implicitly, invited a recognition between actors and audience of the need for personal, social and political change.

Dialogue with an audience within these 'theatre events' might be understood as a series of translations: associative connections or 'internal' images discovered by the actor, translated into dynamic 'external' forms – as images in sound movement and words – 'read' by an audience, and translated, by them, back into associative connections or 'internal' imagery. Dialogue between characters as it might be understood within naturalistic theatre was virtually non-existent, and often replaced by direct address.

The last performance of *Nightwalk*, which was also the last performance by the Open Theater, was in December 1973, at the University of California, Santa Barbara.

The piece was concerned with the perception of disconnection within society, and a longing for wholeness. In its last image, the actor Raymond Barry, facing the audience, gestured with his right arm in a vibrating movement suggesting, simultaneously, both dividing and connecting energies. The sense of both presence and absence is implicit in the words, and the silences between them:

> There was himself and herself and herself and himself
> and between us
> there was himself and herself and herself and himself
> and between us
> there was each self and each other self, each self and each other self
> and between us
>
> (Malpede 1974: 150)

All four projects attempted to remain true to the integrity of the aims of the Open Theater as stated in the programme note of their first performance. The original impetus for the company, however, had been to 'explore things', to be a research theatre, and Chaikin felt that, although the group had found a common language within the context of the forum which was the Open Theater, it had taken things as far as it could – without becoming a production company.

In 1973, the Open Theater disbanded. A year before it ended, it became clear to Chaikin that this had to happen for a further reason. In 1974 he went into hospital for open heart surgery and it was uncertain whether he would recover. After that time – despite further heart surgery and an aphasic stroke in 1984 – Chaikin moved back and forth between interpretative work on 'inherited' plays, and experiments within further investigative and collaborative projects.[16]

Chaikin was still alive, and working, when the first edition of this book was published. He died in 2003.

Post script to the second edition – the perfect people exercise

In an interview with William Coco, published in the Performing Arts Journal in 1983 – after his heart surgery, and just before his aphasic stroke – Chaikin reflected on what he called 'the main artery' of his passion, that of 'exiled emotions' such as 'gentleness' or 'mourning'; and he linked this passion with his continuing interest in precise expressiveness. The task was, above all, to find and explore the relationship between the 'inner' and the 'outer' and the route towards that expressive language remained the evolution of exercises. Whilst structures such as 'the sound and move-ment exercise' provided a means to express the 'inside' of a character, a final example of such an evolution that I would like to mention concerned the embodiment of the 'outside' of a character. It was called 'perfect people' and had its provenance in exercises such as Viola Spolin's 'parts of a whole' that, in its turn, became a series of machine exercises in which actors embodied the interrelated parts of an invented machine.

The first improvisations that developed from the 'perfect people' exercise were ones in which the actors only used slogans and clichés in speaking to each other, and resulted in characters that were as two-dimensional as people in advertisements appeared. They were intended to reflect a satirical awareness of the way in which the media influence ideas of how people feel they *should* appear. A layer of social comment as well as humour was introduced when these 'perfect people' were placed in three-dimensional, often incongruous situations, in which their supposed perfection was sustained. Further developments led to 'unnoticed actions' in which, for example, the characters might sustain a 'perfect' verbal dialogue in a situation which required it, whilst, at the same time, gesturing socially unacceptable 'imperfect' impulses. For example, an improvisation might portray a group of upright citizens attending a church service, but during the ceremony – which is followed verbally – these 'upright citizens' might also be physically fondling each other in suggestive ways.[17]

After his stroke in 1984, Chaikin's need to rediscover words engaged him in working with people with special needs, and in making, with others, a number of pieces about aphasia. His own disability, his own 'imperfection', he recognised, placed him in yet another 'place', 'yet another SPHERE'.

> Now, that I am Aphasic,–
> I am, – 'The Other'.
> I under-stand more – about vul-ner-a-bi-li-ty . . .
> What is normal?
> Who sets the standard?[18]

Chaikin continued to ask questions and continued to change and to 'strive to be alive' to all that he could imagine possible. In reaching for words to tell the story of what had happened to him, and referring back, perhaps, to his sense of the 'levels' from which an actor might address an audience, he said 'I am thinking about the stars – not down – but up'.[19] At the time of the writing of the first edition of this chapter, in the summer of 1998, he was teaching a master class in New York for twelve actors and four directors, entitled *From Shaw to Shepard*. In the new year he directed Samuel Beckett's *Endgame* in New York.

Chaikin had directed Beckett's texts for a number of years, and shortly before Beckett died in 1989, he dedicated his last poem to him (Knowlson 1997: 703). Entitled 'what is the word', it ends:

> glimpse –
> seem to glimpse –
> need to seem to glimpse –
> afaint afar away over there what –
> folly for to need to seem to glimpse afaint afar away over there what –
> what –
> what –
> what is the word –
> what is the word
>
> (Joseph Chaikin archives)

In *The Presence of the Actor*, Chaikin observed that whilst Stanislavsky had directed other people's plays, Brecht had directed his own. Perhaps he might also have conceded that in searching for a new language for performance, and in exploring different possible relationships between 'the word' and sound and movement imagery, he himself had challenged the twentieth century's ideas and practices of play 'wrighting'.

Moreover, his collaborative investigations and explorations into actor training – although never aspiring to be a system – placed the actor at the heart of the creative process, and at the heart of transformation and change within that process. Ideas and practices of theatre making which, at the beginning of the twenty-first century, seem familiar, would be less so, had it not been for his influence.

Notes

1   In his Foreword to *The Presence of the Actor*, Chaikin formally states that, despite using the term 'he', in speaking of 'the actor', he means both women and men (Chaikin 1972: x).

2   Chaikin has been awarded six Obies, including an Obie for lifetime achievement in the theatre. His other awards include the Drama Desk Award, the Vernon Rice Award, the Brandeis University Award for Distinguished Actors, the New England Theatre Conference Award, the Edwin Booth Award, as well as two Guggenheim fellowships and grants (inventory prepared by Christine McBurney-Coen, Joseph Chaikin archives, Kent State University).

3   Influenced by the theories of Antonin Artaud, the Living Theatre was to become by the late 1960s one of the best known, and one of the most attacked, cultural experiments of that decade.

4   Members of the ensemble, at different times, included Joyce Aaron, actress; James Barbosa, actor; Shami Chaikin, actress; John Dillon, production manager; Brenda Dixon, actress; Ron Faber, actor; Gwen Fabricant, designer; Peter Feldman, director; Rhea Gaisner, workshop director and assistant director; Jayne Haynes, actress; Jean-Claude van Itallie, playwright; Ralph Lee, actor; Tom Lillard, actor; Ellen Maddow, actress and musician; Peter Maloney, actor; Howard Meyer, electrician; Richard Peaslee, actor; Marianne de Pury, composer, musician and administrator; Mira Rafalowicz, dramaturg; Mark Samuels, actor; Jo Ann Schmidman, actress; Sidney Schubert Walter, actress; Tina Shepard, actress; Roberta Sklar, co-director; Megan Terry, playwright and director; Barbara Vann, actress; Stan Walden, actor; Lee Worley, actress and workshop director; Susan Yankowitz, playwright; and Paul Zimet, actor.

5   This movement was paralleled in Europe with experiments led by Peter Brook and Jerzy Grotowski, and to an extent there was a certain amount of transatlantic cross-fertilisation between their ideas and practices. Chaikin collaborated with Brook on US in 1966; and in 1967, Grotowski came to work with the Open Theater (Pasolli 1970: 97, 114). In 1968, Chaikin was invited to work with Brook's company in Paris (Mitter 1992: 30, 31).

6   Chaikin also invented a number of exercises to explore different possible relationships or ways of 'connecting' with an audience. 'The first step, that of dedicating, is choosing, closing in on a place of contact between you and another . . .' (Chaikin 1972: 143).

7   This image has been pieced together from a number of scattered fragments (Chaikin 1972).

8   Chaikin recommends that an acting company invents its own exercises, especially in looking for alternative ways to represent character (Chaikin 1972: 17).

9   Descriptions of the exercises contained within this chapter and analyses of the dynamics within them are derived from personal practice, contact with other practitioners, and the application of Chaikin's thinking to the structure of the exercises. Published sources are cited in the bibliography; unpublished sources are housed in the Joseph Chaikin and Open Theater archives at Kent State University.
    Brief descriptions of many other exercises may be found in *A Book on the Open Theatre* by Robert Pasolli. Eileen Blumenthal's *Joseph Chaikin* places the workshop investigations more substantially within their context.

10   The outline of the 'colours' exercise is based on an undated, unsigned manuscript in the Open Theater archives, Kent State University.

11   This term refers to the title of R.D. Laing's book, *The Divided Self*. It is beyond the scope of this chapter to discuss, in any detail, the intriguing parallels which may be drawn between Chaikin's thinking and practice and those of R.D. Laing.

12   The outline of this exercise, in its beginning stages, is based on Peter Feldman's account in 'The Sound-and-Movement Exercise as Developed by the Open Theatre'. In this paper, Feldman (co-founder, and director with the Open Theater between 1963 and 1970) discusses the connections between this exercise and Stanislavsky's 'as if'.

13   In this outline, the way in which the 'chord' exercise might be developed to include move-
      ment is noted by Eileen Blumenthal (Blumenthal 1981: 74).
14   The process of development, editing and shaping was a complex and often problematic one,
      which varied from project to project. Eileen Blumenthal's *Joseph Chaikin* vividly documents
      examples of this process.
15   *The Mutation Show* was not credited with a writer. However, two successive writers in residence,
      W.E.R. La Farge and John Stoltenberg, contributed to the exploratory work for the piece.
16   Chaikin's collaborative ventures have included *Tongues* and *Savage/Love* with Sam Shepard
      (Daniels 1994); an adaptation, with the director Steve Kent, of Samuel Beckett's *Texts for
      Nothing* (Chaikin 1981); *Imagining the Other*, a project with Arab and Israeli actors (Joseph
      Chaikin archives); and *The Winter Project* with dramaturgs Mira Rafalowicz and Bill Hart.
      This latter group met for a few months each year between 1976 and 1983, and five 'works-
      in-progress' were generated by them. Eileen Blumenthal's *Joseph Chaikin* documents examples
      of these investigations, and Chaikin's other work, until 1981.
17   This outline of the 'perfect people' exercise is based on Susan Pomeroys's unpublished notes
      in conversation with Chaikin (1966–67). Eileen Blumenthal also notes that the public 'out-
      sides' of characters such as the corporate wives gossiping and discussing the native cuisines
      of the counties they exploit, and the Wall Street businessmen in *Tourists and Refugees* were, in a
      way, mutant descendants of the 'perfect people'. (*Tourists and Refugees* was a piece emerging out
      of *The Winter Project* exploring the themes of 'home' and 'homelessness'. It is referred to by
      Eileen Blumenthal in *Joseph Chaikin*).
18   This is part of a speech Chaikin made in 1989, for the Aphasic Society, at City Hall, New York
      (Joseph Chaikin archives).
19   In conversation, summer 1998.

Bibliography

Context

Chaikin, J. (1964) 'The Open Theatre', interview by R. Schechner, *Tulane Drama Review*, 9 (2):
      191–97.
—— (1968) 'The Actor's Involvement: Notes on Brecht', interview by Erika Munk, *The Drama
      Review*, 12 (2): 147–51.
—— (1969) 'Chaikin Fragments', *The Drama Review*, 13 (3): 145–47.
—— (1970) 'The Context of Performance', in T. Cole and H.K. Chinoy (eds), *Actors on Acting*,
      New York: Crown.
—— (1972) *The Presence of the Actor*, New York: Atheneum.
—— (1974) 'Notes on Acting Time and Repetition', in K. Malpede (ed.), *Three Works by the Open
      Theater*, New York: Drama Book Specialists/Publishers.
—— (1977) 'Joseph Chaikin', interview by Andrzej Bonarski, *Performing Arts Journal*, 1, (3):
      117–23.
Coco, W. (ed.) (1983) 'The Open Theatre (1963–73) Looking Back', *Performing Arts Journal*, 7 (3):
      25–48.
Kellman, A. (1976) 'Joseph Chaikin the Actor', *The Drama Review*, 20 (3): 17–26.
Mitter, S. (1992) *Systems of Rehearsal*, London: Routledge.
Schechner, R. (1969) 'An Interview with Joseph Chaikin', *The Drama Review*, 13 (3): 141–44.
Shank, T. (1982) *American Alternative Theatre*, London: Macmillan.
Tytell, J. (1997) *The Living Theatre*, London: Methuen.

Exercises

Blumenthal, E. (1981) *Joseph Chaikin*, Cambridge: Cambridge University Press.
Feldman, P. (1977) 'The Sound and Movement Exercise as Developed by the Open Theatre'
      (interview by Peter Hulton), in P. Hulton (ed.), *Arts Archives*, Theatre Papers: No 1, The First
      Series (1977–78), Exeter: Arts Documentation Unit.

Hulton, P. (1977) 'From Action to Theatre Image', in P. Hulton (ed.), *Arts Archives*, Theatre Papers: No 2, The Second Series (1979–80), Exeter: Arts Documentation Unit.

James, W. (1977) 'What is an Emotion?', in P. Hulton (ed.), *Arts Archives*, Theatre Papers: No 5, The First Series (1977–78), Exeter: Arts Documentation Unit.

Laing, R.D. (1959) *The Divided Self*, London: Tavistock Publications.

Meckler, N. (1994/95) *Ways of Physicalising Thoughts, Feelings and Text*, in Peter Hulton (ed.), *Arts Archives*, Exeter: Arts Documentation Unit.

Pasolli, R. (1970) *A Book on the Open Theatre*, New York: Avon Books.

Performance

Beckett, S. (1974) *Texts for Nothing*, London: Calder and Boyars.

Chaikin, J. (1981) 'Continuing Work', (interview by Peter Hulton), in P. Hulton (ed.), *Arts Archives*, Theatre Papers: No 1, The Fourth Series (1983–84), Exeter: Arts Documentation Unit.

Daniels, B. (ed.) (1994) *Joseph Chaikin and Sam Shepard: Letters and Texts, 1972–1984*, New York: Theatre Communications Group.

Dillon, J. (1972) 'The Development of Performance Material in the Open Theatre', manuscript, Open Theater archives.

Itallie, J-C. van (1966) 'Playwright at Work: Off Off-Broadway', *Tulane Drama Review*, 10: 154–58.

Knowlson, J. (1997) *Damned to Fame*, London: Bloomsbury.

Malpede, K. (ed.) (1974) *Three Works by the Open Theater*, New York: Drama Book Specialists/ Publishers.

The Open Theater (1969) *The Serpent*, New York: Atheneum.

Yankowitz, S. (1997) '1969 Terminal 1996: an Ensemble Work', *Performing Arts Journal* 19 (3): 80–106.

[N.Y. 10023–7498] Videotapes of performances referred to in this chapter may be viewed in the Theatre on Film and Tape Archive, at the New York Public Library for the Performing Arts, New York.

The Joseph Chaikin archives and the Open Theater archives are housed in the University Libraries Department of Special Collections and Archives at Kent State University, Ohio.

Chapter 11

Lorna Marshall and David Williams

PETER BROOK: TRANSPARENCY AND THE INVISIBLE NETWORK

OUR PRIMARY CONCERN IN this chapter is to outline the evolution of Peter Brook's ideas on the preparation of actors. Our particular focus is the development of two interrelated qualities that are prerequisites for performers in his own company: a state of openness and immediacy he calls 'transparency'; and a state of connectedness and responsiveness he calls 'the invisible network'. As we shall see, both of these qualities are conceived and explored on internal and external levels. Indeed, like self and other, actor and character, performers and audience, for Brook inner movement and external action must always be in a dynamic relationship of exchange.

CONTEXT

Peter Brook's extraordinarily productive career as a director spans the half-century since the end of the Second World War, and includes over seventy theatre and opera productions and a dozen films. It will be useful in this context to divide his extensive body of work into three periods, despite the fact that such historiographic 'dismemberings' will inevitably be simplifications.

The first phase (1945–63) covers the years of Brook's professional apprenticeship in a wide range of performance contexts, forms and styles. At the age of twenty-two he was already a director at the Royal Opera House, Covent Garden; and by 1963, when Brook was thirty-eight, he had directed over forty productions, including nine Shakespeare plays and seven major operas. Landmark productions included a luminous *Love's Labour's Lost* for the Royal Shakespeare Company (1946), an explosive reworking of Strauss's *Salomé* (1949) designed by Salvador Dali, a startling *Titus Andronicus* (1955) with Laurence Olivier and Vivien Leigh, and an elemental, absurdist *King Lear* (1962) with Paul Scofield.

Although he was known primarily as a director of classical theatre, Brook also juggled productions of major twentieth-century European playwrights (Cocteau, Sartre, Anouilh, Genet, Dürenmatt) and works by seminal modernists (including Eliot

and Miller), plus overtly commercial projects – boulevard comedies, musicals and
television drama. Brook's trajectory reflects his deliberate immersion in a contradictory array of experiences, seeking to find a complex, composite reality through the
exploration of opposites. In retrospect, he has referred to this period as 'a theatre of
images', informed by an escapist aesthetic of illusionist decoration and artifice – a
theatre in which the world of the stage was wholly separated from that of spectators,
and where the director's 'vision' was omnipotent.

The *second phase* (1964–70) constituted a period of reappraisal, maturation and
proactive research. Brook was becoming increasingly disaffected with the existing
processes and forms of much contemporary theatre – a short-sighted, convention-
bound theatre he stigmatised as 'deadly' (Brook 1968: 11–46). In his search for
theatre languages that could more accurately reflect contemporary reality, he
questioned the theatrical *status quo* at every level. Rejecting ossified ('deadly') processes, he returned to core constitutive questions:

> Theatres, actors, critics and public are interlocked in a machine that creaks
> but never stops. There is always a new season in hand and we are too busy
> to ask the only vital question which measures the whole structure. Why
> theatre at all? What for? Is it an anachronism, a superannuated oddity,
> surviving like an old monument or a quaint custom? Why do we applaud,
> and what? Has the stage a real place in our lives? What function can it
> have? What could it serve? What could it explore? What are its special
> qualities?
>
> (Brook 1968: 44)

This period of work reached fruition in a remarkable series of productions Brook
has characterised as a 'theatre of disturbance' (see, for example, Trewin 1971: 199).
An explicit shift in his concerns and processes became evident in an experimental
project conducted under the aegis of the Royal Shakespeare Company, with a group
co-directed with Charles Marowitz. Public 'work-in-progress' showings of this early,
tentative research in 1964 were entitled the 'Theatre of Cruelty' in homage to
Antonin Artaud. The culmination of this research occurred with the celebrated production of Peter Weiss's *Marat/Sade* (1964), a collectively devised response to the
Vietnam War ambiguously entitled *US* (1966), and a choral, ritualised *Oedipus* (1968)
in an abrasive new version by the poet Ted Hughes.

This transitional phase was also characterised by a growing awareness of the
importance of the actor within an ensemble. The creativity of actors would be
instrumental in challenging the complacency of prevalent practices and creative
hierarchies, as well as finding theatrical forms as multifaceted as Shakespeare's. Brook
took Elizabethan dramaturgy as his model; he particularly admired its shifts of gear in
the mix of comedy and tragedy, its vivid language, and the directness of its forms.
Shakespeare was his prototype for a conflation of the 'rough' and the 'holy' into a
textured totality he called the 'immediate'.[1] This area of Brook's research reached
its apogee with his swansong with the RSC, a joyously airborne production of *A
Midsummer Night's Dream* (1970), which radically dismantled received ideas of the play.
In this work, Brook and his group of actor-acrobats created a counter-image to the
harrowing, confrontational tenor of the earlier work of this period, with a bright,
circus-inflected celebration reuniting stage and auditorium.

In retrospect, the 1960s marked a period of significant development for Brook in
terms of his conception of the training of actors. He used detailed exploration of

Figure 11.1 Peter Brook: Stick exercise with the American Theater of the Deaf, Paris (1971).
Source: Photo, CICT.

improvisatory techniques to dislodge actors from reductive psychological behaviour-ism, and, as they began to tap other energies, Brook was able to recognise their creative primacy: 'It takes a long while for a director to cease thinking in terms of the result he desires and instead concentrate on discovering the source of energy in the actor from which true impulses can arise' (Brook 1998: 83).

Brook's goal, to amplify actors' capacities as instruments responsive to all the sources of the creative process, has been pursued and refined by him to the present day. Eventually, it took him from the restrictive working conditions in commercial theatre in England, and led him to a new base in France.

The third phase comprises Brook's work since 1970 with his international group in Paris, the International Centre for Theatre Research (CIRT). Its focus has ranged from private research behind closed doors, to explorations of theatrical communication in the field (on journeys to Iran, Africa and the USA), to forays into the fantastic inner landscapes of neurological disorders for the production of *The Man Who* (1993). Core projects have included *Orghast* (1971) in the tombs of Persepolis, Iran; *Timon of Athens* (1974); adaptations of Colin Turnbull's anthropological study of the demise of a Ugandan tribe *The Ik* (1975–76); a presentation of a twelfth-century Sufi poem *Conference of the Birds* (1979); *La Tragédie de Carmen* (1981); a nine-hour version of the Hindu epic *The Mahabharata* (1985–88); and spartan and illuminating stagings of Shakespeare's *The Tempest* (1990), with the African actor Sotigui Kouyaté as Prospero, and of *The Tragedy of Hamlet* (2000), with the young black British actor Adrian Lester as a sensuous, physical Hamlet.[2]

So, after almost four decades with his own company, what are the qualities Brook most admires and requires in his actor-collaborators? And what are the recurrent impulses and characteristics of the performances they have made together?

Briefly, all of Brook's work with the CIRT has been marked by continuing attention to the following ideals:

1   The development of actors with a capacity to articulate the trajectories of inner impulses, conveying these impulses in external forms with clarity and immediacy – 'transparency' (Brook 1998: 224) – and the search for a charged simplicity and economy in those forms, a 'distillation' (ibid.).
2   The actor as a primary creative source in an ensemble conceived as a 'storyteller with many heads' (ibid.: 197) – a team of players. Therefore actors need to be open, complicitous and responsive to the requirements of an embodied transformability Brook has called 'lightness'.[3]
3   The extreme pragmatism of improvisation as the key to the preparation of performers. Related to this, the importance of direct experiences of differing performance conditions and audiences. Work in progress is often presented in unconventional spaces to unfamiliar audiences (in schools, hospitals, prisons etc.). Such experiences aim to unsettle actors' habitual responses and open them up to different energies and qualities of exchange.
4   The absolute necessity for structure, and the conviction that forms can engender freedom for actors. Structure and play are seen as counterbalancing elements, interwoven supports for each other.
5   Research as 'self-research'; a process of evolution and individual development in which theatre serves as potent site and means, but rarely as the exclusive end. In other words, theatre as a means to go beyond theatre – theatre making as the site for what James Hillman has called 'soul-making'.
6   The act of theatre as affirmative 're-membering' (Brook 1998: 225), in which a mythical narrative or fable is actualised here and now: 'reuniting the community, in all its diversity, within the same shared experience' (Brook 1978: 7).

Ultimately, all of Brook's work with the Centre at its base at the Bouffes du Nord theatre in Paris has been driven by the desire to discover what makes theatre 'immediate' (or 'un-deadly'). His diverse training exercises and rehearsal methods have been developed and endlessly reinvented to support and realise this desire. When examining Brook's work, it is essential to understand its open endedness; he has no single form or style in mind, no preconceived vision of a desirable end product. Moreover, he has often reiterated the instability of the relationship between surface forms and the underlying processes and impulses that 'in-form' them: in other words, between 'means' and 'meanings'.

He suggests that all of his theatre productions possess two distinct, if closely interrelated, aspects. First, the external *mise-en-scène* is comprised of contextually determined forms emerging from the performance's physical conditions. Second, beneath these specific patterns of images, no more than tips of invisible icebergs, lies what he terms 'the hidden production': 'an invisible *network* of relationships' that can give rise to other forms and patterns without forfeiting a work's 'essential meaning' (Brook 1998: 151–52). In this context, it may be fruitful to view Brook's preparation of actors through the lens of this metaphor – as a collaborative 'weaving' of an 'invisible network' that feeds, generates and energises all aspects of theatrical communication.

EXERCISES

Preparation

Given the importance of actors' processes in Brook's work, appropriate training is evidently essential. However, 'preparation' is a more useful term than 'training' when considering the Centre's approach. Brook is not engaged in developing the skills of the actor from the ground up, in 'forming' actors for his own particular style of work. In general, Brook's actors come to the company with a distinguished track record. Most have had years of training within a particular theatre culture – in Japanese Noh, Balinese Topeng, African storytelling and dance, English or Polish classical theatre, and so on; and all have performed extensively in a variety of contexts. By most standards, they are already 'fully trained'. Their bodies, emotions and voices have already learned how to respond to the demands of different kinds of theatre making.

At the same time, all of the CIRT's projects include an element of physical and vocal work geared towards further extending the actors' technical skills. Sometimes this takes the form of training in particular styles of physical or vocal work (for example, Tai Chi). At other times the approach is less familiar. During the Centre's early research, Brook often arranged contact with groups with particular perceptual

Figure 11.2 Peter Brook's production of Shakespeare's *La Tempête* (1990). Ferdinand (Ken Higelin) explores a tropical paradise generated by 'invisible spirits' – Pierre Lacan, Tapa Sudana, Bakary Sangare (Ariel).

Source: Photo, Gilles Abegg.

abilities – for example, deaf practitioners (such as the American Theatre of the Deaf) and deaf audiences, who were usually children. Interaction with their amplified tactile and visual sensibilities was perceived to be as informative as any other more conventional 'specialist' training – perhaps even more so. In addition, performers in particular projects are exposed to appropriate training regimes under the direction of specialists within the group. For example, the CIRT performer Alain Maratrat passed on his extensive knowledge of south-east Asian martial arts to the Mahabharata company, as did practitioners of certain South Indian forms (such as Kathakali and Kalarippayattu).

However, the main thrust of Brook's 'training' lies in another direction. Through the preparatory work, the actors encounter the absolute imperative for responsiveness, openness and the ability to operate as team-players within the group. Their earlier training is useful in terms of the depth of theatrical experience it can afford, and of the self-discipline required for a profession that is an ongoing process of learning to learn. But with Brook they are invited to work beyond or beneath enculturated theatrical conventions, whether it be the 'psychological truths' of Western naturalism or the codified gestures of Asian forms. Brook's processes resemble the via negativa of Grotowski; they necessitate an un-learning, a peeling away of habit and the known in favour of the potential and the 'essential'.

Brook's ideal actor has moved beyond ego-driven virtuosity to a kind of psychosomatic integration that he calls 'transparency'. Alive and present in every molecule of their being, they have 'the capacity to listen through the body to codes and impulses that are hidden all the time at the root of cultural forms' (Brook 1998: 167). At the moment of transparency, as in certain kinds of possession in which consciousness does not disappear, actors become a site or conduit for the manifestation of the 'spirit' or 'life' of words, song, dance – a 'life' that Brook believes exists beneath theatrical forms. At the point of transparency, it speaks/sings/dances them. Thus, actors need to become

> instruments that transmit truths which otherwise would remain out of sight. These truths can appear from sources deep within ourselves or far outside ourselves. Any preparation we do is only part of the complete preparation. The body must be ready and sensitive, but that isn't all. The voice has to be open and free. The emotions have to be open and free. The intelligence has to be quick. All of these have to be prepared. There are crude vibrations that can come through very easily and fine ones that come through only with difficulty. In each case the life we are looking for means breaking open a series of habits. A habit of speaking; maybe a habit made by an entire language.
>
> (Brook 1987: 107)

It was with such a goal in mind that, for example, Brook invited the internationally renowned Feldenkrais teacher Monika Pagneux to prepare the young cast of his Don Giovanni in Aix-en-Provence (1998) – to unsettle received bel canto habits, to stimulate individual and collective dexterity and economy and to encourage a fluid openness and integration.

The starting point for Brook's training is responsiveness: the ability to sense and play with, and off, material in a simple, direct way. This 'material' can be impulses arising within the actor or suggested externally, in the relationship with another performer or performers, or in elements of the text itself. Performers are encouraged to develop and exercise a tripartite attentiveness: to inner impulses, to fellow performers and to the space. For Brook, initially such 'respons-ability' is developed physically through the body and its intuitive intelligence, rather than intellectually through analysis or discussion. His preparation of actors realigns the assumed relationship of mind and body in Western cultures, reversing the conventional Cartesian hierarchy and traditional point of access to 'meaning':

> It is always a mistake for actors to begin their work with intellectual discussion, as the rational mind is not nearly as potent an instrument of discovery as the more secret faculties of intuition. The possibility of intuitive understanding through the body is stimulated and developed in many different ways. If this happens, within the same day there can be moments of repose when the mind can peacefully play its true role. Only then will analysis and discussion of the text find their natural place.
>
> (Brook 1993: 108)

Although the body is initially privileged as mediator of experience and storehouse of knowledges, the ultimate ideal is an actor who has developed to the point where all available channels – those of the body, the intellect and the emotional faculties – are open, interconnected and active (Brook 1987: 232). Research and training thus constitute a 'clearing of paths' (Brook 1973). As in Gurdjieff's system of 'harmonious development', to which Brook's work is indebted, personal evolution stems from simultaneous work on the three core centres of body, thought and feelings. Once this internal network of relationships is active, it permits openings and connections to others, the wider 'network of relationships' that Brook refers to above.

In *There Are No Secrets*, Brook describes the preparatory process for *The Tempest*. The group began by withdrawing from its familiar base in Paris, and moving to a secluded rehearsal space in the cloisters of a former monastery in Avignon. Scripts of the play were ignored completely for the first ten days, as the actors prepared their bodies and voices through group games and improvisations whose sole purpose was 'to develop quick responsiveness, a hand, ear and eye contact, a shared awareness that is easily lost and has to be constantly renewed, to bring together the separate individuals into a sensitive, vibrant team' (Brook 1993: 107).

Such activities are not warm-ups before performers turn to the 'real' task of acting, as is often the case in contemporary theatre. Instead, they are oriented towards amplifying spontaneity, responsiveness and complicity, whilst exercising the 'muscles' of intuition and the imagination.

In practice, these activities take many different forms: leader/led 'conversations' between actors involving physical and/or vocal exchange; collective exercises in rhythm, polyrhythm and counterpoint, of both auditory and spatial kinds; choral work in which individual actions feed and sustain collective images; and improvisatory play focused around simple objects – balls, cloths, doors, boxes, sticks. Brook compares this kind of preparatory work to the training of a sports team: 'only an acting team must go farther; not only the bodies, but the thoughts and feelings must all come into play and stay in tune' (ibid.).

'Tuning' here is a musical or orchestral metaphor. It represents a quality of listening and interaction in which the personal (individual instruments) needs to serve the supra-personal (the orchestral collective). Paradoxically, the recognition of the primacy of the whole over its individual parts – the team over the player – can enable a deeper 'individuality' and sense of self to flourish in 'the projection of a collective imagination far richer than our own' (Brook 1998: 183).

In *The Invisible Actor*, Yoshi Oida describes one of the many exercises that invite heightened attention to the circulation of energies underpinning the 'invisible networks of relationships'. Two people exchange a conversation using only the actions of one hand. Each person 'listens' to physical impulses offered by the other, and responds to them, in a direct and immediate way, using their own hand. Oida is at pains to point out that these puppeted hand languages should not be referential, like a code to be deciphered 'like sign language or a game of charades':

> Instead, you try to concentrate your whole existence into that one hand. It is a kind of strange animal, communicating to another equally strange animal. When you find the genuine life of this creature, and it is able to develop a real and varied relationship with the other animal, it is fascinating to watch.
>
> (Oida 1997: 75–76)

The aim is to condense the full sensitivity and expressivity of the body into one isolated part. Oida suggests that the quality of deep attention brought to bear in such seemingly banal interactions is crucial. When a connection is established, the space between the two hands is animated in a kind of small, energised dance of relatedness. Here 'drama' is generated via the combustion of contact between two 'life forms', their particular qualities amplified because they are reduced and distilled:

> What is interesting is the exchange. The 'acting' doesn't reside in the hand of each actor; it exists in the air between the two hands. This kind of acting is not narrative, not psychology, not emotion, but something else, something more basic. It is very difficult to describe exactly what it is.
>
> (Oida 1997: 76)

On a micro level, therefore, this exercise represents a provocation to concentration (inward towards one's own hand) and openness (outward towards the other's hand). At the same time, it reflects the quality of exchange desired on a macro level within the company as a whole, and ultimately with those present as spectators. The network links the actor to self, to partner, to ensemble, to audience.

It is important to note that all such exercises can, and should, be remade for particular contexts. The exchange could be exclusively vocal, such as improvised responses to the sounds of an existing text; or it could involve any parts of the body, with or without voice. There is no stable vocabulary of exercises, no immutable 'box of tricks'. What is central here is the exchange and its subtle repercussions – the pleasure of the changes it instigates:

> You have to work at a level deeper than that of the intellect. As a result, each time you 'exchange', something inside you changes in reaction. From moment to moment you alter and respond. In this way, as the sounds and movements are exchanged, your inner being constantly shifts.
>
> (Oida 1997: 78–79)

Responding to text

Once the sense of an ensemble has begun to be established, and individual 'instruments' are 'tuned' and able to 'play' in relation to each other, then the group turns to language. Often tied to habitual responses, words can enforce the 'deadly' and impede an immediacy of communication. Brook's preparation of actors includes a re-examination of all aspects of their use of language.

Like other external stimuli employed to provoke internal responses, texts are initially treated as materials to be explored and 'understood' physically and emotionally, rather than intellectually in terms of their surface content and meaning. In this context, the kind of responsiveness Brook seeks in his actors has little to do with intellectual understanding per se, or even with the ability to establish personal emotional identification with the words in question. It is something more fundamental, like glimpsing the particular topography of a world or landscape. Brook's discourse in this context often describes patient and sensitive physiological discovery. He has talked, for example, of the voice as a mountain with many caves that the actor needs to explore, or of the imperative to treat a new word like a blind man finding a butterfly (Smith 1972: 76, 130).

As with any existing cultural formation or expression, Brook wants his actors to disinter elements underlying language through a sensitisation to its deeper resonances. The actors are invited to taste the textures and qualities of energy – the 'music' – underpinning its particular forms and to listen to the ways in which this 'music' impacts on their inner landscapes. To return to Brook's description of preparation for *The Tempest*:

> After a few days our study included words, single words, then clusters of words and then eventually isolated phrases in English and French to try and make real for everyone, including the translator, the special nature of Shakespearean writing.
>
> (Brook 1993: 108)

Indeed Brook believes that it is possible to respond with integrity to a given text even when the actor cannot understand the referential meanings of the words. In the early 1970s, this belief was the axis of the language work which culminated in the performance of *Orghast* at Persepolis. Brook describes his multicultural group's imperative to side-step the assumed consensus of an existing shared language:

> The theme of the first year's work of the International Centre of Theatre Research was to be a study of the structures of sounds. Our aim was to discover more fully what constitutes living expression. To do this, we needed to work outside the basic system of communication of theatres, we had to lay aside the principle of communication through shared words, shared signs, shared references, shared languages, shared slang, shared cultural or subcultural imagery.
>
> (Brook 1987: 108)

In preparation for *Orghast*, the actors initially experimented with the sound qualities of swear words, but soon moved on to the creation of their own language constructed from an accumulation of simple sounds. Oida explains:

> We took words from various languages and jumbled them up together to
> create interesting sounds, e.g. 'Bashta hondo stoflock madai zutto'. We
> had to create a meaning for this phrase according to the situation that was
> being improvised. Working with a partner (who obviously didn't know
> the literal sense of your words), you had to communicate what you
> wanted to say through your uses of intonations and clarity of intention.
> We worked a great deal in this created language . . .
>
> (Oida 1992: 47)

Subsequently, they experimented with 'dead' languages that had once communicated
specific meanings through words and grammar, but that were unknown to all of
the actors in the group. One exercise involved ancient Greek, a language in which
the meanings of words are known to scholars, whilst their precise articulation in
speech still remains the subject of conjecture. Brook describes how a passage of
ancient Greek was given to the actors as a single unbroken unit, without any of
its usual verbal or compositional divisions. Like any newly encountered word, this
'nugget of "unknowingness" ' (Brook 1998: 168) had to be explored for its musical
potential: 'It was not divided into verses, nor even into separate words; it was just a
long series of letters, as in the earliest manuscripts. The actor was confronted with
a fragment: ELELEUELELEUUPOMAUSFAKELOSKAIFREE-NOPLEGEIS' (Brook 1987:
108).

   The actors were invited to approach this fragment 'like an archaeologist,
stumbling over an unknown object in the sand' (Brook 1987: 108), deciphering its
deeper layers by means of their own intuitive sensitivities and 'knowledges':

> The actor's truly scientific tool is an inordinately developed emotional
> faculty with which he learns to apprehend certain truths, to discriminate
> between real and false. It was this capacity that the actor brought into
> play, tasting the Greek letters on the tongue, scanning them with his
> sensibility. Gradually the rhythms hidden in the flow of letters began to
> reveal themselves, gradually the latent tides of emotion swelled up and
> shaped the phrases until the actor found himself speaking them with
> increasing force and conviction. Eventually every actor found it possible
> to play the words with a deeper and richer sense of meaning than if he
> had known what they were meant to say.
>
> (Ibid.: 108)

Once again, Brook's linguistic model is musical: a communicative medium of the
senses in which means and meaning are indissolubly interwoven. For Brook, such
music represents an untranslatable language sufficient unto itself: pre-intellectual,
emotional, physically rooted and potentially transcultural.

Inside/outside

Brook has endeavoured to illustrate key elements of his perspectives on acting processes with reference to a familiar shorthand: acting as from the 'inside-out', and
from the 'outside-in'. Although these two terms are often used to describe two
mutually exclusive approaches to creativity in acting, for Brook they are complementary and inseparable.

In the early 1990s, during a public forum on the Centre's work, he invited those present to enact and experience these different, but interrelated, approaches in a simple and direct manner. First of all, they were asked to respond to their own internal impulses in an external action:

> Make a movement with your right arm, allow it to go anywhere, really anywhere, without thinking. When I give the signal, let it go, then stop the movement. Go! Now hold the gesture just where it is, don't change or improve it, only try to feel what it is that you are expressing. Recognise that some sort of impression cannot fail to emanate from the attitude of your body. I look at all of you, and although you did not attempt to 'tell' anything, to try to 'say' anything, you just let your arm go where it wished, yet each of you is expressing something.
>
> (Brook 1993: 68)

A movement is triggered without conscious intellectual volition or compositional shaping; although it is of course in some sense 'chosen' by the individual participants, for they are its origin and site. Once this movement has been arrested at an externally determined point, participants are encouraged to explore this attitude; they are invited to 'taste' its expressive particularity and informational resonances and associations, as if it were a film still that they temporarily inhabit. No gesture will be neutral or void, Brook suggests, for each one represents an 'attitude' in both senses of the word – a 'dis-position'. Each can be read in many different ways from both the inside and externally.

Brook then proposes something slightly different using exactly the same starting point, an unpremeditated arm movement stopped at a particular moment:

> Now hold the attitude just where it happens to be and try, without modifying your position, to feel a relationship between the hand, the arm, the shoulder, up to the muscles of the eye. Feel that it all has a meaning. Now allow the gesture to develop, to become more complete through a minimal movement, just a small adjustment. Feel in this minute change, something transformed itself in the totality of your body, and the complete attitude becomes more unified and expressive.
>
> (Brook 1993: 68)

Here the emphasis is on sensing relations between the parts and a whole, physically and then cognitively. The endeavour to transform an accidental attitude into a form that has 'meaning', through minimal adjustment, engages the will and imagination. The perspective used in this compositional refining is sensory and internal; at the moment 'meaning' comes into being, 'inside' modifies 'outside'.

At this point, Brook returns to the beginning of the exercise, once again shifting its parameters:

> Instead of making a movement that is your own, take a movement that I give you; place your hand, open, in front of you, the palm facing the outside. You do not do this because you feel you want to, but because I'm asking you to, and you are prepared to go along with me without yet knowing where this will lead. So welcome to the opposite of improvisation: earlier you made a gesture of your own choice, now you are

doing one that is imposed. Accept doing this gesture without asking yourselves 'What does it mean?' in an intellectual and analytical manner, otherwise you will remain on the outside. Try to feel what it provokes in you.

(Brook 1993: 69)

Here the physical attitude is defined from the outside, then projected inwards. Participants are invited to 'listen' and experience the inner associations thus triggered, without trying to decipher or impose conceptual signification; so 'outside' refashions 'inside'. However, once it has been allowed to resonate, and is both 'heard' and accepted, a fresh imaginal response arises within the actor, which in turn informs the external physical attitude. As Brook explains, this bridging of inner and outer constitutes a moment of openness in which energy circulates freely – in other words, a moment of transparency:

Something is given to you from the exterior, which is different from the free movement you made previously, and yet if you assume it totally, it is the same thing, it has become yours and you have become its. . . . The true actor recognises that real freedom occurs at the moment when what comes from the outside and what is brought from within make a perfect blending.

(Brook 1993: 69)

Figure 11.3 Peter Brook: *Le Mahabharata* at the Bouffes du Nord, Paris (1985).

Source: Photo, Michel Dieuzaide.

Note: An archery contest. Bamboo sticks are used to suggest weapons and to construct a dynamically layered space. The actor-storytellers aim to produce an energized depth of field, rather than absolute uniformity.

Perception and reception now become active and creative, rather than passive. Inner/outer, subject/object and structure/freedom are now in dynamic coexistence, rather than being mutually exclusive (as they are so often assumed to be). Whereas a great deal of conventional acting is constituted by adding gesture to feeling, or vice versa, Brook looks for a state of responsive connectedness where feeling and gesture are indivisible and synonymous. If acting comprises the process of making the 'invisible' visible, the exchange between inside and outside needs to be two-way and continuous.

PRODUCTION

The desired confusion of inner and outer, invisible and visible, is one of the corner-stones of Brook's preparation of actors from the Marat/Sade to The Man Who and beyond. For example, during an intensive study period in the preparation of The Ik, members of the group copied the postures of members of the Ik tribe, as recorded in documentary photographs. These postures were recreated in painstaking detail, with the actor 'listening' to information provided by the physical form. Whilst others observed and corrected, the actor would then improvise the action or movement immediately preceding or following the instant captured in the photograph. Through this highly disciplined form of 'outside-in' improvisation, where the precise still-point of a photograph would be passed through as if it were one frame in a continuum, actors were able to access internal responses and echoes outside the limitations of personal biographical experience. As Brook remarks:

> This was a far cry from what is usually understood by 'free improvisa-tion'. We found it enabled European, American, Japanese, African actors to understand something quite directly about playing starving people, a physical condition none of us has ever experienced and therefore cannot reach by imagination or memory.
>
> (Brook 1987: 135)

For the production of Conference of the Birds, on the other hand, the group worked with Balinese Topeng masks to facilitate a storytelling transformability that reflected the fable's rapid shifts in reality. Brook viewed these particular masks as objective, archetypal manifestations of essential types which would help actors clarify and crystallise their own impulses. Extending their earlier study of the physiological attitudes of the Ik, the actors scrutinised and manipulated the masks at arm's length (like Balinese performers); then, at the moment of putting masks on, they would modify their own facial expression in the direction of the mask's physiognomy. In this way, actors aimed to make intimate skin contact with 'the face of a very strong, essential type' (Brook 1981: 63). Paradoxically, Brook conceives of such masks as 'anti'-masks that uncover, offering 'a soul-portrait, a photo of what you rarely see . . . an outer casing that is a complete and sensitive reflection of the inner life' (Brook 1987: 62). Potentially these masks – like all such external stimuli employed to pro-voke internal movement – are both transformative agents of understanding for their wearers and 'lie-detectors' amplifying dissonances in circuits and flows:

> A mask is two-way traffic all the time; it sends a message in, and projects a message out. It operates by the law of echoes; if the echo-chamber is

perfect, the sound going in and the one going out are reflections; there is
a perfect relation between the echo-chamber and the sound; but if it isn't,
it's like a distorted mirror.

(Ibid.: 63)

Similar processes were employed in preparing the production of The Man Who.
Through first-hand observation of, and contact with, patients in a Parisian hospital,
the small, collaborative team involved in the project evolved detailed physiological
impressions of the symptoms of particular neurological conditions. By imitating in
detail the external forms of internal states, the actors' imaginations were activated.
Recently, Brook has described a moment in the production's first public run-through
that seems an apt summation of our discussion of certain core components in
Brook's practice: inside/outside, transparency, distillation, immediacy, the invisible
network:

> There came a moment when I felt we had found a link with what we had
> attempted in Africa when we had first put a pair of shoes on the carpet in
> front of the audience to establish a common ground. In The Man Who, the
> pair of shoes was replaced by a table, a candle and a box of matches. Yoshi
> Oida came to the table, lit the candle with special concentration and
> then for a long time gazed intently at the flame. Then he blew it out, took
> another match, lit the candle and blew it out again. As he started once
> more, I could feel the tension in the audience increasing. The audience
> could read into the simple actions far more than they apparently
> expressed; . . . it understood directly what was going on.
>
> (Brook 1998: 223–24)

Finally, let us return to the notion of the actor as 'team-player'. We have already seen
how part of the actor's preparation focuses on amplifying sensitivity towards fellow
actors. This 'tuning' in turn supports their ability to meet what is required of them in
an ensemble of storytellers. Yoshi Oida uses Brook's sporting metaphor to describe
collectivist ethics and practices of storytelling in The Mahabharata:

> As in Conference of the Birds, we were a team of storytellers . . . [Brook] used
> the image of football to help us understand what he wanted. As if the
> play were a game of football, there were twenty-two team members and
> one ball, the ball being the story. Since we were all on the same team, it
> didn't matter who played which part, or if you changed characters in
> the middle. Together we told one story, keeping one ball in play. In order
> to continue telling the story, you had to be ready to pick up the ball when
> your scenes arrived.
>
> (Oida 1992: 172)[4]

However, the imperative to 'pick up the ball' goes beyond training, rehearsal and
even onstage performance. Oida has also described how actors did not stay in their
dressing rooms during performances of the Mahabharata. Instead, they would stand in
the wings, watching and listening to the way in which a sequence was unfolding
prior to their entrance. In this way, they could sense how to adapt their entrance and
performance in order to keep the 'ball' in play (Oida 1992: 173). So the necessity for
connection to the 'invisible network' even affected actors' behaviour offstage.

Therefore, one can see how the notion of a dynamic relationship between the inside and the outside ('transparency') manifests itself at many different levels of the creative process – from a sensitising of the individual actors to their own impulses and those of others, to methodologies for revealing hidden layers of texts, and for enabling character transformation that is not merely reduced to personal biography. It also influences particular choices of tools and artistic forms, both in rehearsal and in performance. The masks, for example, precisely enact Brook's propositions concerning 'transparency' and the 'invisible network'. The way in which such concepts permeate all aspects of his company's performances is characteristic of Brook's pragmatism. Concepts are only ever sanctioned in terms of usefulness; and more often than not with Brook, they arise from working processes, rather than being imposed upon them.

Notes

1   For a detailed discussion of the characteristics of 'rough theatre' and 'holy theatre', and their conjunction in a prismatic totality Brook calls 'immediate theatre', see Brook (1968).
2   For further details of all of the CIRT's work since 1970, with extensive bibliographies, see Banu (1991), Hunt and Reeves (1995), Williams (1992), Todd and Lecat (2003), and Kustow (2005).
3   In conversation in 1986, Brook described the quality he most admired in one of his actors, Maurice Bénichou, in terms of 'lightness'. This quality can be understood through Paul Valéry's suggestion that 'one should be light as a bird, not light as a feather'. In other words, one must recognise and bear the substantive weight of what it is one enacts, its gravity; one must remain present, engaged and embodied in the doing that takes us into the world – but with a lightness of touch that is buoyant and playful, that enables one not to be encumbered or consumed, but to take off, to move on, to be 'free'.
4   For an analysis of the workings of this storytelling model in performance, see David Williams (1991), in particular pp. 117–92.

Bibliography

Banu, Georges (1991) *Peter Brook, de Timon d'Athènes à La Tempête*, Paris: Flammarion.
Brook, Peter (1968) *The Empty Space*, Harmondsworth: Penguin.
—— (1973) 'Brook at the Brooklyn Academy of Music', workshop sessions transcribed by Sally Gardner, September–October, unpublished, unpaginated, CICT archives.
—— (1978) 'Lettre à une étudiante anglaise', in Shakespeare, *Timon d'Athènes* (adapted by Jean-Claude Carrière, 1974), Paris: CICT.
—— (1981) 'Lie and Glorious Adjective', *Parabola*, 6 (3) (August).
—— (1987) *The Shifting Point*, London: Methuen.
—— (1993) *There Are No Secrets: Thoughts on Acting and Theatre*, London: Methuen.
—— (1998) *Threads of Time: A Memoir*, London: Methuen.
Hunt, Albert and Reeves, Geoffrey (1995) *Peter Brook*, Cambridge: Cambridge University Press.
Kustow, Michael (2005) *Peter Brook: A Biography*, London: Bloomsbury.
Oida, Yoshi, with Marshall, Lorna (1992) *An Actor Adrift*, London: Methuen.
—— (1997) *The Invisible Actor*, London: Methuen.
Smith, A.C.H. (1972) *Orghast at Persepolis*, London: Eyre Methuen.
Todd, Andrew and Lecat, Jean-Guy (2003) *The Open Circle: Peter Brook's Theatre Environments*, New York: Palgrave Macmillan.
Trewin, John C. (1971) *Peter Brook: A Biography*, London: Macdonald.
Williams, David (ed.) (1992) *Peter Brook: A Theatrical Casebook*, London: Methuen.
—— (ed.) (1991) *Peter Brook and the Mahabharata: Critical Perspectives*, London and New York: Routledge.

Chapter 12

Lisa Wolford

GROTOWSKI'S VISION OF THE ACTOR: THE SEARCH FOR CONTACT

JERZY GROTOWSKI IS ARGUABLY one of the most influential figures in the development of experimental theatre and actor training techniques over the past thirty years. Whilst only a relatively small number of people had the opportunity to witness the productions of the Laboratory Theatre or to undergo extended apprenticeship with Grotowski or the actors of his company, the techniques of performance training that these artists helped to develop have been widely disseminated through print sources as well as through workshops, productions and classroom teaching. 'Unfortunately', as Peter Brook observes, 'this ultra-rapid diffusion has not always gone through qualified people, and around the name of Grotowski – like a rolling stone – have come to attach themselves, to graft themselves, all kinds of confusions, excrescences and misunderstandings' (in Schechner and Wolford 1997: 379). In a somewhat more acerbic tone, Thomas Richards relates that he is

> aware that many people have experienced 'Grotowski workshops' con-
> ducted by someone who studied with Grotowski in a session of five days,
> for example, twenty-five years ago. Such 'instructors', of course, often
> pass on grave errors and misunderstandings. Grotowski's research
> might be mistakenly construed as something wild and structureless,
> where people throw themselves on the floor, scream a lot, and have
> pseudo-cathartic experiences. Grotowski's connection to tradition, and
> his link to Stanislavski, run the risk of being completely forgotten or not
> taken into account.
>
> (Richards 1995: 4)

The phenomenon to which both Brook and Richards allude has serious implications, and I would not argue against their assertions that misrepresentations of Grotowski's work are magnified by dubious modes of dissemination.

A tendency to emphasise the experimental aspects of Grotowski's work with the Laboratory Theatre or to focus on selected elements of the company's aesthetic (e.g. the extreme physicality of the actor's work, the non-naturalistic style of presentation,

Figure 12.1 Jerzy Grotowski, Chicago, April (1995).

Source: Photo, Panco Colladetti.

or the ritualistic aspects of the group's productions) has indeed, as Richards argues, had the effect of downplaying the indebtedness of Grotowski's practice to the work of Stanislavsky. 'For many people', Grotowski observed, 'it is difficult to differentiate between techniques and aesthetics' (Grotowski 1980: 121).

A generation in rebellion against the tenets of naturalistic theatre created a false polarisation between Grotowski's approach and that of the Russian master, failing to recognise that both directors' work was underpinned by concrete principles of craft that could be applied in a range of theatrical styles and aesthetic circumstances. Indeed, throughout his life, Grotowski always acknowledged Stanislavsky as a primary influence on his work, emphasising points of continuity and confluence in their respective projects over aesthetic differences. He recounts that, as a young student, he was 'possessed' by Stanislavsky, convinced that Stanislavsky's teachings provided 'a key that opens all the doors of creativity' (Grotowski 1980: 193). A central element of Grotowski's approach to actor training, like Stanislavsky's, was the effort to help the actor live more truthfully on stage; the difference between the directors' styles arises in their respective perceptions of how that 'truth' might best be expressed within an aesthetic framework.

Grotowski, who was also influenced by the work of Vsevolod Meyerhold, shared Meyerhold's belief that a naturalistic emphasis on simulating the surface aspects of daily social existence often obscured a more profound level of Truth. Yet whilst

Grotowski's incorporation of codified physical training methods might owe more to Meyerhold's practice than Stanislavsky's, his emphasis on the 'total act' and on guiding the actor to develop the most subtle nuances of inner life within the framework of the role had little to do with the principles of constructivist theatre.

Privately, Grotowski would sometimes recount that when he studied directing at the State Institute of Theatre Art in Moscow, his teacher, Yuri Zavadsky, often remarked on the uncanny similarity between the young Grotowski's way of working with actors and that which he remembered as characteristic of Stanislavsky. Grotowski also voiced a strong conviction that Stanislavsky's work in the domain of physical actions was the most vital and enduring discovery of his remarkable research into the foundational tenets of the actor's craft. Had Stanislavsky lived longer, Grotowski observed, he would have continued even beyond this vital discovery. In a sense, Grotowski implied that his own research could be seen to mark the continuation of Stanislavsky's investigation, taken up from the point to which it had evolved at the time it was interrupted by Stanislavsky's death.[1]

How can the influence of Stanislavsky be traced in Grotowski's theatrical and post-theatrical work, despite the apparent dissimilarities of their respective projects? What are the essential characteristics of Grotowski's approach to actor training? What elements can be seen as consistent throughout the various phases of his work?[2] Is it possible, as Jan Kott queries, to apply Grotowski's methods in a theatre with different aesthetic and ideological aims? (in Schechner and Wolford 1997: 135). To what extent can the methodologies of actor training developed by Grotowski and his collaborators be incorporated in naturalistic theatre or other types of performance that differ radically from the aesthetics of the Laboratory Theatre? These are some of the questions this chapter sets out to address.

Rather than focusing primarily on detailed descriptions of selected physical and vocal training techniques, I will examine certain basic elements and underlying principles of Grotowski's approach to performance that I would argue are fundamental to understanding his theatrical practice. I take this approach for several reasons. First, because descriptions of physical and vocal training techniques are already available in Grotowski's own writings, particularly in *Towards a Poor Theatre*. Furthermore, in the years after publishing his book, Grotowski became increasingly wary about providing descriptions of specific physical and vocal exercises, as he observed a tendency to fetishise such techniques as if they provided a 'recipe for creativity'. Exercises, he warned, serve only as the preparation for genuine creativity. He cautions against a tendency to believe that physical training techniques have value in themselves, noting that it is tempting for actors to use exercises as a type of 'absolution' for not giving themselves fully in the context of the role. Physical exercises can prove useful in helping to prepare the actor's body as instrument, and especially in allowing the actor to address specific limitations (e.g. a lack of stamina or strength or flexibility), but are not in themselves sufficient to enable the actor to accomplish the task of revealing him/herself in performance. 'In the training of the actor', Grotowski warns, 'in exercises, it is always possible to find a false satisfaction that permits one to avoid the act of personal sincerity' (Grotowski 1980: 196). In order to avoid unintentionally providing more 'recipes', I will refrain from speaking of the precise elements of Laboratory Theatre training in any way that might be interpreted as an indication of 'how to do' these exercises.

Throughout the course of his creative work, Grotowski warned actors to be wary of 'methods ready-made for each occasion', which he asserted were creatively inhibiting and could only lead to stereotyped portrayals (Grotowski 1975: 185).

Grotowski was dubious of not only the efficacy of such methods, but also the impulse behind the desire for recipes and easy solutions:

> We want to learn means: how to play? How best to pretend to be something or someone? . . . But if one learns how to do, one does not reveal oneself; one only reveals the skill for doing. And if someone looks for means resulting from our alleged method, or some other method, he does it not to disarm himself, but to find asylum, a safe haven, where he could avoid the act which would be the answer.
>
> (Schechner and Wolford 1997: 218)

Grotowski consistently denied that any such thing as a 'method' associated with his work could be said to exist, arguing that only a handful of theatre practitioners – most notably Stanislavsky – have ever developed an approach to performance training that is sufficiently detailed and systematic to be accurately described as a method (Grotowski 1975: 174).

> When I came to the conclusion that the problem of building my own system was illusory and that there exists no ideal system which could be a key to creativity, then the word 'method' changed its meaning for me. There exists a challenge, to which each must give his own answer. . . . The experience of life is the question, and the response is simply through true creation. It begins from the effort not to hide oneself and not to lie. Then the method – in the sense of a system – doesn't exist. It cannot exist except as a challenge or as a call.
>
> (Grotowski 1980: 193)

In a discussion of the Laboratory Theatre's training techniques, Jennifer Kumiega suggests that if 'the only method that deserves the name of the Grotowski method is that of having no fixed and universal method at all', then what remains are techniques and ethics. 'Techniques we can understand as the minutiae of method', she elaborates, 'the practicable directives which, in certain combinations, produce the verifiable results which are usually classed as method. Ethics are what inform the use of technique . . .' (Kumiega 1985: 111). Kumiega concludes that it is 'the ethic, the attitude with which [these techniques] are discovered, researched and performed, that is of primary significance' in understanding Grotowski's approach to performance (ibid.: 112).

My own experience of working with Grotowski and a number of his close collaborators confirms the wisdom of Kumiega's directive. I am firmly convinced that it is more productive for artists interested in developing their own independent practice to look for inspiration in the *ethos* and fundamental tenets of Grotowski's work than through importing codified exercises. Whilst my discussion of Grotowski's vision of the performer and his approach to actor training will focus primarily on his work with the Laboratory Theatre, my analysis will also be informed by my experience as an actor in Grotowski's Objective Drama programme at the University of California-Irvine, in which I participated for several years (1989–92), and on my observations of the research conducted at the Workcenter of Jerzy Grotowski and Thomas Richards in Pontedera, Italy (1986–1999).[3] I have chosen to concentrate on certain basic principles of physical training as developed by Grotowski and his collaborators. Whilst Grotowski's approach to vocal work is also profoundly significant, this is a complex matter better dealt with in its own right than subsumed in a discussion of physical training; also, the importance of song in the latter phases of Grotowski's research makes it difficult to speak of voice work solely in relation to the 'Theatre of Productions' phase of his creative activity.[4]

POOR THEATRE: THE ART OF THE ACTOR

Although the nature of Grotowski's creative practice underwent many changes over the course of his lifetime, one element that remained consistent was his emphasis on sustained and methodical research involving the fundamental principles of the actor's craft. In *Towards a Poor Theatre*, Grotowski articulated the need for a type of performance laboratory modelled after the Bohr Institute (Grotowski 1975: 95–99), a forum for investigation of the principles governing artistic creativity. Whilst he rejected any possibility of discovering formulae for creation, which he asserted would be inevitably sterile, Grotowski voiced a desire to demystify the creative process, seeking to define a methodology of performance training that would free the actor to accomplish his or her work without obstruction and also without waiting for random inspiration.

The Teatr Laboratorium, the group Grotowski founded in Opole, Poland in 1959, became known for a distinctive performance style that emphasised the encounter between actor and spectator as the core of the theatrical exchange. Reacting against what he foresaw as the encroachment onto theatre of film and other new technologies, Grotowski asserted that rather than trying to compete with new media, the theatre could best survive by emphasising that which set it apart from other forms of representation: the living presence of the actor, 'the closeness of the living organism' (Grotowski 1975: 41). Rejecting what he described as a 'kleptomaniac theatre', a theatre 'rich in flaws' that promiscuously combined elements from a range of plastic and performing arts in order to create engaging spectacle, Grotowski and his collaborators developed an aesthetic that minimised reliance on autonomous costume, make-up, scenery and lighting (Grotowski 1975: 15–53).

> Elimination of plastic elements which have a life of their own (i.e. represent something independent of the actor's activities) led to the creation by the actor of the most elementary and obvious objects. By his controlled use of gesture, the actor transforms the floor into a sea, a table into a confessional, a piece of iron into an animate partner, etc. Elimination of music (live or recorded) not produced by the actors enables the performance itself to become music through the orchestration of voices and clashing objects.
>
> (Ibid.: 21)[5]

Because Grotowski's theatre positioned the actor at the centre of the theatrical event, performers were expected to be capable of extraordinary acts beyond the reach of the spectator. Grotowski was not interested in a theatre that concerned itself only with the banalities of daily life, nor with an actor whose work consisted of representing mundane behaviour. Ninety per cent of what goes on in daily life, he said, is not the material from which great art can be made; likewise, the ability to speak naturalistic text in a relatively believable manner or to mimic social behaviour was never, for Grotowski, a measure of the actor's skill. 'If [the actor's] body restricts itself to demonstrating what it is – something that any average person can do – then it is not an obedient instrument capable of performing a spiritual act' (Grotowski 1975: 33).[6]

The actor as envisioned in Grotowski's theatre was a holy figure, a type of 'secular saint' whose extraordinary discipline and ability allowed him or her to cast aside daily life masks in order to accomplish an act of self-penetration and disarmament. Poor Theatre made extreme psychic and physical demands on the actor without offering the prospect of material success or widespread public recognition; consequently, those who were drawn to this type of work were motivated by other needs. Central to Grotowski's conception of performance was the notion of the 'total act', a culminating moment in the actor's role in which s/he is able to transcend the performance score and the technical demands of the part, revealing a truth that is paradoxically both personal and universal. It is an act of self-sacrifice, requiring that the actor reveal in the presence of the spectator that which is most secret and essential, an impossible truth that transgresses the barriers of the admissible. In speaking of the 'total act', Grotowski's language was highly metaphoric; he described it as a giving of oneself in totality, 'in one's deepest intimacy, with confidence, as when one gives oneself in love' (Grotowski 1975: 38). Such an act cannot be willed, cannot be achieved by means of technical skill, but can arrive only in a moment of grace to one who is in a state of passive readiness.[7]

Actors in the Laboratory Theatre were not concerned with questions of character in the recognised sense or with placing themselves in the given circumstances of the fictional role. As Philip Auslander observes, 'Grotowski privileges the self over the role in that the role is primarily a tool for self-exposure' (Auslander 1997: 64). Rather than concerning themselves with portraying the character as delineated in the dramatic text, actors in the Laboratory Theatre constructed a form of testimony that drew on the deepest and most secret experiences of their own lives, articulated in such a way that this act of revelation could serve as a provocation for the spectator:

> If the actor, by setting himself a challenge publicly challenges others, and through excess, profanation and outrageous sacrilege reveals himself by casting off his everyday mask, he makes it possible for the spectator to undertake a similar process of self-penetration. If he does not exhibit his body, but annihilates it, burns it, frees it from every resistance to any psychic impulse, then he does not sell his body but sacrifices it. He repeats the atonement; he is close to holiness.
>
> (Grotowski 1975: 34)

Auslander notes that the 'object of their performance was not to communicate an image of an affective state but to produce a state of self-contemplation in the spectator by example' (Auslander 1997: 25). By accomplishing an act of transgression and self-sacrifice, a 'magical act' which the audience was 'incapable of reproducing', the actor served as a type of proxy, inviting the spectator to measure him/herself against the truth revealed in the performance (Grotowski 1975: 41). This was the essence of the communion that Grotowski viewed as one of the unique possibilities of live performance, inducing a type of cathartic process not dissimilar to that attributed to the theatre of ancient Greece.[8]

Despite his concern for creating communion between actor and spectator, Grotowski discouraged actors from 'publicotropism': catering to the whims of the public. He claimed that such 'flirtation' inevitably reduces the actor's revelation to coquetry and prostitution. He insisted that the actor must not take the audience as his or her point of orientation, but neither could he or she ignore their presence, as this would inject a degree of falsehood into the very basis of his work (Grotowski 1975: 181). Thomas Richards suggests that in the productions of the Laboratory Theatre, character functioned as a type of 'public screen' protecting the actors, behind which they could explore an intimate process in relative security (Richards 1995: 108). The actor's testimony, his or her total act, is offered to the spectators' view, accomplished in their presence, but never *for their sake*. The communion Grotowski speaks of as central to the theatrical exchange is thus inherently paradoxical, based on a complex dialectic of presence and absence, since both actor and spectator perceive one another obliquely, through a mediating veil.

PSYCHOPHYSICAL TRAINING

Grotowski asserted that a primary aspect of Stanislavsky's legacy, his great service to the profession, was his emphasis on the need for the actor to commit to daily training and ongoing professional education in addition to his/her work on performances (Kumiega 1985: 110). Grotowski consistently upheld this mandate, requiring the actors under his direction to engage in regular physical and vocal training. Rather than contributing to the development of a particular role (e.g. as an actor might practise juggling or dance in order to accomplish a particular fragment of stage business), the daily commitment of performing these training structures functioned as a type of 'work on oneself' in the sense articulated by Stanislavsky, serving to

Figure 12.2 Teatr Laboratorium 13 Rzędów, Opole (1964) with Rena Mirecka and Zygmunt Molik.

Source: Photo, Ryszard Cieslak. Courtesy of the Archive of the Grotowski Institute.

Figure 12.3 Teatr Laboratorium 13 Rzędów, Opole (1964) with Rena Mirecka and Andrzej (Gaston) Kulig.

Source: Photo, Ryszard Cieslak, courtesy of the Archive of the Grotowski Institute.

develop the foundational level of the actor's capacities. Physical and vocal training as practised under Grotowski's direction were not concerned with teaching the actor *how to do* – how to perform virtuosic physical feats, for example – but rather contributed to what Eugenio Barba describes as the pre-expressive level of the actor's work. As Barba observes, 'before representing anything at all the performer must *be*, as a performer' (Barba 1995: 105). Training not only serves to strengthen the actor's physical and receptive capacities, but also has value as a discipline, an embodied commitment to constantly struggling to supersede the limits of one's abilities.

Grotowski adamantly rejected any form of training that sought to develop in the actor a collection of skills or 'bag of tricks':

> I don't agree with the kind of training in which it is believed that various disciplines, applied to the actor, can develop his totality; that an actor should, on one hand, take diction lessons, and on the other hand voice lessons and acrobatics or gymnastics, fencing, classical and modern dance, and also elements of pantomime, and all of that put together will give him an abundance of expression. This philosophy of training is very popular. Almost everywhere they believe this is how to prepare actors to be creative and they are absolutely wrong. . . . An actor can dance, it's true. He can do modern or classical dance, meaning he can make fairly disciplined dance movement. So if he must dance on stage, he'll be able to dance; he won't create his own dance, he'll be able to repeat a dance dictated by someone else. Afterwards . . . he does some elements of pantomime, he learns to walk in place, how to make the signs of panto-mime. So if there are some bits of pantomime in the production, he can use this. But observe that, in this way, he always uses things which are not

a result of the creative process, which are not personal, which come from another domain.

(Grotowski 1979: 7)

Grotowski argued that whilst actors trained in this manner might display virtuosity or technical skill, their performances almost always lack any line of living impulses. Impulse, in Grotowski's terminology, refers to a seed of a living action born inside the actor's body which extends itself outward to the periphery, making itself visible as physical action. ' "In/pulse" – push from inside. Impulses precede physical actions, always. The impulses: it is as if the physical action, still almost invisible, was already born in the body' (quoted in Richards 1995: 94).

Grotowski maintained that one of the most profound and persistent misunderstandings about the work of the Laboratory Theatre has been the tendency to think of the group's training in terms of a collection of exercises, something that pertained solely or even primarily to the corporeal aspect of the actor's work. He suggested that it would be more apt to speak of *psychophysical* training, since the work conducted under his direction had the aim of developing the actor's imaginative and associative capacities, his or her ability to respond to stimuli, whether tangibly present in the space (e.g. arising from the actor's connection to his/her partner) or emanating from the actor's memory. Whilst the training of Laboratory Theatre actors indeed served to develop important physical capacities such as strength, agility, stamina, flexibility and gestural articulation, the goals of the training were also directed towards more subtle ends. Grotowski described his methodology of training as a *via negativa*, a process of elimination. In contrast to training programmes that aim to give the actor a set of skills, the objective of Grotowski's methodology was to take away from the actor all that obstructed him or her in regard to movement, breathing and, most importantly, human contact (Grotowski 1975: 177). Like Stanislavsky, Grotowski emphasised contact with the acting partner as a primary route to discovering truth and organicity on stage. 'Don't do anything for [the audience]', Stanislavsky advised, 'do everything only for your partner. Check, through your partner's reaction, if you are acting well' (Toporkov 1979: 86).

Although numerous elements of the exercises practised by actors in the Laboratory Theatre were physically demanding and could be interpreted as athletic or even acrobatic, the primary goal of the work was 'not a muscular development or physical perfectionism, but a process of research leading to the annihilation of one's body's resistances' (Grotowski 1975: 114). Rather than focusing primarily on the external level of the actor's physical capacity – e.g. the ability to perform acrobatics or execute codified movements – the types of training developed by the Laboratory Theatre were intended to enhance the actor's receptivity to impulse and to eradicate blockages, both physical and psychological, so that no obstruction might interfere between the germination of a living impulse and its manifestation through physical action.

> The actor who undertakes an act of self-penetration, who reveals himself and sacrifices the innermost part of himself . . . must be able to manifest the least impulse. He must be able to express, through sound and movement, those impulses which waver on the borderline between dream and reality.
>
> (Grotowski 1975: 35)

Corporal exercises

In developing the training structures that came to be regarded as characteristic of their work, Grotowski and his collaborators drew from a number of existing psycho-physical disciplines and methods of actor training. Grotowski cited Stanislavsky's work with physical actions, Meyerhold's biomechanics and the Delsarte system as particularly fruitful in the development of his own practice, along with the work of Vakhtangov and Dullin. He acknowledged having been inspired by the training methods of Kathakali, Peking Opera and Noh Theatre, but eventually came to the conclusion that Western actors were better served by looking to Asian theatre practices as a model for a rigorous work ethic than by attempting to appropriate codified exercises. The actors of the Laboratory Theatre also experimented with Hatha Yoga as an element of their training structure, but found that work with yoga positions resulted in an introspective state unsuitable for the work of the actor. They discovered, however, that 'certain yoga positions help very much the natural reactions of the spinal column; they lead to a sureness of one's body, a natural adaptation to space. So why get rid of them? Just change all their currents' (Grotowski 1975: 208).[9]

By instructing actors to remain attentive to external stimuli and receptive to interaction with colleagues whilst practising elements derived from Hatha Yoga, Grotowski shifted the practitioners' attention from the internal focus characteristic of traditional yoga practice to an outward-directed and dynamically shifting focus better suited to the actor's craft. Using the yoga positions as a point of departure, Grotowski and his collaborators developed a series of exercises that came to be known as the *corporels*. These corporal exercises included a range of headstands, shoulderstands, rolls, somersaults and leaps that developed the flexibility of the spinal column and allowed the actor to test the range of the body's equilibrium. Grotowski suggested that a primary purpose of the corporal exercises was to help the actor regain a sense of trust in his/her own organism:

> There is something to be accomplished and it is beyond you. Don't prevent yourself from doing it. Even a simple roll in the corporal exercises – risky, within a limited sphere, certainly, but still risky, with the possibility of pain – all that's needed is to not prevent yourself from taking the risk. The corporal exercises are the groundwork for a kind of challenge to surpass ourselves. For the participant, they should be nearly impossible, but even so, he should be able to do them. He should be able to do them. I say this with a double meaning. On one hand, they should appear impossible to do and even so, he should not prevent himself from doing them; on the other hand, he should be capable of doing them in an objective sense; in spite of appearances, they should be possible to do. Here begins the discovery of trust in your own self.
>
> (Grotowski 1979: 16)

The corporal exercises were an important element in training not only for the Laboratory Theatre, but also in latter phases of Grotowski's research. Participants in Objective Drama worked with a range of somersaults, headstands and shoulderstands similar to those described in *Towards a Poor Theatre*. Initially, we worked with each of the headstands and shoulderstands in a technical way, learning to execute the positions correctly. Once we were able to find the positions, we were encouraged to play with displacing balance and moving the spinal column in such a way as to test the limits of the body's equilibrium. As a further step in the process of working with the corporal exercises, we were encouraged to create sequences of improvised, non-verbal 'dialogue' with other participants, using selected elements of the corporal exercises as a point of departure and trying to find a type of organicity and flow in the sequence, whilst still maintaining the precision of the positions. Our daily training structure concluded with these sequences. When I observed the training of the research team led by Thomas Richards at the Pontedera Workcenter in 1992, I witnessed a more physically demanding sequence structured around the corporal exercises; in this instance as well, the positions were incorporated into a type of improvised dialogue amongst the members of the research team.

The emphasis on maintaining contact with a partner outside the self, whether physically present in the space (e.g. an acting partner) or summoned from the actor's memory, was a consistent focus of the psychophysical techniques developed by Grotowski and his collaborators. The training structure employed during the Objective Drama phase of Grotowski's work required that participants develop a number of individual exercises designed to address each actor's specific limitations.[10] The exercises were initially set on a technical level under the supervision of the workleader, with each participant working separately. Once participants were able to execute the basic structure of the exercises, we were instructed to develop a score of associations in conjunction with each segment of the training, and to explore these associations each time we performed the training. Such associations might involve relation to a person or object in the room, an image, or a specific memory. Even during exercises, Grotowski counselled that it was necessary for the actor to 'justify every detail of his or her training with a precise image, whether real or imaginary' (Grotowski 1975: 103).

For example, a segment of my own training structure involved sit-ups, with the basic intention of improving abdominal strength. So as not to perform the exercise in an absent-mindedly repetitive or mechanical way, I was instructed that I should be aware each time I rose from the floor of why I was doing so, what motivated the movement, for example, what I might be reaching for. I was instructed that the association should be as specific as possible, never something 'in general'. Whilst the external structure of the exercises used in the training structure was supposed to remain unchanged, improvisation was encouraged in relation to the flow of associations, as was interaction amongst the members of the group. Characteristically, participants would adjust their way of performing a particular exercise, allowing the tone or tempo-rhythm of their movement to be influenced by contact with another actor in the space, allowing improvised 'dialogues' to emerge. Under all circumstances, however, participants were expected to maintain the score of their personalised training structure and to perform each exercise with full effort and attention.

As someone who struggled with balance and other aspects of the physical work, requiring days of effort before I could manage even a simple headstand with reasonable control, I discovered that working in connection with a partner was the most effective means of 'not preventing myself' from accomplishing something beyond my preconceived notions of what I could and could not do. If my attention shifted from preoccupation with a difficult task that I felt was beyond me, to interacting with a partner in the space, I often found that obstacles disappeared. 'You won't fall', Grotowski observed, 'if it is truly your nature which guides you' (Grotowski 1979: 17). Connection with the other was what was necessary to allow me to tap into the directive of my nature instead of following the dictates of my discursive mind.

Figure 12.4 Teatr Laboratorium 13 Rzędów, Opole (1964) with Rena Mirecka.

Source: Photo, Zygmunt Samosiuk, courtesy of the Archive of the Grotowski Institute.

A similar process can occur if one enters into dialogue with a non-human partner (an animal, a natural force), so long as one remains truly responsive to the actions and reactions of the other. At least in relation to my own process, I have observed that the temptation to follow the discursive voice becomes stronger when interacting with a memory or imaginary stimulus – there is always the possibility of allowing the conscious mind to manipulate the image/memory, playing it back as one would play a film, or elaborating it with the deliberation of an author writing a fictional scenario. The purpose of the work with memories and images was not to play them out in this way, as a type of internal projection, but rather to arrive to a state in which one does not anticipate or prescribe what details will emerge.

Plastiques

The emphasis on spontaneity within a structure that characterised the training of the Laboratory Theatre is epitomised by the sequence of exercises known as *plastiques*. The *plastiques* are in a sense less physically demanding than the corporal exercises, focusing more on precise detail and on the articulation of movements emanating from the spine and tracing their way outward towards the periphery of the body. Influenced by Dalcroze, Delsarte and other European systems of actor training, the sequence involved a number of relatively codified movements which the actors learned to perform with careful precision – e.g. an impulse emanating from the spine and manifesting through an abrupt movement of the trunk, or a particular way of rotating the wrist and hand.

Once the external details of the plastic elements were mastered, actors were encouraged to improvise in relation to the sequence, combining the individual elements in spontaneous dialogue or contact with the acting partner or responding to other external stimuli. Grotowski elaborated that the process of working with these elements required that the actor begin by fixing and memorising precise details, then look for the way to transform these details – to make them alive, so that they would become spontaneous and organic, rather than mechanical or calculated – by rediscovering personal impulses within the frame of the codified forms. It was necessary for the actor to be able to combine the elements in different sequences, to change the order and the rhythm, not in a premeditated way, but with the flow dictated by his or her own 'body life'. 'It is thought that the memory is something independent from the rest of the body', Grotowski asserted. 'In truth, at least for actors – it's something different. The body does not *have* memory, it *is* memory. What you must do is unblock the *body-memory*' (Grotowski 1979: 13). He explained that if the actor performs the *plastiques* by directing himself with the conscious mind, treating the body like a puppet guided by a puppet master, then it is impossible for the actor to engage the body-memory. If, however, the actor begins to work in such a way that s/he maintains the precise details but does not consciously manipulate sequence or rhythm of the plastic elements, 'almost like taking the details from the air', then it is possible to awaken the body-life.

> That's how the *body-memory/body-life* reveals itself. The details exist, but they are surpassed, reaching the level of impulses, of the *body-life*. . . . The rhythm changes and the order. And one after the other, the *body-life* 'eats' the details – this happens by itself – which still exist in the exterior precision, but it's as if they explode from the inside, from the vital impulse. . . . We have freed the seed: between the banks of the details now flows the 'river of our life'. Both spontaneity and discipline at the same time. This is decisive.
>
> (Grotowski 1979: 13–14)

The notion that spontaneity and discipline, rather than being mutually contradictory, actually reinforce one another was a central principle of Grotowski's work which can be seen not only in relation to training but also in the actor's work on the role in performance. Grotowski articulated this principle as *conjunctio oppositorum*, a conjunction of opposites, asserting that the actor's mastery of an established structure – his or her ability to accomplish something, whether a performance score or a sequence of codified movements that is fixed in its details – paradoxically allows for a kind of freedom. Without the presence of some type of established structure, Grotowski warned, the actor's work quickly descends into chaos; it is impossible for the actor to be truly creative if he lacks discipline and the capacity for precision. Training both tests and develops these capacities within the actor, specifically in regard to his/her ability to maintain the precise details and exterior structure of the plastic exercises. Once the individual elements of the plastic exercises were fully mastered – sufficiently absorbed by the actor that they become, in a sense, unconscious – then the actor was instructed to shift the emphasis of her attention to exploring contact with something outside the self, to the flow of life that can emerge within the frame of the set details.

An analogous dynamic operates in the actor's work in performance. Vasily Toporkov notes that the 'secret' discovered by Stanislavsky in the final period of his work was that 'through the correct execution of physical actions, through their logic and their sequence, one penetrates into the deepest, most complicated feelings and emotional experiences' (Toporkov 1979: 87). Grotowski emphasised the necessity for the actor to develop an established score – precisely fixed, not at the level of blocking or gesture, but at the level of physical actions. 'It is easy to confuse physical actions with movements', he explained.

> If I am walking toward the door, it is not an action but a movement. But if I am walking toward the door to contest 'your stupid questions', to threaten you that I will break up the conference, there will be a cycle of little actions and not just a movement. This cycle of little actions will be related to my contact with you, my way of perceiving your reactions; when walking toward the door, I will still keep some 'controlling look' toward you (or I will listen) to know if my threat is working. So it will not be a walk as movement, but something much more complex around the fact of walking. *The mistake of many directors and actors is to fix the movement instead of the whole cycle of little actions (actions, reactions, points of contact) which simply appears in the situation of the movement.*
>
> (quoted in Richards 1995: 76, emphasis mine)

Physical action consists not of the bare fact of walking, which in itself is only an activity, but in the actors' awareness of *why* and/or *for whom* they are walking; the movement itself is only a pretext or a means. In constructing her work on a role in performance, the actor must fix the structure not as a sequence of movements – i.e. blocking – but in regard to the points of contact with the partner. This score must be precisely elaborated and absorbed to such a degree that it becomes fully memorised; once fixed, it should not be abandoned or altered (except by conscious choice, e.g. through the intervention of the director). Yet within this structure, the actor should discover an ever-changing flow of life that arises from contact with his or her partners. Grotowski often compared the actor's score to the banks of a river which guides and contains the flow of life: the cycle of living impulses.

CONCLUSION

On a profound level, the demands of the training structures developed by Grotowski and his collaborators served to prepare the actor not only by enhancing their physical abilities (such as strength, flexibility, agility and gestural articulation), but more importantly by engaging the associative and imaginative faculties, calling upon the actor to participate in training with the whole of his or her being. In a very tangible sense, the types of psychophysical work developed under Grotowski's direction allowed the actor to exercise not only his or her body, but also responsiveness and receptivity to contact. This quality of receptivity, both in the sense of permeability to the subtle impulses that emerge from within the body – the ability to manifest these impulses without obstruction – and in the sense of being able to maintain a living, organic contact with one's acting partners, comprised a central aspect of Grotowski's vision of the actor's craft.

'Performer', Grotowski wrote in a text pertaining to the final period of his work, 'must develop not an organism-mass, an organism of muscles, athletic, but an organism-channel through which the energies circulate, the energies transform, the subtle is touched' (in Schechner and Wolford 1997: 376). In a more pragmatic tone, he often said that acting is reacting, that the most fundamental actions are watching and listening. *Really* listening – actively, honestly, fully – not 'showing' listening.

The fact that such a statement is not particularly revolutionary or unique, that it is thoroughly familiar to those who know the teachings of Stanislavsky or Vakhtangov, does not make it any less essential or any less true. It is a basic principle, the efficacy of which is not confined to any particular aesthetic or style of theatre. If I were asked to convey in a few words the most fundamental aspect of what I learned as Grotowski's student in California or as an observer of the research team in residence at his Italian Workcenter, this would be one of the first things that would come to my mind: the indispensable necessity for the actor to live in relation to something or someone outside the self.

Rather than trying to disseminate his ideas broadly, making his techniques and approaches to acting craft available to as wide an audience as possible through short-term workshops and descriptive publications, Grotowski preferred to work in a deeper, more intimate way with select individuals, striving to transmit essential lessons about artistic (and extra-artistic) matters in a format of extended apprenticeship and exchange. Richards, whom Grotowski described as his 'essential collaborator' in Art as vehicle, worked with Grotowski intimately and systematically from 1985 until Grotowski's death on 14 January 1999. Mario Biagini, who emerged as an important workleader in the final phase of Grotowski's practice, studied with him for nearly as long, beginning with the founding of the Pontedera Workcenter in 1986. The body of work to which Grotowski devoted his life continues to be developed under their auspices. Whilst the research conducted by Richards and Biagini at the Workcenter cannot easily be contained within the category of 'theatre', at least as the term is understood in contemporary Western parlance, I am confident that their ongoing work will continue to yield insights about performance craft that will prove valuable for a new generation of theatre artists and performance practitioners, even if the source of that influence remains almost invisible from the vantage of more conventional forms of theatre.

Grotowski often made reference to 'The Well' hexagram of the I Ching in describing his conception of the relationship between the work of a relatively secluded laboratory such as the Workcenter and the more recognisable practice of what he called Art as presentation. '[T]he well can be well dug and the water inside of it pure, but if no one draws water from this well, the fish will come to live there and the water will spoil' (in Richards 1995: 134). Grotowski was an artist and a teacher of extraordinary wisdom and accomplishment, a master of a calibre that is seen only rarely in a given generation, but the living water in the well of which he spoke existed for countless generations before his birth, and will survive his passing.

Notes

1   In addition to Grotowski's essay, 'Reply to Stanislavski', Thomas Richards' 1995 book, *At Work with Grotowski on Physical Actions*, provides an extremely valuable and detailed exploration of the connections between Grotowski's practice and Stanislavsky's.

2   For a comprehensive analysis of the various stages of Grotowski's work (Poor Theatre, Paratheatre, Theatre of Sources, Objective Drama and Art as Vehicle) see Schechner and Wolford 1997.

3   The final phase of Grotowski's practice was characterised by a renewed emphasis on the actor's craft; the results of this research are by no means insignificant for practitioners involved in more conventional forms of theatre practice. For further details about the culminating stage of Grotowski's investigation, see Schechner and Wolford 1997: 365–453.

4   For a discussion of the more complex and subtle aspects of vocal work in Art as vehicle, see especially the full-length version of *The Edge-Point of Performance* (Richards 1997).

5   Rather than serving a decorative or mood-establishing function, scenography in Laboratory Theatre productions was used in such a way as to suggest a specific relationship between the viewer and the performance event; each of Grotowski's well-known productions created a different spatial relationship between the actor and the audience, metaphorically 'casting' the spectator by suggesting a perspective and point of view from which they should approach each performance. Spectators at the Laboratory Theatre's production of Marlowe's *Doctor Faustus*, for example, were metaphorically positioned as guests at Faust's last supper, seated around a table on which the major actions of the performance took place. The stage design for Grotowski's production of *The Constant Prince* was meant to suggest a type of operating theatre, in which spectators viewed the action from an elevated space. See *Towards a Poor Theatre* for further details of architectural arrangement in these and other Laboratory Theatre productions.

6   It is perhaps useful to historicise Grotowski's early work within the context of a theatre system dominated by Soviet realism and naturalistic performance styles. At the time that Stanislavsky began to articulate his approach to actor training, the idea that an actor's body might be able to convincingly recreate 'ordinary life' on stage was in itself somewhat revolutionary.

7   In an essay printed in appendix to Richards 1995, Grotowski discusses the work of Ryszard Cieslak in the role of the Constant Prince, critically recognised as one of the most extraordinary performances in the history of the Laboratory Theatre and a quintessential example of the actor's 'total act'. See Richards 1995: 122–24. For critical responses to Cieslak's performance in this role, see Schechner and Wolford 1997: 116–68 *passim*.

8   Auslander's essay ' "Holy Theatre" and Catharsis' (reprinted in a collected volume *From Acting to Performance* 1997) provides an insightful exploration of the approach of the dynamics of the cathartic process in the relation between actor and spectator both in Grotowski's 'Poor Theatre' period and in his post-theatrical work.

9   The cat exercise described in *Towards a Poor Theatre* (Grotowski 1975: 103) provides a quintessential example of a corporal exercise, and is perhaps the best-known and most frequently copied of the exercises developed by actors of the Laboratory Theatre.

10   During the time I participated in the programme, the structure of the training consisted of six individual exercises and a number of activities performed collectively by the group as a whole (running and walking sequences, along with the corporal exercises); the training structure varied during earlier phases of the programme.

Bibliography

Auslander, Philip (1997) *From Acting to Performance*, London and New York: Routledge.

Barba, Eugenio (1995) *The Paper Canoe*, London and New York: Routledge.

Grotowski, Jerzy (1975) *Towards a Poor Theatre*, London: Methuen. First published Denmark, 1968 by Odin Teatrets Forlag.

—— (1979) 'Exercises', originally published in *Dialog* (unpublished translation from French and Italian by James Slowiak).

—— (1980) 'Risposta a Stanislavskij', trans. Carla Pollastrelli, in Fabrizio Cruciani and Celia Falletti (eds), *Stanislavskij: L'attore creativo*, Florence: La casa Usher.

Kumiega, Jennifer (1985) *The Theatre of Grotowski*, London: Methuen.

Richards, Thomas (1995) *At Work with Grotowski on Physical Actions*, New York and London: Routledge.

—— (1997) *The Edge-Point of Performance*, Pontedera, Italy: Documentation Series of the Workcenter of Jerzy Grotowski.

Schechner, Richard and Wolford, Lisa (1997) *The Grotowski Sourcebook*, New York and London: Routledge.

Toporkov, Vasily (1979) *Stanislavski in Rehearsal: The Final Years*, trans. Christine Edwards, New York: Theatre Arts Books.

Chapter 13

Simon Murray

JACQUES LECOQ, MONIKA PAGNEUX AND PHILIPPE GAULIER: TRAINING FOR PLAY, LIGHTNESS AND DISOBEDIENCE

I regard play as a form of art.
(Sir Herbert Read: poet, soldier, art critic and anarchist, 1893–1968)

CONTEXT

APART FROM DAVID KRASNER'S chapter on Strasberg, Adler and Meisner, framed within the context of Method acting, this is the only essay in this volume which presents the practices of three contemporary theatre pedagogues as a 'set' to be considered together. At once, for both author and reader, this raises questions about motive, justification and methodology.

Each warrants his or her own account within theatre historiography, and indeed in the decade since 2000, after an unjustified and inexplicable silence for too long, a range of writings by and about Lecoq has been published. Little has been seen in written form about the teaching practices of Pagneux and Gaulier, although in the three years since 2006 the latter has burst charismatically and idiosyncratically into print and I identify these contributions below.

Unlike Strasberg, Adler and Meisner, each of these three figures would strenuously deny that their teaching practice represents a 'method', and most certainly would be dismayed to have their work yoked together in a common 'system' or 'technique'. Paradoxically, one of the principles which unites Lecoq, Gaulier and Pagneux is their common rejection of a 'method'. Here one might also note a shared scepticism about the ability of academic writing to capture and communicate any lived sense of their pedagogy: its aims, strategies, inflections and underlying dynamics. Nonetheless, in his own books (*The Moving Body*, 2000 and *Theatre of Movement and Gesture*, 2006) Lecoq wrote poetically and reflectively about his teaching. He was also preparing (with Simon McBurney) a book on what, some have argued, lay at the heart of his whole project, the Laboratory for the Study of Movement (LEM)[1] at the point of his death in 1999. Gaulier, too, has published several works, including a book of bouffon plays (2008a); a Socratic investigation of his own teaching and

philosophy of theatre, appropriately entitled *The Tormentor* (2007); an elegantly produced book on 'handwriting, the imaginary and the theatre' (Editions Filmiko website) called *Letter or No Letter* (2008b); and a novel, *Left or Right* (2008c). Gaulier attests
that *Letter or No Letter* is 'my artistic testament. I have never been so precise on the
subject of the imaginary and the theatre' (Editions Filmiko website). Of the three,
only Pagneux has not written of her work in theatre, or sanctioned others to document it in any way. Annabel Arden[2] notes that:

> Monika has always resisted her work being written down, photographed
> or recorded in any way, insisting that it exists in the work of her students,
> and how they develop and transmit their own practice.
>
> (Arden 2008)

At last, however, this is due to change with a forthcoming collection of writings
collated by Dutch theatre artist Loes Hegger, and with Pagneux herself preparing a
publication of photographic images of her work. Writing about Lecoq, Pagneux and
Gaulier together within a single frame is an act of celebration, certainly a work of
pleasure. Almost a playful experiment of imagining a conversation between them,
enjoying a glass or three of good enough red wine: a conversation of silences,
reflections, laughter, sporadic melancholy, lightness, (faux?) indignation, disagreement, gossip and moments of deep seriousness. Any temptation towards nostalgia
and sentimentality punctured by wryness, mordant wit and the resolve always to
share and test a new discovery, to look forward, and to imagine 'another way of
looking . . . (another) angle of aberrations' (Gaulier, 2007: 165).

At one level the yoking of the three together is obvious, given their 'proximity'
in various manifestations over the last three decades of the twentieth century. Gaulier
and Pagneux were both students of Lecoq and teachers at his school until they left
together to found their own establishment in 1980. And, as exemplified by many
members of Complicite (until recently Theatre de Complicité),[3] countless performers, artists and theatre makers from within both the mainstream and the visual/
physical theatre 'fringes' have trained with all of these three teachers since the early
1970s. And, more significantly, such people have experienced their teaching as being
mutually complementary and enhancing, notwithstanding different inflections of
focus, emphasis, context and pedagogical approach.

In the account that follows I will briefly attempt to suggest a range of connections, continuities and serendipitous 'dialogues' in their preoccupations, aspirations
and strategies for preparing the physically articulate and attentive performer. It is
tempting to harness these shared qualities into a particular kind of paradigm – not to
be confused with 'method' – for contemporary actor training and theatre making. A
paradigm that stands in opposition to the psychologism of Stanislavskian and Method
School approaches, and which embraces a *preparation* for the toil of theatre significantly
beyond – and aside from – the conventions of naturalism and realism.

Despite the risk of flattening out the rich complexity of their respective
pedagogies, this essay suggests that together Lecoq, Gaulier and Pagneux offer a way
of preparing for (and imagining the work of) contemporary theatre making which
positions their practices significantly apart from the weighty traditions of mainstream
Western actor training.

Annabel Arden, Complicite co-founder and performer/director, suggests that
around their common preoccupation with the 'work' of theatre one can position
Lecoq, Gaulier and Pagneux slightly differently. Acknowledging the contingent

nature of this schema she proposes that whilst Lecoq's primary relationship is to the 'universe' (of theatre and the world of which it is part), Gaulier's is to the dynamic between performer and audience and Pagneux's to the particularity of the actor as a potentially creative artist. Of course, as Arden allows, these parameters are porous and do not constitute an analytical framework, but they nonetheless offer a helpful compass bearing as we begin to map some of their qualities and orientations as theatre teachers.

In the three sections which follow – 'Histories', 'Lightness of play' and 'Internationalism as pedagogy, practice and process' – I shall trace a number of dispositions, preoccupations and strategies which seem to be shared by Lecoq, Pagneux and Gaulier in their teaching, whilst attempting to identify differences in either substance or nuance when they occur. In 'Lightness of Play' I provide a small number of examples of practical exercises, emblematic of the teaching of each of these figures.

HISTORIES

Jacques Lecoq (1921–1999), Monika Pagneux (1927–) and Philippe Gaulier (1943–) were born within twenty-two years of each other, close enough to the mid twentieth century to be marked by the cataclysm of the Second World War, with all its attendant scars and imprints on both memory and the landscape of post-war Europe. In 1939 Lecoq was a young man of eighteen, Pagneux only twelve, and Gaulier was a war baby of two by 1945. Gaulier and Lecoq grew up in France, whilst Pagneux, 'born into a Prussian landowning family of rural gentry, both conventional and eccentric' (Arden 2008) moved with her mother and sisters to Berlin as the Red Army occupied the family estate in 1945. This particular configuration of time and place in the young lives of all three inevitably had a bearing on the dispositions and 'ways of seeing' which have shaped and framed the nature of their teaching for a regenerated post-war European theatre. The internationalism espoused unambiguously or implicitly in their teaching, and the structures which deliver it, is positioned emotionally, culturally and politically in this place and time. And so, too, in the metaphors often employed by Gaulier and Lecoq – as when, for example, the former analogises his disparagement of an actor's 'heaviness' with the feet of marching Fascists; and when Lecoq metaphorically invoked journeys, dispersals, uprootings and diasporas in offering narrative stimuli for his students. Searching with students for the gestural dynamics of 'saying goodbye' in neutral mask was rooted for Lecoq not simply in emotions and personal relationships, but in the cultural and social conditions of separation engendered by war, capture, disappearance and emigration.

Jacques Lecoq's young professional life before founding his Paris school in 1956 has been documented autobiographically in The Moving Body (2000) and by others such as Murray (2003) and Frost and Yarrow (2007). As a boy and young man he was actively involved in sport as both participant and teacher, training initially to be a sports physiotherapist before joining the Association Travail et Culture (TEC) as a performer. TEC had been the cultural limb of the French Resistance movement and, in the immediate post-war years, helped in the social, economic and psychological reconstruction of France. Lecoq noted that he performed

> in Chartres to celebrate the return of prisoners of war . . . and in Grenoble
> where we participated in two large celebrations: one for the liberation of

the city, and the other for the May Day holiday in honour of the work
undertaken by men who had been liberated at last.

(Lecoq 1987: 108)

In 1948 Lecoq travelled to Italy and worked with emerging figures of Italian theatre.
First in Padua, where he embarked on a partnership with mask maker Amleto Sartori,
and his son Donato, which had an enduring impact on his subsequent research and
teaching in the Paris school. In 1951 Lecoq moved to the Piccolo Theatre in Milan,
where he joined, amongst others, Paulo Grassi, Giorgio Strehler and Dario Fo. At the
Piccolo Lecoq developed his skills as mask performer and teacher, becoming part of a
popular theatre movement with an explicit anti-Fascist ideology and a commitment
to reaching working-class audiences.

Returning to Paris in 1956, Lecoq opened his first school and moved through
various unsatisfactory teaching spaces until 1976, when, with his wife, Fay, he

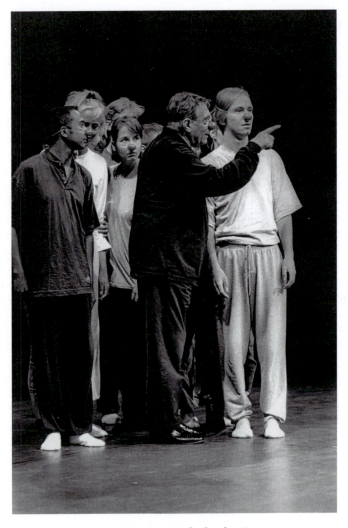

Figure 13.1 Lecoq with students at his international school in Paris.

Source: École Internationale de Théâtre Jacques Lecoq.

discovered 'Le Central' at 57 Rue du Faubourg Saint Denis in the 10th arrondissement. 'Le Central', a beautiful but dilapidated gymnasium devoted to boxing, had inspired Marcel Carné's film *Air de Paris* (1954) and is 'redolent of the 1930s world of the Popular Front' (Bradby 2002a). By the time of his death in 1999, Lecoq (with Fay as business partner and an evolving team of teachers all taught by him) had turned the school into the world-renowned institution that it remains today.[4] Of those students and teachers two were, of course, Monika Pagneux (1963–1979) and Philippe Gaulier (1968–1979).

The working life of **Monika Pagneux** is equally resonant, but it is only its broad contours that are known beyond her immediate circle of family, close friends and working partners. Annabel Arden, as a founder member of Complicite, is one such confidante and has also collaborated with Pagneux as movement director on several operas. Arden records how, initially, Pagneux began her training as a dressmaker, or couturier, within the design department of a Berlin theatre school. Dressmaking was useful, said her mother, 'something you could do with your hands' (Arden 2008), but her passion was for theatre and dance and, through a teacher at the school, Margaret Dietz, she became a member of Mary Wigman's dance company. Customarily, the main influences on Pagneux's work are ascribed to Lecoq and to the Israeli movement practitioner and theorist Moshe Feldenkrais (although it was not until 1975 that she first encountered the latter). Arden notes, however, that Pagneux's practice, 'particularly her compositional work with ensemble, is more influenced by Wigman than by Feldenkrais . . . in fact a whole hinterland of European movement traditions was laid down in the young Pagneux before she ever came to Paris' (ibid.).

From Berlin, Pagneux danced in Wigman's company, and in Switzerland she spent a season working with Cirque Knie ('Switzerland's national circus') in Rapperswil before moving to Paris in the early 1950s. Pagneux's relationship with Lecoq goes back to the early days of the school in 1963 and she was there until 1979. During the 1970s she began an association with Peter Brook's International Centre for Theatre Research (CIRT) at the Bouffes du Nord and was movement director on a number of Brook's productions. In 1980 she and Philippe Gaulier left Lecoq to establish their own 'École de Formation Théâtrale' in a basement studio in the smart 17th arrondissement behind the Champs-Élysées on rue Alfred de Vigny. Here, until 1987, Gaulier and Pagneux offered an integrated programme of four- or five-week courses which, depending on the extent of enrolment, would be taught in the morning and afternoon. Since 1988, Pagneux has run workshops around the world and has collaborated with companies like Complicite as movement director on a range of projects. Even such a brief biography indicates the richness of experience over a working life of more than fifty years that Pagneux brings to both her teaching and partnerships with theatre companies and artists.

Philippe Gaulier was born in occupied Paris in 1943 'at five minutes to midnight' (www.ecolephilippegaulier.com), and from the age of twenty-five studied for two years at Jacques Lecoq's school. At this juncture Lecoq's school had yet to reach Le Central and was located in an industrial building that used to manufacture aeronautical balloons on rue de la Quintinie. Significantly, Paris became a centre – and the symbolic heart – of international student rebellions and worker uprisings which promised, in a brief moment, to overturn the capitalist order. Les *évènements* marked Lecoq's school as much as the far larger universities of the Sorbonne and Nanterre. Lecoq, and doubtless Gaulier too, had considerable sympathy towards the aspirations of the students and, in response to their demands for greater autonomy, introduced what subsequently has become one of the defining elements of the school's

Figure 13.2 Gaulier observing students' work in Japan.

Source: Private collection of Philippe Gaulier.

curriculum – *autocours*. In response to student demands that they should 'teach themselves', Lecoq introduced weekly sessions where small groups of students would subject work they had made themselves to the critique(s) of their tutors. Here the skills, dispositions and challenges of devised and ensemble work were developed and rehearsed as an integral part of the curriculum. For anyone who has encountered Gaulier as teacher, colleague or friend, it is clear that the anarchic spirit and dispositions of 1968 continue to embody and inform his practice.

Upon finishing as a student with Lecoq, Gaulier became a member of the teaching team at the school whilst continuing his own work as clown, director and writer. In 1970 he began working with Pierre Byland to form the Compagnie Byland-Gaulier and wrote what was to become an iconic clown double act: *Les Assiettes*. Throughout the early and mid1970s Gaulier and Byland performed *Les Assiettes* over three hundred times and within this span smashed 'at least 60,000 plates'. As we have seen, from 1980 Pagneux and Gaulier established their own school which for seven years offered

Figure 13.3 Pagneux leading a workshop in Spain.
Source: Personal collection of Annabel Arden.

short workshop courses on play, clowns, bouffons, melodrama, neutral and character mask, tragedy, directing and pedagogy. After 1987 Gaulier and Pagneux ceased to integrate their courses, but Gaulier continued to teach his own programme of workshops from the basement studio on rue Alfred de Vigny. In 1991, following an invitation from the Arts Council of England, Gaulier took his school across the Channel and for eleven years was based at three different venues in north London. In 2002, Gaulier returned to Paris to re-establish his school in the city of his birth, and at the time of writing his teaching studio is in Sceaux, in the Parisian suburbs. Somewhat mournfully, Gaulier states on his website that 'in London, the school was happy. So was I'. He has always enjoyed the English, finding their eccentricities a source of much pleasure, rich in anecdote and a valuable reference for teaching material.

Gaulier's working life since the early 1980s has blended an energetic teaching programme – workshops across the world as well as at his own school – with writing (poetry and plays), directing and photography.[5]

THE LIGHTNESS OF PLAY

> Play is the highest phase of a child's development
> > (Friedrich Froebel, cited in Sutton-Smith 1997: 131)

> A nip is but a nip
> And a boojum
> Is but a butterfly
>
> > (after Lewis Carroll)

> . . .
>
> (Play) can yield the most mysterious of transformations
> > (Sutton-Smith 1997: 1 and 139)

Play is possibly the most significant 'condition' in the lexicon of teaching invoked by Lecoq, Pagneux and Gaulier, and perhaps the most elusive. At a simple level it is both noun and verb which we all apparently understand. We know the order of permission that is being granted when told that we can 'go and play'. We think that we can instinctively identify the territory when invited 'to play' and what sort of behaviours might be permitted or outlawed within such activity. Play is at once so straightforward and so full of contradictions, layers and (creative) tensions.

The manner in which singly and together these three figures engage with the term illustrates just such complexity. In this section, using the umbrella of play, I try to identify the most emblematic strategies and qualities of their teaching, and first consider how each articulates their understanding of play and then review the extent to which there is some common inflection or disposition between them, particularly by focusing on the quest for *lightness*.

The motors of play*

> Two characters pass, each one meets the other's eye and comes to a stop, and a silent dramatic situation arises from this meeting. Then a third person comes along and observes the first two. Then a fourth who watches the first three etc.
>
> (Lecoq 2000: 33)

In the *The Moving Body* (2000) Jacques Lecoq uses *play* and *replay* in a number of different modes. In some contexts 'to play' is synonymous with 'to act' or 'to perform', but he also uses *play* as a quality to be sought and expressed through action and interaction. Early in the Paris school's two-year course students are introduced to the improvisational exercise of *replay*, which is silent. Lecoq describes it thus:

> Replay involves reviving lived experience in the simplest possible way. Avoiding both transposition and exaggeration, remaining strictly faithful to reality and to the student's own psychology, with no thought for spectators, students bring a simple situation to life: a classroom, a market place, a hospital, the metro. *Play* (acting) comes later.
>
> (Ibid.: 29)

In this context, replay is a distillation of action unmediated by any attention to audience, spatial context, acting technique, or theatrical genre. Here, Lecoq is enjoining students to attend to the dynamics and rhythms of movement entailed in apparently straightforward actions and scenarios. Later, through the neutral mask, students are invited to open themselves up both to the space around them and to materials they may encounter, as an initial step along a journey towards becoming an actor and theatre maker. Significantly, replay is enacted silently, but this is little to do with some banal notion of mime, but engages a fundamental proposition of Lecoq's that action prefigures language. He says that 'the imposition of silent performance leads the students to discover the basic law of theatre: words are born from silence' (Ibid.: 35).

> Gesture precedes knowledge
> Gesture precedes thought
> Gesture precedes language
>
> (Felner 1985: 150)

Beyond and within these usages of play and replay, Lecoq engages with a more complex, nuanced and fluid articulation of play which – as we shall see – resonates with both Gaulier and Pagneux's teaching. Here, arguably, we are reaching something fundamental to Lecoq's whole project, namely a search for the underlying dynamics, dispositions or 'driving motors' of performer action and interaction. Scanning Lecoq's various writings on pedagogy it becomes clear that play is the *driver* of creativity. Without a disposition – and ability – to play it is impossible to produce the conditions whereby the actor/performer is a creator rather than simply interpreter. While the divisions between being a *creative* as opposed to an *interpretive* actor are neither rigid nor impermeable, Lecoq is proposing a model of performing where the actor is the (co-)author-maker of material whether it is physical, spoken, musical or imagistic. For Lecoq, the creative performer has acquired a disposition to play generically under any conditions, but combines this ability with an embodied understanding of the specific demands of playing tragedy, melodrama, clown or bouffon, for example. It is for these reasons that companies like Complicite have usually drawn upon actors who have what one might call a generic disposition to play, who have acquired the vocabulary and language of play, and who will approach devising and rehearsal with that spirit of invention, generosity and openness which Lecoq also calls *disponibilité.*[6]

In *The Moving Body* and during the second year of the curriculum, Lecoq examines the motors of play in different theatre forms, and here he speaks often of the 'universal laws of theatre'. While there is no space to scrutinise what Lecoq means in any detail by 'universal laws' he is proposing that, for example, there are a number of necessary propositions about the playing of, say, tragedy which must be harnessed regardless of text and context. And for Lecoq these propositions are neither abstract nor academic rules: they engage dynamics, rhythm and the laws of motion which are deeply embodied within the form in question.

> We seek to discover the *motors of play* . . . so that it may inspire creative work . . . to promote the emergence of a theatre where the actor is playful. It is a theatre of movement, but above all a theatre of the imagination.
> (Lecoq 2000: 98)

Hence, for example, the playing of tragedy necessitates that actors develop a kinaesthetic understanding of being pushed and pulled by fates beyond their control. Here the rhythmic dynamics of the chorus in relation to the tragic hero must be mastered by any actor working in this dramatic territory. It is important to grasp that Lecoq is not proposing that there is a rigid or timeless formula for playing tragedy, but that a series of historically rooted driving motors which embody this form must be translated into whatever context is chosen by actors, writer and director.

Pulling and pushing: the dynamics of tragedy in the choral voice

> Experiencing the choral voice where you no longer speak as an individual. *You are spoken* – someone speaks through you. Working in pairs, face your partner. One begins to speak a choral text. After a while, the other takes the words from his partner and also starts to speak. Shortly you are speaking the text together with the same rhythm, cadence and volume. You become one voice.
>
> (Murray 2003: 145)

There are few of these propositions about play that Philippe Gaulier would not espouse, yet play suffuses the moment-by-moment reality of his teaching in a manner which suggests a fascination about the pleasure of play that is in a different register from either Pagneux or Lecoq. This is not a matter of grading the respective importance which each ascribes to play, but rather, on the one hand, to note differing modes of articulating and siting play within acting and theatre making and, on the other, to acknowledge Gaulier's preoccupation with the partnership between performer and spectator in the construction of the live event.

Since 1980, when he began working in partnership with Pagneux, Gaulier has always designed his curriculum on the basis of four or five week-long courses, the sequence of which he suggests is most certainly not 'haphazard'. For the student making a commitment to the whole package of courses, Le Jeu (play) is the first of a cycle and engages with the core of Gaulier's philosophy which will underpin and permeate everything that follows. Le Jeu offers students the opportunity to acquaint themselves with the vocabulary or scaffolding of acting. Here, students learn to embody the basic teaching terms Gaulier uses in all his courses: complicité, fixed point, learning to play in major and minor keys and, above all, about the pleasure of play. He explains:

> Why begin with the 'jeu'? Because 'jeu' — game and play — is the source of everything: of the pleasure and desire to be an actor. Playing in the theatre is the same as playing at running, jumping, fighting as people and animals do; playing cowboys, Indians, soldiers, doctors and with dolls.
>
> (Philippe Gaulier: www.ecolephilippegaulier.com)

And in a chapter entitled 'Truth kills the joy of imagining' in his book The Tormentor (2007) he elaborates on play and pleasure in relation to nature:

> I am talking about the movements of nature which explode all around you at Easter time. Have you watched the hundreds of wild horses who play in the countryside near Brisbane, galloping to their hearts content, copulating, whinnying with joy? They play . . . everyone plays so as to discover life, nature, sex and light. Play is as vital a function as breathing or laughter.
>
> (Gaulier 2007: 193)

Significantly, like Lecoq through his work on the neutral mask, Gaulier returns to the analogies and metaphors of nature to find a way of explaining and capturing the human qualities he is searching for and provoking in his students. It is also important to note here that the pleasure of play is fundamentally about action, about agency and about movement. It is not, at heart, about psychology, nor is it about passivity.

So for Gaulier — as with Lecoq and Pagneux — play is an embodied and emotional disposition which, although not psychological in any habitual sense of the term, is certainly psycho-physical.

The 'Game of the Scarf'

Two actors each tuck a scarf into the back of the top of their trousers. The game consists of trying to take the other person's scarf, by moving here and there, dodging about. The teacher nominates one student to play in Major and they set the rhythm. The other student follows this rhythm. Both students can take the scarf, one by setting rhythm and the other by following it. When a student gets hold of the scarf, the teacher shouts 'stop': a fixed point. The classmates look at one another. The winning student shows the joy of someone who is playing in Major. The looser is in Minor.

(Gaulier 2007: 207)

The blocks which inhibit or prevent play are more likely to lie in the psyche than narrowly in the musculature: the student who tries too hard (*trop fort, trop voluntaire*) – who is anxious, mentally brittle or stiff, and frozen by lack of confidence – will find it difficult to play. Equally, lacking both generosity and *disponibilité*, the brash, strident and self-centred performer, suffering from a surfeit of confidence, will also find it impossible to play. More significantly, perhaps, an over-identification between actor and role or character will make it hard for that performer to play on stage. Here, Gaulier's use of the word shifts slightly as he extols play as one might talk about the 'play' in a bicycle chain, or a piece of string or rope. In other words, the actor should discover where there is slack, looseness, a relaxation of the sinews which connect performer to character. To find this quality, the ego has to loosen its control over the actor's desire to succeed, to get it right, and to find the answer. By circling and keeping some slack in the chain that connects performer to role, the actor will remain open to discovery, will stay *disponible* and therefore in a perpetually creative relationship with her material and the performance of it. Australian performance maker and teacher Barry Laing[7] puts it like this:

This is part of his stringent refusal and deprecation of the performer 'knowing too much' . . . It might be possible to say that Gaulier's assumption could be that the performer's 'self/ ego' . . . too often 'identifies' with the task or text, with all its received associations and traces of 'normalising' assumptions and judgments. These carry 'weight' . . .

(Laing 2002: 171)

Finally, we must note that the game of playfulness – the pleasure of play – is embodied and taught by Gaulier through employing the very same quality. His relationship with any student is one of playful provocation, constantly teasing, often elliptical, always exploring the 'angle of aberrations'. On the receiving end of a witheringly concise dismissal – '*bien, suivant*' – for some constipated action or response, the student may well fail to detect playfulness and its attendant pleasures, but Gaulier's language (spoken or written) is always suffused with the élan and impulse of play. There is a strong connection here too for Gaulier between the pleasure of pretending – the play of fiction and the imagination – and what he regards as the tyranny of truth seeking. With this, Gaulier, like Lecoq, is positioning his teaching (and the theatre which it aspires to serve) at a distance from psychological approaches to acting, with their evangelical search for truth and truthfulness. Gaulier exhorts us to

enjoy pretending to feel, without feeling. The pleasure of lying will give your lies the appearance of truth. You will be believed. People who look for the real truth in the theatre, rather than the not-real truth, are fanatical preachers and true (not pretend) arseholes. What a shame! Truth kills the joy of imagining.

(Gaulier 2007: 196)

From 'Ring o' Roses' to *Antigone*

In the summer of 1987 Philippe Gaulier ran a workshop in London on 'Tragedy'. Members of Complicite and other professional theatre makers, including me, participated. Two small groups (men and women) hold hands, skip in a circle and sing 'Ring o' Roses'. One group begins and, at a signal from Gaulier, stops on a fixed point; the other takes the impulse rhythmically and begins the rhyme in counterpoint. This is repeated until, at another signal, the song is substituted with text from *King Lear, Antigone* or *Macbeth*. The group of men surround the women, now tightly bunched. One by one each woman turns to the man behind and articulates a speech from *Antigone*.

Monika Pagneux has regularly been described – and for some, pigeonholed – as a 'movement teacher', and whilst this is not untrue in a literal sense, the epithet tells us little about the deeper and more nuanced propositions of her process and pedagogical strategies. Between 1993 and 1995 Barry Laing 'trained' with Gaulier and Pagneux as well as members of Complicite. Laing suggests that both offered him:

> A way of seeing as much as a collection of exercises and strategies for generating performance . . . working principles with sufficient slippage addressed to *the peculiarity of the performer* . . . ways-in rather than methods.
>
> (Laing 2002: 147)

My own experience of spending a year training with Pagneux and Gaulier in Paris in 1986/7 suggests that Laing's *Bergerian* 'ways of seeing' might be complemented by acknowledging that Pagneux's teaching also nurtures and produces a 'quality of attention' in students. This may be an attention to their own bodies (but never in a narcissistic or self-referential manner), to their consequent interactions with other bodies, or to their encounters with the material world. If Gaulier's locus of attention is the student-performer's engagement – *complicité* – with audience, Pagneux's concern with play follows an arc which grows experientially from the minute relationship of, say, one limb against another through to the light – but fully engaged – playfulness of all members of a whole class (or cast) with each other.

The sequence and flow of movement

> Lying on your back, knees up in 'recovery' position. Right arm lying as straight as possible on the floor above head. Right elbow on the ground so the arm will be slightly bent. Raise elbow off the ground and register movement in the hand. Raise elbow further off the ground and let the hand follow – the tips of the fingers are the last to leave the ground. Now raise arm even further off the ground, finding a wave in the movement – shoulder blades will begin to move – and producing an undulation reflected in the whole body.
>
> (Exercise from a class with Monika Pagneux, 1987)

Pagneux's teaching begins and ends with the body, and as she draws on – and adapts – an elaborate portfolio of movement exercises which have their lineage in the work of Moshe Feldenkrais, she begins to explore how movement travels through the body. 'Economy of movement' seems a particularly dry way of describing what Pagneux is searching for in her students, but it suggests one partial dimension of her pedagogy. A corporeal translation of E.M. Forster's maxim 'only connect' might equally capture what Pagneux is seeking as she guides students or actors through a range of exercises that trace the journey a movement may take through a body without distortion, unnecessary effort and without encountering psycho-muscular blocks. With this work Pagneux is initially inviting students to discover the tiny possibilities of play between, say, the wrist, the fingers and the lower arm, or the movement consequences for shoulders, spine and pelvis when the right hand of a standing figure reaches out towards the wall opposite. So, at a very simple level, 'play' at this point in the arc of her teaching may be equated with movement or plasticity, but not in the quest for virtuosity or learning a particular acting technique. Annabel Arden joyfully paraphrases a Pagneux commentary as she invites students to experience what happens when exploring a particular move:

> If I lift my arm I can feel the movement in my little toe. *Tout participe.* Put the pieces together. Who pulls who? My eyelids lead my cheek, my cheek leads my jaw, my neck, my shoulder, my ribcage, my lumbar, my pelvis, my knee . . . I TURN!
>
> (Arden 2008)

One might say here that she is preparing the body for a second level of play – a corporeal approach towards finding that *disponibilité* which she will be exploring later through ensemble and collaborative practices. This stage of her teaching also has its parallels in Lecoq's work with the neutral mask. One could suggest that – insofar as the neutral mask is inviting its wearer to rediscover a pre-linguistic, pre-cultural[8] relationship with matter, with nature – Pagneux's teaching is preparing the body for the fluidity and responsiveness necessary for effective work with the neutral mask. Arden clarifies the purpose behind this aspect of her teaching:

> she is suspicious of the idea that you can 'train' actors, which implies for her a certain obedience, that they graduate with a defined set of skills. She says she *forms* them, rather than *deforming* them . . . and stresses that there is no 'body of an actor' which you can acquire by training. Rather, each person must explore their own specific body in order really to inhabit it, and allow expression of the unexpected parts of the self, the hidden registers.
>
> (Arden 2008)

These exercises, which work initially with the actor's own body, are also serving another linked purpose, and that is to exercise the muscle of attention. Without mystification, rhetoric or metaphysics Pagneux is establishing conditions whereby bodies can attend better and more sharply, not only to themselves, but also to the perpetual stimuli of the human and material world around them. These exercises help to nurture a generous and responsive alertness which will prepare them for theatrical play at another stage in their development. It is also important to stress here that for Pagneux this quality of attention is not to be directed inwards, towards some fixed and mythical centre of authenticity. Rather, as Barry Laing puts it, the performer undertakes 'the seeming "impossibility" of simultaneously being "near and far" – from the text, "character", emotion and the full dynamics of movement . . . not "holding too close" the identifications of text, emotion or even the movement itself' (Laing 2002: 174).

On those rare occasions that Pagneux's work has been described in the writing of others, her practice has been firmly anchored in the work of Feldenkrais, with an occasional nod towards other influences garnered throughout her long career. Arden, however, points out that Pagneux came late to Feldenkrais, after dancing with Mary Wigman and already teaching with Lecoq. She argues that in fact Pagneux's teaching continues to draw very much on the chorus work, theatrical expressivity and the musicality of the body as explored and practised by Wigman. Arden quotes Wigman to illustrate Pagneux's preoccupation with the connections between the body's musicality and the world beyond:

> Teach your students to see and absorb with waking eyes the manifold eventfulness of their everyday life . . . teach them to think in terms of big dimensions. The spatial relationships do not tolerate any narrow-minded limitations.
>
> (Wigman 1966: 107/111)

Pagneux's teaching typically travels between work on the minute detail of a move-ment or sequence of movements in an actor's body, through to ensemble exercises inspired by her early experiences with Wigman. At no point in this pedagogical arc is she concerned with virtuosity for its own sake, rather that every activity is focused on 'waking up the senses' (Arden 2008), whether this be through a Feldenkrais exercise following the sequence of movement from the turn of a head to the lifting of a leg, or twenty students moving pleasurably and musically together to a simple choreo-graphic design whilst incorporating rhythmic clapping, chanting or percussive sound. In everything the exercise is simultaneously 'near and far', a performance in itself whilst always only a small step in a process, a journey without a terminus. Throughout, both the small and the big 'dance', the minute play of limbs moving fluidly, and the collaborative delight of twenty bodies working attentively and musically together. The pleasure of things becoming.

Understanding feet

> Stand normally. Sense and 'mark' the places where your feet have contact with the floor, and note any particular points of pressure. Take a mental x-ray. Note the relative position of each foot. Take a piece of paper and draw your feet, shading in areas of contact, marking pressure points. Exchange your drawing with another student and now try to stand in exactly in the way indicated by your (new) drawing. Register how your new stance affects your legs, pelvis, back, shoulders, head etc.
>
> (Exercise from a class with Monika Pagneux, 1987)

That a significant part of this essay has been devoted to reflecting on how Lecoq, Gaulier and Pagneux engage with play in their teaching is a measure of how funda-mental this disposition is in their imaginings about the theatre they hope their pedagogies will inspire and construct. Within the intricate but ubiquitous weave of play, the quality of lightness appears for all three figures as both condition and consequence of successful play. Here, I briefly examine both the grain and politics of lightness as partner and corollary to play in the work of Lecoq, Gaulier and Pagneux.

For Gaulier, lightness is an imperative quality or texture in how an actor conducts him/herself in relation to the material of performance, to space and objects, to movement, to speech and sound, to fellow performers and – above all – to spectators. He is particularly preoccupied with the *instant* of performance: a combination of qualities that will remove the moment from the void of deadliness and bring it soaring into life, regardless of style or genre. Gaulier invokes lightness almost as much as he does *play*, *pleasure* or *élan*, for example. The quality of lightness sought is Gaulier as pedagogical Icarus, creating the conditions where flight may just be possible and where gravity and weight may be defied if only for an instant. It is also about the generative possibilities of lightness as performative photosynthesis, and here he is marking territory where intellectual or academic analysis would seem to close down and preclude the likelihood of creative play. Gnomically, he claims that 'the creative play of the actor takes place in the light. It is hopeless to seek refuge in a cave of repentance and remorse' (Gaulier cited in Wright 1990: 8). We may 'illuminate' Gaulier's interpretation of lightness by way of Italian author Italo Calvino, who, in *Six Memos for the New Millennium* (1988), cites and celebrates the poet Lucretius, whose 'chief concern is to prevent the weight of matter from crushing us' (Ibid.: 8). He goes on to say:

> Were I to choose an auspicious image for the new millennium, I would choose . . . the sudden agile leap of the poet philosopher (Cavalcanti) who raises himself above the weight of the world, showing that with all his gravity he has the secret of lightness.
>
> (Ibid.: 12)

Richard Raskin poetically summarises what lightness means for Calvino in a way which encapsulates those qualities that Gaulier is looking for in the moment of performance:

> Lightness for Calvino is identified with such properties as mobility, agility of spirit, knowledge of the world, subtlety, multiplicity, the precarious-ness of things as they are, levitation and freedom. Correspondingly, heaviness is linked to inertia, opacity, petrification, sluggishness, density, solidity and the crushing of life.
>
> (Raskin 2004: 104)

So, for Gaulier, lightness, pleasure and play are mutually interdependent qualities and dispositions. Together they form the kernel of his pedagogy which invites the actor:

- to discover pleasure in the act of performing regardless of text, style and genre;
- to lighten the weight of the text by circling it, by coming to it at a tangent, through an indirect glance, playfully and with generous disrespect;
- to loosen and relax the sinews attaching performer to character, to find an engaged distance, to avoid knowing too much and trying too hard.

Laing summarises this lightness, this circling, the importance of pleasure in Gaulier's practice:

> The pleasure of the *performer* – as distinct from, though not necessarily
> opposed to, the 'character' – contains all of the lightness of tactics and
> game playing. It is, Gaulier intimates, almost a contradiction in terms to
> be unhappy with your own tactic. It is this lightness and pleasure that is
> then addressed to text, character, and the 'choreography' of a scene.
>
> (Laing 2002: 171)

For Pagneux, one might say that her focus is an embodied translation of many of the
principles articulated above. For her, lightness is no less important than for Gaulier,
but the quest is focused on what Annabel Arden calls 'the fun of moving without
effort, with the lightness that comes when the body is centred' (2008). Here, lightness is the kinaesthetic and experiential condition achieved when action and effort
are in perfect balance or harmony. However, unlike many movement teachers who
would subscribe to something similar, seeking this quality for Pagneux is never
simply a 'mechanical' accomplishment of mind and musculature finding the most
fluid and economic partnership. It also – and only – arises from acknowledging the
singular humanity of each student, each actor. So, lightness is a psychophysical quality
and one which has a contextual dimension as well as a narrowly corporeal one.

   Arden describes how Pagneux taught acrobatics at Lecoq's school and thereafter,
pointing out that she was never interested in the technical virtuosity of a somer-
sault, a cartwheel or a back-flip. After initially matching students of similar ability
she would pair a physically adroit student with one who was less competent. At this
juncture the more skilful student was to imitate exactly the more rudimentary
cartwheel of their partner. This was the moment when something interesting and
performatively dynamic might begin to occur. Arden identifies what was happening:

> first, the poor student would improve, second the gifted acrobat would
> find a new expressivity and humanity in the movement, third a possible
> improvisatory dialogue and relationship would emerge so that a scene
> could be played between the two, using the dynamic of their difference. It
> was all play – that was the secret.
>
> (Arden 2008)

For Pagneux, therefore, lightness is born out of the body and its ability and willingness to move economically, responsively and fluidly in space, but is only fully realised
in the context of play – play between performers, play with text and objects, play with
the imagination and – finally – in the play of *complicité* with an audience.

A trip to the zoo

In the early autumn of 1986, whilst taking 'Le Jeu' with Gaulier and Pagneux, all
students are required to make a visit to the Paris zoo. Here we are enjoined to observe
most carefully the way large beasts – elephants, rhinos, hippos, giraffes, bears, bison
and, of course, the big cats – move through space. The point is to notice, and indeed
marvel, at the way in which these huge creatures negotiate their mobility with such
delicacy, lightness and – apparently – unselfconscious precision.

Lecoq does not appear to 'name' lightness in the way both Gaulier and Pagneux
do in the daily discourse of their pedagogies; nonetheless it is an unspoken condition

or assumption that lies within every aspect of his teaching. Lightness of action and of the haptic (touch) is an indispensable quality of work with the neutral mask. This work frames the students' journey through the school, and Lecoq says that 'such fundamental things occur with this mask that it has become the central point of my teaching method' (Lecoq 2000: 36). This is not the moment for a deep investigation of the neutral mask[9] or the debates around its cultural provenance, but it is important to grasp that the 'neutral mask is a way of understanding performance, not a way of performing' (Eldredge and Huston 1995: 127). If by 'understanding' we assume a corporal and embodied disposition (and not merely a cognitive one), then this is an assertion with which, I imagine, Lecoq would have agreed. There is a sense in which the role of neutral mask within Lecoq's curriculum serves a similar purpose to Gaulier's opening course, 'Le Jeu'. Whilst Gaulier also offers a course on the neutral mask later in his sequence, both invite the student to open themselves up to the world of nature, objects and materials. Lecoq's work with the neutral mask is a process of demystification and sensitisation, of inviting the mind-body of the actor to renew their experience of the world without the *weight* of accrued knowledge. For Lecoq there is no sense that this is an achievable goal, rather a heuristic strategy for discovery and for unlocking the imagination. 'Of course' he says 'there is no such thing as absolute and universal universality, it is merely a temptation' (Lecoq 2000: 20).

Waking up

This for both Lecoq and Gaulier is almost the first exercise a student will undertake with the mask, and here Pagneux's lightness and fluidity of movement becomes both tool and embodied quality of any action undertaken. Lecoq describes the task:

> In a state of repose, relaxed and lying on the ground, I ask the students to 'wake up for the first time'. Once the mask is awake, what can it do? How can it move?
>
> (Lecoq 2000: 39)

Lecoq, it would seem, tends to use variations around 'freeing' the body or of giving 'freedom' to the student rather than the term 'lightness' as such. It is this freedom – constructed, as it were, through the neutral mask – which enables the student to become *disponible*, in 'a state of discovery, of openness, of freedom to receive' (Ibid.: 38). Another clue of a shared disposition toward lightness between the three is evidenced by a comment by Lecoq, similar in tone to Gaulier's prohibition on actors 'seeking refuge in a cave of repentance and remorse', as he insists:

> It is essential to have fun and our school is a happy school. Not for us, tortured self-questioning about the best way to walk on stage: it is enough that it be done with pleasure.
>
> (Ibid.: 65)

INTERNATIONALISM AS PEDAGOGY, PRACTICE AND PROCESS

I began this essay by noting that notwithstanding the twenty-two years which separate the oldest (Lecoq) and the youngest (Gaulier) of the trio, all three grew up

Figure 13.4 Theatre de Complicité's production of *The Elephant Vanishes*, inspired by the short stories by Haruki Murakami, directed by Simon McBurney, British production (2003).

Source: Photo, Tsukasa Aoki, courtesy of Setagaya Public Theatre.

in Europe before, or in the immediate aftermath of, the Second World War. Forcefully, but in different ways, this marking of time and place has shaped the political and cultural contours of their teaching. In an affecting encounter between Lecoq and Dario Fo shortly before the former's death in 1999, recorded on film by Jean-Noël Roy and Jean-Gabriel Carasso, we are witness to a conversation recalling their shared early years as young theatre makers in post-war Europe:

> DF: But there was a very important phenomenon that we were going through at the time. We were living among extraordinary renewal. We had to throw away everything and construct a world. The world had to be made all over again.
>
> JL: There were no more rules. There were no more rules. We had to make up the game again – find new rules.

> (Roy and Carasso 2006)

What this dialogue particularly evidences is that sense of optimism, following the defeat of Fascism, that artists must empower themselves to invent afresh the rules of their creative practice. For Lecoq and Fo, firmly on the left of the political spectrum, this meant both a denial of nihilism and a commitment to theatre which had a critical role to play in this project of renewal. Whilst for Lecoq this was a less publicly articulated practice than it was for Fo, it remained quietly central to his teaching for nearly fifty years. Lecoq's political radicalism is expressed not in one single element of his teaching, but in various linked strands of commitment which emerged and became more clearly defined in the school's practice as each decade passed. We might summarise these as follows:

- The school as *international* laboratory: a crucible where different cultures could play together to establish their differences and their commonalities in a shared making of theatre.
- An exploration, a commitment and a refinement of collaboration and ensemble through autocours and other strategies.
- An extraordinary and detailed sensitivity to the particular qualities and idiosyncrasies of each student: a challenging but never indulgent form of attention.
- A willingness to move critically, but reflectively, to acknowledge the temper of the times: 'students are often contradictory. We must hear what they say without listening too much' (Lecoq 2000: 23).
- A commitment toward theatre training as imaginative but structured playground of possibilities: more Bauhaus than boot camp.

Lecoq, Gaulier and Pagneux have always taken considerable pleasure in the mix of nationalities and cultures represented on their courses. At one level this multiplicity provides rich material to be worked on and around – with humour, through sonic and vocal inflection, and through gesture, action and movement. All three navigate and explore complexities and tensions between the distinctive and singular features brought by students to the class, and their 'universal' and species-specific qualities. Gaulier particularly invokes national stereotypes as provocation, which serves both to unsettle and 'unbalance' actors, whilst at the same time providing reassurance that their idiosyncrasies are rooted in characteristics beyond themselves.

For all three figures this radicalism is both disposition and mind-set, but more significantly, it is articulated through the warp and weft of their teaching and in the context of particular courses: melodrama, clown, bouffon and tragedy, for example.

In Gaulier's teaching this emerges particularly through the transgressive potential of bouffons and the clown. For Gaulier and Lecoq the clown, far from being merely an irritatingly twee 'personage' with a red nose, has a dissenting quality for overturning or denouncing order and the comfort of stability. In reaching the conclusion (quite early in the life of his school) that models of circus clowning had limited potential for theatre, Lecoq – and later – Gaulier align themselves with Beckett in finding the late twentieth-century clown the perfect vehicle for the hopelessly hopeful, but perpetually dissident survivor. Samuel Beckett's signature in *Worstward Ho*, '*Ever tried. Ever failed. No matter. Try again. Fail again. Fail better*' (Beckett 1983: 7–8) could be the clearest injunction for the Lecoq–Gaulier student of clowning.

Arguably, however, it is the subversive qualities of bouffons which most resonate with Gaulier's anarchist spirit; a sense that to challenge and often to offend, whilst sustaining pleasure, lightness and laughter, is at the heart of his project. Although Gaulier's teaching of bouffons has its roots in Lecoq's curriculum it is clear that over a period of twenty years he has pushed this practice considerably further than his old mentor, and in his writing on bouffons, the locus of Gaulier's political passion and anger – often disguised through humour – reveals itself:

> The bouffon is he or she (sick, handicapped, mad, gay, a prostitute, a witch etc) whom the 'pure of heart' have shown the way to the ghettos. These same 'pure of heart' at times made them parade through the village streets so that their ugliness and deformity could chase away the plague or cholera. Gargoyles were given the same job: to repel successive attacks that the devil planned against the churches. The bouffon parodies those

bastards who have always pointed out the way to the concentration camps, and will always do so.

(Gaulier 2008a: 9)

Although too young to experience the war, Gaulier grew up in its immediate aftermath, and from this text above it is clear that his performative framing of the bouffon is far more than 'bleeding heart' compassion for the dispossessed, but lies rooted and contextualised in the holocaust and, indeed, in any articulation of Fascism. As was indicated at the beginning of this account, Gaulier's almost obsessive preoccupation with lightness is often given meaning and potency by contrasting this elusive quality with the *weight* and *darkness* of stamping – Fascist – boots.

Pagneux was born six years after Lecoq, and one can only speculate what imprint being a child in Hitler's Weimar Republic of the 1930s has left on her. Annabel Arden tells of Pagneux's work as a young dancer in post-war France, working with her husband for an international youth theatre organisation in Le Maison des Jeunes. Like Lecoq, in the Association Travail et Culture she was committed to opening up artistic activities for young working-class people. Arden believes that Pagneux 'lives her politics on a micro level . . . the group is the work, the group is the heartbeat' (Arden 2008), and here she is referring to the deep political dynamics of ensemble, of collaboration and of shared process. In her regular classes the absence of one or more members without advance warning would incur profound displeasure from Pagneux – 'we *felt* your absence. We missed you' (Pagneux cited by Arden 2008) – not for reasons of control or discipline, but because of the disturbance such an absence would have for the subtle, complex chemistry and process of the group. Although all three figures have a finely tuned eye and ear for what each student is offering – or refusing – Pagneux particularly is searching for what Arden calls 'something more delicate, hidden, the absolutely unusual in people . . . often discovering through human fragility qualities which the actor did not know he had . . . which have been buried' (Ibid.). However, Pagneux's immensely detailed attention to the individual bodies of her students and her quest for *disponibilité* is neither for therapeutic reasons, nor to make her students feel happier. It is in the service of a psychophysical sensitising and attuning of performing bodies for collaboration in the making and performing of theatre. Actor and collaborator with Peter Brook, Yoshi Oida, puts it like this:

> What is interesting is the exchange. The 'acting' doesn't reside in the hands of each actor; it exists in the air between the two hands. . . . As a result each time you 'exchange', something inside you changes in reaction. From moment to moment you alter and respond.
>
> (Oida 1997: 76)

This essay has attempted to map out a field of training possibilities which have characterised the theatre making and teaching practices of Jacques Lecoq, Monika Pagneux and Philippe Gaulier over a period of nearly sixty years. The significance of these pedagogies has marked the body of world theatre through the work of thousands of performers, theatre makers and other artists who have had the distinction of being 'formed' by one or more these three teachers. Together and singly, Lecoq, Pagneux and Gaulier have proposed an alternative model of 'training' from the paradigm of 'Method', 'System' and their attendant preoccupations with psychology and motivation: a paradigm which remains dominant – but not uncontested –

throughout the West. It is training, in part, to 'untrain', and one that celebrates the creative tension, or paradox, of exquisite attention to the individual with the belief that theatre is, first and last, a practice of collaboration, of comradeship and of ensemble.

> Perhaps the false is the dress rehearsal for the true. No doubt! The one is less tiresome than the other. Most certainly.
>
> (Gaulier 2008b: 5)

Notes

1   LEM continues to be taught at the Paris school, but is separate from the two year course. Available to students within the school but also to others outside, LEM is preoccupied with experimental scenography and its relationship to the performer's body. For fuller accounts of LEM see Lecoq (2000: 155–57) and Murray (2003: 86–91).
2   I must thank Annabel Arden, who has given me considerable help and advice in writing this essay, particularly around the work of Monika Pagneux. This account draws significantly on an unpublished essay on Lecoq, Gaulier and Pagneux by Annabel in 2008, and a telephone interview I conducted with her in May 2009.
3   Complicite (as Théâtre de Complicité) was founded in 1983 by Simon McBurney, Annabel Arden and Marcello Magni. McBurney and Magni had just spent two years together at the Lecoq school, while the former had also been a student at Cambridge University with Arden.
4   A more detailed account of the curriculum at Lecoq's school may be found in Lecoq (2000) and Murray (2003).
5   In 1988 Philippe Gaulier had a public exhibition of photographs entitled 'Gargoyles and Bouffons'.
6   For a fuller explanation of what Lecoq meant by *disponibilité* and *complicité* see Murray (2003: 65–70) and Murray and Keefe (2007: 146–47).
7   I must thank Barry Laing for his advice and insights around the teaching of Philippe Gaulier and Monika Pagneux, and particularly for introducing me to Italo Calvino on 'lightness'. In this essay Barry's words are quoted from his unpublished PhD thesis (2002), but interested readers should also see his writing in an essay entitled 'A Horse Throwing its Rider' in D. Fenton, L. Mercer and J. Robson (forthcoming 2009) *Live Research: Narratives of Practice-Led Research in Performance*, Brisbane, Australia: Postpressed.
8   'Pre-linguistic' and 'pre-cultural' are of course highly contestable claims with which I cannot deal in this essay. However, in *Jacques Lecoq* (2003) I argue that Lecoq was under no illusion that such an essentialist 'pre-cultural' state was possible to achieve, rather, that the neutral mask was a heuristic tool of discovery for students and that total 'neutrality' was of course a myth, 'a temptation'.
9   See Lecoq (2000: 36–45), Murray (2003: 72–78) and Eldredge and Huston (1995: 121–28) for a detailed account of neutral mask teaching.
*   This exercise, and the seven which follow, are presented in a different font. They represent 'snapshots' of teaching practice from each of the three subjects in this essay. They offer associations, rather than illustrate, the text.

Bibliography

Arden, Annabel (2008) Unpublished essay and interview with author.
Beckett, Samuel (1983) *Worstward Ho*, London: Calder.
Bradby, David (2002a) Unpublished interview with author, London, 23 May.
Bradby, David and Delgado, Maria (2002b) *The Paris Jigsaw: Internationalism and the City's Stages*, Manchester: Manchester University Press.
Calvino, Italo (1988) *Six Memos for the Next Millennium*, Cambridge, MA: Harvard University Press.

Chamberlain, Franc and Yarrow, Ralph (eds) (2002) *Jacques Lecoq and the British Theatre*, London: Routledge.

Eldredge, Sears A. and Huston, Hollis W. (1995 [1978]) 'Actor Training in the Neutral Mask', in Philip B. Zarrilli (ed.) *Acting (Re)Considered*, London: Routledge.

Felner, Myra (1985) *Apostles of Silence: The Modern French Mimes*, Cranberry and London: Associated University Presses

Frost, Anthony and Yarrow, Ralph (2007) *Improvisation in Drama*, Basingstoke: Palgrave Macmillan.

Gaulier, Philippe (2007) *The Tormentor*, Paris: Éditions Filmiko.

—— (2008a) *Bouffon Plays*, Paris: Éditions Filmiko.

—— (2008b) *Lettre ou pas lettre*, Paris: Éditions Filmiko.

—— (2008c) *Left and Right*, Paris: Éditions Filmiko.

Laing, Barry (2002) 'Rapture: Excursions in Little Tyrannies and Bigger Lies', unpublished PhD thesis, Melbourne, Australia: Victoria University.

Lecoq, Jacques (1987) *Le Théâtre du Geste*, Paris: Bordas (unpublished translation by Gill Kester 2002).

—— (2000), *The Moving Body*, London: Methuen.

—— (2006), *Theatre of Movement and Gesture*, ed. David Bradby, London: Routledge.

Murray, Simon (2003) *Jacques Lecoq*, London: Routledge.

Murray, Simon and Keefe, John, (2007), *Physical Theatres: A Critical Introduction*, London: Routledge.

Oida, Yoshi (1997) *The Invisible Actor*, London: Methuen.

Raskin, Richard (2004) 'Italo Calvino and Inevitability in Storytelling', *Danish Journal of Film Studies*, POV no.18, December: 103–8.

Read, Herbert (1944) *Education through Art*, London: Faber and Faber.

Sutton-Smith, Brian (1997) *The Ambiguity of Play*, Cambridge, MA and London: Harvard University Press.

Wigman, Mary (1966) *The Language of Dance*, trans. Walter Sorrell, London: MacDonald and Evans.

Wright, John (1990) 'Philippe Gaulier: Genius or Egotist', *Total Theatre*, Winter, London: Mime Action Group, pp. 8–9.

Websites

Éditions Filmiko: www.filmichiko.com

Gaulier, Philippe: www.ecolephilippegaulier.com

DVD

Roy, Jean-Noël and Carasso, Jean-Gabriel (2006) *Les Deux Voyages de Jacques Lecoq*, Paris: On Line Productions/CNDP.

Chapter 14

Ian Watson

TRAINING WITH EUGENIO BARBA: ACTING PRINCIPLES, THE PRE-EXPRESSIVE AND 'PERSONAL TEMPERATURE'

CONTEXT

EUGENIO BARBA, THE DIRECTOR of the Odin Teatret, is one of those rare theatre people who combines the creativity of an artist with the more reflective skills of a researcher, theorist, and teacher. Since 1964, when he founded the Odin, he has created over sixty original works, ranging from intimate theatre pieces to large-scale outdoor spectacles. He has established one of Western Europe's only government-funded theatre laboratories, the Nordisk Teaterlaboratorium (NTL), which, apart from researching performance, incorporates a publishing house, a film and video archive, and production facility. He also heads the International School of Theatre Anthropology (ISTA), which he founded in 1979 to investigate the connections between traditional Eastern and contemporary Western performance. In addition to his practical successes, Barba has produced many articles as well as books which together encompass important writings on actor training, dramaturgy, performance, and theatre sociology. Besides this published material, Barba has also lectured and taught on both the practical and theoretical aspects of his work in Europe, North, and Latin America, as well as in Asia. He is an advisory or consultant editor to journals such as TDR: The Drama Review and New Theatre Quarterly. Barba's combination of insightful theatre scholarship and artistic achievement has garnered him numerous international awards. These include honorary doctorates (from the universities of Aarhus, Ayacucho, Bologna, Havana, Warsaw and the Estonian Academy of Music and Theatre), the 'Reconnaissance de merité scientifique' from the University of Montreal, an award from the Danish Royal Academy of Science and Letters, the Pirandello International Prize, and the Sonning Prize from the University of Copenhagen.

Barba's personal history in many ways mirrors the cultural pluralism of his professional development. He is an Italian who, as a young man, settled in Norway. He is also a former member of the Norwegian Merchant Marine whose journeys took him to various parts of Asia. He studied theatre for the first time in Poland in the early

1960s with Jerzy Grotowski, following which he founded the Odin Teatret, in Olso, Norway, only to move his theatre to Holstebro, Denmark within two years. One of the original models for his company and its work methods was the Kathakali school in Cheruthuruthy, India that he had visited while still living in Poland. The Odin has consisted of actors from many different countries over the years, most of whom do not share a common native language, leading to a creole of sorts both in the rehearsal room and in its productions; while the company is rarely at home, since it and Barba tour extensively, especially in Europe and Latin America. Barba also spends an appreciable amount of time in Bali, Japan, India, and Brazil working with the artists who attend the various ISTA gatherings. It is hardly surprising that he has characterised his sense of place as corporeal rather than one contained within national boundaries, going so far as to say, 'My body is my country' (1988a: 293). But, even though his life challenges the very idea of national identity, Barba views his professional heritage in familial terms, seeing himself as a descendant of Stanislavksy, the 'father' of modern Western theatre (1988a: 292).

Barba's contention aside, his theatrical lineage is much closer to Meyerhold than it is to Stanislavsky. Granted, Stanislavsky conducted the major study of the actor's art in the early years of the century, but Barba has rejected the very basis of Stanislavsky's system (psychological realism), embracing instead a theatre that explores a language of its own rather than one that simulates daily life on stage. He has developed a theatre in which the *mise en scène* takes precedence over interpreting the author's vision, in which causal connections between scenes have been rejected in favor of an episodic montage, and in which the actor/audience relationship and the performance space are adjusted for each production. All of these are ideas more often associated with Meyerhold than Stanislavsky.

Despite his European heritage and what he has termed his 'period of [theatrical] apprenticeship' (1986: 239) with Grotowski, Barba has always been fascinated by the East. This fascination began with an interest in the Asian religions in his youth and gradually moved to its theatre after his exposure to Kathakali. Barba maintains that the root of this fascination lies in understanding presence. Why is it that if you are watching two actors on stage, even if you are unfamiliar with their theatrical form and cannot understand what they are saying, you are unable to take your eyes off one of them while the other is of no interest at all? (1985a: 12). His search for an answer to this question lies at the root of most of his performance research, even today. In keeping with his denial of borders, his research encompasses not only the icons of contemporary European theatre such as Stanislavsky, Meyerhold, Eisenstein, Decroux and his mentor Grotowski but also Asian performers and theoretical treatises such as Kathakali, Noh, the onnogata, Barong, Rukmani Devi, Mei Lanfang, Zeami, and the *Natyashastra* (1988b: 126; 1995: 42). Barba's professional identity is that of the theatrical polyglot.

The breadth of Barba's professional identity is nowhere more obvious than in his approach to training. The latter is central to Barba's vision of the theatre. It is the foundation of his entire aesthetic: training provides the basis for his unique dramaturgical and rehearsal processes; it is the origin of his major production styles – the studio/theatre performance and the open-air street spectacle; and the research orientation of the Odin's current training continues to inform Barbra's creation of new theatre pieces.

Training has been a major factor in Barba's approach to theatre since the Odin was formed. The group's initial working sessions were devoted entirely to it and the actors have continued to train ever since. This training usually consists of separate physical and vocal sessions because Barba believes it is necessary to explore physical and vocal rhythms independently to ensure that neither one dominates the other.

Barba's initial ideas on training were influenced by several factors. The single most important of these was his role as Grotowski's assistant immediately prior to forming the Odin. During Barba's years in Poland, Grotowski initiated his now famous 'poor theatre' performer training and research programme, which introduced Barba to a theatre that touched a personal chord. His formative education was in a military school in Naples where discipline and authority were all important. Barba rebelled against this approach to education at the time, but he saw it reflected in Grotowski's research with his actors and in the Kathakali academy he visited in India. Barba was well aware of his lack of formal theatre training when he formed his fledgling company in Norway; he was equally cognizant of his young actors' limitations. Unlike Grotowski's performers, who were all trained professionals, his actors were high school students who had been rejected by the national theatre school in Oslo. They needed training. He lacked the background to provide it. But, he had seen what authority and discipline could achieve. So, with the models of Poland and India, filtered through his experience in Naples, he established an intensive training regimen when he formed his new company. This regimen focused on the acquisition of skills and later evolved into using training as a research tool.

Unfortunately, Barba and his actors not only lacked basic theatre skills, they also wanted for the funds to pay teachers. This latter disadvantage, like so many in Barba's history, proved to be instrumental in establishing his future course. Due to the fact that he could not afford teachers, the actors taught themselves. Members of the company with skills, no matter how rudimentary, taught them to the others. Thus, gradually, the original members of the group developed a body of skills that formed the basis of their subsequent training and which they were able to teach new actors as they joined the company.

Yet the group's training was not as hermetic as this description may imply, since several external factors have contributed to its development over the years. A series of workshops Barba organised when the group first moved to Holstebro exposed the Odin actors to Western performers and directors like Grotowski, Ryszard Cieslak, Etienne Decroux, Jean-Louis Barrault, and Dario Fo, as well as Oriental masters that included the Noh actors Hisao and Hideo Kanze, the Kyogen performer Mannojo Namura, and the Odissi dancer Sanjukta Panigrahi. In addition to these contacts, the actors attended workshops conducted by Asian performers of Kathakali, Noh, and Topeng at the Third Theatre gatherings in Belgrade (1976) and Bergamo (1977); and at these same gatherings other groups similar to the Odin demonstrated and discussed their approaches to training. ISTA expanded the pool of Eastern master teachers the company came in contact with to include the Japanese Nihon Buyo performer Katsuko Azuma, and various Balinese performer/teachers, while at least one member of the company has studied Butoh (Watson and colleagues, 2000: 78), and several Brazilian Candomblé (in fact, company member Augusto Omolú is a Brazilian modern dancer with deep roots in traditional Candomblé). However, except for a few obvious examples, such as the influence of Grotowski, it is difficult to establish a direct connection between these experiences and developments in Barba's training methods. But, given the correlation between the Odin's present training and Oriental theatre, it is clear that at least this early exposure to Eastern masters has influenced the evolution of Barba's and his group's training considerably.

The most important feature of this evolution has been the gradual shift in emphasis from skill-oriented training to the use of training as a form of performance research. In the Odin's early years in Holstebro there was a large turnover of new actors joining and leaving the group. But, as the company stabilised and ceased to take in new actors, the need to teach and learn basic skills became less of a necessity. In the best tradition of the autodidact, the actors, under Barba's guidance, turned their attention to developing their own training programmes. The performers no longer concerned themselves with accumulating skills, but rather with testing and exploring their potentials and limitations. Training for Barba became something created and shaped by each of the actors individually.

TRAINING [1]

Training, according to Barba, is:

> . . . a process of self-definition, a process of self-discipline which mani-
> fests itself indissolubly through physical reactions. It is not the exercise in
> itself that counts – for example, bending or somersaulting – but the
> individual's justification for his own work, a justification which although
> perhaps banal or difficult to explain through words, is physiologically
> perceptible, evident to the observer.
>
> (1986: 56)

Since the exercises are less important than how the actor chooses to use them in training for Barba, he has not developed a prescriptive body of exercises or systematic hierarchy of information that a neophyte actor has to master in order to perform. For this reason, the only way to understand his training methods is to consider how they have developed over the past thirty-plus years at the Odin Teatret. It is with the Odin actors that he has formulated his understanding of training, it is with them that he has realised a rehearsal methodology that is rooted in his approach to training, and it is with them that he has created and directed all of his major theatre pieces.

When Barba began working with his Odin actors in the early 1960s, his training was collective. The actors trained together and everyone learned the same basic acrobatics, gymnastics, pantomime skills, and vocal techniques. Even during this early collective training phase, however, Barba had already established what was to become the hallmark of his training methodology: he rarely taught anything in the conventional sense of the word; the actors taught what they knew to each other while he remained witness and guide to their endeavours. [2]

It was during this period that Barba first came to realise the importance of individual rhythm in the training process. This realisation led to a gradual change of focus in the exercises, from an emphasis on skill to an emphasis on the individual actor's pace and rhythm (Barba 1979: 65). At the same time as this shift was taking place in Barba's thinking, his actors began to explore material that Barba eventually shaped into what he terms composition exercises.

Composition, which owes somewhat of a debt to Barba's mentor Grotowski, does not consist of specific exercises like body rolls or head stands. In fact, it can involve virtually any series of movements because the focus is on the physical ideograms created by the composition of body elements during the movements, instead of on the movements themselves. These ideograms can have their source at a

Figure 14.1 Barba: Training at the Odin Teatret in the early 1970s.
Source: Odin Teatret.

purely technical level, as in dividing the body so that one half moves rapidly while the other half moves slowly in order to express an inner physiological tension, or they can involve physical expression of a mental association, such as using the image of a flower's growth from germination to maturity and death to influence how one moves through space. As one of Barba's Odin actors, Torgeir Wethal, describes it:

> You allowed an inner action sequence to live within these exercises. You were in a completely personal situation in a particular place at the same time as you were doing the exercise, precisely and concretely. Your inner movie has a great influence on the details of an exercise, the rhythm, the tempo.

> (Christoffersen 1993: 49)

Figure 14.2 Barba: An Odin Teatret training session.

Source: Photo, Christoph Falke, courtesy of Odin Teatret.

In a composition exercise the actor concentrates on the balance of muscular tensions and/or psycho-physical association, rather than on executing a task correctly. These concerns emphasise process over product, that is, doing the exercise rather than learning a specific skill.

The shift towards process in Barba's thinking about training was accompanied by an increased use of improvisation. Barba has employed improvisation to develop performances during rehearsals since his first production *Ornitofilene* in 1965. But, until his production of *Min Fars Hus* in 1972, almost ten years after the company was formed, these improvisations were based on texts written prior to rehearsal. *Min Fars Hus* was the first production developed entirely, from its inception through to the *mise en scène*, by Barba and his actors during rehearsals. This development included the creation of a fabricated language as well as explorations of biographical and literary material related to Dostoyevsky, whose life and works were the inspiration for the piece. Drawing upon their vocal training, Barba and his company developed a language loosely based on the phonetic quality of Russian for the production. In conjunction with these linguistic explorations, the company created a physical score from improvisations based on the actors' reactions to and associations with events in Dostoyevsky's life.

Influenced by the emphasis on composition in the group's training at the time, the *mise en scène* was the combination of a dynamic physicality and an operatic-like vocal score. This score consisted of incantations, singing and dialogue, all in a language that required the audience to focus on its musicality rather than its semantic content. The work, rooted in parallels between the performers' lives and Dostoyevsky's experiences, was deeply personal, and, in keeping with the Odin's earlier productions, far removed from realism.

The increased emphasis on improvisation in Min Fars Hus placed the creative responsibility entirely upon the performers and the director since they no longer had a single, cohesive literary source to guide their rehearsals. This change in the use of improvisation fed back into the training and, combined with the focus on process in composition and the emphasis on individuality in rhythm, led to the creation of a new type of training altogether.

In the latter stages of rehearsals for Min Fars Hus one of the actresses, Iben Nagel Rasmussen, began to develop her own training. This training consisted of an improvised series of physical and vocal exercises that she felt best challenged her own abilities and weaknesses. Despite the fact that the collective training continued during this period, her experiments did not go unnoticed, and there was a great deal of discussion between her, Barba, and her fellow actors. Barba encouraged others to develop their own training, and eventually collective training was abandoned altogether. Each actor now explored what she felt was important for her, but within the supportive environment of a single room where others were engaged in similar research.

Barba, while following these changes in the Odin's training, began a systematic study of Oriental theatre with the express aims of discovering the source of the presence in the traditional Asian forms, and exploring its possible relevance for Western actors (1986: 115). From these comparative studies he concluded that the two fundamental elements of Oriental forms that contribute to the actor's commanding stage presence are the use of learned body techniques designed to break the performer's automatic daily responses, and the codification of principles which dictate the use of energy during performance.

In daily life much of our physical action is automatic, due to constant repetition. Our body 'knows' how to accomplish relatively complex tasks, like walking and climbing stairs, without having to think through the various muscular adjustments involved because we have done them so often. In Eastern traditional forms such as Kathakali and Noh, on the other hand, the body is intentionally distorted, particularly through the positioning of the feet and legs. In Kathakali the performers stand on the outer edges of their feet with their legs in an open position, and in Noh the actors lock their hips and bend their knees, altering the line of the spine and the distribution of weight. These 'distortions' constitute what Barba refers to as extra-daily technique, that is, learned technique which establishes a pattern of performance behaviour which is different from daily behaviour. According to Barba, this extra-daily technique is a major source of actor presence during performance, since it establishes a pre-expressive mode in which the actor's energies are engaged prior to personal expression (1986: 119–20).

Personal expression in traditional Eastern performance is rigidly codified and can vary greatly from one form to another. Barba's studies revealed, however, that, despite these differences, the codes incorporate similar principles that dictate the body's use of energy. Principles such as the use of opposing body tensions to create a dynamic on stage, a balance between energy expended through space (i.e. motion) and energy expended through time (i.e. dynamic inertia), and the use of distorted equilibrium to alter muscular tensions during performance. An example of distorted equilibrium may help clarify Barba's point. In Noh, Odissi dance, and Balinese dance drama the performers use precarious balance to engage their performance energies. The locked hips, bent knees, and the way the actor walks by sliding his feet across the stage without lifting them in Noh change the normal position of the spine, alter the center of balance, and engage the trunk as a single unit. All of which creates opposing

Figure 14.3 I Wayan Bawa leading a training session of Balinese classical dance principles for participants at XIII ISTA, Seville, Spain, 2004.

Source: Photo, Fiora Bemporad, courtesy of Odin Teatret.

tensions in the upper and lower parts of the body that require the performer to find a new point of equilibrium. In Odissi dance the 'tribangi,' which is a major component of the form, requires the dancer to manipulate her body as if the letter 'S' were passing through the hips, trunk, and neck. This position, which distorts the line of the spinal column, affects the performer's balance and thereby alters the normal relationship between body weight, center of gravity, and the feet. Similarly, in many Balinese forms of dance drama the performer pushes down on the soles of the feet while at the same time lifting the toes, thus reducing contact with the ground. To compensate, the dancer widens his gait and bends his knees, which alters the center of gravity and the normal position of the spine. These adjustments increase the level of muscular activity which, as in similar distortions in Odissi dance and Noh, produce a dynamic, rather than static, physical state.

Through his knowledge of the few similarly codified Western forms, such as mime and ballet, Barba realised that many of the principles in Eastern performance are shared by their Western counterparts. The principle of opposing body tensions, for example, is a major component of mime, and the alteration of normal equilibrium is a fundamental element of ballet. He further, and more importantly for the evolution of his own idea on training, realised that his Odin actors were employing similar principles (1995: 6).

Barba began to publish the results of his research, which, combined with the influence his discoveries had on his work and on his discussions with his actors, led to a further development in his individualised training method. There was a gradual shift in emphasis from composition, with its focus on physical expression, to an exploration of the principles underlying performative action, that is, to the source of the pre-expressive. Training for Barba today is, as one of his Odin actresses described it, 'improvisation structured by the application of principles' (Carreri 1985). A simple example, quoted by another company member, clarifies what she meant:

> To stand on one's head involves mastering particular technical skills such as placement of the hands, legs, and head, and the adjustment of body weight and balance. It also involves the principle of shifting the body's weight quickly so that one is off-balance, finding a point of equilibrium which is held for a period, and returning to the normal body position. Standing on one's head is a skill that has to be learned, the principle underlying it, meanwhile, can be applied to many situations including walking, sitting, and working with a requisite [hand prop].
>
> (Wethal 1985)

Barba's system of training focuses on exploring this and similar principles, rather than mastering skills. Consider a typical training session I observed at the Odin in the mid 1980s:

> There are five actors in the room, three women and two men, all working separately. Following a brief warm up, consisting of simple stretch exercises, the actors begin to work on their individual activities. Actress 1 is sitting in a deck chair. She moves her right arm across her body, then her left arm. She moves her head from right to left, then up and down. All actions are slow, precise, and punctuated with a brief pause. She sits up in the deck chair, she sits back, she sits up again, then repeats this up and down action several more times. During these actions her trunk appears to move as one unit, with no curve in the spine or separation between chest and waist.
>
> Meanwhile, Actor 1 moves to the back of the room and begins to do a tap dance-type shuffle. He raises his arms in the classical ballet position and spins around several times. He lowers his arms and begins what appears to be a simple dance. The top half of his body does not seem to be engaged in the dance. He stops suddenly and does several shoulder stands, returning to the upright position each time. He lunges into the shoulder stands, but has great control and executes them precisely. He returns once more to a simple dance and moves around the room, occasionally breaking into the tap dance shuffle he began with.

There are no clearly identifiable skills being learned, the actors are not doing scenes from a play, nor do they seem to be exploring ways of creating a character, and, despite the fact that people are together in a room, each is concerned with her own work. The focus is elsewhere, as the actress working with the deck chair told me following the session. She explained that she had been working with several principles that day, including moving with one part of the body at a time, leading all movement with the eyes, and segmenting various sections of the body. What appeared to be haphazard movements were, in fact, actions strictly monitored by adherence to consciously chosen principles.

TRAINING AND PERFORMANCE

The fact that many of Barba's Odin actors continue to train today, even though most of them have worked with him for over twenty years, suggests a great deal about the connections between training and performance in Barba's understanding of theatre.

One aspect of training for Barba is parallel to physical exercise. Just as aerobics are an ongoing process which maintains one's fitness without continually having to learn new skills, training for Barba is a daily workout that exercises the actor's means of expression in preparation for performance.

But this is a long way short of the entire story because the daily regimen of training has ramifications beyond merely tuning one's physical instrument. Even though Barba rejects training as a means of learning techniques, it continues to be an indirect way of developing new skills. Similarly, it plays an important part in maintaining the actors' physical and mental disciplines, as well as providing a means of honing the skills they have already learned. It also prepares the Odin actors for Barba's somewhat unusual way of creating productions, and is a source of personal development as well as of social cohesion within the group.

The secondary role of skill acquisition in today's training at the Odin stems from Barba's emphasis on acting principles. The performers may no longer be concerned with learning new gymnastic exercises or perfecting the high-pitch singing technique of Beijing opera, but they are continually exploring ways of mastering the principles of acting. These explorations include devising solutions for physical and vocal problems (how to control a particular fall, for example, or how best to use one's voice in street performances) while remaining faithful to the principles they are working with. This problem solving often expands the actors' skills because their solutions frequently demand an ever-increasing repertoire of physical and vocal techniques, even if this expansion is not the primary focus of their research.

Discipline has always been an important factor in training for Barba. In the Odin's and Barba's formative years, this discipline was imposed by Barba himself. But, as individual training became more important, the onus of discipline shifted to the actors, and they continue to be responsible for the schedule and content of daily training. The most obvious aim of this daily discipline, as touched on earlier, is to maintain the actors' performance conditioning. The Odin actors continually exercise their bodies and voices in order to ready their physical and vocal instruments for performance. Barba maintains that this preparation is not only directed toward expression, because continual training also helps the actor tap the pre-expressive. This pre-expressive mode is based on mastery of the very principles that the actors use in their training. It is based on the use of alteration from one's normal daily balance and centre of gravity, for instance, or on control of opposing tensions in the body. It can also be based on what might best be described as the deconstruction and reconstruction of the body in traditional Eastern performance training; that is, using training to break the normal patterns of behaviour in order to discover a cohesive physical and vocal grammar of performance that engages the body differently from our daily activities and speech (Barba 1986: 115–22).

Training not only develops pre-expressive and expressive skills but also prepares the actors for the rehearsal process. New productions at the Odin usually begin with little more than a theme and/or fragments of texts that are explored in rehearsals. These explorations invariably have their roots in improvisations by individual actors which are then lengthened, shortened, altered, and/or combined in different ways by Barba to develop a single montage of different scenes that constitute the final piece.[3]

The use of improvisation in creating new works is connected to its use in training for Barba. In training, improvisation is an integral part of the daily work. In dramaturgy, on the other hand, even though the final production montage is set and repeated in each performance, improvisation provides the raw material for the production. The actors rarely develop this material during training, but their studio research builds a lexicon and grammar of improvisation which they draw from during rehearsals to create new pieces. As Carreri put it, 'I keep training in order to be ready to respond, to be able to meet the demands of the new performance' (1985).

Barba regards training as a form of mental conditioning as much as a way of exercising and investigating the means of expression (1985b: 15; 1985c). The ongoing process of developing one's own training (of self-discipline, research, and concrete physical and vocal tasks) manifests an attitude towards what is happening. The actors are thus exploring their physical and vocal potentials not only through exercise but also through a process of mental discipline. Most days at the Odin there is a prescribed time when the actors enter the training studio and work for an hour or more. During this time, their minds as well as their bodies are directly concerned with exploring the principles they are working on and indirectly with developing their improvisational skills. Their minds are thus daily focused on the work at hand, and on its potential implications for the next production. Barba maintains that this mental focus is as much part of the training process as are the physical and vocal exercises because, just as these exercises build a physical routine, the daily mental engagement builds an intellectual discipline. The body and the mind are equally engaged.

Apart from the mental and physical components of Barba's approach to training, there are important personal ramifications involved. One of Barba's aims in making each actor at the Odin responsible for their own training is to make them autonomous, to allow them to create their own training without relying on specific techniques or particular teachers. Through this process, the actor is attempting to discover what Barba refers to as their own 'personal temperature', that is, their own rhythm, their boundaries, their abilities, and what is unique about each of them as a performer (Barba 1988a: 298). Thus, when they begin work on a new production, they do not merely apply a set of learned techniques to interpret a text or the director's vision, as say a Stanislavsky actor might, but rather they use improvisation to explore the relationship between themes suggested by Barba and their own 'personal temperature'.

This 'personal temperature' is also an important factor in the *mise en scène* for Barba because of the dichotomous tension between the role and the actor during performance. He maintains that performance is neither entirely the fictional world of the play, nor the actor's experience in portraying it. It is the dialectic between these two, what he calls the anatomical theatre: a theatre in which the relationship between the 'external surface of the actions and their internal parts' (1986: 112) is the central core of any production.

In Barba's theatre, an actor portrays not only the fictional score (i.e. the physical actions and vocal delivery decided upon in rehearsal and repeated in each performance), but also their meeting with it. Ryszard Cieslak, Grotowski's leading actor, in talking about this process in an interview with Richard Schechner, used the metaphor of a candle contained inside a glass to explain the difference between the score and his meeting with it during performances of *Akropolis*:

> The score is like the glass inside which a candle is burning. The glass is solid, it is there, you can depend on it. It contains and guides the flame.

But it is not the flame. The flame is my inner process each night. The flame is what illuminates the score, what the spectators see through the score.

(Schechner 1977: 19)

Cieslak goes on to describe how the score remains the same, but that the flame varies from performance to performance.

Variations in the flame, in the meeting with the score, are based on several factors in Barba's approach to performance: the audience's reaction to the piece, the actor's psycho-emotional responses to events on stage as well as in the theatre, and the actor's personal associations with particular actions and/or situations in a work he has developed with his colleagues during rehearsal. The tensions between these variables (i.e. the flame) and the score provide the means of realising the anatomical theatre, since the score provides a structured resistance ('the external surface of the actions') against which the actor struggles in order to display his inner processes:

The performance is a tightly woven net, which we must break through in order to liberate, in an unforeseen moment, fragments of our past and our experiences.

Every evening the actors struggle with this net. Every evening they try to dissolve, to annul the rigid iron structure through which they reveal themselves and which makes them into actors and those who surround them into an audience.

The resistance that the performance opposes to testimony makes the play into an organism which changes form and turns the rehearsed gesture of the actor into a gesture which appears to have the force of an improvised reaction.

It is through the convergence of these opposite forces, that our personal experiences can reach others. . . .

(Barba 1986: 181)

This convergence has its beginnings in Barba's individuated training. It is in the studio, where each actor confronts their strengths and limitations daily, that each actor prepares himself/herself for their 'struggle with this net'.

The struggle is, nevertheless, a social act; the actor engages the dramaturgy during each performance for the spectator. But, this engagement must be affective, it must have 'the capacity to stimulate affective reactions' (Barba 1997: 130) in the audience. This effectiveness, like so much in Barba's theatre, lies in the training. It is the individual actor's ability to perform what Barba terms 'real actions' as opposed to simple gestures or movements that generates a change of perception in the spectator (ibid.: 128). Real actions for Barba are those that produce 'a change in the tensions of your whole body' (ibid.: 128) because they have their origins in the spine: 'it is not the elbow that moves the hand, not the shoulder that moves the arm, rather, each dynamic impulse is rooted in the torso' (ibid.: 128). These dynamic impulses are learned actions that have their origins in the principles that form the basis of each actor's training regimen.

Barba's emphasis on an individualised training that draws its inspiration from various cultures as well as different teachers has inevitably led to a diversity of skills and techniques among his Odin actors. Should another group of actors choose to embrace his training ideas, the results would no doubt reflect a similar diversity. But one must understand that skills take second place to intention in training for Barba. As William Farrimond, a researcher who followed the Odin in the early 1980s, noted about the company, 'It is only in the principles and not in the techniques . . . that one can trace an element common to the whole group' (1981: 92). Barba's training is concerned with how performance principles, the pre-expressive, and individual creativity come together in productions. His emphasis on the research and process orientation of training engenders a continual cycle of growth and renewal in which training, rehearsals, and performance are inextricably linked.

Notes

1   Due to the limitations of space, I will only discuss Barba's physical training. For further information on his vocal training techniques see Watson, 1995: 63–68.
2   Voice training was somewhat of an exception. Barba taught the basics of Grotowski's resonator voice training in the Odin's early days. Once the actors had grasped the rudiments, however, they developed their own vocal training based on this initial instruction.
3   For a more detailed description and discussion of Barba's rehearsal and dramaturgical methodologies see Watson, 1995: 73–103.

Bibliography

Barba, Eugenio (1979) *The Floating Islands*, Holstebro, Denmark: Odin Teatret Forlag.
—— (1985a) 'Interview with Gautam Dasgupta', *Performing Arts Journal*, 3 (2): 8–18.
—— (1985b) *The Dilated Body*, Rome: Zeami Libre.
—— (1985c) Interview with the author, Nordisk Teaterlaboratorium, Holstebro, September 5.
—— (1986) *Beyond the Floating Islands*, New York: Performing Arts Journal Publications.
—— (1988a) 'The Way of Refusal: The Theatre's Body in Life,' *New Theatre Quarterly*, 4 (16): 291–99.
—— (1988b) 'Eurasian Theatre', *The Drama Review*, 32 (3) (T119): 126–30.
—— (1995) *The Paper Canoe*, London and New York: Routledge.
—— (1997) 'An Amulet Made of Memory: The Significance of Exercises in the Actor's Dramaturgy', *The Drama Review*, 41 (4) (T156), 127–32.
Carreri, Roberta (1985) Interview with the author, Nordisk Teaterlaboratorium, Holstebro, Denmark, 26 August.
Christoffersen, E.E. (1993) *The Actor's Way*, London and New York: Routledge.
Farrimond, W. (1981) 'Actor Education: An Interdisciplinary Approach – An Analysis of the Training and Performance Principles Applied by Eugenio Barba and the Actors of the Odin Teatret in 1981', PhD dissertation, Copenhagen: University of Copenhagen.
Schechner, R. (1977) *Essays in Performance Theory: 1970–1976*, New York: Drama Book Specialists.
Watson, I. (1995) *Towards a Third Theatre: Eugenio Barba and the Odin Teatret*, London and New York: Routledge.
Watson, I. and colleagues (2002) *Negotiating Cultures: Eugenio Barba and the Intercultural Debate*, Manchester: Manchester University Press.
Wethal, T. (1985) Interview with the author, Nordisk Teaterlaboratorium, Holstebro, Denmark, 2 September.

Chapter 15

Helen E. Richardson

ARIANE MNOUCHKINE AND THE THÉÂTRE DU SOLEIL: THEATRICALISING HISTORY; THE THEATRE AS METAPHOR; THE ACTOR AS SIGNIFIER

> I consider that the theatre must be political, and historical, and sacred, and contemporary, and mythological. It's only the proportions that change from production to production.[1]

CONTEXT

ARIANE MNOUCHKINE HAS CONSISTENTLY created an epic universe on stage: fierce in its consideration of the unrelenting momentum of history and human passions, while intimate in its focus on the individual's struggle to survive and, when possible, to act their conscience. Her stage images are rarely matched in the theatre and evoke the power of such masters of the cinema as Eisenstein and Kurasawa. She has inspired a vast public, engendering one of the most popular avant-garde theatres of the last forty-five years. Throughout her career Mnouchkine has sought to regenerate the dynamic interchange, traditionally found in popular theatre forms, between performer and audience, while exploring socially relevant and compelling themes. A significant part of the company's effort has been toward developing a rapport between the actor and the public that produces a sense of community, so that everyone becomes part of an extended global theatre family, the Théâtre du Soleil.

Although the vision of the Théâtre du Soleil is that of Ariane Mnouchkine, the troupe's strength comes from the ensemble nature of the company, which was founded in 1964 as a workers' collective. Everyone in the troupe – whether their position is administrator, technical support, or performer – is paid the same. During its long history actors have participated collectively in helping build the props and set, as well as cooking the meals and maintaining the theatre. Depending on the production, they work at the canteen during intermission, serving the audience meals and

Figure 15.1 Mnouchkine at the Kabul, Afghanistan workshop 2005.
Source: Photo, Virginie le Cöent.

refreshments. Roles for the play are not distributed by Mnouchkine: instead, each
actor has the possibility of working on whatever role he or she is attracted to. Over a
period of time, it becomes clear to everyone which actor is most suitable for which
role. A 'star' system is rigorously avoided; however, certain actors, through their
efforts and talents, may consistently achieve principal roles. Actors often play several
characters in one production, and are expected to contribute to the creation of other
actors' roles as well. In the case of collective creations, the actors engage in the
generation of character and text. Mnouchkine believes in the 'pedagogy of the humble copy' (Féral 2001: 73), the traditional Eastern approach to training, where the
student copies the master. The actors are present at all rehearsals and, when they are
not on stage, they observe the work of the other actors intently in order to learn
from their efforts. As the audience enters the performance area at the Théâtre du
Soleil they can watch the actors preparing themselves, putting on last bits of costume
and observing their characters in the mirror, or communing with fellow actors and
familiar members of the audience, thus establishing a direct link between audience
and performers.

The overarching goal of the troupe has been to create a viable, socially engaged, popular theatre in the face of the almost insurmountable competition from film and television. Throughout its development, the company has, with the inspiration and guidance of Mnouchkine, investigated and incorporated into its work most known forms of popular theatre: from the mask work of the *commedia dell'arte* to puppetry, ancient Greek theatre, Shakespeare, and traditional Asian forms such as Beijing Opera, Japanese Kabuki and Bunraku, Indian Bharata Natytam and Kathakali, and Balinese Topeng. It has explored the texts of Aeschylus, Euripides, Shakespeare, and Molière, as well as collaborating with the writer Hélène Cixous.

Ariane Mnouchkine is as compelling as the theatre she creates with her ensemble of international theatre makers. She is easy to spot at a performance as she moves about with a sense of mission – sporting a thick mane of silver grey hair – attending to the business of running her theatre with what the French press characterises as a soft voice and hand of iron. Her strength of will, power of personality, idealism, pragmatism, and genius for the *mise-en-scène* have been an important source of the vitality animating the Théâtre du Soleil. Visitors to the Cartoucherie,[2] the home of the company, will notice that Mnouchkine seems to be everywhere at once. As well as directing and administering her company (some forty-plus members) Mnouchkine is very much engaged in a direct relationship with the audience. She can be seen selling tickets at the box office before a show. It is she who opens the door at performance time, welcoming the public and guiding them to their seats, taking special care that places can be found for everyone in an often sold-out house. At intermission she may serve refreshments at the canteen or greet visitors, many of whom have been coming to see the Théâtre du Soleil for many years. During a post-show talk Mnouchkine is prepared to challenge audience members to regard themselves, as she regards herself, as 'world citizens'. Speaking out on the fate of international refugees, the world's poor, and current political affairs, she will remind the audience of the importance of theatre as a place of communal social engagement, and speak to the accomplishments of the masters of theatre such as Artaud, Brecht, Copeau, Dullin, Jouvet, Meyerhold, and Jean Vilar, and the necessity to continue their legacy. As the audience exit, she remains available to converse with those visitors who linger, many of them from all parts of the globe.

Mnouchkine is very much at home in her self-appointed role as a world citizen, interested in exploring theatre from various regions and different eras as a forum for witnessing the human condition. Essential qualities underpinning her theatre ethics are: a global vision, a belief in the mission of theatre as embracing humanity in all its complexity and diversity; the idea that theatre can make a political difference; a commitment to the principle of collective creation; a powerful aesthetic sensibility that demands theatre be an artistic experience that is beautiful as well as meaningful; a desire to experiment and continually innovate; and a dedication to a rigour that expects the best from her theatre ensemble and her audience. Although Mnouchkine exudes a powerful presence in her theatre, her approach calls on the actor, designer, playwright, technician, and administrator to be an active co-creator in the work, helping her to construct a utopian community of collective responsibility and vision.

The work of Mnouchkine has gone through several incarnations during the life of the Théâtre du Soleil. From her first work as a director of theatre, the production of *Genghis Khan* by Henri Bauchau in 1961, to her signature piece *1789*, about the French Revolution, in 1970, to more recent endeavours such as *Le Caravansérai* (2003), about international refugees, and *Tambours sur la Digue* (1999), a parable about the displacement and destruction of human life caused by environmental abuse, Mnouchkine has used a variety of forms to realise her vision. She has, however, consistently embraced history as her framework, and most often the role of 'the people' within it as her focus. The collective creation 1789 tells the story of the French Revolution from the point of view of those who participated in it, from the peasant to the revolutionary leader Marat. Significantly, it is the voice of the collective, the people, which resonates throughout the piece, culminating in the account of the taking of the Bastille, the eighteenth-century prison, by those who were there: namely, the people of Paris.

Mnouchkine was born on the eve of the Second World War, 3 March 1939, in Paris, to the prominent film producer Alexandre Mnouchkine, a Jewish Russian émigré, and June Hannen, a British actress. Her family hid in the Bordeaux region of France during the war, but her grandparents decided to stay in Paris, were denounced, and perished in the concentration camps. This was to have a strong impact on Mnouchkine influencing her life-long consideration of the role of the individual and the community during historically challenging times, when moral imperatives can make the difference between death and survival.

Mnouchkine grew up on film sets where her father was engaged as a producer, and she was nourished by the rich cinematic period that followed the war in France. However, she chose theatre over the commercial pressures of the film world, preferring to have the freedom to follow her own vision. She was strongly influenced by the work of Brechtian directors such as the Italian Giorgi Strehler and the French Roger Planchon, as well as by Eastern theatre that she saw at the Théâtre des Nations in Paris, such as Kathakali and Chinese Opera. In 1959, a student of psychology at the Sorbonne, Mnouchkine founded ATEP (the Theatre Association for Students of Paris), with the blessings of Roger Planchon, as a counter to the more traditional established campus theatre organisation. Sartre was among the first invited to speak at the ATEP, and the group sponsored work by Genet. In 1962 Mnouchkine chose to take a year off and travelled through Asia, which was to make a profound impression on her, one that has resonated throughout her creative work.

Part of Mnouckine's journey has been to seek the sources that lead to the foundation of theatre. Like so many of her generation, including Brook, Grotowski, and Barba, she has been influenced by the impulses of Artaud, and the need to revitalise theatre by returning to its origins and by looking to the East for inspiration. For Mnouchkine, the theatre is first and foremost the telling of a story about people by the people through a form characterised by a total theatricality. And, as often found in traditional Asian theatre, where music, text, character, dance, audience, and place are integrated, the performance event is as much to be remembered as the historical events contained within the play. Space is of paramount importance to Mnouchkine, and she has been known to abandon a production because she could not envision the theatrical space for the piece. For her, 'Each show has its own set of laws' (Miller 2007: 103–4). Once she knows what form a production will take she can begin to enter into telling the story.

In order to understand the development of the actor at the Théâtre du Soleil, one must take into consideration the troupe's constantly evolving history of experimentation with form. Although a certain aesthetic marked by hyper-theatricality characterises the work of the troupe, each production has its own unique signature and process of preparation. Mnouchkine offers no single approach to training. Even though mask work is fundamental to the formation of the actor at the Théâtre du Soleil, few of the productions use actual masks in the performance, but the concept of the actor as 'masked' prevails. Whilst Mnouchkine has a fundamental vocabulary that she uses to inspire the actors, she does not practise a single methodology consciously.

Mnouchkine often relies on experts to train the actors in forms that she plans to integrate into the creation of new work, from Tibetan traditional dance, or the Bharata Natyam of India, to Korean drumming.

In 1964, Mnouchkine directed Gorki's *Le Petit Bourgeoisie*, the premier production of the Théâtre du Soleil, as the troupe members tried to confront their own bourgeois origins. Stanislavsky's *Creating a Role* in hand, Mnouchkine demanded that the actors find their own motivations. Some actors quit the rehearsal process, complaining that Mnouchkine did not know what she was doing, since she refused to tell them what to do. Her second production, an adaptation of the French nineteenth-century novel *Le Capitain Fracasse*, about an itinerant theatre troupe in the seventeenth-century, involved extensive improvisation by the actors and an exploration of *commedia dell'arte*. This approach suited Mnouchkine and from then on she sought even greater involvement by the actors, as well as continuing her research into popular theatre forms.

The company's breakthrough came with its 1967 production of *The Kitchen*, by the British playwright Arnold Wesker, which told the story of alienated kitchen workers in a large London restaurant. Mnouchkine had recently seen the Living Theatre's production about US military prisons, *The Brig*, in Paris. She was impressed with the Living Theatre's theatricalisation of the ritual demeaning of United States marines in prison and sought to capture the same visceral sense of oppression in her production. The actors did research by taking jobs in restaurants, while Mnouchkine attended classes at the Lecoq school and devised a rigorous training based on exercises from the Living Theatre. She created a charged choreography in which the actors had to move at high speed to keep up with the accelerating rhythm of the restaurant's kitchen. She rehearsed the actors by throwing broken dinner plates, which the actors had to catch in mid-air.[3] The production created a sensation and the audience included members of the Restaurants' Union, who testified to the authenticity of the actors' work.

A Midsummer Night's Dream followed in 1968. The set was a floor of sheepskin, over which the actor-dancers crawled and tumbled their way through a nightmarish world of forest spirits, and where the only spot of comfort was that offered by the mechanicals, whose dedication to their craft and collaborative spirit, naïve as it might be, promised some hope in a world gone mad. May 1968 saw the student revolt and a profound questioning on the part of French theatre makers as to whether theatre should be abandoned for more direct political action. After long hours of debate, the Théâtre du Soleil took its inspiration from the artisanship characterised by the mechanicals in *A Midsummer Night's Dream* and renewed its dedication to its craft.

The company's next piece, *The Clowns*, explored the day-to-day challenges of contemporary life, using the form of the clown as a point of departure. Each actor created their own clown character and many hours of improvisation were developed, which Mnouchkine ultimately edited down to four hours. This caused a serious crisis among the actors, as much of their work was discarded. *The Clowns* (1969–70) reflected a difficult time for the company, internally as well as externally. The May 1968 revolution had failed politically, leaving a deep sense of discontent. The work of the actors in *The Clowns* had been individually focused on their characters, leading to a sense of personal alienation which strained the collective nature of the company. Moreover, the form, with its broad physicality, was difficult for many of the actors, who left the company in frustration.

Faced with the malaise within the company, Mnouchkine strove to find a direction that would engage the enthusiasm of the whole troupe. The result was *1789, or The Revolution Must Only Stop at the Perfection of Happiness*. This piece presented the French

Revolution as the start of social change that had yet to be realised. The topic not only inspired a renewal of the company's vision, but also engaged the French audience still trying to come to grips with the failures of May 1968. During this time the Théâtre du Soleil was able to acquire a home, the Cartoucherie, an old ammunitions factory, which it rented from the local government for a nominal fee, and where it has resided ever since.

The Théâtre du Soleil continued its investigation of the Revolution in the production 1793 (1972), and then turned its attention to contemporary history using the form and masks of the *commedia dell'arte*. *L'Age d'Or* (1975) involved various scenes about the condition of émigrés in France. The persons in the play were based on traditional *commedia* characters such as the miser Pantalone and the servant Arlequino, transformed into the rapacious contractor-businessman Volpis and the poor émigré worker Abdallah.

After *L'Age d'Or* Mnouchkine refocused the direction of the troupe by taking on a film project, *Molière* (1977), in which the story of the trials, tribulations, and

Figure 15.2 Théâtre du Soleil's *L'Age D'Or* with Philippe Caubère as Abdallah, asleep in the workers' dormitory.

Source: Photo, Paul Jenewein.

triumphs of Molière and his troupe became an allegory for the history of the Théâtre du Soleil, as experienced over its first decade. Mnouchkine began more consciously to define her journey as a theatre artist as she explored old theatrical forms in order to create new forms for the present. She would continue to do this periodically, 'returning to school' as she put it, investigating theatre forms of the past, whether Molière, Shakespeare, or the Greeks, as a preparation for finding a more effective way of telling stories about the present.

Although the Théâtre du Soleil had achieved critical success over the decade, French reviewers continued to be sceptical of the achievements of the company, charging that its collective collaboration, though filled with spectacular theatricality, resulted in weak texts. Mnouchkine had hoped for the arrival of talented writers at the Cartoucherie, but so far no writer had materialised. With the next production, *Mephisto* (1979), Mnouchkine tried her hand at playwriting by adapting the novel *Mephisto* by Klaus Mann (the son of Thomas Mann), which focused on the various choices made by German actors in the face of Hitler's rise to power and the tragic consequences that followed.

After *Mephisto*, Mnouchkine tried writing a play about Cambodia and its devastation by the Khmer Rouge. However, she found her writing tended towards cinematic realism, and she turned to the works of Shakespeare in the hope that engaging his texts would help her to understand the genius of his dramaturgy, in terms both of how he handled history and how he constructed metaphor. Mnouchkine ambitiously sought to do *Richard II*, *Henry IV, Parts 1 and 2*, and *Twelfth Night*. After several months of cliché-ridden improvisations on *Richard II*, Mnouchkine, having recently seen Kurasawa's film *Kagemusha*, directed the actors to consider forms of Asian theatre as a way of matching the theatricality of Shakespeare's language and dramaturgy. Mnouchkine's search for the appropriate form for a production, in terms of both space and acting style, was the guiding impulse as she considered how to best express the hierarchic ritual world of medieval England. Among the questions posed was 'How does a king walk?'. By alienating Shakespeare and transposing, in the Brechtian sense, the world of feudal England into the world of feudal Japan, the company was able to find the gestus of the characters and the ritual of power politics that was implicit in both worlds. The aesthetic of the Shakespeare productions became a hybrid of Elizabethan and Eastern styles of theatre, borrowing from traditional Japanese and Indian performance in particular.

The Shakespeare plays can be seen as the beginning of a new era in Mnouchkine's approach to *mise-en-scène*, with a stripped down space and a greater emphasis on the theatrical virtuosity of the actors. Freed from developing their own text, the actors of the Théâtre du Soleil focused with a passion on form; Mnouchkine gave them a beautiful empty space and encouraged the actors to incarnate Artaud's notion of the actor as an 'athlete of the heart'. Mnouchkine regards the discovery of the importance of the representation of the sacred on stage as coming from this period. This was a characteristic of the traditional Asian theatre which had so inspired Artaud. For Mnouchkine, the genius of the East is its theatrical form and the methods it provides for the training of the actor, while the genius of the West is its dramaturgy and its emphasis on text. (Féral 1998: 39).

> What interests me in Asian theatre is that actors are creators of metaphors. Their art consists of showing passions, recounting the interiority of human beings [. . .] the actors' aim is to open up human beings, like a

pomegranate. Not to display their guts but to depict what is internal and transform it into signs, shapes, movement, rhythms.

(Williams 1999: 87)

The exploration of Eastern theatre helped Mnouchkine continue to evolve a theatricality in which the actor occupies both a metaphorical and metaphysical space, and must embody his character not only as a human being in action, in a certain time and place, but as a symbol participating in a collective sacred drama about the history of mankind, and in which the actor becomes both sign and signifier. This demands that the actor invent gestures that read on two levels: both as stage actions and on deeper levels, be they metaphoric, symbolic, or iconic, for example. One such moment occurred in her production of *Richard II* where Henry of Bolingbroke supports the body of his childhood friend and rival, Richard II (murdered by Henry's henchmen), evoking the image of a pietà but also signifying the sacrifice of Richard on the altar of power. These examples suggest both an iconic image and a symbolic action rather than just stage action. Mnouchkine uses this image of the pietà again in her production of *L'Indiade* (1987), where a cart comes on stage to take away the bodies of Hindus and Moslems who have killed each other during the partition of India and Pakistan. In the cart is the body of the Hindu man who had just before killed the Muslim whose body is now deposited next to him. Forming a pietà with his killer, *this action creates* a metaphor of their mutual destiny and a reflection on the metaphysics of existence. As they are taken off to be buried in the same grave, the image created by the actors becomes both a comment on the futility of violence and a reflection on the sacred intimacy of their shared fate found in death.

Figure 15.3 Théâtre du Soleil's production of Shakespeare's *Henry IV* (*Part* 1) with Georges Bigot, John Arnold and Maurice Durozier (1984).

Source: Magnum Photos, photo, Martine Franck.

During the Shakespeare productions Mnouchkine formed a relationship with the Algerian born feminist writer Hélène Cixous, who had written several plays. She asked if she would be willing to attempt to write a play, with the Théâtre du Soleil, about Cambodia. Cixous agreed and a long-term collaboration began which has included *L'Histoire terrible mais inachevée de Norodom Sihanouk, roi du Cambodge* (1985), *L'Indiade ou l'Inde de leurs rêves* (1987), and *Tambours sur la Digue* (1999), among other plays. Cixous brought a rich lyricism to the texts of the Théâtre du Soleil which complemented the hyper-theatricality of Mnouchkine's *mise-en-scène*. The Théâtre du Soleil's productions took on an epic scope, lasting anywhere between four and eight hours, as Mnouchkine and Cixous constructed contemporary morality plays exploring periods of history in which human conscience is swept away by extremist ideology, the struggle for power, and greed, resulting in the breakdown of human conscience. The creative process involved collaboration between Cixous, Mnouchkine, and the actors. Cixous brought her writing to the rehearsals and the actors improvised with the characters and text, which Cixous then transposed into her poetic language, while Mnouchkine ultimately determined the final text and *mise-en-scène*. During this period Mnouchkine continued her experimentation with forms including Bunraku as a model for creating human puppets on stage in *Tambours sur la Digue*, where actors were costumed to appear as Bunraku puppets and handled by other actors as if they were puppets. She continued her exploration of mask work in *Sihanouk* (1985) and in *Et soundains des nuits d'éveil* (1997), and she staged *The Oresteia* (1990–92) by Aeschylus, and Euripides' *Iphigenia at Aulis* (1990) in order to 'return to school' and delve into theatre as a ritual articulation of a community in crisis. During this period dance and music took on a new level of importance in the work, and actors were challenged to achieve a high level of physical virtuosity and theatrical engagement as they incarnated character, created text, learned complex athletic dances, recreated puppets and animals, and became master drummers.

In recent productions Mnouchkine has returned to the collective creation of text by the actors. *Le Dernier Caravansérail* (2003) evoked the fate of the millions of today's refuges escaping from political and economic oppression. *Les Ephémères* (2007), on the other hand, focused on the intimate lives of people, and their day-to-day struggles in the face of personal and political adversity. Both productions employed a new form of scenography devised through Mnouchkine's cinematic approach to these works. She felt the need to frame the characters and establish their circumstances quickly in a play that moved continuously from one part of the world to another. Through experimentation, the actors helped to find a solution: the characters and their environment were pushed on and off the stage on wheeled platforms by other actors, creating a montage of the movement of history and people's lives. At this point, Mnouchkine, seems to be looking to capture the individual story within an accelerating humanity, taken over by global politics on the one hand, and an increasingly materialistic and depersonalised world on the other. In the case of *Le Dernier Caravansérail* the stories came out of many interviews with exiles, as well as the personal experiences of the actors and their readings and research, whereas *Les Ephémères* was more directly based on personal experience of members of the company. Both pieces leave the audience with a flood of images of disrepaired lives, whose survival rests on the fragile gesture of another's concern. Hope is symbolised by a lone seagull flying against a storm or by an individual's willingness to sit quietly and listen to another.

Figure 15.4 Théâtre du Soleil's production of *Le Dernier Caravansérail Part II* (2005).
Source: Magnum Photos, photo, Martine Franck.

THE TRAINING

> I do not say to myself 'what technique should I put to work?' Afterwards, on
> reflection, I perceive that having believed I had no method, fundamentally, there
> was one. In watching *Au soleil même la nuit*,[4] I told myself: at base, there is a method,
> but I am not conscious of it. They are the adventures of each instant, the moments
> where I am there and I say: I will embark.[5]

Mnouchkine's methodology is rooted in the demands of the moment and an intuitive
understanding of the creative potential of the actor poised on the edge of the
unknown. She knows what she wants when she sees it but she must depend on the
actor to reveal it. In essence, Mnouchkine proposes a situation and the actors respond
with their imagination and willingness to play. Mnouchkine's genius is her ability to
inspire, recognise, nurture, and give shape to meaningful choices made by the actor.
This method of creation is very demanding on the actors, since they must be willing
to make that step, with a guiding push from Mnouchkine, that may just as often lead
them to stumble as to discover. One of her favourite refrains is that the actor must be
like a child, with a certain openness and willingness to enter the world without
preconception; yet this child must also be actively inventive and able to fill an empty
space with their own particular imagination, demonstrating a strong ability to tell a
story through the body as well as words.

   Mnouchkine's approach to creation is through the senses. She sets the actors off
on their journey by establishing an atmosphere that is rich with images and sound.
Whilst inspiring her actors to find a more accessible approach to Shakespeare's *Henry
IV*, Mnouchkine conjures a specific world: 'Think of a village, on this high plateau, on
the border of the Himalayas, at the end of the dirt trail, the caravan stops and plays for

the last time this history before the village becomes blocked by the snow . . .' (Double Page 1984). Mnouchkine will provide specific pictures, photos, and descriptive stories as inspiration to the actors. Jean Jacques Lemêtre, the resident musician and composer and Mnouchkine's longtime collaborator and sounding board, who has been with the company since 1978, will offer up musical accompaniment from the moment the actor sets foot on stage, creating themes for each character and an appropriate, dynamic atmosphere that carries the story along. Lemêtre is at every rehearsal, sometimes with as many as three hundred different instruments from all over the world, and several assistant musicians, improvising music and adjusting instruments in response to the actors' improvised actions. Lemêtre's musical impro-visations, in turn, inspire further choices by the actors. By performance time, the music and the actors' actions are totally integrated, so that the piece is scored throughout. This synthesis of live music and action during the improvisational rehearsal period is a fundamental aspect of Mnouchkine's method and an important factor in the success of her work. Mnouchkine believes in approaching the dramatic character as someone living through a series of changing and evolving emotional states (états) which the actor must find and incarnate. The music supports the actors in their search for the emotional state of the character, transporting the actor and helping sustain the state as the actor moves through the character's actions.

For Mouchkine, costume, like music, is fundamental to creating the sensate experience of the character and action on stage:

> The costume is the actor's second skin, and the only skin of the character. Getting costumes is re-finding one's childhood: joy, disguise, proces-sionals, and metamorphoses. It's thanks to costumes that actors become other.
>
> (Féral 1998: 33)

During rehearsal the actors cannot go on stage in their street clothes; materials for creating costumes are available from day one, and the actors improvise their own costumes for whatever characters they are working on. Each rehearsal starts with the actors taking the time to 'disguise' themselves, with the help of the costume designer and assistants, who provide a large choice of cloth and costume items within which the actors can transform themselves into their characters. Over time, in collaboration with Mnouchkine and the costume designer (who is present at rehearsals), the overall look of the costumes is developed. Actors remain in costume throughout the rehearsal day, always ready to go on stage even if it turns out they will not get to work on a scene that day.

> [. . .] the theatre is a metaphor, metaphor of gesture, of the word, and [. . .] what's beautiful is when an actor transforms a feeling, a memory, a state or a passion. No one sees pure passion unless the actor transforms it into performance, that is to say into a sign, into a gesture.
>
> (Williams 1999: 102)

There is one reading of the text at the beginning of rehearsal, with actors taking turns reading different characters, and then they are on their feet, learning the lines as they move about, script in hand, improvising their actions. At the rehearsals the actors divide into groups working on the same scenes, which they then present to the whole group. Actors can volunteer to work on certain roles. Mnouchkine discourages the psychologising of a role by the actor, and reminds the actor to focus on the theatricalisation of the character, finding the external gesture and emotional state that represents the character's inner and outer conflicts. Mnouchkine is interested in a character's choices in the face of moral and social imperatives rather than purely personal issues. In her most recent work, the line between realism and theatricalisation has diminished as she tells the story of contemporary people in crisis in a day-to-day world. One might compare Mnouchkine's efforts recently to those of the film director Jean Renoir, who was painstaking in finding realistic details while at the same time pushing the character into a theatricality that suggests a type. Even when the actors are not rehearsing with them, the masks of the Théâtre du Soleil are close by to serve as inspiration. Though the acting is large in scope, any grandstanding is quickly scrubbed away by Mnouchkine's demand that the actors listen and that they keep their actions simple, authentic, and truthful.

Since Mnouchkine tells her stories through an epic structure that highlights history and the character's social action within its flow, characters tend to appear, disappear, and reappear, and actors play many different roles in a production. In recent plays, the audience has been taken from one part of the world to another, and so the narrative is constantly moving between different places, times, and people. This is not to say, however, that the actor's depiction of character is generalised. Mnouchkine is rigorous about specificity; just as a good mask is crafted down to the last detail, Mnouchkine asks the same of her actors as they shape their characters. The gesture of the actor is not only an action but also a sign that evokes a universal image. In the production of L'Age d'Or the actor Philippe Caubère played an immigrant labourer who must find a place to sleep in a room that is already completely filled with other sleeping workers. The crowded room, represented by a large empty space, is in the imagination of the actor and, by extension, in the imagination of the audience: it is sufficient for the actor to roll onto his shoulder, his body extended into the air above him while his feet fall back towards his head, for us to understand how crowded the room really is (see Fig 15.2).

Mask work

> I think that the mask does not hide the actor but rather the self. In fact, it hides nothing at all, it reveals. It's a magnifying glass to the soul, an eye into the soul. [. . .] With the mask, suddenly, all the laws of the theatre are there.
>
> (Féral 1998: 29)

Mnouchkine's training of the actors at the Théâtre du Soleil rests on mask work. She studied at the Lecoq school in the 1960s and learned there that the mask does not lie, that the truth of the actor's actions and the essence of theatricality can be determined through observing the actor in mask. Mask work is the framework through which she auditions new actors into the company. Every two years or so Mnouchkine holds a mask workshop, which two hundred to eight hundred actors attend.[6] The workshop has a theme such as the Resistance or the Occupation. In the first days of the workshop Mnouchkine sets up several improvisations without masks, first with two actors, then with larger groups, including various circumstances: a dispute over an inheritance; the morning before a funeral; a day at the ice rink where passions explode; a public transport bus at the moment when the inspectors get on to check if people have valid tickets. She gives each of the actors their actions in confidence, and the improvisation begins, accompanied by some recorded music such as Holst's *Symphony of the Planets* in order to create an atmosphere of powerful emotional states. The goal of the improvisation is to find strong clear actions based on l'*état* (the state or internal landscape) of the character. From the moment the improvisation begins Mnouchkine wants to see the state of the character; the line of their movement; their 'musique interieur', an inner rhythm that propels them across the stage; and the atmosphere of the scene. Rather than the character's inner thought process, she is interested in the character's condition, which is reflected through the sensate world of movement and vocal quality. This does not mean that there is no interior life; on the contrary, the inner life is demonstrated through the theatricality of the actor's performance. Where a realistic approach might demand that the actor interiorise their character's feelings, Mnouchkine asks the actor to externalise the inner life of the character. She also asks the actor to focus on l'*état* (the condition) rather than a specification, thus actions manifest as a result of the actor's receptivity to the character's condition: 'The actor receives. He does not search, he does not find. He waits to receive; he is in a state of reception, of availability. He waits' (Féral 1998: 26).

An improvisation can last as short as thirty seconds. Mnouchkine will announce a definitive 'Stop!' if the actors do not establish themselves as being present in the moment. Being present is not necessarily manifested by a great deal of activity. It is clear (as one observes) whether the actor has brought life to a character or whether we still feel the self-conscious actor's presence beneath the unrealised other. After the improvisation, Mnouchkine asks the actors to critique themselves. She asks questions: Were they in the moment? Did they have the generosity to receive from their fellow actors? She notes that it is through listening and observing the action of other characters that the actors will discover their own. She observes that the actor, however, must be careful not to be a parasite, clinging to a fellow actor, in order to feed off their action. The actor must dare to enter the space as an individual, even though they are part of a group. She persists by asking whether they found 'the interior music' of each character and remarks: 'I hear the noise, but not the music.' For Mnouchkine, each character has his or her rhythm and leitmotif, which should be apparent at the entrance of the character: 'Was the character present from the moment you entered? You must do something without thinking about doing it. What was the state of the character? Were the actions clear? If you are illustrative, you kill theatre.'

Several days into the workshop Mnouchkine introduces the mask. The Théâtre du Soleil has an extensive collection of wood masks from the *commedia dell'arte* and Balinese comic mask tradition, including masks made by Erhard Stiefel, who studied with the master of mask making Sartori and has worked with Mnouchkine since their days studying together at Lecoq. These masks are of the highest quality and evoke, by their very presence, a pleasure that is in itself irresistible; the beauty of the mask invites the actor to engage. Mnouchkine demonstrates the rules of mask work. The actor must respect the mask: 'With the mask it is you who must yield.' The mask must be held carefully on the sides of the face, never on the nose or through the eyes, and never placed with the mask face down. Through observation of the mask the actor should 'seek a humble and loving encounter with your character.' Once the actor has observed the masks and chosen one to which she has an affinity, she must find the appropriate costume for that mask. In the case of the mask work, the disguise offered by the costume must be complete. Skin, hair, arms, legs, hands, and feet must be covered in order to create a complete theatrical effect and to avoid any allusion to realism. The actor is provided with exquisite costumes from past productions at the Théâtre du Soleil as well as yards of beautiful fabric to make into turbans, belts, leggings, and so on.

Mnouchkine invites individual actors to choose a mask that they are drawn to. She watches attentively as the actor prepares by putting on their costume and observing the masked character in the mirror. The mirror is always there for the actor to check in with their character, should they lose touch with it. The room is quiet. The actors of the Théâtre du Soleil are present at the periphery and offer help in costuming the novice actor. Once the actor is ready and up on stage, Mnouchkine engages the character by asking questions and giving them directions. She uses her skill as a coach to draw out and help the actor ground the character: Where are you from? Do you have family? What work do you do? Where are you going? Show me what you want. And so forth. After several days of individual work, the actors are encouraged to find a group of four to eight actors to work with on the theme that has been suggested by Mnouchkine. The actors go off into their groups and develop their scenario and characters based on the masks they will be working with. The subject is the Resistance.

A group volunteers: the actors go up on stage to try out their scenario. Mnouchkine stops them, 'How can there be so much preparation and then you walk on stage as if walking down the street? I love theatre. I want theatre! Out! Next! Fear of the mask is a wholesome fear such as one might feel when a god descends.'

She goes on to make several points:

- It is important to remember that once one enters on stage, one enters another continent, one begins a voyage where day-to-day language, vulgarity and the prosaic cannot be used.
- Don't touch your mask or the mask of the other or you'll break the magic.
- Share the mask with the audience. Work with the mask demands frontality on the part of the actor as they establish a direct rapport with the public.
- A mask cannot lie. The mask reveals all artifice; it demands truth, but not realism.
- The actor must ask what the mask's emotional state is before entering on stage.
- It is important to become like children when creating theatre: 'Children love the act of playing. The presence of the masks keeps us from forgetting to play.'

One group devises a scene in which members of the Resistance set dynamite to the statue of the hated invader, with the intention of blowing it up. As soon as the bomb has been set, two lovers (not masked) arrive for their assignation under the statue. They are in love and totally absorbed with each other. The members of the Resistance are in a state of great agitation, not wanting to kill anyone, just blow up a statue. They decide to disable the bomb in order to avoid hurting the young couple, while trying to not call attention to themselves. The couple leave and they reset the bomb, and the couple return, just as the bomb is about to go off. Frustrations are high but the choice is made to disarm the bomb again. The lovers exit, oblivious to the impact they have had on others.

Mnouchkine compliments the group. The scenario was simple, with strong choices. The actors established a group rhythm. They maintained their individual characters' leitmotifs. The actors shared their masks with the audience, keeping the frontality that is necessary in order to create a rapport. Costuming was done carefully, such that the line of the character was clearly delineated. The actors were in the moment and open to each other and avoided muddying their actions. 'One can only commit one action at a time.' The gestures were specific and economical, clear of any unnecessary business. The actors found rests and stops in the action, which supported the rhythm of the scene. Each actor understood how to do the minimum to achieve the maximum. They demonstrated the intense energy demanded in mask work through their commitment to the physicality and emotional states of the characters. Mnouchkine makes some specific points to the group:

- Without stops, there can be no rhythm, form creates rhythm. As in musical notation, there have to be rests and stops, in order to feel the rhythm.
- Don't explain yourself, but learn to be.
- Take the time to finish. Complete your action and remember you can only play one action at a time, even if actions come one after the other very quickly.
- To be like a child in the work is not to infantilise the character.
- Do not make your characters into bizarre and ugly creatures; in every creature there is beauty.
- The monologue doesn't exist in this form of theatre: one is always talking to someone, even if it is only the audience.
- Find the design of the mask that's to be embodied in your whole person. Ask yourself: do my movements, my costume, complete the design of the mask?
- These masks are complete beings: find the contradictions. You can't see the rays of the sun if you can't see the dirt beneath you.
- Have the humility to imitate those whose work you respect, but it is not a question of imitating from the exterior, but from the interior.

Although Mnouchkine's actor training varies from production to production, in rehearsal she is consistent in her advice, which reflects the same concerns that she emphasises in the mask workshops. The contribution of the actors to the training process is also significant. In some cases, actors are given travel grants before the rehearsal of a production in order to go to various parts of the world to engage in formal training with Indian, Balinese, Korean theatre masters, for example, and to bring back what they have learned.[7]

During the rehearsal and performance period the actors do a warm-up that is led by those actors with the appropriate training in movement and voice. The warm-up is set for each production and includes exercises that are specific to the needs of the piece. For example, in the latest productions the actors have had to push wheeled platforms (transporting set and actors) on and off stage effortlessly. Games using a large inflated ball were devised to help build the necessary upper-body strength. For the Shakespeare plays the actors had to run five miles a day to keep in shape. Games designed to help actors become more aware of the importance of rhythm are also part of the training. Yoga provides a basic element to the warm-up. If, during rehearsals, the actors are struggling with the improvisations, Mnouchkine may take a day to refocus the actors. She may ask them to take a scene and work on telling the story physically, without words, using the musical accompaniment devised by Lemêtre as inspiration. Rehearsals average about six months, and much of what is devised in rehearsal is discarded as Mnouchkine searches for the precise gesture and mise-en-scène.

THE PRODUCTION OF 1789

The creative process of 1789 reflects the fundamentals of Mnouchkine's approach to theatre, in particular when she is creating new work. 1789 involved intensive historical research by the actors. This included university lectures, reading history books, and viewing popular films on the French Revolution (which had shaped the French people's understanding of this pivotal moment in their history). Having determined that the space would be an open-air market of eighteenth-century Paris, where 'the people' encountered the popular theatre of the time and heard the latest news of the Revolution, the company engaged in a four-month period of extensive improvisation, exploring various popular theatrical forms associated with the street theatre of eighteenth-century France, including puppetry, commedia, mime, and acrobatics. At every rehearsal the troupe would divide into several groups; each would work on the same event leading up to the French Revolution. Then the groups would perform their versions in front of the company and the best improvisations would be kept, expanded upon, and refined. The final piece consisted of an epic narrative showing the pivotal moments in the French Revolution during the year 1789. It was during the process of creating the performance that Mnouchkine immersed herself in the work of Meyerhold. She was inspired by his concept of a theatre space without limits and by the theatre of the fairgrounds, which he had extolled. The company devised a set that replicated the outdoor theatre of the eighteenth-century where various entertainers performed on large wooden platforms as the populace passed by on their way to market.

The audience had the option of standing in the open space at the centre of the event, surrounded by the stages, or to sit in risers that overlooked the enormous space. The action took place around the audience, sometimes the same action happening on all of the platforms, at other times the actors moving from one platform to the next or descending into the crowd. The audience were also integrated into the action of the play so that they became the people of Paris in the year 1789, watching the story of the Revolution unfold around them. The audience became engaged in the great debates of the time as the actors playing leaders of the Revolution addressed them directly. They laughed and hissed at the ineptitude of the royal family as they watched the king and queen satirised in farcical puppet shows and commedia burlesques; they celebrated the taking of the Bastille with those who had been there; they were told at gunpoint by the Marquis de Lafayette that the Revolution was over and it was time to go home; and they were exhorted by Citizen Marat at the end of the play to continue the fight even as the bourgeoisie pre-empted the Revolution by shutting 'the people' in a locked box. There were times when the actors struggled to bring the public's attention back to the action of the play, as the audience snake-danced through the open space and became caught up in the euphoria of the Revolution. The Théâtre du Soleil opened to much acclaim at the Piccolo Theatre in Milan, which invited it to perform at its space after the city of Paris had refused its request to perform in the large open market space, Les Halles. The production 1789 played over a span of three years, to almost 300,000 spectators from France to Berlin, London and Belgrade. In 1973 a film was made of it.

Mnouchkine is a synthesist in her practice as a director and in her work with the actor. She reaches back to various forms of actor training originating in both Eastern and Western popular theatre traditions, in order to inspire her actors to animate the stories of the present. She and her company, the Théâtre du Soleil, strive toward a direct rapport with the audience, as experienced in popular theatre, while taking on the weight of transformative engagement – as witnessed within the sacred. In order to manifest such a 'whole-souled' theatre, Mnouchkine demands the utmost commitment of each actor and audience member to engage as a prescient child might, unexpectedly faced with the profound movement of history.

Notes

All translations from the French are the author's unless otherwise indicated.

1   Ariane Mnouchkine during the rehearsal of Le Denier Caravansérail in 2003, quote recorded by Françoise Lauwaert. See: www.lebacausoleil.com/SPIP/article.php3?id_article = 284. A webpage that is part of a website of the Théâtre du Soleil (www.lebacausoleil.com) dedicated to various articles and information on the history of the Théâtre du Soleil.
2   Located in the Bois de Vincennes on the eastern periphery of Paris.
3   Mnouchkine, 'Le Théâtre du Soleil ou La Quête de Bonheur', in Marie Louise Bablet and Denis Bablet (eds), Diapolivre 1, Paris: CNRS, p. 8.
4   A documentary on Mnouchkine's Afghanistan workshop by Eric Darmon and Catherine Vilpoux.
5   See www.lebacausoleil.com/SPIP/article.php3?id_article = 284.
6   The following description of the workshop and all subsequent quotes from Mnouchkine on mask work and the work of actors were recorded during the mask workshop at the Cartoucherie, April 1988, unless otherwise noted.
7   The following details of rehearsals are taken from an interview with Théâtre du Soleil actor Duccio Bellugi-Vannuccini on 14 July 2008.

Bibliography

Bablet, Denis and Bablet, Marie-Louise (1979) Le Théâtre du Soleil, ou la quête de la bonheur (Diapolivre 1) Ivry, Paris: Center National de la Recherche Scientifique. Including 84 slides, 1 sound disc, 2 booklets.
Bablet, Denis and Jacquot, Jean (eds) (1977) Les Voies de la Création Théâtrale 5, Paris: Editions du Centre National de la Recherche Scientifique.
Bellugi-Vannuccini, Duccio (2006) 'A Sun Rises in Afghanistan: An Actor's View,' Theater, 36: 78–81.
Bradby, David and Williams, David (1988) Director's Theatre, New York: St. Martin's Press.
Bryant-Bertail, Sarah (1994) 'Gender, Empire and Body Politic as Mise en Scène: Mnouchkine's "Les Atrides" ', Theatre Journal, 46 (1): 1–30.
Champagne, Lena and Kourilsky, Franise (1975) 'Political Theatre in France since 1968,' The Drama Review, 19 (2): 43–52.
Cixous, Hélène (2004) Selected Plays of Hélène Cixous, London: Routledge.
Copfermann, Emile (1971) 'Entretiens avec Ariane Mnouchkine et le Soleil: Différent – Le Théâtre du Soleil,' Travail Théâtral, Lausanne (La Cité): 3–33.
Delgado, Maria and Heritage, Paul (eds) (1996) In Contact with the Gods? Directors Talk Theatre, New York: St. Martin's Press.
Donahue, Thomas J. (1991) 'Mnouchkine, Vilar and Copeau: Popular Theater and Paradox,' Modern Language Studies, 21 (4): 31–42.
Double Page (1984), Les Conseils d'Arane Aux Comédiens Pendant Les Répétitions de Henry IV, photographs by Martine Franck, Double Page, 32, Paris: Editions SNEP.
Féral, Josette (1998) Trajectoires du Soleil: autour d'Ariane Mnouchkine, Paris: Editions théâtrales.
—— (2001) Dresser un monument à l'éphémère: Rencontres avec Ariane Mnouchkine, Paris: Editions théâtrales.
Féral, Josette and Husemoller, Anna (1989) 'Mnouchkine's Workshop at the Soleil: A Lesson in Theatre,' The Drama Review, 33 (4): 77–87.
Féral, Josette, Husemoller, Anna and Mnouchkine, Ariane (1989) 'Building up the Muscle', The Drama Review, 33 (4): 88–97.

Kiernander, Adrian (1993) *Ariane Mnouchkine and the Théâtre du Soleil*, New York: Cambridge University Press.

Kirkland, Christopher D. (1975) 'Théâtre du Soleil: The Golden Age, First Draft,' *The Drama Review*, 19 (2): 53–60.

Meineck, Peter W. (2006) 'Ancient Drama Illuminated by Contemporary Stagecraft: Some Thoughts on the Use of Mask and 'Ekkylema' in Ariane Mnouchkine's 'Le Dernier Caravansérail' and Sophocles' "Ajax" ', *The American Journal of Philology*, 127 (3): 453–60.

Miller, Judith G. (2007) *Ariane Mnouchkine*, London: Routledge.

Mnouchkine, Ariane (1979) *Méphisto, le roman d'une carrière*, Paris: Solin/Théâtre du Soleil.

—— (1990) 'Méphisto', trans. Timberlake Wertenbaker in *Theatre and Politics: An International Anthology*, New York: Ubu Repertory Theatre Publications, 361–469.

Picon-Vallin, Beatrice (2000) 'Le Soleil, de Soudain des nuits d'éveil à Tambours sur la digue: Les longs cheminements de la troupe du Soleil', *Théâtre Publique*, 152: 4–13.

Richardson, Helen (1990) 'The Théâtre du Soleil and the Quest for Popular Theatre in the Twentieth Century,' PhD dissertation, Berkeley, CA: The University of California, Berkeley.

Scheie, Timothy (1994) 'Body Trouble: Corporeal Presence and Performative Identity in Cixous's and Mnouchkine's "L'Indiade ou l'Inde de leurs reves" ', *Theatre Journal*, 46 (1): 31–44.

Théâtre du Soleil (1971a) *1789: La révolution doit s'arrêter à la perfection du bonheur*, Paris: Stock.

—— (1971b) '1789', trans. Alexander Trocchi, *Gambit*, 5 (20): 5–52.

Wehle, Philippa (2005) 'Theatre du Soleil: Dramatic Response to the Global Refugee Crisis', *PAJ: A Journal of Performance and Art*, 27 (2): 80–86.

Williams, David (ed.) (1999) *Collaborative theatre: the Théâtre du Soleil sourcebook*, London: Routledge.

Videos and filmography

Bellugi-Vannuccini, Duccio, Sabido, Sergio Canto and Chevallier, Philippe (2006) *Un soleil à Kaboul . . . ou plutôt deux*, Paris: Bel Air Media/Théâtre du Soleil/Bell-Canto-Laï/Voltaire Production.

Darmon, Eric and Vilpoux, Catherine with Mnouchkine, Ariane (1995) *Au Soleil même la nuit*, Paris: Agat Films/La Sept ARTE/ Théâtre du Soleil.

Mnouchkine, Ariane (1974) *1789*, Paris: les Films Ariane.

—— (1976–77) *Molière ou la vie d'un hônette homme*, Paris: Les Films du Soleil de la Nuit/Claude Lelouche; DVD, Paris: Bel Aire Classiques/SCEREN-CNDP.

—— /Théâtre du Soleil (1989) *La Nuit Miraculeuse*, dialogues by Hélène Cixous, Paris: France Telecom/ La mission du Bicentenaire/et al.

—— (2002) *Tambours sur la digue: Sous forme de pièce ancienne pour marionettes joué par des acteurs*, Paris: Le Théâtre du Soleil/ARTE France/ Bel Air Media.

—— (2006) *Le Dernier Caravansérail* (Odyssées), Paris: Bel Air Classiques/ SCEREN-CNDP.

Vilpoux, Catherine (1999) *Film d'après La Ville Parjure ou le réveil des Erinyes*, Paris: Vidéo de Poche/Le Théâtre du Soleil.

Zitzerman, Bernard (2009) *Les Ephémères*, Paris: Arte Editions/Bel Air Classiques.

Websites

www.theatre-du-soleil.fr/
www.lebacausoleil.com/

Chapter 16

Alison Hodge

WŁODZIMIERZ STANIEWSKI: GARDZIENICE AND THE NATURALISED ACTOR

CONTEXT

THE CENTRE FOR THEATRE Practices 'Gardzienice' has produced few performances – just seven in more than thirty years[1] – but they have placed this Polish group at the forefront of international theatre. Richard Schechner recognises Gardzienice as 'one of the world's most important experimental and community-based performance groups'.[2] In their introduction to Gardzienice's British tour in 1989, Richard Gough and Judy Christie described the Company as 'pursuing an artistic endeavour that merges with a "Life Project" ' (Gough and Christie 1989: 3), while Susan Sontag has identified Gardzienice as 'one of the few essential theatre companies working anywhere in the world today'.[3]

Gardzienice's founder and Artistic Director, Włodzimierz Staniewski, has been the principal architect of this notional 'Life Project'.[4] Since the group's inception in 1977, he has led an intensive artistic programme which has evolved from expeditions to indigenous communities and village gatherings. At the Company's rural home in eastern Poland, international symposia, building restoration, work demonstrations, lecture tours and an Academy of Theatre Practice interrelate with the Company's own ongoing artistic research and training. Ultimately, all of these activities function to serve the main purpose – that of making a unique song theatre.

The ideological foundation of Staniewski's work can be identified early in Gardzienice's development through his notion of a 'new, natural environment of theatre' in which he proposed a rejection of the urban environment in favour of rural surroundings. In 1979 Staniewski outlined certain prerequisites that he felt this demanded of the actor:

- leaving the town, leaving not only the theatre building but also the city street,
- addressing oneself to people – the audience, consumers, who are undefiled by 'routine behaviour', undefined by . . . modelled reactions or a stereotypical scale of values, a conventional scale of assessment,
- entering the space that is unknown or that has been abandoned by theatre.

By space, I do not mean yet another 'closed circle', fortified by dry rules, rituals. I do not mean yet another stage. By space I mean an area and the substance of land and the substance of the sky bound by that area. I am not concerned with background or with idle poetic contemplation of nature. My concern is that these substances become the living participants in the event.[5]

In prioritising the theatre's symbiotic relationship with rural environments, and the indigenous people who live there, Staniewski identifies the immediate context in which the actor works as a primary source of creativity and an active partner in theatre making.

By re-integrating the actor with the rhythms and sensibilities of the natural environment, Staniewski has been alert to the urgent ecological concerns that have haunted the late twentieth and early twenty-first centuries: 'It is space that is crucial – finding and creating spatial forms and conditions which are ecologically sound. . . . "Ecos" in Greek means home, while creativity I understand as a dialogue with the spirit of the space (*genius loci*).'[6] It remains Staniewski's deeply held belief that both the theatre and its audience can no longer afford to ignore the nature of this sensitive, interactive relationship which demands a re-awakening to the totality of human experience:

To perceive means to be able to absorb with all the senses. This is no longer part of our education, nor is it allowed. The result is that the most fundamental human relationships become aseptic, sport-like, quite banal.

Figure 16.1 Włodzimierz Staniewski leading a master class at Columbia University, New York.
Source: Gardzienice Theatre Archive, photo, Maciej Znamierowski.

And what is it that we are afraid of in this reduction, all this castration? Are we afraid to be similar to nature, to animals? Why are we afraid that we have senses, that we can be absorbed? What does it mean, this desperate will to isolate ourselves from wholeness, from the world?

(Staniewski 1993: 16)

Resisting what he regards as the reductive, isolating tendencies of contemporary Western life, Staniewski has created an allegorical song theatre; a 'polyphony' of sound, body and text within a reverberating space which engages all the senses. At the Company's base in the village of Gardzienice, audiences are invited to watch a repertoire of performances in one evening. Each may be staged in or outside the restored buildings. The evening is shaped by the old and new performances in dialogue with each other and audiences move from one to another via torch-lit walks. The whole event (known as 'Cosmos') is built on the importance of encounter not just with performance but with the natural environment in which the work was formed.

Gardzienice's emphasis on the relational corresponds with a particular sense of reciprocal engagement found in many indigenous cultures where intimacy with nature, sense of community and maintenance of an ancestral relationship confirms an unbroken dialogue between people, place and tradition. By choosing to live and work alongside fast-disappearing traditional practices in Middle and Eastern Europe, Staniewski also recognised the value of the actor learning directly from sources which could offer archetypal patterns, fragments of behaviour, songs, music, rhythms and gestures which are 'ancient, hidden, forgotten':[7]

How does this work serve theatre? I believe that it teaches theatre and art, from the contact with their roots, not academically, but [it] teaches:

- [how] to see light
- the truth of gesture
- music
- truth in action
- ostensible unnaturalness is naturalness, that what seems unmannerly, immoral, is true and profound.[8]

Within Gardzienice's theatre ecology, the classical Western anthropocentric image of the actor has been exchanged for one which Staniewski refers to as 'eco-centricity'[9] where the actor is no longer centre stage, but is always a partner in a process of reciprocity with all that is energising and animating the theatrical event. This exemplifies Staniewski's search for 'Ecos'.[10] It is a state in which the actor can reconnect with ancient and traditional practices, using powerful physical and vocal techniques, to construct a visceral performance language which is metaphorical, urgent and passionate. It is not surprising, therefore, that Philip Arnoult describes the company's work as a 'ritualistic, almost religious experience' (Strausbaugh 1986: 30). The Polish academic and critic Leszek Kolankiewicz terms Gardzienice's style as *ethno-oratorio*, and associates its earlier performances with the pageants of the Middle Ages:

European theatre was born perhaps twice: in the ancient times and in the Middle Ages, both times from the spirit of music. And both times its true background was folk song. In Gardzienice Theatre, we witness how a Mystery Play is born, yet again, out of the spirit of music.[11]

Staniewski's emphasis on music and musicality in training is the key to the company's rigorous performance technique. It is through Gardzienice's advanced application of musicality that the central themes of ecology, indigeneity, the archaic, and reciprocity coalesce. Staniewski believes that musicality has a deep, spiritual relationship to theatre:

> We have to do something with the training of our senses, our memory, so that musicality can still be part of our way of communicating with the world, and with 'holiness'. There are three aspects to my process: one is concerned with the expansion of our system of perception; the second with how to find ways to absorb and introduce musicality into our practice; and the third with how to frame it within a performance.
>
> (Staniewski with Hodge: 2004)

ORIGINS AND INFLUENCES

De-urbanisation

De-urbanisation is an important part of the history of twentieth-century actor training. Stanislavsky, Vakhtangov, Copeau and Brook have all, at some point, sought rural retreats for their work. In the early 1970s Jerzy Grotowski also moved the focus of his practice from the city of Wrocław to Brzezinka in rural Poland. It was here that he began a series of paratheatrical projects which moved away from theatre to a more ritualised process of communication and exchange between participants. He sought to abolish the distinction between actor and audience through simple, non-theatrical meetings: 'Examining the nature of theatre . . . we came to the conclusion that its essence lies in direct contact between people' (Kolankiewicz 1977: 24). The qualitative value of this 'direct contact' could be measured by its ability to remove the debilitating social mask which Grotowski had consistently sought to strip away. The rural environment stimulated this interactive work and, as one participant reported: 'Habits brought from the city slowly die out: the defensive attitude (necessary there), the dullness of the senses, and the indifference. . . . Gradually we become sensitive to one another, we feel our constant, tangible, warm presence' (Kolankiewicz 1979, quoted in Kumiega 1987: 172–73).

Włodzimierz Staniewski joined Grotowski in 1971, and was a key collaborator in his paratheatrical work. By 1975 he had left the Laboratory Theatre to form his own group with Tomasz Rodowicz.[12] They gathered a small group of collaborators, most of whom were university graduates, and work began in a disused sixteenth-century chapel in the village of Gardzienice.[13]

Significantly, Staniewski's understanding of the importance of the context in which to work went much deeper than the de-urbanisation of previous practitioners. The social context, the eastern villages and their inhabitants were a primary concern. The group did not isolate themselves in the rural quiet – rather they went straight to the local people with their performances. Staniewski's express desire was to make theatre: 'For me it was very important to make something with its own performative architecture, possessing more than changing rituals and ceremonies . . .' (Staniewski 1987: 159).

Expeditions and gatherings

Staniewski, Rodowicz and their colleagues travelled to the borderland villages of eastern and south-east Poland seeking traces of the region's diverse communities. The dominant Catholic Church coexisted with marginal Roma, Belorussian, Łemko and Ukrainian cultures as well as with traces of Jewish traditions. It was an area rich with the songs and stories retained by the elderly inhabitants. Many of these rural communities were on the brink of extinction as the younger people migrated to the towns.

Rehearsing and training as they travelled into this isolated territory, Gardzienice performed its first show, *Spektakl Wierczorny* (*Evening Performance*) in 1977 (based on Rabelais' *Gargantua and Pantagruel*) to villages en route. After the performance, the group found that people stayed, and some started singing: 'Singing was the most open channel of communication. We saw that certain stylistic "figures" were emerging. We saw ourselves facing a tradition that had always existed' (Staniewski 1987: 141). This response inspired the idea of theatre meetings between the group and the villages. These 'Gatherings', often overcrowded in anticipation of the artistry of the occasion, became encounters where songs, dances, rituals and oral histories could be remembered, enacted or retold, and in which Gardzienice also sang and presented sequences of its developing work. For Staniewski, a Gathering still offers valuable insights for both actor and director because it contains 'the fundamental structure and principles of drama. It has enormous theatricality and dynamism' (Staniewski with Hodge 2004: 54). The actor must respond to the event with intuition, ingenuity and dramaturgical skill, whilst the director learns to build the momentum of the evening's exchanges effectively. In the early expeditions, the gathering was not only a form of communicating, but also a way of 'awakening the cultural undercurrents of a given social enclave' (Gough and Christie 1989: 14).

These meetings inspired the actor's physicality in performance, but not through simple reproduction. 'I never took entire themes from their dances, but certain electrifying gestures – a bowing of the head, or a hand movement which seemed to me to be a particularly significant expression of the person through their body' (Taranienko 1997: 133). Gardzienice's leading actor, Mariusz Gołaj, stresses that gestures are not explored for their psychological content, nor are they simply copied:

> I don't believe in copying because you never know exactly what emotions the village people have. Very often they know how to dance the body, how to use the gestures, and very often they are doing this cold. And this is its strength.[14]

Mikhail Bakhtin

The Gardzienice project was formulated in the political context of a Poland which had experienced nearly forty years of Communist rule. The government's cultural programme promoted Socialist Realism, encouraging an idealisation of the rural through a sanitised image of folk culture. The authorities celebrated a homogeneous version of peasant life which obscured the underlying diversity (and deprivation) of many rural areas.

Gardzienice's early expeditions were especially informed by Mikhail Bakhtin and his theories of carnival and grotesque realism, which had themselves been developed in the authoritarian climate of Stalinism.[15] Bakhtin's celebration of carnival – the inversion of the social order, the dynamic opposition of high and low culture, and the honesty of physical expression, free of political and social restriction – found echoes in Gardzienice's own political environment, and was directly explored through its use of Rabelais' texts in its first performance, *Spektakl Wierczorny*.

Bakhtin continued to be an influence in later productions which, for example, contained sounds and imagery modelled on principles of the grotesque body. In Gardzienice's seminal third performance, *Avvakum*[16] the use of Russian Orthodox iconography was directly referred to through opposites and contrasts, synthesised within the actor's own physique. The effect is an ambiguity within images which invites the spectator to unravel an enigma, to decipher the body rather than a spoken text. Halina Filipowicz recognised the depiction of reality in the performance as:

> [. . .]entirely problematic, existing in a constant of destruction and reconstruction. This fluid dramatic structure reflects a view of human nature as something infinitely malleable to control and transmutation, and thus succeeds where causal and discursive dramaturgy might fail. The obsessive stream of images is in a process of continuous, kaleidoscopic transformation which divests the work of permanence and closure.
>
> (Filipowicz 1987: 153)

Polish Romanticism

Staniewski's belief in the importance of a reconnection with sensuality through nature and culture is also strongly influenced by the work of Poland's leading Romantic poet and exiled playwright, Adam Mickiewicz, whose own ethnographic work recognised and celebrated the value of an ancient Slavic folk culture. He regarded it as a revitalising source for his country's cultural identity. Throughout the twentieth century Romanticism remained a dynamic cultural influence in Poland. It reached beyond literary and artistic concerns, towards an idealistic, political and philosophical movement that expounded ideals of freedom and identity. As with many of the Polish Romantic artists who experienced oppressive eras of occupation, Staniewski acknowledges the problem of identity as a key component of his work: 'How do you look for your identity? The material I select relates to this investigation, which concerns the *heritage* of my soul, the *heritage* of my mind, my people and my context' (Staniewski with Hodge 2004: 106).

Gardzienice's theatre has spanned two political realities in Poland: in 1989 Soviet-led Communism gave way to a political democracy based on Western models but the ideological base for the work, a theatre of ecology, has remained unchanged. Staniewski's theatre continues to respond to what he identifies as 'the temper of the times' through a dialogue between contemporary life and the philosophical and cultural ideas of historical periods in which Staniewski finds an enlightening correspondence.

This rich conflation of influences – environmental, historical and cultural, with echoes of a Romantic sensibility and a Bakhtinian subversion of the deadening and repressive political order – has helped shape Gardzienice's theatre model. In performance, the actors are the adept engineers of the theatrical language; it is through their skill, energy and extreme physical and vocal expression that the work is realised. And it is in the actor training that the values, aesthetics and principles of the work are embedded.

THE TRAINING

'Training with us is an open matter; there is no method in the sense of an applied normative system' (Staniewski 1987: 153). Staniewski avoids a formulaic approach to training. Each new phase serves to develop a new performance. His preliminary ideas; the themes, rhythms, songs and texts (including material gathered on expeditions) are worked on through the training: 'Training does not merely serve to prepare an actor for their role. It may be applied – for example, some acrobatic exercises can be transformed to become part of a role, to support the acting' (Taranienko 1997: 131).

But despite the fluidity of Gardzienice's training, two fundamental principles have consistently informed the work: musicality, with its complex relationship to the actor's physical and vocal technique; and mutuality – a particular way of perceiving.

Musicality

Staniewski defines the term 'musicality' as a specific feeling for music which corresponds with the Pythagorean concept of the harmonia mundi: 'I am utterly convinced that the earth is musical, that it has musicality and that every part of nature can be musical' (Staniewski 1993: 11). He regards musicality as the vital source for his theatre: 'everything in our theatre practice comes from musicality and ends in musicality' (Staniewski 1993: 31). It is Staniewski's belief that musicality has a spiritual significance, that the original power of life originated in sound, and that consequently sound and spirit are very closely connected.

This proposal, with its proximity to the Pythagorean cosmological view (and later that of the Renaissance) of an 'invisible harmony of the spheres', is a concept to which Gardzienice's work has repeatedly turned. Staniewski suggests that if the Gardzienice actors can achieve a sensibility to the musicality of the natural environment, they will find themselves within a language which is the essential sound of the natural world. This will allow them to re-act: to find the responsiveness which is integral to Gardzienice's 'naturalised' performance. Intuitive and instinctive processes of reaction are referred to in all aspects of Gardzienice's activities:

> I believe in instinct and intuition. Soon we will forget them. We will forget that they are parts of our nature. We already find for them sophisticated terms such as para-natural and para-psychical, and by alienating them from our human nature we cut the umbilical cord which holds us to our origins. But I believe that instinct and intuition are real and I also believe that they cannot exist without musicality.
>
> (Staniewski 1993: 11)

The actors do not attempt to imitate the sounds of nature but try to find their own organic rhythmic sounds and gestures that express states of body/consciousness. These are rehearsed repetitively with the precise momentum of a musical phrase. The actors are concerned with contacting their inner musicality – finding a personal melody which can lead their work.

The creative potential of this approach has received further confirmation through Staniewski's discovery of related techniques found in other cultures. Gardzienice has made several expeditions to Lapland where the Sami people are known for their unique vocal technique:

> Yoikers have a very particular way of expressing what they do with the voice. They never say what they are singing. They say that they are Yoiking. . . . Usually when we sing, we sing about something. They say rather that they are 'yoiking something'. . . . You are sitting in front of me and I can try to Yoik you. This does not mean that I improvise a song about you or that I try to describe you. It means, in my terms, that I am reading you. But it is a particular way of reading you, in which I am not thinking about you, so much as somehow trying to touch the spaces, the shapes of you, your measurements, your softness or hardness, your height, your nerves.
>
> (Staniewski 1993: 14)

Traditional songs, which are treated as living phenomena, are learnt orally and through repetition. The actors learn a particular way of singing which engages the whole body – a reflection of their encounters with people such as the Sami, where spontaneous movement and gesture frequently reinforce the song. Mariusz Gołaj stresses the importance of partnership: 'When you are singing with somebody all the time, you have to be in correspondence with the voice, with the rhythm, with the colour of the voice. You have to be mutual.' Singing forms the basis of the actor's technique; it initiates movement and therefore provides the opportunity for the actors to develop their skills. Gołaj continues: 'You are not controlling yourself by your dreams but by concrete situations; through music, your position in space, your relationship with your partner and with energy.'

The training is extended through exploring vocal phenomena such as breathing patterns, an actor's personal sounds (sighs, cries and shouts), rhythmic exercises based on laughter and ritualistic vocal traditions such as lamentation. The actors explore harmony, polyphony, antiphony and dissonance, rhythm and counterpoint. The work extends the actor's responsiveness. For example, antiphonal dialogue is concerned with a particular kind of partnership of actors *re-acting* to each other through the stimulus of the voice. The questions may be put in a variety of tones – provocative, conspiratorial, pleading – but in such a precise way that the partner is forced to respond or 'is obliged to answer'. Staniewski maintains that the deeper and more precise the question, the clearer the answer.

Mutuality

This obligation to answer – an unforced, impelling dynamic of musical reaction and interaction – is intimately bound with Gardzienice's second key principle: *mutuality*. Practised in all aspects of Gardzienice's activities, it is simply a way of perceiving, absorbing or dialoguing with a partner and, by extension, with the environment in which the actor works. Reminiscent of Martin Buber's[17] philosophy of 'I and Thou', the intersubjective process of encounter is not exclusively psychological but an attempt to absorb the wholeness of the person on a number of levels. By engaging in an intimate relationship with a partner, the actor develops subtle ways of communicating meaning beyond verbal language, through musicality, space, touch, gestures, sound, breath, rhythm and energy. Mutuality disallows Gardzienice's training process to become a system: 'Training, as I understand it, is necessarily a mutuality of two live presences. It is sharing energy, warmth. . . . How is it possible to make a method or a catalogue out of that?' (Staniewski 1987: 153).

The spine

Nevertheless, some elements of the training are permanent, in particular, the use of the spine. In colloquial Polish the spine is called 'the cross.' It is regarded as one of the most important parts of the body, as its foundation. Staniewski sees that it is the source of our basic human energy:

> We know that the strength and the power of life are located there. We know that work with the spine releases physical and mental energy. . . . The attitude (posture) of the cross when the solar plexus is exposed, is an attitude of questioning, inviting, it's a challenge, readiness, and the beginning and end of action. The importance of the cross for dialogue in partnership, for cooperation of one actor with another, is unquestionable. It evokes a certain state. Without it the work of one actor with another doesn't work; there's no true partnership, only an imitation of it; only token signs of it.
>
> (Taranienko 1997: 149)

Training often begins with a series of exercises which warm up and draw attention to the spine. Twists and turns are explored to facilitate the more acrobatic work that follows. During partnership work the spine becomes the origin of movement for the whole body, and this demands a total physical commitment. The actor is forced to communicate through this often unfamiliar focus, personally challenging and dismantling any preconceived self-image. The flexibility of the spine is maintained through rhythmical and flowing acrobatic exercises which enable the Gardzienice actors to fully explore the extreme physicality of their performance imagery. Furthermore, Staniewski is concerned with analysing the spine's cultural connotations:

> We began from the so-called Alexander Principle, but the really interesting things appeared when studying iconography during our work on *Avvakum* . . . In the entire Russian iconography, the human profile is reduced to a drawing of the 'cross'. If we were to 'undress' the figures presented [in the icons] from their clothes, their body mass, a sign of the cross would remain.
>
> (Taranienko 1997: 147)

Acrobatics

For Staniewski, acrobatic training is not only concerned with muscle building, flexibility or stamina; nor solely with the satisfaction of completing specific exercises.

It is an energising group situation in which the actor can affirm their fully articulate body through physical contact with others. Consequently, the particular exercises are not as important as the mutuality experienced through them. Acrobatics are practised in many different situations: both indoors and on the meadows of Gardzienice, as a morning wake-up, in the late afternoon or in preparation for a late evening rehearsal. The changes in circumstance alter the character of the exercise.

This is useful information for the actor who is tuning the instinctive and intuitive responses necessary for Staniewski's performances. Each time an exercise is done, it is a different experience. The moves may be the same but there is a new relationship, a new spine, body weight, time of day and not least the personal circumstances which an actor brings, all of which inform the quality of the contact made. Exercises are frequently broken down into smaller components. For example, the initial gesture of an actor signalling the execution of a handstand to the supporting partner may be practised many times before the move is carried out. It is the quality and intention of the action that is of prime importance – the execution is secondary.

Assistance

Acrobatic moves are assisted by a third (and sometimes a fourth) actor, who looks for the moments, and areas of the body, which might need additional support. Assistance is a vital element of the training and reinforces the sense of mutuality: that is, the necessity of being alert to the present action, responding instinctively to support others, ensuring safety and at the same time serving the action. Both the actions and intentions stemming from this find a resonance within the performances.

Figure 16.2 Physical morning training in the grounds with Włodzimierz Staniewski, Mariusz Gołaj and members of the Academy for Theatre Practices (2009).

Source: Gardzienice Theatre Archive, photo, Agnieszka Mendel.

Figure 16.3 Physical morning training in the grounds with Mariusz Gołaj and members of the Academy for Theatre Practices (2009).

Source: Gardzienice Theatre Archive, photo, Agnieszka Mendel.

Night running

All the training exercises stem from the symbiotic principles of mutuality and musicality. The activity which embodies the values of Gardzienice's training better than any other is night running. This process was introduced by Staniewski in the early stages of Gardzienice's training and has remained a constant touchstone ever since.

The night run is led by precise rhythms sustained through the stamping feet on chalk paths that lead into the forest. The group bunches in behind the leader, collectively affirming the initial rhythm through those who run behind and in front, sometimes in complete darkness. The ground may be uneven and unseen branches or logs may block a path; in such situations the actors run supporting each other with their arms. As the bodies warm up through the intimate, physical exertion, breathing becomes audible. The actors may stimulate counter rhythms through the breath which punctuate or play with those of the feet. The circulating energy and the organic rhythms that emerge from the common (and frequently playful) experience of the group are also responsive to the changing landscape. Night running can last for up to an hour or more.

> When you run through the night, when you run together with other people, you search for rhythms, for a common rhythm, for rhythm as dialogue, rhythms in which you look for the relationship with the person who is next to you, on your right side, on your left, ahead or behind of you. When you run, you search for certain dynamics which occur

through repetition, through the continuity of the breath, through continuous rhythms, as in *ostinato* in music, and you feel your inner self is growing, extending somehow.

(Staniewski 1993: 24)

As in the acrobatic and assistance exercises, there are elements both of danger and of safety within this situation. For some, the initial and unfamiliar experience of the dark – and the possibility of falling – can create a nervousness which needs to be overcome. This is countered by the care and physical contact maintained by the group, creating sensitivity amongst the participants. 'A particular mutuality is one kind of phenomenon which occurs during the running . . . your relationship to others is very strong; you feel that you are in a very intimate relationship with other people' (Staniewski 1993: 24).

At the same time, running through the forest puts actors in direct contact with the natural elements, whilst the reduction of visibility greatly enhances the other senses. Gołaj describes the experience:

> You experience nature through the senses. It's dark, you can't see the way. . . . You can feel the wind and you can hear the breathing and touch the bodies of partners. It's a very full experience which integrates the group and is also working on many levels. You have the feeling that you are dealing with nature, that you are part of it.

For Staniewski, the practice can also serve as an opportunity for testing material, part of the 'naturalising' process. Initially, pieces of music were introduced into the structure of the run – body gestures and scenes then followed. When it was impossible to incorporate these elements, they were done within pauses. Staniewski found this to be a way of rhythmicising work, of discovering how the performance material is directed by natural stimuli. He believes that actors make discoveries within this form of rehearsal that would not be possible in the closed rehearsal space: 'Suddenly the run creates an incredible pulsation of a given song . . . you are pumping your diaphragm, you are opening your throat – it happens naturally. You don't have to use artificial methods, you are naturally opening yourself. . . .'

When the night run is done prior to rehearsal, it 'awakens the body' and the breathing provides the concrete and audible link between the two experiences. In the rehearsal that follows, the action is energised through rhythmic coordination signalled by the exhalation of breath which supports each move. Actions are punctuated by the actors' musical and articulate language of breathing.

Night running is not exclusively intended for actor preparation. On a deeper level, the process is regarded as an existential one which embodies the fundamental values of Gardzienice's practice. Staniewski believes that it helps to develop the actor's perception:

> The gate of your perception is open, and in this way you can deal with many things around you. . . . Physiologically you could explain this by saying that your senses are reacting more sharply, that your blood is circulating more strongly.

(Staniewski 1993: 25)

This exposes what is perhaps the central project of Staniewski's work: that of accessing the *harmonia mundi*. He continues:

> It is comparable to the way Artaud talked about the multiplied actor, the actor who can transform himself into many existences, the atomised actor who can deal with many realities at one and the same time. I believe this is possible.
>
> (Staniewski 1993: 25)

Artaud's own appreciation of the physiological influence of nature on the artist was nowhere more evident than on his trip to Mexico in the 1930s. During a speech he gave in Mexico City he declared that:

> The organism of man functions in harmony with the organism of nature and governs it. And in so far as science and poetry are a single and identical thing, this is much the business of poets and artists as it is the business of scientists.
>
> (Artaud 1976: 373)

Whilst he was in Mexico, Artaud visited the Tarahumara Indians in the remote Sierra Madre region. He did not witness the running for which the Tarahumara are renowned, but his appreciation of an intense harmony between the landscape and its people was confirmed by Staniewski's own visit.[18]

> My trip . . . confirmed for me the truth of Artaud's heritage. It is the experience of a magical reality. The earth of the Tarahumara Indians has such a musical scenario, that everything that Artaud wrote should be considered a precise description.
>
> (Taranienko 1997: 143)

Staniewski was invited to participate in the Tarahumara's traditional *rara-muri* run. Whilst running is part of the Tarahumara's everyday existence, this particular event, where one lap can cover 12 kilometres, lasts for anything up to 16 hours. The main participants are divided into two teams and they run continuously throughout the night, by torch light:

> They run with naked feet . . . down through the valley and up through the rocky paths, quite high. Then they circle round and come back, making a kind of figure of eight . . . all the time kicking this ball, through the forest, up the mountains . . . It meant, to me, that running could be a way of living: . . . that during the run, life could be lived to the fullest.
>
> (Staniewski 1993: 23)

The causing actor

Gardzienice's concentration upon the expressive potential of the material body has led to the actors achieving a performance aesthetic drawn more from behavioural rather than psychological impulses. The concern is not with what could be explored within the actor's so-called 'inner, private emotions' but with what can be achieved through direct vocal and physical actions in relation to the external stimuli. Staniewski describes the actor's performance as principally based on 'facts'.

> I am concerned with the actor who causes facts. I very much like the word *Causer* instead of actor . . . In Polish *sprawca* is a minor hooligan . . . someone who did something, who has made something happen that is out of the ordinary and which has consequences . . .
>
> (Staniewski 1993: 25–26)

Staniewski's 'causing' actor demands, questions or provokes the partner (or the ensemble) to react to a song, word or action. Physically the actor must 'build a practice of actions similar to a musical score [. . .] the key to the character is one characteristic gesture or a certain behaviour' (Staniewski 2008). To find these emblematic patterns of behaviour, the actor refers not only to daily life but also to specific iconography chosen for each performance. The 'causing' sequences (which switch between action, word and song) created by one character are interwoven into a web of complementary themes and events by Staniewski which he frequently describes as a 'dramaturgical fugue'.

The acting model is much closer to Meyerhold's than to Stanislavsky's. A Gardzienice actor's rhythmicised, iconographic, causing sequence resonate with Meyerhold's externalized, codified actions driven by tempo-rhythm. Staniewski's 'truth' is sought in the allegorical theatre language *itself* rather than any attempt at self-examination or a faithful representation of daily life:

> [. . .] the causative moment comes when the first one of the two partners acts entirely for the second one. When a confessor has a confidant (regardless of hierarchy), a beloved has a lover, an afflicter has a wretch, a fighter has a foe or an ally, a beggar has a benefactor. I stop trying to 'be myself' because . . . I am 'with him or towards him'.
>
> (Staniewski 2008)

Through Staniewski's personal work with each actor, he slowly integrates the training into the complex layering of images, texts and songs that will constitute the performance. Within this intimate process Staniewski acts as a partner to the actor; challenging, encouraging, berating and questioning. Long-standing company member Joanna Holcgreber[19] recognises the deliberate challenge of Staniewski's rehearsal process:

> He gives the actor the space to create [. . .] He never shows the actor how to perform, though in the moments of desperation it happens (very rarely) that he does some actions himself and it is quite amazing. I mean he is very able to do many things but he doesn't want to treat the actor as a tool to realise his ideas [. . .] He leads the actor, giving him or her directions, 'signposts', suggesting the tools they can use; and later on being very demanding and sorely critical, and able to motivate the actor to use his or her potential that he or she didn't even realise existed. The tasks always seem at the beginning too difficult, even impossible to realise.[20]

Iconography

As the work has progressed, the cultural and historical references have widened. Staniewski acknowledges the need for the actor to begin with the particularity of their own culture but then to work in a broader field:

> in reference to that which is old, ancient, forgotten . . . somehow universal. So you have to have the ability to transcend your own culture. If somebody is saying, 'I am Swedish and that's me!' I am saying it means that the only thing you can do is contained within the limitations of today. It means nothing else, just a replica of today, a cliché. Ideally, I am going even further, not only demanding that you transcend your own culture, but your own sex. The real 'acting out' is when a man is able to break through the limitation of his male condition and assumptions, to reach the enigma of the female body. But, of course, you cannot find it without identifying with the female soul. And the same the other way round. This is not that big a revelation because it is the old knowledge; of Eastern theatre, of Ancient Greek theatre. But now it is extremely difficult to reach it.
>
> (Staniewski with Hodge 2004: 96)

One of the actor's main routes to the transcendence of their own culture is through understanding the philosophy and cultural themes of another. For Gardzienice, a specific historical period becomes a visual and aural source for new training. There have been four key periods, indigenous European (including influences from Brueghel and Chagall), Russian Orthodoxy, the Middle Ages and finally Ancient Greece (especially the iconography from the vase paintings: 6th to 4th centuries BC). By altering the dynamics of the body in each new performance era, the Gardzienice actor effectively recomposes it. This is a typically practical process which is based on physical training that corresponds with each new musical environment.

PERFORMANCE

Since the mid-1990s the orientation for Gardienice's theatre has shifted significantly from living sources to historical ones. Staniewski has led an artistic programme of research to 'excavate' the roots of Western theatre through a practical study of ancient Greek culture. Staniewski refers to this process as 'theatrical archaeology'. The Company has reanimated archaic forms of music and gesture, interwoven with classical texts. However, the reference points of ecology and indigeneity remain key coordinates; the archaic fragments of music were cross-fertilised with others from living Hucul and Peloponnesian cultures. And each performance continues to be 'naturalised' through this specific process of development.

Staniewski's most recent trilogy of performances reintroduce music and dance as central to the performance of Greek tragedy. Staniewski refers to these productions of *Metamorphoses*, *Elektra* and *Iphigenia at Aulis* as theatrical essays. Each performance is framed by a practical and theoretical introduction by Staniewski and the Company which enables the audience to follow the 'archeological' and organic process that led to the productions. For example, the actors' development of a vocabulary of expressive gestures corresponding to the vase paintings and supported by fragments of music are introduced, whilst images of the original vases are projected behind the actors. Staniewski refers to this latest development of gestural work as 'Cheirono-mia'.[21] In performance, each gesture involves the whole body and is punctuated with sound, breath and word as the actors move fluidly from one to another.

In *Iphigenia at Aulis*, the collective body enacts the Cheironomia which charge the events and actions. They can be performed with different energetic and rhythmic qualities: sometimes aggressively towards an individual character, at other times presented provocatively. Their function can be to reinforce plot themes, emotions and crisis points but can also serve as a leitmotif for individual characters. The Cheironomia has become the basis for the new performance language underpinning both *Elektra* and *Iphigenia at Aulis* and out of which individual character work emerges. Holcgreber recognises that for the actors, 'the training with iconography, the long intercourse with the images, creates a way of thinking with the body'. The alignment

Figure 16.4 Joanna Holcgreber presenting the cheironomia technique in relation to the image from an Ancient Greek vase.

Source: Gardzienice Theatre Archive, photo, Piotr Znamierowski.

of text, sound and body in these gestural sequences create a powerful energetic affect. Yana Sistovari-Zarifi acknowledges their complexity: 'This alphabet of gestures is not simply a set of word-image-movement-sound correspondences, but an ecstatic language rooted in the spirit as much as in the flesh.'[22]

Performances develop over a long period, 'naturalised' by the processes which surround them. In the recent series of Greek work, text has served a more central role than ever before. In *Iphigenia at Aulis*, Mariusz Gołaj plays Agamemnon.[23] He describes a detailed research process involving thematic discussions with Staniewski, close analysis of Agamemnon's speech and actions in Euripides' text, the study of imagery, exploring the character's mentality, making personal associations and finding emblematic actions. He searches for 'means, images, forms . . . in fact for every scene, every passage, every moment of silence'. Gołaj stresses three main points of orientation for the actor working on the role: the text, work with the partner and tasks set by Staniewski. The importance, Gołaj believes, is in the sense that the work is always open-ended:

> This work is unfinished, all the time stimulated by Włodek and the partners, invoking personal associations and emotions, images, gestures, postures - commemorated by centuries; people's feelings processed into a series of musical, rhythmical and kinesthetic sentences. Work on the character, work on the role, absolutely disciplined, aiming at an expressive effect.

In many ways the process of the Gardzienice actor's stylisation is similar to that of Japanese Noh Theatre, in which the performance is based on two potentially opposing forms: the lyricism of song and dance, and the reality of character type. The fluidity of movement complements the articulation of the character. In Gardzienice,

Figure 16.5 Staniewski's production of *Iphigenia at Aulis according to Euripides* (2007).

Source: Gardzienice Theatre Archive, Photo, Piotr Znamierowski.

the character emerges *through* the repetition of precise rhythms and iconography, and through the 'lines of life' of the songs. Mariusz Gołaj acknowledges that often his initial understanding of a role is through rhythm – a reflection of traditional cultures whose gestures are usually intimately connected to music. For him, it is from the precision of movement that the character's emotions evolve, although he never entirely loses himself in feeling: 'We can divide ourselves into different parts, part of me can be embraced by the task to be [the character], and part can have a distance or control, and ask – "what am I doing now?" '

Ultimately, it is not the music, the multi-layered performance text, nor the actor's interpretation of it which is of primary concern, but the interconnection of all these things. Staniewski stresses that: 'The issue, the subject, the theme is not only that which is spoken or written. It is the way of creating the whole world with the body, with the music, with the spine.' This is reminiscent of Artaud's recognition that the theatre's domain is a physical, rather than psychological, language. In saying this, however, Artaud was careful to insist that the argument should not be based on a straightforward comparison:

> This does not simply mean assessing whether theatre's physical language can attain the same psychological resolutions as words or whether it can not express emotions and feelings as well as words, but whether there are not attitudes in the field of intellect and thought which words cannot assume, which gestures and everything inclusive in this spatial language cannot attain with greater precision than them.
>
> (Artaud 1974: 52)

The articulate language in which Gardzienice's work is expressed is predicated on a particular state of presence which demands that the actor's 'gate of perception is open'. The actor must find a highly tuned state of instinctive response. Staniewski describes the actor's cognitive process as an intelligence 'of the heart'. Within the performance, the Gardzienice actor aims to achieve multiple states of presence, in order to deal with many realities simultaneously. This form of awareness goes beyond the notional duality of the actor's consciousness (identified in Diderot's paradox) to realise a heightened state of performance consciousness which Artaud had reached for as an ideal.

Gardzienice's work is a realisation of a form of theatre which, Staniewski believes, defies the reductive tendencies of contemporary Western culture. Commentators have found that it manages to reconnect the actor with instinctive processes and invites the audience to experience the work, not solely intellectually, but through all the senses. Others have recognised Gardzienice's reconnection with everyday life, with actors and their environment and, in performance, reality with transcendence.

Notes

1   *An Evening Performance* (Spektakl Wiełczorny) 1997, *Sorcery* (Gusła) 1981, *The Life of Archpriest Avvakum* 1983, *Carmina Burana* 1990, *Metamorphoses or The Golden Ass* (According to Lucius Apuleius) 1997, *Elektra* by Euripides 2002, *Iphigenia at Aulis* by Euripides 2007.

2   See Paul Allain 1997: back cover.

3   See Włodzimierz Staniewski with Alison Hodge (2004): 1.

4   Włodzimierz Staniewski was born in Bardo, Poland in 1950. He graduated in Humanities from Kraków University before becoming an actor in the renowned student theatre group, Teatr STU. From 1970 to 1976 Staniewski collaborated with Jerzy Grotowski in his Laboratory Theatre's paratheatrical projects before leaving to form Gardzienice Theatre Association in 1977.
5   The speech was made at the congress of the International Theatre Institute in Sofia, Bulgaria, 1979.
6   An extract from an unpublished paper 'Theatre Practices in Relation to Ecology' given by Staniewski at the International Theatre Symposium, September 1991, Gardzienice, Poland.
7   Extract from 'Theatre of the Ruins', a speech Staniewski made in June 1996 at an international training workshop in Gardzienice.
8   A second extract from Staniewski's 1979 speech in Bulgaria.
9   Extract taken from DVD (2004) *Gardzienice Practicing the Humanities*.
10   Ecos form the Greek *Oikos*, meaning habitation, home, place or world.
11   From a speech made by Leszek Kolankiewicz 'On Gardzienice', presented at the International Theatre Meetings, Warsaw, 1988.
12   Co-founder Tomasz Rodowicz was a leading actor with the group from its inception. He was Staniewski's close collaborator in the musical research, and in establishing the first group. He left Gardzienice in 2004 and leads the Theatre Association Chorea.
13   The informal ensemble was initially composed of Włodzimierz Staniewski, Tomasz Rodowicz, Jan Tabaka, Wanda Wróbel, Waldemar Sidor, Jan Bernad, Henryk Andruszko.
14   Unless otherwise stated, all quotes from Mariusz Gołaj are taken from a personal interview with the author in Ghent, July 1998.
15   See Mikhail Bakhtin's seminal work: *Rabelais and His World*, 1965, trans. Hélène Iswolsky, Cambridge, MA: MIT Press.
16   *Avvakum* was based on the life of the Russian Archpriest, Avvakum. His autobiography is regarded as one of the masterpieces of 17th Century Russian literature.
17   Martin Buber (1878–1965) Austrian-born Hasidic theologian who articulated a philosophy of encounter.
18   Staniewski visited the Tarahumara Indians in 1987. His participation in the ritual of running is fully discussed in his interview with Peter Hulton (Arts Archives 1993).
19   Joanna Holcgreber has been a core member of Gardzienice since 1995.
20   All quotes from Johanna Holcgreber are taken from a personal interview conducted in April 2009.
21   *Cheironomia*, after the ancient art of gesture depicted in Egyptian hieroglyphs.
22   The extract is from Yana Sistovari-Zarifi's forthcoming chapter, 'Staniewski's Secret Alphabet of Gestures – Dance, Body and Metaphysics', to be published in 2010 in Fiona Macintosh (ed.), *The Ancient Dancer in the Modern World: Responses to Greek and Roman Dance*, Oxford University Press.
23   Mariusz Gołaj's comments on his role as Agamemnon come from a personal interview conducted in April 2009.

Bibliography

Allain, Paul (1997) *Gardzienice: Polish Theatre in Transition*, London: Harewood Academic Publishers.
Artaud, Antonin (1974) 'Oriental and Western Theatre', in *The Theatre and its Double*, London: Calder and Boyars, pp. 50–54.
—— (1976) 'Artaud in Mexico', in S. Sontag (ed.), *Selected Writings*, New York: Farrar, Straus and Giroux.
Bakhtin, Mikhail (1965) *Rabelais and His World*, trans. Hélène Iswolsky, Cambridge, MA: MIT Press.
Filipowicz, Halina (1987) 'Gardzienice: A Polish Expedition to Baltimore', *The Drama Review*, 113 (1): 137–63.
Gough, Richard and Christie, Judy (eds) (1989) Gardzienice Theatre Association booklet, to accompany 1989 UK and Ireland tour, Cardiff: Centre for Performance Research.
Hunt, A. (1993) 'An Introduction', in *Gardzienice, Poland*, Włodzimierz Staniewski, in conversation with Peter Hulton, ed. Dorinda Hulton, Exeter: Arts Archives, Arts Documentation Unit.

Kolankiewicz, L. (1978) 'On the Road to Active Culture', trans. B. Taborski, unpublished collection of papers, Wrocław: Instytut Laboratorium.

—— (1977) 'What's up at Grotowski's?' in *The Theatre in Poland*, 5–6: 24–25.

Kumiega, J. (1987) *The Theatre of Grotowski*, London and New York: Methuen.

Mickiewicz, Adam (1986) 'Lectures on Slavic Literature Given at the Collège de France', introd. and trans. Daniel Gerould, *The Drama Review*, 111 (3): 92–97.

Sistovari-Zarifi, Y. (2010) 'Staniewski's Secret Alphabet of Gestures – Dance, Body and Metaphysics', in Fiona Macintosh (ed.), *The Ancient Dancer in the Modern World: Responses to Greek and Roman Dance*, Oxford: Oxford University Press.

Staniewski, Włodzimierz (1987) 'Baltimore Interview with Richard Schechner', *The Drama Review*, 113 (1): 137–63.

Staniewski, Włodzimierz (1993) *Gardzienice, Poland*, Włodzimierz Staniewski in conversation with Peter Hulton, ed. Dorinda Hulton, Exeter: Arts Archives, Arts Documentation Unit.

Staniewski, Włodzimierz with Hodge, Alison (2004) *Hidden Territories: The Theatre of Gardzienice*, book and CD-Rom, London and New York: Routledge.

Staniewski, Włodzimierz (2007) *Gardzienice: Practising the Humanities, a Theatrical Essay*, DVD, Lublin: Gardzienice Archives.

Staniewski, Włodzimierz (2008) 'Obecno 岌 aktora' ('The Presence of the Actor'), in Malgorzata Dziewulska (ed.) *VIth volume of lectures, in the Warsaw National Theatre*, Warsaw: National Theatre.

Strausbaugh, J. (1986) 'Feast of a Fest', *The Baltimore City Paper*, 6 June: 30.

Taranienko, Z. (1997) *Gardzienice: Praktyki Teatralne Włodzimierza Staniewskiego*, Lublin: Wydawnictwo Test (unpublished trans. A. Zubryzcka).

Zeami, Motokiyo (1984) *On the Art of the Nō Drama: The Major Treatises of Zeami*, introd. and trans. J. Thomas Rimer and Yamasaki Masakazu, Princeton, NJ: Princeton University Press.

Website

Gardzienice's website: www.gardzienice.art.pl

Chapter 17

Royd Climenhaga

ANNE BOGART AND SITI COMPANY:
CREATING THE MOMENT

CONTEXT

DIRECTOR ANNE BOGART OFTEN ascribes the start of her theatre career to a transformative moment when, as a teenager, she saw Adrian Hall's 1968 production of *Macbeth* during his tenure as Artistic Director at Trinity Rep in Providence, Rhode Island. Though she says she did not understand what was happening, she was nonetheless drawn into the event through the actors' energy and focus, and the carefully crafted staging of the work. She realised that 'theatre is not about understanding what's going on. It's about meeting something you don't know.' (Bogart 2001c: 2) She has developed that simple idea throughout her varied career, creating work that reclaims theatre as an arena for action in which audiences are communally engaged, rather than consuming a product that is presented to them.

Bogart began to apply creative developmental techniques to her directing early in her career. In 1972 she attended Bard College, where she created a collage-based reflection on Ionesco for her senior thesis production, and joined Via Theatre, a group dedicated to exploring Jerzy Grotowski's ideas and techniques. After graduation she moved to New York, where she began work in the experimental hotbed of the downtown theatre scene. She worked on her Masters degree at New York University in the Department of Drama (soon to become the Department of Performance Studies), which was led by Richard Schechner. After receiving her Masters, Bogart began teaching in the newly formed Experimental Theatre Wing at the university, and developed her experimental techniques in pieces with the students there.

Bogart went through a period of intense interest in contemporary German theatre at this point, particularly that of Peter Stein. She incorporated ideas of the German avant-garde into her own directing, and was eventually invited to Germany to continue her work in this area. But while in Europe, Bogart suddenly realised the importance of her identity as an American – not simply because it was the place she came from, but more profoundly because of her awareness of how America had shaped the way she thought and moved. She returned to New York and worked at a series of venues, directing radical adaptations of plays and musicals, creating new works, exploring site-specific theatrical events and, throughout the 1980s, establishing herself as a director of uncommon vision.

In spite of her growing reputation as an experimental director, Bogart was asked to take over from the retiring Adrian Hall as Artistic Director of the more conventional Trinity Rep. Her first and only season in the large, regional theatre was full of daring and iconoclastic works, created with many of her friends from the downtown theatre world, which inevitably alienated the largely conservative subscriber base. After a battle with the Board, Bogart agreed to leave, but, despite the trauma of that chaotic season, she considers that year a defining moment in her career. It propelled her into a new league of artistic possibility, working at respected theatres both in New York and regionally.

Among the new opportunities was one that combined many of her past interests: she collaborated with playwright Charles L. Mee and producer Anne Hamburger[1] to create the site-specific *Another Person is a Foreign Country*. This pageant play of outsider status paired Mee's interests in collage structure with Bogart's ideas of presentational staging. The piece created a new form of theatrical engagement housed in and around the run-down courtyard of the abandoned Towers Nursing Home on the Upper West Side of Manhattan. The innovation lay in the choice of space, the material, and the actors, many of whom were drawn from non-theatrical backgrounds and noticeably identified with various qualities of 'difference': blind, dwarf, transvestite, or simply a seventy-two-year-old retirement home resident who stumbled upon rehearsal one day and asked to be in the piece. The performers essentially played a version of themselves. This created an arena for exploring the very nature of theatricality that Bogart had been disassembling to that point. Although much of her later work would not as radically re-imagine the theatrical act of presentation, the qualities of this work ushered in many of the concerns that Bogart has continued to develop for the rest of her career.

This idea of 'engagement' has led Bogart to conceive of orchestrating time and space differently from more conventional directing practices. In her work, the stage space shifts to become an open invitation rather than a place of telling. The articulation of a world is still vitally important, but the emphasis changes from directing that communication outwards, to inviting the audience in. Creating an environment where you can 'meet something you don't know' demands a different set of tactics from the director, both in her staging and in the preparatory work with actors. As Scott Cummings has noted, 'she directs plays with the mind of a choreographer, scoring the motion of bodies in time and space with a keen eye towards rhythm, visual composition, and other formal principles' (Cummings 2006: 6).

This emphasis on the active physical condition of the actor in time and space leads to a vital connection between an actor and his or her body. Actor/director and teacher Cecil O'Neal claims that the 'physical connectedness her people use answers an increasing problem in young people we see today. They simply have no connection with their bodies. All vanity, no sensuality' (qtd. in Anderson 2008: 81).

Bogart's directing process has utilised and adapted The Viewpoints as developed by Mary Overlie at NYU (see below). Beyond its impact on her directing work, Bogart's version of Viewpoints creates the potential for a dynamic base in actor training; one that is continually expanding in undergraduate theatre programs in America, and that has aroused considerable interest elsewhere. Still, Viewpoints training is only one leg on which the work stands.

In 1990 Bogart was asked to go to Japan to meet with director Tadashi Suzuki[2] and to see his work. Though she didn't know it at the time, Suzuki was looking for a collaborator to start a new international theatre enterprise, and Bogart was invited. The two agreed that the operating principles would be a combination of Suzuki's own training methods and Bogart's approach, resulting in a company of actors equally trained in both disciplines. They established an American base at Skidmore College in Saratoga Springs, NY, creating the Saratoga International Theatre Institute (SITI). After the initial productions were performed in Japan and at Skidmore, the company set up its permanent home in New York City as SITI Company.

Inherent in the formation of this company was the importance of ongoing training and teaching. Most of the actors had been training in Suzuki's rigorous physical technique and had combined that with Viewpoints training, while a few performers who had worked with Bogart previously were introduced to Suzuki's training. The emphasis on training was built into SITI's mission statement:

- to create bold new productions
- to perform and tour these productions nationally and internationally
- to train together consistently
- to train theatre professionals and students in an approach to acting that forges unique and highly disciplined artists for the theatre
- to create opportunities for artistic dialogue and cultural exchange.

(Bogart 2007: 44)

Bogart and her company members always express disbelief at the lack of ongoing training for actors. 'Dancers have barre work. Singers do their scales. Musicians wouldn't dream of not practising. Yet we think because we can walk and we can talk, that we can act' (Bogart 2001c: 15). The training is a means of building awareness and presence on stage and in the moment. It is a vital part of the work, but it shouldn't be confused with performance itself. The plays and new works that SITI develops are underpinned by the training they share, but each piece addresses its own needs in staging. 'Training helps you play characters, situations, create new forms, but it's not about doing a play in a style of Viewpoints or Suzuki or whatever it is' (Bogart 2001c: 16).

After training together and performing new works in Japan and in America for four years, the company expanded and began touring. It also created specific teaching situations to further the practice and integration of its training. The summers spent in Saratoga Springs from 1991 to 1995 led to a Summer Intensive Training programme, which has grown to include around sixty people working with Bogart and company members on a mixed course of Suzuki training, Viewpoints and Composition work. The company also offers training sessions in New York, Los Angeles and elsewhere, with individual company members teaching at a variety of schools around the country as well.

Today SITI Company keeps a hectic schedule of touring, developing new work, the Summer Intensive and other training sessions and outside work. Despite the demands of such as schedule, the emphasis on training is reinforced, with the group becoming more determined to find time to work, to train and to grow together. They carefully guard the Summer Intensive as a time to come together and focus on training. Several company members also try to make regular return visits to Japan to re-establish contact with Suzuki training at its source.

SITI Company actors are trained to be open to the world that surrounds them and to contribute to the creative process. Ever wary of imposing a stated objective on the ensemble, Bogart works to create the conditions that allow for action and then gives the actors the necessary openness to exist in that moment, and to be alive in it. This is a key part of the training, and is achieved through concentration on the details of presence. Too many actors work to achieve emotion, thinking 'If I feel it, the audience feels it.' As Bogart says, 'I feel more and more militantly against the Americanized, misunderstood version of Stanislavsky we seem to suffer under' (Bogart 2001a: 2). Bogart prefers to focus on details and let the emotional component come out of the precision, intensity and focus of the stage action. She continues:

> I don't get actors to emotional places. I try to create an environment in which many-colored emotions might occur. I find that if I try to *make* emotions happen, the environment is cheapened. So I try to create the circumstances in which emotions can be free. Now what I find is, in rehearsal, if you concentrate on detail, things start happening. The trick is to keep working on *something*. And eventually the emotions that need to happen – the arc of the scene – emerges, not because you're trying to make it happen, but because you're taking care of the things around it.
>
> (Bogart 2001a: 5)

This emphasis on detail is combined with a more expansive questioning of the basic assumptions of what is occurring on stage. Bogart explains that her study of sociology and anthropology (in the form of a nascent Performance Studies program at NYU) was in fact the best director training possible. 'To actually think, what are we doing instead of how do we do it' (Bogart 2001c: 4). That exploration of the very nature of the work comes up time and again in rehearsals as actors are pushed to consider the impact of the act they create on stage, but it is always grounded by an equally in-depth questioning of the specificity of the action and the way it exists on stage. 'What is it? and What is it really?' become the common mantra of the actor at work on SITI Company pieces (Cummings, 2006: 226). What are the basic assumptions and generative conditions that create this moment, and what is actually happening on stage? Part of SITI's training is always focused on opening up this level of exploration.

A further component of Bogart's work is the necessity of spontaneity and reacting to the moment. She describes it in terms borrowed from choreographer Yoshiko Chuma,[3] who would set certain parameters and then turn to her dancers and energetically prod them with '1, 2, 3 – GO!' (qtd. in Cummings 2006: 235). The point is to respond viscerally to the conditions that have been set and let something happen, bypassing a more intellectual response to get at the essential core of the action. The initial reaction creates something to work with and against, developing into a continuing network of response.

Bogart's work with her company requires and feeds off of this intricate balance of specificity and openness, spontaneity and permanence. Once something is dis-covered in rehearsal, it is meticulously crafted into a concrete and repeatable moment on stage, brought to life through the active presence of the actor.

THE TRAINING [4]

SITI Company training entails the married practices of Suzuki work and Viewpoints. Both disciplines are kept separate, yet they intersect at complementary points of awareness and presence and combine to create something much deeper than either individual practice. Composition work builds on this foundation, and moves it towards performance in the form of creative exercises with participants in the Summer Intensive, and as a developmental practice for the company in creating new work.

For Bogart, training is in part about tapping into a hidden reservoir of experience and finding ways to connect to it. Her belief is that we are creative heirs to the invisible history of our theatrical past. 'The theatre carries its own history inside of itself. Every performer's body contains every body that ever performed' (Bogart 2007: 121). Each moment in performance is built on a past that runs deep, both personally and collectively. Training also enables you to bring your own past into the moment and to build a shared past with a collaborative ensemble.

Both Suzuki and Viewpoints training highlight the actor as a point of attention and awareness. You respond in the moment to the stimuli around you, and you practice to build your perceptual awareness of yourself (Suzuki training) and your connection with others and the world around you (Viewpoints training). It is that multivalent engagement that leads toward a sense of aliveness on stage, and it comes out of hard and regular work. Ultimately, you work toward presence, toward being alive in the moment. Company member Leon Ingulsrud explains:

> There is something that . . . when you take away the costume, the play, the production, character, there is still acting – that there is something fundamental that an actor is doing that exists even when you strip all the trappings away from it. There is still that core of energy in the activity called 'acting' that is discernable from daily life, and that is not dependant on the behavior of a character.
>
> (qtd. in Bond 2002: 247)

The core of energy that Ingulsrud describes comes out of the connection between individual awareness and the group. Viewpoints training, in particular, helps to develop open awareness and your responsibility to creating a group dynamic. Ellen Lauren describes what she gets from Viewpoints as a 'sense of compassionately working toward revelation in the other' (qtd. in Bond 2002: 249). The combined elements of Suzuki training and Viewpoints help her as an individual actor to find her own placement, but also to reach out and find completion in the combined effect of mutual support in collaboration.

Suzuki training

Suzuki training begins with the actor's grounded connection to the earth. Specific exercises are developed to help actors identify and work from their centre as a generative connection to movement, breath, and placement in space. Most people associate Suzuki work with the heavy stomping that connects the body to the earth through the forceful release of energy and the resonance of striking the flat of the foot against the floor. It is certainly the most dynamic part of the training, but Suzuki gives

Figure 17.1 Suzuki Training with Ellen Lauren, Stephen Webber, Will Bond, SITI company.
Source: Photo, Michael Brosilow.

equal emphasis to the preparation before the release, the held tension of a sitting or standing statue, the immediacy of action in hitting a position, and the controlled release of tension in a slow up or down motion or movement across the space.

The training is as much about awareness and placement as it is about exertion. Many of the activities are indeed physically taxing, the more so because they require as much control as they do force. Each exercise becomes a personal assessment of where and who you are at that given moment, and how you are in your body. The positions of the body for basic exercises #1, #2, #3, or #4 (all essentially quick reactions to gather energy, and forceful stomps to release) are specific, but geared to the actor's own body. The position I take will be different than that of the person next to me, though they are both moving toward an ideal toward which we both reach. The teachers may be closer to that ideal through more extensive practice, but they too are testing themselves against criteria that can never be completely met. You do not arrive at perfection – you are in a constant struggle to get closer to it. The work is not about achieving something so much as being present in the effort to achieve something.

The training combines work on those stomping postures, walks across the floor in various poses, standing and seated statues from positions of held tension (often involving speech in the moment of extremis), slow movements across the floor, and combinations of these actions in narrative exercises. Teachers maintain a respectful and disciplined environment and you quickly leap into action, often without much prior explanation, figuring things out as you go. You put yourself in the moment and are forced to respond to how you are in your own body. You have to find a point of integration if you are to continue.

What appears to be one of the simplest exercises actually draws on all levels of an actor's awareness to achieve its grace and beauty. The Slow Cross begins with two groups of performers standing in lines at either side of the stage. As music starts, you

Figure 17.2 Suzuki Training with Barney O'Hanlon, Stephen Webber, SITI company.

Source: Photo, Michael Brosilow.

move across the floor as a group, intersecting and passing through the other group at centre stage before reaching the other side, turning and heading back. The difficulty comes both in the attempt to regulate your own cross so that it is a slow and constant progression, giving the appearance that you are slowly gliding across the space, and in working collectively as a group to reach your destination in unison. The basic parameters of this cross were developed from the image of a ghost in Japanese drama, and the goal is to create a sense of that ghost-like progression, so that when you reach the opposite wall it feels as if you could just as easily keep gliding on right through it. To achieve this, you need to be keenly aware of your centre of gravity and carefully work to allow it to describe a straight line steadily moving forward. With your knees bent, you move forward with consistent fluid steps, holding tension through each step in order to achieve the shared quality of slow motion. The ethereal quality of consistent motion is nearly impossible to sustain, but only nearly, so that you are constantly checking yourself against the potential for success and continually working to get closer to the ideal. You have both to work from within your own body and maintain a degree of objectivity in order to monitor your progression across the floor.

All of that would be challenging enough, but the real grace and beauty of the exercise come in the quality of unified movement. While focusing awareness on your own presence in the moment, you also need to constantly observe those around you, so that your movement across the space is as unified as possible. The goal is to create a singular line, like a bank of fog that rolls out across the floor and intersects with that other line of ghosts coming toward you at the precise centre of the stage, heading to the opposite side and turning in unison both with your group and with the others on whom your back is now turned. It is the simplest and yet most profound act of collaboration to give yourself over to the group and become one with the inexorable movement across the stage and back. The apparent simplicity of this exercise belies the monumental act of engaged bodily presence, awareness, and expression. When executed with conviction it becomes beautiful to watch, simply to see what comes from actors fully committed to an act of collaborative presence. Acting, in this instance, is literally doing, but it is not what you accomplish that affects an audience so much as the quality of your investment in the act itself.

The Viewpoints

Viewpoints requires an equal level of entering into the moment and as disciplined a focus as Suzuki training, but the emphasis is more on an open awareness and interaction with others in the room (and the room itself). Rather than fixed exercises or body postures, the training here consists of awakening a consciousness of specific qualities of presence in time and space and being responsive to them, usually in a more improvisatory way. There are some specific exercises to help isolate individual Viewpoints, but mostly the aim is a balance of multiple possibilities sustained for a number of people. As you progress, Viewpoints can lead toward more direct connections to the play or piece being developed through the incorporation of character relationships, language, and elements from the world of the performance.

Mary Overlie was the first to identify Viewpoints as a method of training and developing performance, derived from her work as a dancer and choreographer in the New York Modern Dance scene of the 1970s. Overlie articulated six fundamental aspects of dance practice that she called the Viewpoints of Space, Story, Time, Emotion, Movement and Shape (SSTEMS). She based her creation of performance on audience perception. 'The first tenet of this system is that the audience's perceptual abilities provide the basis for the structuring of performance. The audience in this analysis is not cast in social or cultural modes, but is defined by the perceptual potential they bring to the performance situation' (Overlie undated: 1). Overlie continued to develop her work on the Six Viewpoints with Wendell Beavers, with whom she collaborated on new pieces at Danspace Project in New York. She also experimented with different strategies as a teacher in the Experimental Theatre Wing at New York University.

Working with Tina Landau,[5] Bogart redirected and expanded the original Six Viewpoints into nine more formal qualities of stage presence broken into two categories:

- Viewpoints of Space: Shape, Gesture (further broken into Expressive and Behavioural Gesture), Architecture, Spatial Relationship and Topography
- Viewpoints of Time: Tempo, Duration, Kinaesthetic Response and Repetition.

Although consideration of these various points of awareness is constantly in flux, the basic nine Viewpoints have remained the cardinal points of departure of SITI Company's training.

The first thing you notice in initial work with Viewpoints training is the degree to which you are forced to let go of preparatory thinking in order to simply react. You work to juggle multiple awareness, leaving you to experience the connections you create with others in the room as you create them. 'Things happen' in Viewpoints work and, without foresight, you need to let things happen, see them happening, and then respond simultaneously.

This is the main component of the Viewpoint of kinaesthetic response – an awakening of physical and visceral connection where you feel the appropriate action to take and respond before you have the chance to intellectualise the consequences of your action. Someone walks by and, without thinking, you follow, only to turn sharply when someone across the room sits down. But in that seemingly unrelated string of actions, relationships are built that lead to the next action, until mini-dramas of visceral intent are played out. That level of response, placed within the formal condition of your existence in space and time, is the engine that drives Viewpoints work. As Bogart says, 'you cannot make things happen; you can only create the circumstances in which something might occur' (Bogart 2007: 54).

One simple exercise that helps to isolate kinaesthetic awareness involves working with groups of five or seven performers. Each performer is given a lane to work within and a series of simple actions: standing, walking, squatting. You move back and forth within your lane, starting, stopping, squatting, but attempt to open up your awareness and let the actions of others dictate when you perform any given action. There is no right or wrong response, but you train your own focus to relinquish choice and allow outside elements to dictate the conditions of the experience. You may respond to the person in the lane next to you, or to someone across the room, so that you are working individually but creating a group dynamic of interaction. There are series of exercises intended to help isolate individual Viewpoints and provide practice at keeping awareness open. After you establish a familiarity with one Viewpoint, you add another, and another, until you are juggling multiple levels of awareness.

Once a working vocabulary of the nine Viewpoints is in place, open Viewpoints work usually begins with the class leader simply stating 'Five up'. As in Suzuki class, there is no hesitation, you jump up to become part of the work, and after some jockeying to arrive at the desired five actors (or seven or nine, as the case may be) you establish a spatial relationship with each other and with the architecture in the room. SITI Company often works with music in open Viewpoints that you carefully play with and against, never letting it dictate the action, but feeling the weight of its presence and mood and responding to it. Someone initiates an action, from walking across the space, to sitting down, to creating a shape with their body, to jumping, and that sets off the chain reaction of responses that come as a process of your own awareness of the various Viewpoints of space and time as well as your growing relationship with the group. You are carried along on the stream of reactions and interactions.

There are times when not much takes place in a Viewpoints session, and others when there are strings of poignant moments that seem to come from nowhere. In both cases, however, you continue to develop your capacity to see more broadly outside of yourself, to constantly focus on your relationship with others, and to respond in the moment through active awareness. With continued work, those traits begin to become ingrained in your body, and this is what you bring to the rehearsal process and, finally, into performance. You work to create a more live sense of presence.

Equally important to the Viewpoints class is the time you spend watching others work, looking for moments from the outside and being able to see how a world, a relationship, a connection is expressed. It teaches you to see with fresh eyes and begin to recognise connections not readily apparent. Concentrating on the exactness of various elements of the stage and the way they are drawn together has the effect of slowing down time, giving you the chance to see the world as it rushes past you. You can pay attention to those connections from the perspective of an audience member from the outside, or from within, where you are now poised to act in response. Viewpoints work enhances your listening, with all your senses and perceptions. Bogart describes this trait as 'listening with the whole body'. The actor brings attention to the world around them and the growing dynamic connection to others in the room, and out of that heightened presence, things happen. In the midst of a situation, all elements of the work coalesce into an overall conscious liveness.

A class leader may choose to emphasise certain facets of the work or add in restraints or new elements. The environment changes when a few chairs are added to the mix, or if you can use speech. When adding in speech, for instance, restricting available utterances to a few lines from the play you are considering allows for their more spontaneous inclusion. Simply allowing any speech handcuffs the participants by forcing them to make prior choices and doesn't allow them to react in the moment. By the time you make a choice, the moment is gone and you are not able to ride the wave of the action that happens in spite of you. You are trying to dictate action rather than to let things happen. Restricting possible speech to a few set lines reduces the decision to two options, to speak or not, and that is something that can happen faster than the speed of thought, creating an event that you then commit to fully.

In teaching Viewpoints, SITI Company members stress the importance of recognising the point of focus in the developing scene, or 'Who's Hamlet,' as it is known. As the exercise develops, someone becomes the point of focus. They are Hamlet for the moment. The others recognise this and add to the moment as it is created, supporting the scene until it shifts and the spotlight falls on someone else.

Building familiarity with that dynamic interplay of energies is invaluable as you work to create compelling moments on stage. Groups like SITI Company who have worked together in this way for years are able to easily discover a balance with each other on stage, but I have seen the increased potential that even a short introduction to Viewpoints work can provide an ensemble of actors.

Bogart and SITI Company members underscore open awareness in Viewpoints training and in letting the form itself dictate the content. Any context that is created comes from response to the elements and the developing action in the room, and relies on the varied formal facets of space and time. Wendell Beavers visited our class during the Summer Intensive in which I participated and offered a slightly different perspective. Working from two of Overlie's original six Viewpoints, Emotion and Story, you enter into the created world from another angle. Attuning yourself to story and emotion is dangerous territory and can easily lead toward attempts to dictate response but, carefully handled, they can also add new dimensions to the experience. One important point of focus that uncovers these other Viewpoints is eye contact. The choice to look, or look away and look again immediately sets up relationships and imminent stories that you still respond to as they develop in the moment, but that can carry you in different directions than the formal elements alone.

During work on *Who Do You Think You Are*, SITI Company's recent piece about the brain, Bogart invited eminent neurophysiologist R. Grant Steen to a Viewpoints workshop and rehearsal. Steen commented afterward: "What I was just watching on stage is how neurons in the brain function" (qtd. in Anderson 2008: 82). Bogart immediately made the connection to her own study of neurons and how synaptic pathways are created to arrange sensory information into perceptual experience. Entering into that process through training in Viewpoints reorients your being, according to Bogart, and provides a means by which an audience can participate in the paradigm shift of theatrical meaning. We are redefining the ways in which theatre functions and how we create meaning through live presence. Viewpoints training puts us in the midst of that perceptual re-imagination.

Composition

If Suzuki training and Viewpoints are the two feet upon which Bogart and SITI Company's work stand, Composition fleshes out the process in bringing life to an established script or developing new work. As with Viewpoints, Composition was born from the fertile period of performance experimentation in Greenwich Village in the 1960s. Bogart derived her sense of Composition work from her teacher at Bard, Aileen Passloff. An active member of the interdisciplinary dance/theatre/ performance scene and known for her collaborations with visual artists and musicians, Passloff began teaching a class in Composition when she arrived at Bard in 1969. Like John Cage's influential Composition classes taught at the New School a decade before, Passloff defined performative Composition as 'putting things together, putting one thing after another, listening to what the content is so you can find out what form it needs to take' (qtd. in Cummings 2006: 126). Composition exercises consist of integrating a list of components, from specific props to attitudes and actions, in order to create new performance pieces that explore the base of the larger work at hand. Bogart may ask her cast to devise short pieces in rehearsal, having been given some constituent parts that relate to the play and twenty minutes in which to work. In the Summer Intensive, we were given a week to work in small groups, devising pieces with elements drawn from *A Midsummer Night's Dream*, SITI's forthcoming performance.

For one Composition exercise, we were asked to include: an offstage action; twenty seconds of stillness; fifteen seconds of top-speed talking; fifteen seconds of simultaneous unison action; fifteen seconds of laughter/crying; reference to a Depression-era photo (SITI Company was basing its work in the dustbowl experience in America in the 1930s); the disorientation of love; something very loud; fighting off a lack of sleep; five interruptions; a meeting that causes physical change; a midstream change of allegiance via magic; a play within a play; sex; someone becoming a donkey without 'physical stuff'; a chase scene; the idea that it is hot and late at night; and the presence of the moon. The whole piece was to take on the structure of a dream, with the actors moving through roles from Mechanicals to Athenians to Fairies and the Director as Puck. All of the text came from Shakespeare's play, but could be chopped up and rearranged in any way we saw fit. We had to use the black box theatre we were rehearsing in, and the piece could only be ten minutes, maximum.

Many of the active formal components, such as twenty seconds of stillness, return in many composition exercises, and Bogart has found they are helpful in delineating stage actions and creating interesting choices. The elements that are derived from the source itself are often a means to find what fits. Gathering up various materials that come from the ensemble's reaction to either an established play or a broader idea under consideration creates the opportunity to experiment and test the impact and weight that certain elements bring to an imagined context. Bogart explains this process of inclusion through what she calls 'Vice'. While filming the stylish 1980s television crime drama *Miami Vice*, the art director determined whether elements worked within the production concept (Vice), or whether they fell outside the tight stylistic palette under which the show was constructed (not Vice). For Bogart, the theatrical world is created through similar means of inclusion, and Composition exercises, in part, help to determine what is or is not 'Vice.'

But the idea extends beyond merely design considerations. Within a Dustbowl-inspired *Midsummer*, a women standing in the corner quietly singing a sad folk ballad from the 1930s may be 'Vice'. A madcap race through the space with opening and closing doors as a devilish sound man manipulates the action from above may be 'Vice'. Or both may work in the context of the composition exercise, but not fit within the larger context of the piece. The elements that are created may be brought wholesale into the developing work, but more often the energy that is developed contributes to the creation of something else in a rehearsal which then transforms again as the final piece takes shape. In this way, Composition exercises leave their mark on the final production, even if it is as a barely perceptible undertone.

Bogart suggests that the sheer multitude of actions and the limited time of a Composition exercise force actors and directors to work on a more intuitive level, making choices, responding and moving on in order to get the work finished in time. The full intention, focus, and commitment to the moment may come from Suzuki training, and the ability to respond and create in the moment is helped through Viewpoints, but the creative leap of putting those practices into evocative form comes from Composition work. It is not a pre-determined creativity, but an active response to crisis; another form of 1, 2, 3 – GO!

The results of training

For many SITI Company members, the ultimate result of training is a confirmation of the act of putting yourself on stage. To risk presence is a leap of faith and you need to check in with your own personal investment in creating that moment. Tom Nelis claims that Suzuki training in particular addresses this idea. 'The underlying reason that you stand on the stage is the thing you need to know before you can do anything' (qtd. in Bond 2002: 245). You establish your own presence on stage out of personal motivation and commitment, and then you invite the audience in, creating a conduit through which they may participate.

The combination of Viewpoints and Suzuki training integrates the entirety of the acting experience. While Suzuki training directs focus and accentuates the individual's connection to the eternal, Viewpoints work opens awareness and explores the actor's placement in the dynamic immediacy of the world around him and in his connection to others in that world. The two together free the actor from an emphasis on achieving emotive states that many other acting techniques call for, and engage the audience in an active process of interpretation.

Bogart refers to the German verb to empathise, *einfühlen*, as a way to explain this more active process. 'Ein-fühlen: to feel *into*. To arrive at empathy, you *enter feelingly*. Empathy in this sense is not something that happens to you; rather, it is an action that you take in the world. You will yourself into another person or event' (Bogart 2007: 66). Bogart is talking about the role of an audience here, but in order to create the conditions by which this active 'feeling into' might occur, the actor needs to be present in a different way. The actor works to invite an audience in rather than delivering emotion out.

About halfway into SITI Company's production of the collage-like *bobrauschenbergamerica*, Bob's Mom pops out of the American-flag painted back wall and chimes, 'Lunch is served.' A bright and silly song blares through the speakers and the actors all jump into a flurry of activity, bringing out a picnic table and all of the makings of a good old-fashioned backyard picnic, with Bob's Mom ushering in a continuous series of corn-on-the-cob, macaroni salad, etc. and placing each dish down with a humbled sense of reverence. After this elaborate, choreographed routine, the song abruptly ends, leaving the collected ensemble in silence eating their fried chicken. They sit in silence for a long time before Allen looks up and points to the night sky. They all look up in wonder as he pulls apart conundrums of time and space, finishing with 'there is a great deal more space than time, you know,' with a flourish of his chicken drumstick.

The pairing of the everyday and the eternal is tangentially connected to the work of artist Robert Rauschenberg on which the piece is based. The piece is not a description of his life in any literal sense, but rather a drama of interconnection, much like Rauschenberg's own eclectic combines. In this case, the grand ensemble gesture followed by a moment of held tension in silence that opens up a majestic and more eloquent idea brings the audience into a similar position of contemplation. The ability to pull it off without slipping into pompous grandiloquence comes from the pairing of elements and pull between the universal and the particular in the training, just as the elements of the picnic itself come from composition studies and ensemble-generated exploration in rehearsal.

Once the audience is engaged in this way, the path has been cleared for a series of revealing monologues, all couched in the various love relationships that are the centre of the piece. They discuss the nature of relationships in idle chatter and gossipy detail

Figure 17.3 *bobrauschenbergamerica* with Ellen Lauren, SITI company.
Source: Photo, Michael Brosilow.

before Susan, who is accused of being irresponsible in her dealings with men, responds with an impassioned defence of 'How it is for women.' The speech is funny and poignant, but made all the more so as we see the character begin to eat from a large sheet cake[6] that is part of the picnic spread. She continues talking as she stuffs more and more cake into her mouth, finally finishing off the entire cake before storming off stage. It's a tour-de-force moment for the actor, and we sit, amazed at her physical achievement as much as at her emotional outburst. We are attuned to the ideas and emotional qualities of the character through a more direct entrance into the theatrical construct. To a large degree, the moment doesn't pretend, it is. The actor, Ellen Lauren, goes through the physical act of eating cake and presenting this monologue, and it is that reality of action rather than any pretense that creates our connection to the character of Susan. That process is mirrored in the physical demands of the training and its demand of awareness and charged presence in the moment.

Figure 17.4 bobrauschenbergamerica with Kelly Mauer, Akiko Aizawa, Leon Ingulsrud, SITI company.
Source: Photo, Michael Brosilow.

A moment later, Phil the Trucker, played as a large and rough-looking character in a Harley Davidson T-shirt by company member Leon Ingulsrud, and Phil's Girl, played as a perky beauty in a bathing suit by fellow company member Akiko Aizawa, create a slip'n'slide martini out of a plastic tarp and bottles of gin, a splash of vermouth and a jar of olives. The incongruous couple have a grand time sloshing through their cocktails before walking off together, having an animated discussion in Japanese. The conversation has no immediate connection to the stage action, it is just one among many images that coalesce to create the impression of this particular stage world.

In performance, this moment is surprising and revealing; it doesn't tell us anything concrete about the story, but it creates an incredible feeling of intimacy and delicacy between these two characters and of how their relationship intersects with the other relationships we see played out before us. In short, it is graceful, and all the more so because it is unexpected to see this character so easily conversing in Japanese, and because it appears superfluous. This little conversation may seem irrelevant, but it also shows the ground on which the piece is built, and the nature of the company's work.

Charles L. Mee ostensibly wrote the play, but it is more accurate to say he scored it in collaboration with the entire company through a long period of development and rehearsal. Mee didn't write this scene with the expectation that any actor playing this role would undertake it in an act of pretense. This simple cross most certainly came out of a moment in rehearsal that was adopted and incorporated into the show. It comes from a real moment that maintains its actual presence.

Though the actor Leon Ingulsrud was born in Minnesota, he moved to Japan at an early age and has studied in Japan for years. He is, in fact, fluent in Japanese, and often translates for Aizawa in rehearsals. The actors were not asked to invent something for this moment, they simply acted, and that real action was recognized as having a weight outside of its original intent and brought into the piece. In that way, it is exactly like the materials that Rauschenberg often used: discarded items seen with fresh eyes and that bring the weight of their past life to bear in being recreated in a new context.

The goal is to train your eye to see things anew and to be able to then weave that into the structure of the work. As the director of the piece, Bogart keeps her eyes and ears peeled for these moments, and she has trained herself in the art of seeing beyond the surface to the potential impact of the unexpected. Her actors' continual training also helps to keep this sense of openness and readiness at all times. You need to be ready for the moment in rehearsal, ready to select it and then be present with it in performance.

The play itself opens a sense of wonder in the audience, and that becomes an operating principle for SITI Company. Its approach to all of its work is imbued with a wide-eyed feeling of freedom, even as it is grounded in rigorous structure. Performance in this case demands attention to what is actually taking place on stage, whether that is lifting a pencil or creating a large-scale picnic. We are not in a world of reference, looking to what these actions point to, but caught in the moment itself, in its real presence.

The combined forces of focus and open connection placed within an enlivened metaphoric space create an intensity of presence, heightening the performance environment to a place of attention and participation. Theatre reconnects with the potency of ritual where we are not simply told a story, but asked to join in to become part of the event. Theatre needs to recover that vitality if it is going to survive the onslaught of images we see flashing before us, from television, to movies, to the internet, all competing to tell us something, give us something, and ultimately sell us something. The stage can be a place for participation of a different sort.

The act of training prepares you to be present at an event of exchange. You are not preparing a product to deliver to an audience, but creating a way of being in a world in which they may share. They feel along side of you, or *feel into* your presence on stage, as Bogart says. You create the conditions that allow for change, that provoke and stir an audience to enter in and finally leave transformed. In Bogart's theatre, the art of live performance is a transformative act, not because the actor has become someone else, but because the audience is helped to shift their own perspective, to see along with the artist within a concentrated and vitalised space and time, and to carry that change with them.

Notes

1   Anne Hamburger established the site-specific presentation company En Garde Arts partly based on earlier collaborations with Bogart.

2   Tadashi Suzuki (1939–) has achieved international acclaim as a director and for his work with the Suzuki Company of Toga. But he is best known for his creation of a physically based training programme derived in part from the traditional Japanese forms of Noh and Kabuki.

3   Yoshiko Chuma has been an influential part of the experimental dance, theatre and performance world in New York for over twenty-five years, working as director of the performance ensemble The School of Hard Knocks.

4   In this section, I draw on my own experience of Suzuki training, Viewpoints and Composition from the Summer Intensive I undertook with SITI Company in 2003, and further training at the SITI studio in New York. I have also incorporated Viewpoints and Composition work into my own teaching and directing.

5   Tina Landau (1962–) further developed Viewpoints through her work with Bogart in the 1980s. She continues to explore Viewpoints in her own directing work and in creating new pieces. She is a member of The Steppenwolf Theatre Company.

6   A sheet cake is a rectangular one-layer cake. They are common in America at large picnics.

Bibliography

Anderson, Porter (1998) 'Approaches to Theatre Training' *American Theatre*, January: 31–34.

—— (2008) 'The Search for a SITI State', *American Theatre*, March: 24–27, 81–83.

Bogart, Anne (1995) 'Terror Disorientation and Difficulty', in Michael Bigelow Dixon and Joel A. Smith (eds), *Anne Bogart: Viewpoints*, Lyme, NH: Smith and Kraus, pp. 3–12.

—— (2001a) 'Balancing Acts: Anne Bogart and Kristin Linklater Debate the Current Trends in American Actor-Training', moderated by David Diamond, *American Theatre*, January, http://tcg.org/publications/at/2001/balancing.cfm: 8pp.

—— (2001b) *A Director Prepares: Seven Essays on Art and Theatre*, London: Routledge.

—— (2001c) 'Forty Years of Passion: Past TCG Board Presidents: Anne Bogart', *American Theatre*, July/August, http://tcg.org/publications/at/2001/bogart.cfm: 16pp.

—— (2006) 'The Role of the Audience', TCG National Conference 2006 – Building Future Audiences, http://tcg.org/events/conference/2006/bogart.cfm: 13pp.

—— (2007) *And Then You Act: Making Art in an Unpredictable World*, London: Routledge.

Bogart, Anne and Landau, Tina (2005) *The Viewpoints Book: A Practical Guide to Viewpoints and Composition*, New York: TCG.

Bond, Will (comp.) (2002) 'SITI: Why We Train', in Nicole Potter (ed.), *Movement for Actors*, New York: Allworth, pp. 243–51.

Cummings, Scott T. (2006) *Remaking American Theatre: Charles Mee, Anne Bogart and the SITI Company*, New York: Cambridge University Press.

Dixon, Michael Bigelow and Smith, Joel A. (eds) (1995) *Anne Bogart: Viewpoints*, Lyme, NH: Smith and Kraus.

Genzlinger, Neil (2003) 'A Collage of Sly Tricks in Honor of a Collagist', *The New York Times*, 16 October: B5.

Herrington, Joan (2000) 'Directing with the Viewpoints', *Theatre Topics*, 10 (2): 155–68.

—— (2002) 'Breathing Common Air: The SITI Company Creates *Cabin Pressure*', *The Drama Review*, 46 (2): 122–44.

Lampe, Elke (1992) 'From the Battle to the Gift: The Directing of Anne Bogart', *The Drama Review*, 36 (1): 14–47.

Landau, Tina (1995) 'Source-Work, the Viewpoints and Composition: What Are They?', in Michael Bigelow Dixon and Joel A. Smith (eds). *Anne Bogart: Viewpoints*, Lyme, NH: Smith and Krauss, pp. 13–30.

Overlie, Mary (undated) 'Six View Points', unpublished manuscript (class handout): 3 pp.

Plagens, Peter (2003) 'Rauschenberg's American Beauties: A Life in Theatrical Collage', *The New York Times*, 12 October: F7.

Chapter 18

Frances Babbage

AUGUSTO BOAL AND THE THEATRE OF THE OPPRESSED

CONTEXT

AUGUSTO BOAL BECAME FAMOUS for his Theatre of the Oppressed, a system of radical performance techniques now widely applied around the world. His work is regularly taught in academic programmes; a theatre syllabus today is as likely to include Boal as Artaud. Yet Boal's initial attempts in the mid-1970s to establish and expand his grassroots theatre movement met with resistance from actors and directors to whom 'theatre' meant the works of elite, principally European, dramatists, respectfully produced on the professional stage. He was then in exile from his native Brazil, living in Portugal. Here he systematised the participatory methods with which he had already begun to experiment.

Frustrated by the responses of fellow artists, Boal wrote: 'Everyone can do theatre: even actors!' This was, he later admitted, 'the sentence that caused me some problems' (Boal 2001: 320). That it did so is unsurprising. Boal's statement had several implications, among them that training and professionalisation in acting are unnecessary; further, that the acquisition of traditional skills might actively impede one's ability to make effective theatre. The assertion does much more than this, of course: it argues above all for the democratic ownership of art, reflecting Boal's conviction that all people have both the ability and the right to act. 'To act' here holds an important dual meaning: one 'acts' in the theatrical sense but also in the sense of taking action, socially and politically.

The majority of Boal's practice over a career spanning more than half a century has centred on this democratisation of the theatrical process. Responding to the diverse contexts and cultures in which he worked, Boal developed a substantial and growing body of methods which he called 'the arsenal' of the Theatre of the Oppressed. These encourage individuals and groups to participate actively in socially engaged, critically reflexive theatre processes and, by extension, to recognise their dynamic and transformative potential in society (Boal 2002: 48).

Theatre of the Oppressed in its various manifestations has had a great impact on popular theatre practice virtually worldwide. This phenomenon can be explained in a

Figure 18.1 Augusto Boal (2008). Photo: Hugh Hill.

number of ways. Firstly, the strategies Boal advocates are designed to be accessible. Secondly, Theatre of the Oppressed methods have proved productive in, and trans-ferable to, diverse cultural contexts; this does not mean that they have not also been adapted, modified and critiqued. Thirdly, there are numerous 'Centres' of Theatre of the Oppressed around the world which collectively demonstrate – through their lists of members and affiliated groups – that there are few countries these practices have not touched.[1] Finally, Boal's own energetic commitment to travelling, teaching and writing helped greatly in the dissemination of his work.

Following the publication in 1974 of his now classic manifesto for radical theatre, *Theatre of the Oppressed*, Boal produced numerous texts on subsequent develop-ments in his practice, as well as an autobiography, *Hamlet and the Baker's Son: My Life in Theatre and Politics* (2001). He taught, lectured and directed all over the world, working with groups as diverse as prisoners (and prison guards), psychotherapists, house-maids, hospital patients, Royal Shakespeare Company actors, favela-dwellers and factory workers. He was the recipient of numerous awards and honours, including the UNESCO Pablo Picasso Medal in 1994; honorary doctorates from the University of Nebraska and Queen Mary University of London (1996 and 2001, respectively); and the Prince Claus Award in 2007. In 2008, he received the Cross Border Award for Peace and Democracy and was nominated for the Nobel Peace Prize.[2]

If *Theatre of the Oppressed* has proved the most academically influential of Boal's books, *Games for Actors and Non-Actors*, first published in 1992, has been the most widely adopted by practitioners. The title of this second work returns us to the starting point of this chapter: the relationship between 'actors' and 'non-actors', trained and untrained, professional and amateur. Although Boal's earlier statement signalled a tension between the established bourgeois theatre and the oppositional popular performance that he was promoting, the title of this later book is essentially non-confrontational, reflecting Boal's insistence that 'While some people make theatre [. . .] we all *are* theatre'.[3] Human beings are necessarily actors, since we act, and we are necessarily spectators, since we also observe (Boal 2002: 15). Equally, there is

little trace in *Games for Actors and Non-Actors* of the radical Marxist analysis that characterises *Theatre of the Oppressed*. One might infer from this that Boal shifted somewhat from
what was originally an overtly oppositional stance – arguing for aesthetic as well as
societal revolution – to a more open and inclusive position. An awareness of the
context that informed the writing of both books is helpful in order to appreciate how
Boal's Theatre of the Oppressed originated, its relationship to wider theatre practice,
and what the work has subsequently become.

For some years Boal pursued chemistry and theatre simultaneously, but it was Boal was born in 1931 to Portuguese parents and grew up in Rio de Janeiro at a
time when Brazil was under Getùlio Vargas's totalitarian government (the *Estado Novo*).
Boal's early years and much of his adult life unfolded in a context of political
upheaval. The history of Brazil over the last century was indelibly marked by a series
of dictatorships, with the country frequently under military rule; 'democracy' has
been temporary and fragile, something to be fought for and never taken for granted.
Boal was always leftist in sympathy, for many years a member of the Workers' Party
(*Partido dos Trabalhadores*, or PT). However, in the political climate of late 1960s and early
1970s Brazil, especially, he effectively became 'militant' – or was perceived as such –
by his association with those who directly opposed the ultra right-wing measures of
the military dictatorship (Boal 2001: 251). Despite the constant presence of such
tensions, Boal's autobiography describes a happy childhood and optimistic adult-
hood. Theatre was always essential to him, whether this meant coaxing the family
goat to imitate a dog, writing plays staged with his siblings, or, at seventeen, pouring
as much energy into his extra-curricular role as 'Cultural Director' at Brazil's National
School of Chemistry as into his academic studies (Boal 2001: 34, 75, 107).

For some years Boal pursued chemistry and theatre simultaneously, but it was
at Columbia University in New York that theatre finally won through. Boal had gone
there in 1952 to study advanced chemistry and also, specifically, to take courses in
playwriting and directing with the critic John Gassner. The impact on Boal of
the theatre programme was such that he pursued a further year's study there; the
experience gained and the contacts made were pivotal in securing the position that
shaped his future work decisively when, in 1956, he was appointed by José Renato as
director and playwright at São Paulo's highly regarded Arena Theatre.

Boal's artistic training in New York reflected the temper of the times. Realism
was a powerful influence on modern American theatre, manifest in new plays by
Arthur Miller, Tennessee Williams and others as well as more generally in dominant
production styles. Boal was able to observe rehearsals at the Actors Studio, then based
at the Malin Theatre under Lee Strasberg's direction. He was already familiar with
Stanislavsky's theories of acting and was fascinated to watch the Method put into
practice. Boal's name is now virtually synonymous with participatory, dialogical
theatre far removed from traditional dramatic realism, but he nevertheless insisted
that the study of Stanislavsky was 'a cornerstone' of his career:

> It was he who systematised a method which helps the actor to seek,
> within him or herself, ideas and emotions attributed to the characters. In
> this sense one of the main functions of the director is to be *maiêutic*, like
> Socrates in his philosophising process – the philosopher is the midwife
> who makes the student discover what s/he already knows, without
> knowing that s/he knows it, by means of questions that provoke reflec-
> tion, thus opening up the path to discovery. That is how the theatre
> director should be: helping the actors *give birth* to characters.[4]
>
> (Boal 2001: 147)

Boal drew many important lessons from his observation of the Actors Studio work as well as from Gassner's tutelage. He was impressed both by the performers' disciplined approach to rehearsal and by the fact that they evidently understood their task as essentially *creative*: the director was not expected to provide solutions. Boal strove to replicate these principles in his own work with Arena – although by his own account he struggled to institute the former, given the more relaxed attitude to timekeeping of his Latin American actors (Boal 2001: 145). However, Boal was critical of the 'excesses' of realist production that he witnessed: the proliferation of representative scenery and properties that could clutter the stage, and the fondness for hugely drawn out pauses within the dialogue to allow actors to go through some complex, but largely invisible, internal process. Application of the Method should not be allowed to lead to the 'hypertrophy of subjectivity' but, he believed, should be tempered by constant awareness of theatre as action in the present, with characters articulated not in isolation but always in dynamic interrelation with one another. Equally, the actors ought never to forget their responsibility to the audience (Boal 2002: 38–39). Like Gassner, Boal favoured a 'selective' realism, in all aspects of dramaturgy, whereby ideas had space to breathe without being smothered by slavish imitation of contemporary life.[5] Other genres influenced him too, however, such as vaudeville and comedy; the plays Boal wrote and directed during these two years experimented with all these forms.

Boal's artistic contribution to Arena, where he worked for fifteen years, was shaped by the unique qualities and histories of that theatre as well as by his New York training. Arena's stage was far smaller than any he had been used to, just five square metres, with spectators on all sides. It was an exceptionally intimate performance space, in which nothing could be hidden from the (150 capacity) audience. On such a stage, 'realism' *had* to be selective; at the same time, lack of money meant that Arena never could have mounted shows on the scale of its highly regarded neighbour, the Teatro Brasileiro de Comédia, even had it wished. Under Renato's direction Arena had gained a reputation for production of Brazilian plays, a policy challenging to sustain in a culture that tended to privilege foreign imports above home-grown drama.[6] Boal followed Renato's lead in two ways. Firstly, he instituted a Writers' Group designed to foster the creation of new work. Secondly, he led a phase of 'nationalising the classics', whereby Arena staged foreign plays but highlighted elements judged analogous to contemporary experience under the dictatorship: Machiavelli's *Mandrágora* was one such, mounted to great acclaim in 1962. Under Boal's direction, the company applied Stanislavskian principles extensively; its aim was to achieve a freshness and 'truth' of characterisation, in contrast to the star system then operative in São Paulo's bourgeois theatre, which preferred 'to *reinforce* the mannerisms and automatisms of each actor [onto which] the characters would be glued' (Boal 2002: 33).

During the same period, Boal was eagerly reading Brecht, in search of a theatrical language that could effectively communicate political subjects to a Brazilian audience. A key production resulting from that search was *Arena Conta Zumbi* in 1965, jointly written by Boal and Gianfrancesco Guarnieri, with music by Edu Lobo. *Zumbi* combined elements of realism with Brechtian distancing, retelling an episode of resistance to despotism from Brazil's history and thereby implicitly condemning oppression in the present. The production was a great popular success and initiated a series of 'protest musicals' from Arena in similar style.[7] *Zumbi* also placed new demands upon the actors: for example, the show used collective narration addressed to the audience; characters, too, were shared between the cast as a whole rather than each being ascribed to a single actor; finally, use of music and an eclectic shifting of styles between farce, documentary and melodrama kept the audience constantly engaged and simultaneously prevented the actors 'settling' into any individual genre. Similar skills would become integral to the Theatre of the Oppressed. Zumbi helped form the Boalian actor: one who creates a character willingly to relinquish it, making the part vivid and 'real' in order that others should recognise and desire to appropriate it.[8]

Zumbi was radical in style and content, but nonetheless was still staged within Arena for an established public. Boal's autobiography details the company's persistent efforts to create a popular theatre that could speak directly to the poorest people of their struggles and incite them to revolt. The ambition proved difficult to realise in practice: in lectures or workshops, Boal often reflected humorously and with humility on the misunderstandings and embarrassments of encounters in which peasant audiences declined to have their lives 'explained' to them by Arena's actors.[9] Such experiences taught Boal and his company what radical Brazilian educationalist Paulo Freire, a contemporary, already knew: that 'the people' were not ignorant of circumstances that shaped their own lives but were intelligent human beings who simply lacked the skills to analyse and thus transform those conditions.[10] It was only when Boal was forced into exile after a period of imprisonment and torture in 1971 that he had the opportunity to explore closely – and with less arrogance – the shape that a genuinely popular theatre might take.[11]

In exile in Peru, Boal became involved in a national literacy campaign conducted by the country's revolutionary government. The methods of the campaign were largely derived from Freire, and Boal led a theatrical strand that adopted Freirean principles and applied these to performance. Where Freire started from the assumption that the peasantry were *already* 'literate' – they just could not read or write in the dominant language of Spanish – Boal began with the language of the human body. The body is already expressive, but he led exercises designed to make it more so, and, importantly, to help participants 'unlearn' habitual patterns imposed by their work and status. Freire was not Boal's only influence. Less obviously, his approach was marked by what he knew of Brecht and Stanislavsky. Brecht emphasised the necessity of defamiliarisation in rehearsal and production, to enable actor and spectator to look afresh and critically at that which they had previously considered 'natural'. Stanislavsky demanded full articulation of emotional feeling: but, as Boal writes elsewhere,

> how can emotions 'freely' manifest themselves throughout an actor's body, if that instrument (the body) is mechanised, automated in its muscle structures and insensible to 70 per cent of its possibilities?
>
> (Boal 2002: 29)

Boal's Theatre of the Oppressed, published following these experiments, outlines a detailed set of techniques used to prepare the body to act, to extend its expressive powers and ultimately to make theatre that operates dialogically and in which the boundaries traditionally dividing actor from spectator are removed.[12] For example, Simultaneous Dramaturgy is a form in which actors improvise scenes suggested by members of their audience; Forum Theatre – perhaps the best-known technique Boal employed – takes spectator participation further by inviting direct physical interventions in the action from all who propose them. Other forms include Newspaper Theatre, consisting of a series of procedures by which the day's news, as reported, is swiftly transformed into lively dialogic performance; and Invisible Theatre, in which actors draw attention to issues of urgent social concern by enacting prepared scenes in public settings, designed to provoke spontaneous reactions and debate among spectators who witness them *without knowing* that these are actors. The building blocks for all these forms are the preparatory exercises and subsequent stages of Image Theatre, a method which allows actors to construct vivid realistic or symbolic expressions of themes, emotions and attitudes and subject these to critical analysis.

After that initial phase of practice in Peru, Boal continued to expand and adapt his Theatre of the Oppressed in response to the diverse contexts in which he worked. Travelling around Europe in the 1980s, he developed a set of techniques termed the Rainbow of Desires, also known as Cop in the Head. Its methods were similar to those already established, but their application had a new, therapeutic dimension designed to address oppressions that are typically hidden and internalised rather than out-wardly manifest (Boal 1995). He returned to Brazil in 1986 (a possibility open to him since the *abertura* or amnesty of 1979) and set up a Centre for Theatre of the Oppressed (CTO) in Rio. Struggling to survive financially, and influenced by the growing popularity of the Workers Party under the leadership of Lula (Luis Inacio da Silva, later to become Brazil's president), the CTO-Rio joined forces with the party in 1992.[13] Through this alliance, and aided by Boal's election to the position of *vereador* (councillor) the same year, Boal developed a process he named Legislative Theatre. Using established Theatre of the Oppressed methods, CTO-Rio's teams would spend time with communities and marginalised groups, working to identify concerns that were then communicated to the council through Boal. In some cases, this ultimately led to the introduction of new laws (Boal 1998).

Since the mid 1990s, the Theatre of the Oppressed has continued to evolve. There has been a series of projects engaging with the Brazilian penitentiary system and another in support of the country's Movement of Landless Rural Workers. In 2006 Boal produced a new book, *The Aesthetics of the Oppressed*. Its title deliberately recalls the study for which he is best known and it is likewise a theoretical work that also describes concrete experiments in practice. In *The Aesthetics of the Oppressed*, Boal elaborates the philosophical principles that have consistently underpinned his work: above all, he insists that creative engagement increases the human capacity to imagine multiple possibilities for our world and, further, that the encouragement of this stimulates the desire to do it. Without such exercise, our brains and modes of per-ceiving and engaging with our fellows are liable to 'harden, becoming opaque and compacted' (Boal 2006: 28). His analysis implies that practitioners of Theatre of the Oppressed are necessarily *always* in training. For both the actor and 'Spectactor' (Boal's term for the spectator-turned-participant), continuous creative, dialogic engagement is vital to prevent diminution of intellectual, emotional and physical flexibility.

When Boal declared that 'even' actors were capable of making theatre, he was being deliberately provocative rather than cynical or sarcastic. His statement reflected humorously on the profession he knew best, in all its characteristic behaviours, aspirations and vanities. Actors should, of all human beings, be the *most* capable of transformation, whether of themselves or in their ability to reveal this potentiality to others. Yet Boal had witnessed actors wedded to a method (in New York, *the* Method) that could become a strait jacket, by which pursuit of the actor's 'art' overtook the imperative to connect with an audience. He observed, in both the United States and Brazil, a star system whereby performers were employed in order to restage, repetitively, the persona for which they had become famous. At the same time, actors should be alive to the social implications of any role they assume, yet Arena itself failed to demonstrate such awareness in its encounters with the people who, it believed, most needed its 'revolutionary' drama. Now famously, in Boal's telling, the peasant farmer Virgílio was so swayed by the actors' passion that he claimed them as fellow-fighters in an immediate revolt against the landowners. The company had then to explain that, as artists, they did not personally intend to run the risks they were urging upon its audience. It was a performance of solidarity, only; it had no basis in action and incurred no threat to the actors' security (Boal 2001: 193–94; and 1995: 2–3). Yet, despite all such frustrations and stumbling blocks, Boal insists that of all professions 'the actor's is the most beautiful: while each is who he or she is [. . .] the actor can be Einstein, Chaplin or Gandhi today and, tomorrow, a refuse-collector, a grave-digger, an illiterate pariah'. He goes on:

> the human being is capable of diving into the depths of the self and emerging with undreamed-of characters, hidden potentialities sub-merged in the recesses of the person. Being an actor means immersing oneself in this plunge into self, awakening the characters bubbling away in the pressure cooker of our unconscious. It is wonderful to be an actor. We are all capable of it – except those who, in their profession as actor, enact only their own character.
>
> (Boal 2001: 321)

TRAINING AND PERFORMANCE

In this section I outline some of the methods Boal employed to structure this 'plunge into self' and examine the relationship of training to performance in Theatre of the Oppressed work. Here I draw not only on Boal's arguments and experiences, but on contributions from other practitioners who apply these techniques in different parts of the world. Such breadth of reference seems appropriate – imperative even – when assessing a mode of theatre-making that was, from its inception, proffered as a movement that could revolutionise the way human beings engage with art, with politics and with each other.

In one sense it is not necessary to train in order to practise Theatre of the Oppressed. Boal's work is founded on the principle that everyone can 'do theatre', and methods such as Forum Theatre invite spontaneous performances from specta-tors, in other words from people normally considered 'non-actors'. However, such events are planned, presented and facilitated; those who take on these responsibilities do require at least some training if the work is to operate effectively. The extent of prior preparation in the methods will, of course, vary enormously among practitioners. One cannot insist on a level of instruction, for several reasons – not least that to do so would countermand the emphasis Boal always placed on accessibility and inclusion. Crucially, given that the Theatre of the Oppressed is still largely practised with groups who are marginalised or otherwise underprivileged, it is unlikely their representatives will have the resources for extensive engagement in training programmes.

A Boalian actor-in-training may have had the chance to work directly with Boal; she may equally be taught by another practitioner in the field; or, like members of Ashtar Theatre in Palestine, she may be essentially self-taught, having used one or more of Boal's books for guidance in the methods. Sometimes courses are offered free, or have free places; this strategy gave practitioners such as Terry O'Leary a first

Figure 18.2 Theatre of the Oppressed workshop, hosted by Cardboard Citizens, February 2008.
Source: Photo, Hugh Hill.

taste of the work, in her case through London's Cardboard Citizens, who make theatre with homeless people.[14] However, in Theatre of the Oppressed, training – the acquisition and refinement of skills – by definition cannot take place wholly inside a studio or its equivalent. As with other forms of participatory performance, the development of a facility in the method necessarily comes through engagement with an audience. Moments of revelation or transformation of consciousness almost invariably come via the responses of Spectactors: those who witness the work may admire or be moved by it, but more importantly, their criticisms and interventions can expose its limits and flaws, and thereby 'teach' actors what they have yet to learn.

Exercises

Boal continually expanded the body of exercises that he used: inventing new techniques, adapting existing ones and stealing them, magpie-like, from the wealth of games, rituals and songs encountered as he travelled. Additionally, both the CTO-Rio and the Théâtre de l'Opprimé in Paris run intensive laboratory sessions from which fresh ideas emerge. As Boal emphasised to participants in a workshop in 2002, 'the techniques don't come out of the blue sky'.[15] Yet while Boal's many publications and associated training programmes collectively provide quantities of exercises and techniques, it would contradict the spirit of his work to accept these as a fixed body of knowledge; more in accord with the underlying philosophy would be to test, modify where needed, or add one's own.

Nevertheless, there are a number of key stages in Theatre of the Oppressed practice that can be considered fundamental. First of these is *Knowing the Body*: one must become familiar with the instrument of expression, learn its habits and tendencies and investigate the extent to which these are alterable. Some of the exercises at this stage are practised alone, but more usually in pairs or groups; some take the form of games, so that participants are hardly conscious they are engaged in a process of training. The purpose is consistent, however: to understand and gradually 'de-mechanise' participants physically, mentally and ultimately at a political level. The methods used make demands on the muscles and the senses; some, still at this preliminary stage, call on the memory, imagination and emotions too. The spirit of Boal's own classes was typically congenial and generous; this did not make the work any less demanding. However, what will be enjoyable and accessible for some may not be so for all. It is an important principle of Theatre of the Oppressed that, rather than being pressured towards risk or achievement, 'no one is compelled to do anything they don't wish to do' (Boal 2002: 49).

Pushing against each other

This exercise is typically conducted early on in the training process – perhaps on day one of a week-long programme – but could usefully become a regular part of warm-up stages in a group's practice. An exercise in *Knowing the Body*, it was also included by Boal in the category of techniques designed to help us 'feel what we touch': in other words, to encourage us to explore and extend the capabilities of our senses rather than remain within the limited spectrum of everyday use.

1   Work in pairs, facing each other. Each place your hands on the other's shoulders. There is a line on the floor between you (real or imaginary). Begin to push, gradually increasing the force used; the object is to employ all your strength, but at the same time to avoid either partner crossing the line. This means that in practice you must achieve a balance in the degree of pressure and resistance applied.
2   *Variation.* The same exercise but standing back to back, leaning against each other. Using the weight of each and maintaining contact of backs, gradually walk away from each other, bending your knees as you do this, so you end up sitting on the floor, still back to back. Then, pushing against each other with your backs, rise to standing again without putting your hands on the floor for support.
3   *Variation.* The same, but facing each other seated on the floor and gripping your partner's wrists. The soles of your feet should be flat on the ground, your knees bent. Using the weight of each, rise to standing, then sink down again to your starting position. A further variation of this last is the 'see-saw': rather than standing and sitting in unison you do this alternately, so that the person seated pulls the other to stand, then, when she sinks back down, her partner begins to rise from the floor.
4   *Variation.* Threes, fours or more. Stand in a circle holding each other's wrists and step backwards until your arms are extended but not taut. As in 3, balance the weight of each to enable everyone to sink down to the floor to the point where you are all seated, the soles of your feet flat on the ground. From here, pull yourselves back to the starting position, always making sure that you work collectively, negotiating each person's weight to achieve balance as a group.[16]

This exercise, in whichever variant, is testing in several ways. Firstly, at the physical level it requires one to expend considerable energy even though the range of movement initially appears limited; one must stretch, twist, pull, push, give and take weight. It can be surprisingly demanding, yet because the task has to be negotiated in order to achieve balance, no one is forced to take more weight than she or he can bear. Secondly, it requires good communication; it is like having a wordless conversation with your partner, using your bodies to respond to the signals of each to arrive at a kind of harmony. Thirdly, there is also, potentially, an emotionally affective aspect: experienced performers may be comfortable undertaking exercises that require them to grapple with one another, but it is a different matter in a workshop whose participants are 'non-actors'; this may be the first moment that group members hold on to each other, making extended one-to-one eye contact, and it helps that the exercise often provokes laughter over both failed and successful attempts to rise to standing, or sink down to the floor. Fourthly, one can regard the exercise politically: simple on the surface, it nonetheless raises issues of power and responsibility, since it requires players to work democratically to achieve the desired result. It is a characteristic of Boal's method that any exercise – from what appears to be a preliminary warm-up through to a complex technique overtly engaging with issues of power or oppression – will be deconstructed by workshop participants. Boal would ask simply 'How was it?' and, from this invitation, quite lengthy analysis might follow. In contrast with training patterns that defer discussion to the point when physical work has concluded, Theatre of the Oppressed workshops are marked by repeated opportunities for critique (although conversations *during* exercises are discouraged). The principle here is that the process should remain dialogic at every stage.

The second exercise is part of a stage titled *Making the Body Expressive*; it is also listed by Boal as an 'Image game'.

Figure 18.3 Theatre of the Oppressed workshop, hosted by Cardboard Citizens, February 2008.
Source: Photo, Hugh Hill.

Animals [17]

Each person is given a piece of paper on which is written the name of an animal, male or female. Assuming even numbers, there will be two of each animal in the group (a fact not initially known by the players). At a signal from the facilitator, the actors perform their animals, all at the same time. They move around the room, their actions realistic or symbolically expressive as they choose. Rather than settling on first ideas for representation, they are encouraged to explore different aspects of their animal: the movement of limbs, or wings, or head; its speed; how it sits, stands or sleeps; how it eats and drinks; how it confronts an enemy; and so on. (The exercise is played without sound, since adding this would create an immediate cacophony as well as offering a 'shortcut' to representation, thereby avoiding its exploratory purpose.) Eventually, the invitation is given by the facilitator for the animals to seek out a potential mate. Players may already have guessed they have a partner in the room, but in any case are now encouraged to look actively, displaying themselves enticingly to those who might be the other half of their couple, 'courting' in ways they deem characteristic of the animal in question. As pairs start to form they leave the playing space and reveal their identities to each other, not by talking but by means of the appropriate animal call (e.g. a lion's roar or cat's meow). If they turn out to be mistaken, they re-enter and look again. Boal adds:

> The animals chosen must be very different from each other: felines, reptiles, fish, big birds, little insects, etc. It is also not a bad idea to slip a 'man' and a 'woman' in among the couples. Very often spectators have some trouble identifying them.
>
> (Boal 2002: 146)

If desired, the facilitator can conclude the game by inviting each pair in turn to come into the centre and re-enact their courtship for the rest of the group to observe. In this way, what was a predominantly experiential exercise becomes performance.

'Animals' is one of many exercises (or 'gamesercises', as Boal occasionally termed them) which are extremely funny to play or watch and which move from initial simplicity to a state of cheerful chaos. The collective scene in the room invariably becomes messy, ludicrous even, and the more this occured the more Boal appeared to enjoy it. Asked by a workshop participant why he often asked them to convey so many different and sometimes 'impossible' things at once, he replied simply: 'because it's very theatrical, and because I am a man of the theatre!'[18] Moments of beauty and imagination may occur in the 'Animals' exercise, but equally important is that participants enjoy themselves: the aim is to encourage players to overcome inhibitions about performing and help them get to know each other. At the same time the game can be physically challenging, since it requires one to move and interact in an unaccustomed way. There can be a political dimension to this, as Boal explains in *Theatre of the Oppressed* when discussing the 'muscular alienation' imposed on each one of us by our work:

> A simple example will serve to clarify this point: compare the muscular structure of a typist with that of the night watchman of a factory. The first performs his or her work seated in a chair: from the waist down the body becomes, during working hours, a kind of pedestal, while arms and fingers are active. The watchman, on the other hand, must walk

continually during his eight-hour shift and consequently will develop muscular structures that facilitate walking. The bodies of both become alienated in accordance with their respective types of work.[19]

(Boal 2000: 127)

As with all Theatre of the Oppressed exercises, the starting point is the bodies of those participating, not bodies 'in the abstract'. The process gently reveals familiar, habitual patterns and encourages exploration of alternatives; there is no imposition of technique with an accompanying set of expectations.

Image Theatre

Image Theatre is the term Boal gives to the core techniques of Theatre of the Oppressed, in which themes identified by the participants – as well as their emotions, experiences and attitudes more generally – are articulated visually. This work is frequently the starting point for the development of other modes such as Forum Theatre, but equally it may be practised as a method in its own right. It may generate performance, or it may remain the basis of a reflexive exploratory process.

Often, the first stage of Image Theatre will be an expressive still pose by one person, either self-created or sculpted by another actor. This may be set alongside another still image, and then others, until the actors in their various positions suggest a 'gallery' of interpretations of a given theme or responses to a provocation. The image may be animated through a series of stages: for example, by addition of a gesture that may be repeated a number of times; by movement across the space; or by presenting a further image or action by which the original actor shows what they believe 'happens next'. The actor may be invited to add a sound to the image, or to

Figure 18.4 Theatre of the Oppressed workshop, hosted by Cardboard Citizens, February 2008.
Source: Photo, Hugh Hill.

utter the words that the image might say 'if it could speak'. Sometimes Boal would ask those in an image – often several actors simultaneously – to deliver a continuous improvised monologue in a low voice that explores what the image might be 'thinking'.

In its initial stages, Image Theatre is generally non-verbal. Boal insisted that visual image making and the dynamics of animation are processes more productive, revealing and less open to misunderstandings than conventional discussion. He often recounted the tale of the 'birth' of the Spectactor, which occurred in Chacalayo when a woman in his audience grew outraged that her instructions to the actor were being ignored. It was only by getting up from her seat and demonstrating her meaning that she was at last understood (Boal 2001: 205–7). This story aside, it would be problematic to assert that actions are necessarily less ambiguous than spoken language; indeed, much of the richness of Image Theatre as a method comes from the multiplicity of 'readings' that participants can draw from even the very simplest stage picture (for illustration, see 'What's the Story?' below). There are other arguments in favour of keeping words out of the first stages of exercises: for instance, participants will be more and less verbally articulate, or may speak different languages from one another. But, perhaps more fundamentally, this way of beginning emphasises the primacy of action and at the same time helps to circumvent any tendencies in participants to mimic dialogue-heavy 'conventional' theatre instead of discovering a stage language more truly their own.

Boal employed a great many Image Theatre exercises, but described above are the elements that inform almost all of these: creation of the still picture; its animation; its analysis, both on its own and as it 'reads' when placed alongside other images. A second key element of the process is the creation of Real, Ideal and Transitional images. The political dynamic of the work should be evident in this. First one depicts a theme or situation 'as it is', or as that participant understands it to be, revealing its tensions or oppressions; next is shown an imagined 'ideal' version of this, what the picture might be if these tensions were overcome. Most crucial, in political terms, is the transition: how could the world as it is be transformed into the world we would like it to be? These three phases need not be explored in this order. For instance, actors may begin by creating images – singly or in groups – in response to themes such as Happiness, or Democracy, and through this might depict their imagined Ideals. They might then explore the inverse of these, or the forces that mitigate against them, again in images. All three phases are necessarily dialogic. It cannot be assumed that the group will share an 'ideal', any more than that individual members would represent an existing problem in the same way. Equally, even if the group collectively establishes a Real and Ideal image, the Transitional stage(s) will be differently envisioned by each.

An example of Image Theatre in practice will help to illustrate how the method is used to expose and then analyse an issue of importance to those present. In Theatre of the Oppressed, Boal describes a workshop where a young Peruvian woman expressed in an image an event that had taken place in her village of Otuzco, when the leader of a peasant rebellion was castrated by the landlords in the main square. The woman

> composed the image of the castration, placing one of the participants on
> the ground while another pretended to be castrating him and still another
> held him from behind. Then at one side she placed a woman praying, on
> her knees, and at the other side a group of five men and women, also on
> their knees, with hands tied behind their backs. [The] young woman

placed another participant in a position obviously suggestive of power and violence and, behind him, two armed men pointing their guns at the prisoner.

(Boal 2000: 135–36)

It was not difficult to agree upon an 'Ideal' image of a peaceful Otuzco, but the 'Transitional' stages were differently conceived by the participants. For example, those who supported the Revolutionary Government focused on the armed figures in the image, moving them so that their guns were turned from the victim to the figure in power or castrators themselves. One woman went first to the kneeling men, and through her modifications they freed themselves and attacked the torturers; for her, 'social changes [were] made by the people as a whole and not only by their vanguard'. Typically, participants did not make adjustments to the image of the kneeling woman. Boal comments that the women in the group, especially, 'did not see in that woman a potential force for revolutionary change'; yet one girl from Lima, 'being more "liberated" ', began with this figure: in other words, 'changing precisely that image with which she identified herself' (Boal 2000: 136).

It should be clear from this example how the initial stages of Image Theatre can be developed as more sophisticated dialogic methods and how one might progress from still images, to their animation, to the more extended scenes of a Forum Theatre show. Fuller training in Theatre of the Oppressed methods will provide the actor with a vast array of exercises and more complex techniques; as suggested, these will generally be variants upon core principles rather than methods entirely new. Commenting on the appetite for learning that he encountered in Brazilian workers, Boal claimed that '[t]he greater the vocabulary, the greater the possibilities of thought' (Boal 2001: 202). That philosophy is embedded in his training: the Boalian actor acquires a body of techniques whose many versions allow subtle application and selectivity in practice. This is vitally important, since Theatre of the Oppressed is fundamentally an interactive process that must have the capacity to respond with sensitivity to the spontaneous reactions – intellectual, emotional, actively physical – of participants. This is nowhere more important than when practitioners offer their work to an audience.

Performance

Theatre of the Oppressed practice may not result in performance as such. Boal's Rainbow of Desires techniques, for instance, were not designed with public presenta- tion in mind; Image Theatre, equally, can be conducted simply as group process. Forum Theatre does require the creation of performance, but this is not its 'end'. Boal insisted that in Forum 'it is more important to achieve a good debate than a good solution'; by the same principle, no play presented to an audience matters more than the reactions – and *actions* – it generates (Boal 2002: 259). A Forum 'show' is offered not as model but anti-model, its purpose to be pulled apart and remade. Boal describes numerous such shows in his books (especially *Games for Actors and Non-Actors*) and one can read accounts of Theatre of the Oppressed events, made with and presented before diverse communities, from other writer-practitioners also.[20] Given this, I have chosen not to single out any individual Forum show, but to explore in broader terms some of the issues and concerns attached to the performance of Theatre of the Oppressed with community groups. I discuss the variety of skills the

Boalian actor must possess, or at least, should seek to acquire, and assess the 'risks' of practising Theatre of the Oppressed when training has been limited. I also consider how the Joker − Boal's term for the facilitator or compère − might be 'trained' in preparation to perform this function.

In Theatre of the Oppressed performance, one is effective as an actor by playing a role with conviction and energy, based on intelligent observation as well as exploration and analysis in rehearsal. The actor must equally be skilled as an improviser, since she will need to show her character's reactions to the spontaneous interventions of Spectactors. Further, she must develop her abilities as facilitator and mediator: someone who performs in a Theatre of the Oppressed show is unlikely also to be its Joker, but must nonetheless support that function. She, as much as the Joker, will interact with those who step in to replace the protagonist, as Forum invites: her responses, in role or out of it, must be such that debate is furthered and not closed down. Moreover, actors will typically take part in any closing discussions, talking with audience members; the capacity to do this with sensitivity is essential if the latter are to remain critically engaged with the issues once the event is over. It should be obvious that if actors withdraw awkwardly to one side, even from timidity, the divisions that the participatory process sought to dismantle are soon reinstated. Beyond this, the Forum event will often occur at the midpoint in the encounter of company and community, part of a process that may last days, weeks or longer. Vidya, a grassroots group that works in the (so-called) 'slums' of Ahmedabad, Gujarat, has found it essential to spend several days in an area, during which period it will engage with community members in a variety of ways prior to and following any performances. Thus the pattern of a week's visit might be: arrival and advertising of the performance (day one); erecting the platform stage and presenting the Forum show, often several times (day two); visiting community members and gathering responses (day three); creation and performance of new 'playlets' based on feedback received (day four); further discussions and informal evaluation among the community (day five). The group will also frequently return to the same area months later to monitor the effects of the work and the progress of any initiatives undertaken.[21] Other companies will operate differently, but the example of Vidya illustrates that the responsibilities of actors in such work extend far beyond performance of a given role.

Unquestionably, the quality of relationship between actors and audience is fundamental to the efficacy of this work. The process may well be eased where performers and spectators belong to the same community − as in Vidya's case − since the closer the connection between those who shape a Forum and those who receive and respond to it, the more likely that what is shown will be judged authentic. Problems occur, as Boal discovered, when actors are outsiders with little understanding of the realities of community experience. Bill McDonnell, who has practised within activist contexts in Britain and Northern Ireland, takes this argument further; for him it is vital that those who do this work recognise the dialogic principles and philosophy of liberation that underpin it. Without this, he believes, you 'get a dangerous belief in a type of technical instrumentality: a belief that methods automatically translate into perception or consciousness'.[22] Practitioners of these techniques must, therefore, have applied them to their own frustrations and desires: oppression, to use Boal's term, cannot be regarded as the experience of other people. Like McDonnell, Theatre of the Oppressed trainer Birgit Fritz, based in Vienna, turns the question of efficacy back to the actor-facilitator who, she suggests, will ideally bring not only 'a strong sense for democracy [but] first hand experience of what it means to be oppressed, or a strong sense of compassion for the oppressed'. She emphasises: 'You cannot ask from others what you are not ready to do (undergo) yourself.'[23]

Critics of Theatre of the Oppressed sometimes fear that a practice which openly tackles themes of power with reference to marginalised groups may inadvertently aggravate the very problems they aim to address: whether because the complexity of issues has not been fully understood, or because techniques are handled with insufficient flexibility to accommodate the experiences participants bring. Prosper Kompaore, who directs the Atelier Théâtre Bourkinabé in Burkina Faso, accepts that a poorly managed Forum can leave audiences

> with a feeling of powerlessness, not to say, and more seriously, with the sense that failure is inevitable [. . .]. It can also happen that bad practice in Forum turns the public off, they feel manipulated and consequently hostile towards Forum theatre in general.[24]

Such risks will be lessened by training and also, obviously, by practice: the implication is that one must risk making mistakes – perhaps painful ones – to gain the experience that would render this less likely. Practitioners with whom I discussed this issue agreed that excessive anxiety about inexperience simply results in stasis. James Thompson, who has applied these methods in war zones as well as prisons, insists that whilst attunement to the ethics and politics of the work is crucial, 'danger is not something that can be screened out'.[25] His view is shared by Mojisola Adebayo, a facilitator who has worked with minority ethnic groups in South Asia, the Americas and the Middle East. Adebayo stresses the 'risks' attached to the issues under scrutiny: 'Even if an inexperienced (or experienced) practitioner leads a session which looks at my abuse in a somewhat clumsy way, it will never be as damaging as the abuse I actually experienced myself.'[26]

One should also recall that Theatre of the Oppressed as a method gained strength (and greater subtlety) through Boal's discoveries of its inadequacies and consequent modifications of both the techniques themselves and his use of them. Effective practice in this field depends on the willingness and ability of those who use it to listen to the communities with whom they work. David Diamond of Canada's Headlines Theatre, whose application of Boal has included engagement with violence, suicide, racism and drug abuse, stresses that the methods do not constitute a 'sacred canon' and cannot be used as such.[27] Boal would not have disagreed: 'I did not invent Theatre of the Oppressed by myself, in my house, nor did I receive it as tablets of stone from God: it was in the interaction with popular audiences that [it] was born, little by little' (Boal 2001: 339). In her own work in African countries, Jane Plastow has found Forum Theatre in particular less readily transferable than it is sometimes assumed to be:

> In some cases I have found straight Forum has simply not worked because it is seen almost as too rude, too direct, unsubtle and unrespectful to tradition, to community feeling or to particular groups. Forum [. . .] cannot expect to work unmodified everywhere. In at least one instance I know of religious figures simply closed down a debate on family planning, saying it was ungodly and that silenced everyone else. I often use elements of Theatre of the Oppressed but just as some useful techniques among many others.[28]

How, then, can actors – perhaps especially Jokers – become better at the art of listening to the communities with whom they engage? Boal offered his own guidelines on this, principally in articles on the conduct of the Joker and the question of how Forum Theatre events might best be prepared and rehearsed (Boal 2002: 253–76). I conclude on this theme of listening, so crucial to the Boalian actor, by describing one further exercise shared with me by James Thompson. One could categorise it as Image Theatre, although it is not a technique I saw Boal himself use. Including it here underlines the extent to which application and development of this work extend well beyond the proposals of its originator.

What's the story? [29]

Two actors stand on stage, one in the centre of the space towards the back and the other forward and a little to the side, so the audience can see both. They do nothing. The Joker asks: What's the story? Those watching offer interpretations of what *could* be happening between these characters, at this moment. The actor at the back then takes a step forward. The Joker asks again: What's the story? The same process is repeated a second and maybe a third time. At one point, the two on stage may be side by side; or, perhaps at the audience's suggestion, one may turn away, or kneel. The emphasis of the exercise is on the spectators and what they 'read'. There is no acting on stage. The Joker's task is to listen and respond to the audience's interpretations, not to offer her own analysis or ideas.

It is the simplest of exercises, yet possibilities for meaning are limitless. Its inclusion reminds us that, in this practice, the ability to create opportunity for participation – intellectual, emotional, physical – is perhaps the most potent skill an actor can bring.

NOTE ON THE TEXT

This essay was prepared in 2008. Very sadly, Augusto Boal died in May 2009, after a long battle with leukaemia. He will be greatly missed, but the legacy of work Boal leaves behind will continue to inspire artists and activists the world over.

ACKNOWLEDGMENTS

My thanks go to Mojisola Adebayo, Yolisa Dalamba, Michele Decottignies, David Diamond, Birgit Fritz, Adrian Jackson, Prosper Kompaore, Fritz Letsch, John Martin, Bill McDonnell, Doug Paterson, Jane Plastow, James Thompson and Tim Wheeler, all of whom responded generously and with great insight to questions about the experience of practising Theatre of the Oppressed methods. I regret that there was not the space to include more of their valuable comments. I am grateful also to Cardboard Citizens and Hugh Hill for giving me permission to reproduce these photographs. Above all, of course, I want to acknowledge and thank Boal himself: I feel his loss profoundly, both personally and professionally.

Notes

1　See for example the Centro de Teatro do Oprimido in Rio (www.ctorio.org.br/), the Théâtre de l'Opprimé in Paris (www.theatredelopprime.fr/), the Centre for Theatre of the Oppressed and Applied Theatre Arts in Los Angeles (www.ctoatala.org/home.html), and the Theatre of the Oppressed Laboratory in New York (www.toplab.org/). This is by no means a comprehensive list.

2　The Prince Claus Fund for Culture and Development is managed from the Netherlands but is an international organisation. The Cross Border Award for Peace and Democracy was conferred by Dundalk Institute of Technology, Republic of Ireland.

3　This phrase is quoted by Doug Paterson in 'Theatre of the Oppressed Workshops', at www.wwcd.org/action/Boal.html (accessed 23 July 2008). It is a statement Boal often made when introducing his work to new audiences.

4　The somewhat obscure term *maiêutic* Boal employs here refers to the Socratic method whereby the questioner seeks to clarify the ideas of others, especially facilitating the conscious awareness and articulation of latent ideas and beliefs.

5　For more on Gassner's analysis of the contemporary American theatre scene, see Gassner (1956).

6　The importance of Arena's contribution to Latin American theatre is discussed in detail in George (1992).

7　Margaret Milleret (1987) provides a detailed assessment of the production and its significance.

8　Through *Zumbi* Boal also developed the 'Joker system', a complex structure of presentation designed to help the audience understand different sides of the conflict presented. 'Joker' has subsequently been adopted as the term for the facilitator of Theatre of the Oppressed processes, especially Forum Theatre. These two uses of the word are only loosely connected, however; the Joker of Forum Theatre does seek to help spectators appreciate the complexity of material, but the elaborate structure Boal described in relation to *Zumbi* is not a part of current application. See Boal (2000: 167–90).

9　Boal was a charismatic storyteller and would often answer a question by means of an anecdote; indeed, the deployment of stories – whether personal or taken from folk tradition – in order to understand ideas was a characteristic of his teaching method.

10　Paolo Freire (1921–97) was a Brazilian philosopher and language specialist who achieved international recognition as a radical educationalist. He is best known for his attack on what he termed the 'banking' concept of education, which regarded the student as empty account awaiting deposit of knowledge from a master. Boal was strongly influenced by Freire's theories as well by the democratic educational practices Freire advocated.

11　For a full account of the worsening political situation and conditions that led up to Boal's arrest and imprisonment, and subsequent exile, see Boal (2001: 231–314).

12　This is only one section of the book. For a discussion of the relationship of the work in Peru to the analysis of 'bourgeois' theatre that occupies the preceding 100-plus pages, see Babbage (2004: 35–65).

13　Lula was elected Brazil's president in 2002 and took office in 2003. He was re-elected in 2006 for a presidential term extending until 2011.

14　For more about this work, see www.cardboardcitizens.org.uk/.

15　The workshop was 'New Techniques from the Theatre of the Oppressed', organised by Cardboard Citizens and led by Boal. It was held at the Union Chapel in Islington, London. 2–3 March 2002.

16　A fuller description of this exercise is given in Boal (2002: 58–61).

17　The earliest description of this exercise is in Boal (2000: 130–31); a longer version is given in Boal (2002: 145–46).

18　'New Techniques from the Theatre of the Oppressed', in Boal (2002).

19　Boal's claim that our bodies become 'alienated' is potentially problematic, as the word seems to imply an original state of physical harmony, or freedom, to which we might return. His point, however, is that our bodies and actions increasingly assume the shape that our work imposes.

20　Recent examples include Babbage (2004: 67–105); Chamberlain (2007); Mohan (2004); Paterson (2008); Szeman (2005).

21   Chamberlain (2007: 24–27).
22   McDonnell, email interview, 30 July 2008.
23   Fritz, email interview, 31 July 2008.
24   Kompaore, email interview, 18 July 2008. My translation from Kompaore's original French.
25   Thompson, telephone interview, 30 July 2008.
26   Adebayo, email interview, 15 August 2008.
27   Diamond, email interview, 16 July 2008.
28   Plastow, email interview, 17 July 2008.
29   The exercise is described in my own words. Thompson did not invent the exercise and does
      not recall seeing Boal use it; however, he has come across it frequently in Theatre of the
      Oppressed 'circles'. Thompson, telephone interview, 30 July 2008.

Bibliography

Babbage, F. (2004) *Augusto Boal*, London and New York: Routledge.
Boal, A. (1995) *The Rainbow of Desire: the Boal method of theatre and therapy*, trans. A. Jackson, London
      and New York: Routledge.
—— (1998) *Legislative Theatre: Using performance to make politics*, trans. A. Jackson, London and New
      York: Routledge.
—— (2000) *Theatre of the Oppressed*, trans. C.A. McBride, M.-O.L. McBride and E. Fryer, second
      edition, London: Pluto Press.
—— (2001) *Hamlet and the Baker's Son: My Life in Theatre and Politics*, trans. A. Jackson and C. Blaker,
      London and New York: Routledge.
—— (2002) *Games for Actors and Non-Actors*, trans. A. Jackson, second edition, London and New
      York: Routledge.
—— (2006) *The Aesthetics of the Oppressed*, trans. A. Jackson, London and New York: Routledge.
Chamberlain, F. (2007) 'Interview with John Martin', in F, Chamberlain (ed.), *Vidya: Theatre as
      Development*, special issue of *Seagull Theatre Quarterly*, 39: 18–34.
Cohen-Cruz, J. and Schutzman, M. (eds) (2006) *A Boal Companion: Dialogues on theatre and cultural
      politics*, London and New York: Routledge.
Freire, P. (1972) *Pedagogy of the Oppressed*, Harmondsworth: Penguin.
Gassner, J. (1956) *Form and Idea in Modern Theatre*, New York: Yale University Press.
George, D. (1992) *The Modern Brazilian Stage*, Austin: University of Texas Press.
Milleret, M. (1987) 'Acting into Action: Teatro Arena's Zumbi', *Latin American Theatre Review*, 21
      (1): 19–27.
Mohan, D. (2004) 'Reimagining Community: Scripting Power and Changing the Subject
      through Jana Sanskriti's Political Theatre in Rural North India', *Journal of Contemporary
      Ethnography*, 33 (2): 178–217.
Paterson, D. (2008) 'Three Stories from the Trenches: The Theatre of the Oppressed in the
      Midst of War', *The Drama Review*, 52 (1): 110–17.
Schutzman, M. and Cohen-Cruz, J. (eds) (1994) *Playing Boal: Theatre, Therapy, Activism*, London and
      New York: Routledge.
Szeman, I. (2005) 'Lessons for Theatre of the Oppressed from a Romanian Orphanage', *New
      Theatre Quarterly*, 21 (4): 340–57.

Index

Theatre, Dance and

www.tandf.co.uk/journals/rtdp

Performance Training

New in 2010

Editors
Simon Murray, University of Glasgow, UK
Jonathan Pitches, University of Leeds, UK

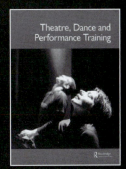

Theatre, Dance and Performance Training is a peer-reviewed journal which acts as a research forum for practitioners, academics, creative artists and pedagogues interested in training in all its complexity.

The journal is dedicated to revealing the vital and diverse processes of training and their relationship to performance making both past and present, a diversity reflected in the journal's international scope and interdisciplinary form and focus.

Theatre, Dance and Performance Training acts as an outlet for documenting and analysing primary materials relating to regimes of performer training as well as encouraging discursive contributions in a range of critical and creative formats. It provides a valuable meeting-point for practitioner-researchers wanting to know more about training before, beneath, beyond and within performance.

Visit the website to:

- submit your research
- request a free sample copy
- register to receive table of contents alerts - this will ensure you are notified of the new research published in the journal twice a year.

Routledge
Taylor & Francis Group

Stanislavsky in America

Mel Gordon

Stanislavsky in America explores the extraordinary legacy that Constantin Stanislavsky's system of actor training has left on acting in the US.

Mel Gordon outlines the journey of Stanislavsky's theories through twentieth century American history, from the early US tours of the Moscow Art Theatre to the ongoing impact of 'The System' on modern American acting.

This fascinating study by a leading theatre critic and practitioner provides hundreds of original acting exercises, used by the pivotal US figures who developed his teachings, such as Lee Strasberg, Stella Adler and Bobby Lewis. By going back to these primary sources, Gordon cuts through the myths and misapprehensions which have built up over time.

Part memoir and part practical guide, *Stanislavsky in America* is an essential resource for anyone wanting to understand Stanislavsky's work and his relationship with American theatre.

HB: 978-0-415-49669-8

PB: 978-0-415-49670-4

e-book: 978-0-203-86877-5

The Lee Strasberg Notes

Edited by Lola Cohen

Foreword by Martin Sheen

The Lee Strasberg Notes reproduces the original teachings of a unique voice in actor training, for the very first time. It is a stunning document in the history and ongoing practice of Strasberg's Method.

Compiled and edited by Lola Cohen, the book is based on unpublished transcripts of Strasberg's own classes on acting, directing and Shakespeare. It recreates his theoretical approach, as well as the practical exercises used by his students, and brilliantly conveys his approach and personality.

The book features Strasberg's teachings on:

• Training and exercises

• Characters and scenes

• Directing and the Method

• Shakespeare and Stanislavski

• The theatre, acting and actors.

Including a preface by Anna Strasberg and a foreword by Martin Sheen, this illuminating book brings the reader closer to Strasberg's own methods than any other, making it a phenomenal resource for students, actors and directors.

HB: 978-0-415-55185-4
PB: 978-0-415-55186-1
e-book: 978-0-203-86313-8

PN 2075 .T94 2010

Actor training

On Directing: Burning the House

'A theatre which is able to speak to each spectator in a different and penetrating language is not a fantastic idea, nor a utopia. This is the theatre for which many of us, directors and leaders of groups, trained for a long time.....'

- from the Introduction

On Directing is Eugenio Barba's unprecedented account of his own life and work. This is a major retrospective of Barba's working methods, his practical techniques and the life experiences which fed directly into his theatre-making.

On Directing is an inspirational resource. It is a dramaturgy of dramaturgies, and a professional autobiography, from one of the most significant and influential directors and theorists working today. It provides unique insights into a philosophy and practice of directing for the beginning student, the experienced practitioner and everyone in between.

HB: 978-0-415-54920-2
PB: 978-0-415-54921-9

Available at all good bookshops

For ordering and further information please visit:

www.routledge.com